COLD WAR ENDGAME

COLD WAR
ENDGAME

ORAL HISTORY · ANALYSIS · DEBATES

Edited by William C. Wohlforth

THE PENNSYLVANIA STATE UNIVERSITY PRESS
UNIVERSITY PARK, PENNSYLVANIA

Library of Congress Cataloging-in-Publication Data

Cold War endgame : oral history, analysis, debates /
edited by William C. Wohlforth.
p.   cm.
Including index.
ISBN 0-271-02237-X (cloth : alk. paper)
ISBN 0-271-02238-8 (pbk. : alk. paper)
1. Cold War.
2. United States—Foreign relations—Soviet Union.
3. Soviet Union—Foreign relations—United States.
4. World politics—1945–1989.
I. Wohlforth, William Curti, 1959– .

D843 .C577312 2003
940.55'8—dc21   2002153327

Contents

Acknowledgments

THIS BOOK IS organized around the transcripts of the conference "Cold War Endgame," held at Princeton University's Woodrow Wilson School on March 29–30, 1996. The conference was sponsored by the John Foster Dulles Program for the Study of Leadership in International Affairs, Princeton University, and the James A. Baker III Institute for Public Policy, Rice University. I am especially grateful to Fred I. Greenstein, director of the John Foster Dulles Program, for organizing the conference and inviting me to contribute to the project. The conference and this book would not have been possible without the support of James Baker, the Baker Institute, and its director Ambassador Edward P. Djerejian. The project also owes a debt of gratitude to Don Oberdorfer, former chief diplomatic correspondent for the *Washington Post*, for providing expert moderation during the conference and crucial assistance in preparing for it.

The scholars who labored over many years to bring forth this book dedicate it to the memory of Joseph Lepgold, who died in December 2001 as a result of injuries sustained in a hotel fire in Paris. Without Joe's encouragement, his trademark enthusiasm, and his wise counsel, this project may never have come to fruition. He enriched our work and our lives; we are better for having known him and will suffer in his absence.

Introduction

William C. Wohlforth

AS THE COLD WAR recedes into memory it is all too easy to forget how potentially apocalyptic it was. For forty-five years the two superpowers faced each other across the globe, each dreading the consequences of ceding dominance to the other. To forestall that outcome, each devoted colossal resources to defense—5 to 14 percent of the economy for the Americans, 15 to more than 25 percent for the Soviets—and maintained a deterrence posture that eventually entailed the acquisition of massive nuclear arsenals jointly totaling over 50,000 warheads.[1] Deterrence amidst such an intense rivalry put a premium on the credibility of their commitments, and largely to defend their reputation for resolve U.S. and Soviet leaders periodically undertook policies that ran the risk of escalating to global thermonuclear war, most notably over Cuba.

It staggers the imagination that a conflict which could have ended civilized life on the planet rapidly drew to a close in the three years leading up to the implosion of the Soviet Union in December 1991. How that transpired is partly a result of large-scale tectonic changes in world politics, but it is also very much a human story of leaders engaged in the responsible pursuit of conflict resolution. How did top decision makers negotiate an end to the Cold War? Why were they able to do it peacefully? What lessons does the experience provide for dealing with other dangerous rivalries? This book is a collaborative effort between scholars and policymakers to answer these questions. Its purpose is to illuminate our understanding of the ending of the U.S.-Soviet rivalry, and also to contribute to the important dialogue between scholarship and foreign policy practice.

Part I presents the record of a critical oral history conference featuring two days of fascinating discussions by former Soviet and American officials of how they managed the tumultuous diplomacy of 1989–91, including German unification, the Persian Gulf War, and the collapse of the Soviet Union. Using the conference transcripts as well as the latest archival and memoir

---

1. U.S. estimates are reported in Aaron L. Friedberg, *In the Shadow of the Garrison State: America's Anti-Statism and Its Cold War Grand Strategy* (Princeton: Princeton University Press, 2000). Soviet estimates are reported in Noel E. Firth and James H. Noren, *Soviet Defense Spending: A History of CIA Estimates, 1950–1990* (Houston: Texas A&M Press, 1998).

evidence, each of the six scholarly chapters that follow tackles a different aspect of the relation between theory, policy, and the Cold War's end. Part II considers a series of unresolved theoretical and empirical puzzles presented by the events of 1989–91, and Part III presents a debate over the causes of the end of the Cold War. In the concluding chapter, Joseph Lepgold offers a framework for addressing these central questions. While his answers may not persuade all readers, they provide a productive way to summarize and incorporate the new evidence and debates presented in this volume.

When Did the Cold War Begin to End?

There are as many answers to the question of when to date the Cold War's end as there are definitions of the Cold War itself. A fully satisfactory explanation for the end of the Cold War would have to deal in depth with the years leading up to the period this book calls the endgame. The decision to focus on the years between 1988 and 1992 was partly pragmatic: an earlier conference and edited volume dealt with the Reagan-Gorbachev period, which in crucial ways laid the groundwork for the ending of the Cold War.[2] But there are sound historical reasons to study this specific three-year period. The preponderance of participants and scholars concur that the international epoch they knew as the Cold War came to an unambiguous end sometime between December 1988 and December 1991.[3] In designating this period as the endgame, the contributors to this volume do not mean to imply that the precise nature of the Cold War's end was foreordained. The oral history and analysis that follow amply demonstrate that decision makers did not know how the Cold War would end, and in particular that it would end so swiftly and peacefully. Nor was there agreement on who the victor would be—or even whether there would be a clear victor.

By "endgame" we simply mean the period in which policymakers were progressively becoming aware that the superpower rivalry and the bipolar order they had known for a generation were coming to an end. Thus, the analogy to chess is accurate in at least two senses. The endgame was a distinct phase of the Cold War when the termination or fundamental alteration of

2. William Curti Wohlforth, ed., *Witnesses to the End of the Cold War* (Baltimore: Johns Hopkins University Press, 1997).

3. For an excellent review of the scholarly literature and primary documents on the end of the Cold War, see David S. Painter and Thomas S. Blanton, "The End of the Cold War," in Jean-Christophe Agnew and Roy Rosenzweig, eds., *A Companion to Post-1945 America* (London: Basil Blackwell, 2002).

the rivalry began to seem to many to be within grasp, although the precise moment when it began was arguable at the time and is still so in retrospect. And, though shorter than the opening and middle game of the Cold War, it was just as important. For many participants in the conference and scholarly contributors, the analogy works in a third sense as well; namely, that in the endgame the normal way of assessing the value of pieces may be highly misleading. A pawn may suddenly be more powerful than a rook. By the end of 1988 Mikhail Gorbachev and close advisers like Anatoly Chernyaev were hoping to translate what by some traditional measures was beginning to look like a weak position into a big win for the Soviet Union and, they would stress, for the world as a whole.

To capture the moment when the action in this book begins, consider the December 27–28, 1988, meeting of the Politburo of the Central Committee of the Communist Party of the Soviet Union. The first item on the agenda was a discussion of Gorbachev's historic December 7 speech to the United Nations General Assembly in which he stressed that universal human values took precedence over the class struggle and affirmed the freedom of all countries to choose their own destinies, thus implicitly revoking the "Brezhnev Doctrine" that Moscow had a right to intervene to preserve allied regimes in Central Europe. The speech followed a turnaround in U.S.-Soviet relations over the preceding two years: negotiations were proceeding on arms control, regional conflicts, and human rights. In December 1987, Gorbachev and U.S. president Ronald Reagan had signed the Intermediate-Range Nuclear Forces (INF) treaty, the first Cold War arms agreement that actually reduced (albeit by only four percent), rather than merely limited the growth of, the two sides' arsenals. But the changes in superpower relations were still mainly intangible: the intellectual ferment prompted by Gorbachev's new political thinking on the Soviet side, a marked softening of the Reagan administration's anti-Soviet rhetoric, and a burgeoning relationship of collegial trust between the highest-level officials of the two governments.

The transcript of the Politburo's session captures a crucial moment in the Cold War's ending when major change was clearly afoot but its precise direction remained deeply uncertain. Gorbachev clearly wanted to go much farther than the deep détente he and Reagan had attained. He stressed to his Politburo comrades that the goal was to undermine the "foundation of the 'Cold War,'" and to "build a new world." To do that, it was necessary to "pull the rug from under the feet of those who have been prattling . . . that the new political thinking is just about words."[4] At the United Nations, he announced major unilateral reductions in Soviet tanks and troops in Europe and Asia.[5] Would this do the trick? Before his colleagues, Gorbachev remained cautious. The problem was that many in the United States and Europe saw Soviet concessions as the result of increased Western power and the "crisis in socialism and communism." They wanted to stick to their hard line and pick up more Soviet concessions. Gorbachev noted that President-elect George Bush and many members of his team appeared attracted to this approach. Further concessions might simply play into their hands. At the same time, the Americans were worried that Soviet initiatives would continue to dominate the international agenda: "They are still concerned lest they might be on the losing side." The U.N. speech had burnished Gorbachev's already stellar status as the world's most visionary statesman. Continuing the current policy course might produce a real breakthrough in the relationship by pressuring or convincing Western policymakers of the need for major change. On balance, Gorbachev concluded that it was necessary to carry on with the new approach. "We cannot allow the future [Bush] administration to take a protracted time out and slow down the tempo of our political offensive."

As the conference transcripts and other sources confirm, Gorbachev's assessment was right.[6] Many officials in the United States and its allied governments were convinced that Gorbachev was driving the global agenda with his innovative policies. They believed that some response was necessary to regain the initiative. If the West responded in kind, Gorbachev hoped, a "tit for tat" dismantling of the Cold War would ensue that would leave all parties—and especially the Soviet Union—much better off. A high-stakes play was under way designed to change the rules of the Cold War game. And competitive impulses (Gorbachev's fellow reformer Aleksandr Yakovlev spoke at the same Politburo meeting of "pulling the carpet out from under the feet of

---

4. "Minutes of the Meeting of the Politburo of the Central Committee of the Communist Party of the Soviet Union (CPSU CC) 27–28 December 1988 (Excerpts)," *Cold War International History Bulletin*, no. 12/13 (fall/winter 2001): 24. The following quotations are from this document.

5. He had vetted the reductions with the General Staff and the Defense Ministry—though not thoroughly enough to satisfy officers opposed to the initiative. See Sergei F. Akhromeyev and G. M. Korniyenko, *Glazami marshala i diplomata: Kriticheskiy vzglyad na vneshnyuyu politiku SSSR do i posle 1985-go goda* (Moscow: Mezhdunarodniye otnosheniya, 1992), 210–14, and L. G. Ivashov, *Marshal Yazov (Rokovoi Avgust 91-go): Pravda o "putche"* (Moscow: Biblioteka Zhurnala "Muzhestvo," 1992), 26–28.

6. See Chapters 1 and 5.

the [U.S.] military-industrial complex") still mingled with visionary hopes of mutual understanding and cooperation. In hindsight, what stands out about the close of 1988 are the mounting challenges to Gorbachev and the Soviet Union—from the economy, hard-liners, and the rising independence movements in East-Central Europe and many of the Soviet republics. At the time, these were balanced by Gorbachev's spectacular success on the world stage and the hope of domestic renewal inspired by his reforms. As the new Bush administration took office in January 1989, it was still unclear whether the Soviet Union's international successes would outpace its growing internal and imperial failures, and how the unfolding drama would affect the U.S. role in Europe and the world.

This book represents a joint effort by scholars and policymakers to understand how the uncertainty and contingency that characterized the end of 1988 was resolved over the course of the following three years. Given the diverse backgrounds and perspectives of the participants in this project, as well as the extraordinarily complex and controversial nature of the Cold War's endgame, it will come as no surprise that the pages that follow contain more than their share of debates—among practitioners, between practitioners and scholars, and most notably among the scholars themselves. Some debates are the kinds that are generated by any major event—for example, the role of deep economic and social causes as opposed to specific policy choices, personalities, and contingency. Others are specific to the case—such as whether the United States missed opportunities to engage Mikhail Gorbachev earlier in 1989 or stuck with him too long in 1991, or whether Gorbachev missed opportunities to salvage better terms for Moscow during the diplomacy of German unification. Such debates are inevitable and necessary for sharpening our understanding of the end of the Cold War and its implications for general theories of international relations and foreign policy.

Notwithstanding its diversity, this book is unified by four crucial concerns. First is a commitment on the part of all the conference participants and the scholarly contributors to getting the story right—a goal that is advanced measurably by the use of the conference discussions in conjunction with other sources. Second, the chapter authors all share a commitment to the empirical testing of theoretical or policy arguments and a conviction that the end of the Cold War is an event that is unusually instructive for that purpose. Third, the chapter authors all locate their arguments at the level of "middle-range theory" rather than the "grand theories" such as realism, liberalism, and constructivism that have framed the scholarly debate thus far. By so doing, they avoid much of the "talking past each other" (that is to say, use of incommensurate language and evidentiary standards) that has characterized the academic debate over the Cold War's end.[7] And, fourth, the debates in the chapters that follow all revolve around the relationship between large-scale tectonic changes, on the one hand, and specific circumstances, perceptions, and choices, on the other. In particular, the book is animated by two central questions: What role did personality, interpersonal interactions, and the evolution of trust among individual policymakers play in explaining the peaceful end of the Cold War? And how do we evaluate the influence of these factors in a context characterized by powerful domestic and international constraints?

Part I: Oral History: The Princeton Conference

On March 29–30, 1996, Princeton University's Woodrow Wilson School, in cooperation with the Baker Institute for Public Policy at Rice University, hosted nine former high officials of the U.S. and Soviet governments who played critical roles in the tumultuous diplomacy of the Cold War's end.[8] Led by former U.S. secretary of state James A. Baker III and former Soviet foreign minister Aleksandr Bessmertnykh, the conferees spent two days analyzing and reliving the major events affecting world politics from 1989 to 1992: the forging of a new political relationship between the incoming Bush administration and the Gorbachev team in the winter and spring of 1989; the collapse of communism in Europe in the fall of that year; the new relationship that developed between Bush and Gorbachev at the shipboard summit in Malta in December; the genesis and management of the "two-plus-four" talks on Germany in early 1990; collaboration between the superpowers against Iraq's occupation of Kuwait, which was cemented by the two leaders at the Helsinki summit in September 1990; and the dramatic domestic develop-

---

7. For further elaboration of this argument, see William C. Wohlforth, "Reality Check: Revising Theories of International Politics in Response to the End of the Cold War," *World Politics* 50, no. 4 (July 1998): 650–80.

8. A small selection of excerpts from the conference was published in Fred I. Greenstein and William C. Wohlforth, eds., *Cold War Endgame: Report of a Conference Sponsored by the John Foster Dulles Program for the Study of Leadership in International Affairs, Princeton University, and the James A. Baker III Institute for Public Policy, Rice University*, Center of International Studies Monograph Series, no. 10 (Princeton: Princeton University Center of International Studies, 1997).

ments in the Soviet Union that culminated in the August 1991 coup and the collapse of the Soviet state four months later.

One of the major dividends of an oral history conference is to re-create the intellectual atmosphere that characterized a major event while participants are still able and willing to do so. The format of the Princeton conference, with the two teams of policy veterans seated at tables and able to react to each other, encouraged such recollections. It allowed spontaneous interactions that mirrored what had occurred years before across numerous negotiating tables. The conference, whose spirit is well captured in the transcripts reprinted in Chapters 1–4 thus added to our historical knowledge and provided a powerful antidote to the hindsight bias of post hoc, ergo propter hoc.

The discussions were extraordinarily frank. While many of these policy veterans have written memoirs, at the conference they were able to argue with each other, prod each other's memories, compare recollections, and debate policy options and possible "missed opportunities" as they relived some of the most important years of their careers. The conferees discussed both domestic politics and grand strategy; they debated underlying causes of events as well as the details of statecraft; they recalled specific meetings and decisions as well as the general perceptions that underlay decision making on both sides.

Chapter 1 presents the first roundtable discussion, which opened with remarks by James Baker and Anatoly Chernyaev on the causes of the Cold War's end and the Soviet collapse that frame the subsequent sessions. The first session examines the recasting of the U.S.-Soviet relationship after the new Bush administration's inauguration and Gorbachev's acceleration of reforms in Soviet domestic and foreign policy. It illustrates both the perceptual gap between the two sides that still existed in this period and the complex relationship between international interactions and domestic coalitions. The fundamental question that underlies the discussion is, why were the Americans so much less certain of Soviet intentions than vice versa? The perceptual gap and the complex links between domestic and foreign policy are dramatically illustrated by the two sides' different reactions to Gorbachev's offer of a "third zero" on short-range nuclear forces, which he conveyed to Baker during the secretary of state's visit to Moscow in May 1989. The former Soviet officials insisted that this offer was not intended to sow discord in the NATO alliance, while the Americans assumed that it was precisely such a classic Cold War ploy.

The collapse of communism in Eastern Europe and the reunification of Germany are discussed in the second session (Chapter 2). The participants debate the extent to which Germany's unification in NATO was a consequence of superior Western statecraft or the unintended outcome of a chaotic and uncontrolled process, with the former Soviet officials tending to accept the latter view. Soviet policy veterans detailed the reasoning behind Gorbachev's acquiescence to American and German terms as well as Moscow's decision not to form a coalition with Paris and London to prevent or slow unification. They contended that Gorbachev and Shevardnadze played a complex, two-level strategic game designed to stave off the polarization of Soviet domestic politics—a game that required unorthodox decision-making procedures. For example, bureaucratic stratagems had to be employed to circumvent internal opponents and present them with faits accomplis. Such tactics help account for the erratic character of Soviet policy in this period.

Chapter 3 deals with U.S.-Soviet cooperation in countering Iraq's aggression against Kuwait and restarting the peace process in the Middle East. The conferees relate how Soviet foreign minister Shevardnadze—against the views of most of his ministry and with only partial advance approval from Gorbachev—agreed to a joint statement with Baker that condemned Iraq's occupation of Kuwait and endorsed an arms embargo; how Moscow came to support U.N. Security Council resolutions on Iraq; how special Iraq envoy Yevgeny Primakov and Shevardnadze battled for Gorbachev's allegiance; and how First Deputy Foreign Minister Aleksandr Bessmertnykh single-handedly revised a Soviet plan presented to Iraqi foreign minister Tariq Aziz by Gorbachev and Primakov that might have derailed U.S.-Soviet cooperation. Chernyaev details Gorbachev's frenetic efforts to negotiate a diplomatic solution, quoting extensively from heretofore unpublished transcripts of Gorbachev's talks with Aziz.

Chapter 4 presents the transcript of the final session, which directly addressed the crucial backdrop to all the preceding diplomacy of the Cold War's end: Soviet domestic politics and the mounting dual crises of the communist system and the Soviet empire. The conferees discussed efforts by Bush, Baker, and U.S. ambassador to the Soviet Union Jack Matlock to warn Gorbachev of an impending coup. Because many of the principals were present, the conference provided an opportunity to clarify the flow and eventual fate of information in this unusual episode. The discussants also explore the collapse of Gorbachev's support and the final crisis and dissolution of the Soviet Union. They engage in a sharp debate on the question of whether the Soviet Union could have been saved in some form, and whether U.S. policy could have done more to support Soviet reforms.

How the Conference Transcript Was Edited

Chapters 1–4 present verbatim transcripts, only cosmetically edited, of two days of intense give-and-take discussions. Emendations were made only to enhance clarity and stylistic consistency. Some minor editorial changes and clarifications are indicated in brackets; larger clarifications are made in footnotes. In no instance was the meaning of the original text altered, and there were no additions of text after the fact.

My procedure for editing was as follows. First, I checked the stenographic transcript against audio tapes of the conference to catch any speech missed or misunderstood by the typist. I resolved conflicts or names or dates by checking the historical record and, in some cases, checking with participants. Second, I edited the text, omitting some material in instances where the discourse was repetitive, speech was unclear, or references were made to goings-on in the conference hall. In a few instances, I removed text containing digressions unrelated to the subject at hand or invalidated by subsequent discussion. In a very few instances, I altered the order of points when a speaker who was enumerating a series of arguments interrupted himself and added commentary to a point made in a previous paragraph. I made the minor grammatical and syntactical corrections that are inevitably necessary to render spoken English more easily readable. Finally, I added annotations in footnotes where clarification seemed necessary. The only more complete source is the original transcript of the audio tapes, which is available from the editor upon request.

Part II: Analysis

Part II consists of two chapters that analyze central empirical and theoretical puzzles presented by the behavior of each of the superpowers in the Cold War's endgame. In Chapter 5, Derek Chollet and James Goldgeier explain U.S. behavior during the "pause" of 1989. When Ronald Reagan left office, he and Secretary of State George Shultz were quite clear that they had effected a transformation of the U.S.-Soviet relationship. But at the start of the next administration, despite the presence at top levels of Reagan holdovers, the Bush team declared the need for a pause. Their own assessment that the Cold War was indeed over did not occur until the Malta summit in December 1989. Was this lag caused by a perceptual bias in officials steeped in a Cold War mind-set? Was it a kind of "adaptive error" that results from the strategic imperatives not to get suckered by an adversary in sheep's clothing? Making use of a large array of memoirs by former U.S. officials, Chollet and Goldgeier explore the role of personal interactions and the phenomenon of trust to explain the gradual acceptance of the Bush team that Gorbachev was sincere. In a conclusion that directly reinforces the views of the Princeton conferees, they find that interpersonal trust developed in face-to-face meetings is the best explanation for shifting assessments of the advisability of closely engaging with the Soviets. The authors forward the implications of their strong finding for international relations theory and our understanding of recent history.

In Chapter 6, Andrew Bennett develops an integrated explanation for the central puzzles of Soviet behavior in 1989–90: Why did the Soviet Union fail to use force in 1989 to keep together the Warsaw Pact, as it had in Hungary in 1956 and Czechoslovakia in 1968? Why did the Soviet bureaucracy apparently fail even to come up with a coherent option for using force in 1989? Why was Gorbachev unable or unwilling to exact a higher price for German unification in 1990? Why did his acceptance of a unified Germany within NATO survive opposition from his foreign and defense ministries, which in this case did propose and push for alternatives? Incorporating an extraordinary range of new material, Bennett tests the strengths and weaknesses of four influential middle-range explanations. He concludes by showing which theories perform best for which aspects of the event, and derives critical lessons for further theory development and empirical explanation.

Part III: Debates

Part III presents a debate on the causes of the end of the Cold War: the "Gorbachev factor" (Vladislav Zubok, Chapter 7); the role of new ideas and intellectuals (Robert English, Chapter 8); and economic constraints on the Soviet Union (Stephen G. Brooks and William C. Wohlforth, Chapter 9). The idea underlying this part of the book is that presenting and evaluating arguments over the causal importance of different variables at play in a complex event as clearly and rigorously as possible helps to define the debate for students and scholars alike. This analytical exercise also sets the stage for interpreting future releases of archival or other evidence by setting forth as clearly as possible the case that can be made for the importance of various factors based on the evidence now available. Each of these three chapters captures a corner of the ongoing debate on these events, and each mines all the most recently released archival and memoir material that bears on the argument in question. Moreover, each chapter is distinguished from existing literature by the clarity and rigor with which the central concepts—leadership, ideas, and material incentives—are operationalized and tested.

In Chapter 7, Zubok provides an original interpretation of the impact of Gorbachev's personality on the Cold War endgame. Mining a massive array of Soviet and Russian memoir materials, he paints a dramatically different portrait of Gorbachev than that propounded by both his admirers and critics in Russia and the West. He shows how this "less than great" but nonetheless historical personality decisively influenced Soviet preferences, strategy, and negotiating tactics in 1989–90. In particular, he explains why Gorbachev was so easily and deeply influenced by specifically *Western* ideas—an important contribution to the explanation of this case that powerfully complements the work of scholars who highlight the role of ideas in international politics.

One such scholar is Robert English, who in Chapter 8 shows how the new thinking shaped the Cold War's end. English seeks to demonstrate the inadequacy of explanations based mainly on material incentives as well as those that focus on ideas merely as instrumental tools that actors use to forward their interests. Exploiting extensive interview and memoir material, he establishes the crucial importance of the *normative* power of ideas. The new thinking, in his analysis, was more a reflection of noninstrumental values and cultural norms than it was a vehicle for solving political, economic, or military problems. The result is a sharp, clean, and persuasive case for the causal importance of ideas in a crucial episode of international change—and one with important implications for how scholars study the role of ideas in international relations

In Chapter 9, Stephen G. Brooks and William C. Wohlforth take the popular economic explanation for the end of the Cold War and subject it to greater empirical scrutiny than other scholars have generally done. They report on research that shows—in contrast to English and Zubok—that economic constraints strongly biased the Soviet Union toward retrenchment, and thus made the Cold War's end on mainly Western terms the most likely outcome. Gorbachev and the new thinkers were swimming with the current of underlying material incentives, not against it, as stronger versions of explanations that emphasize leadership or ideas hold. The effect of leaders and ideas was thus to a significant degree endogenous to changing economic constraints. Given that the economic argument is the one against which most others are pitched, clarifying that argument is useful even to those who ultimately remain unpersuaded by Brooks and Wohlforth's conclusions. In the interests of further clarifying the issues at stake, the authors systematically consider and respond to five popular arguments against an explanation rooted in economic constraints.

Conclusion: The Search for Synthesis

Debates such as that presented in Part III can clarify explanatory and theoretical issues, but they do so at the risk of overemphasizing differences among analysts or oversimplifying complex and contingent events. In the concluding chapter, Joseph Lepgold uses an informal rendition of strategic-choice theory to suggest a way to synthesize the causal arguments presented in Part III, the contending explanations offered in Part II, and the practitioners' perspectives on display in Part I. Although any such effort to "subsume" a complex and contentious body of scholarship and practical knowledge is bound to be controversial, Lepgold is explicit about the costs of his approach. Moreover, the approach he forwards does have the virtue of inclusiveness, not only with regard to contending academic theories, but also with regard to the concerns of practitioners. The gaps that divide scholarly schools of thought as well as the worlds of policy and scholarship will never and probably should never be eliminated. But we do need a language for communicating knowledge across these divides. One way to develop such a language is for a diverse group of scholars and practitioners to join forces in an effort to understand a seminal event. That objective underlies all of the chapters that follow.

PART I
Oral History: The Princeton Conference

1 Forging a New Relationship

THIS CHAPTER PRESENTS the first session of the Princeton conference. It begins with opening remarks by James Baker and Anatoly Chernyaev that frame the debate over the causes of the end of the Cold War that recurs throughout the conference and is addressed by the scholarly chapters in Part III of this volume. The conferees then discussed the forging of the new administration's relationship with Moscow, ending with the December 1989 Malta summit. Following the inauguration of President George Bush in January 1989, the Bush administration cautiously took up the task of dealing with the Soviet Union. After a lengthy and much-criticized policy review, Secretary of State James Baker flew to Moscow in May 1989 to meet President Mikhail Gorbachev and Foreign Minister Eduard Shevardnadze, who were frustrated by U.S. passivity. Baker returned counseling a renewal of U.S. activism. The effort saw its first breakthrough in September in the meeting of Baker and Shevardnadze at the Jackson Hole, Wyoming, ministerial meeting. Shevardnadze displayed astonishing frankness about the situation at home and modified Soviet arms control positions. The Malta "seasick" summit on December 2–3, which had been under discussion in secret channels since midsummer, marked the first meeting of minds between Bush and Gorbachev. For some participants, this meeting marked the symbolic end of the Cold War. It was at Malta that Gorbachev told Bush, "We don't consider you an enemy anymore"; and he emphatically stressed the right of the peoples of Eastern and Central Europe to choose their own governments. Bush, in turn, assured the Soviet leader that the United States would not exploit the turmoil in ways that would harm the interests of a reforming Soviet Union.

Fred I. Greenstein: Welcome. We are going to get rather quickly into a panel discussion in which Don Oberdorfer will be doing the principal questioning. But first we are going to have opening remarks by Mr. Baker and by Mr. Chernyaev, and I thought that just to start things off I would steal a passage from one of the several volumes by participants: Jack Matlock's *Autopsy on an Empire.* "To understand why the Cold War ended in 1989 rather than 2089 and the Soviet Union collapsed in 1991 rather than 2091, and why the latter

occurred with little violence in the empire's heartland, we must think about
the decisions actual people made. Impersonal social and economic trends may
have molded the environment in which decisions were made, but it was decisions made by political leaders that determined the timing and character of
events."[1] Stay tuned for the next two days and you will learn a great deal about
them. Jim?

James A. Baker III: Fred, thank you very much. Let me begin by saying
how pleased I am to be here today at an event which is cosponsored by two
institutions which are very dear to my heart: Princeton University and the
Baker Institute at Rice University. I am truly honored that we have such distinguished participants, both scholars and practitioners, with us. I hope that our
reflections here today will serve to bridge the gap between the world of scholars and the world of practitioners, which is a key tenet of the Baker Institute for
Public Policy, because these worlds have a great deal to offer each other.

Now I do not claim that what I am going to outline here in the next ten
to twelve minutes will be either complete or unanimously accepted. Indeed, I
encourage all of you to take issue with my impressions and my conclusions
when you differ with them. After all, a vigorous debate is a necessary antecedent
to an informed approach to public policy. And, of course, an informed approach
to public policy is the ultimate goal of a conference such as this. In any event,
I hope that my comments will offer us a starting point from which we can proceed—a road map, if you will, for further discussion.

We meet today to discuss perhaps the most important event of this century: the *peaceful* end of a half-century of confrontation that had the very real
potential of annihilating mankind. Let me start with a very simple premise:
that there is, in my view at least, no single explanation for the peaceful end of
the Cold War. All of the people that you see at both tables here today were
fortunate, if you will pardon the expression, to be "present at the expiration."
But that expiration was the result of a multiplicity of factors. The issues presented by these revolutionary changes were enormously complicated, and
these issues offered no shortage of challenges to those who had to deal with
them on a day-to-day basis.

With the benefit of hindsight, I think some rather distinct patterns are
recognizable and that we can generally trace the end of the Cold War and the

---

1. Jack F. Matlock Jr., *Autopsy on an Empire: The American Ambassador's Account of the Collapse of the Soviet Union* (New York: Random House, 1995), 649.

dissolution of the Soviet Union to a confluence of economic, political, and strategic forces that began to emerge in the early 1980s. First and foremost among these was the growing economic stagnation in the Soviet Union. That stagnation prompted Mikhail Gorbachev to move away from the central planning model that had long defined the organization of the Soviet system. By the mid-1980s, indeed, it had become painfully obvious—not just to the Soviet leadership but to the average citizen as well—that the Soviet Union could no longer postpone the choice between guns and butter. That is to say, the Soviet Union could no longer pursue an approach of increasing defense spending while also placating consumers through their very extensive social support network. In trying to satisfy these two conflicting and increasingly urgent demands, investment in infrastructure—that is, infrastructure outside the military-industrial complex—was neglected. There was little choice but to try to reform.

In the face of this, Mikhail Gorbachev devised perestroika, or "restructuring." At heart, it is my view that Gorbachev was a reformer, he was not truly a revolutionary. I think he sought reform as a way to strengthen and renew communism and for that matter to strengthen and renew the Soviet Union as a superpower itself. I think he felt that he could somehow modify socialism without fundamentally altering that system. But soon it became obvious that merely tinkering with Gosplan-organized economy was only going to hasten its collapse.[2] By the late 1980s, the Soviet economy was sagging heavily under its own weight. At the same time, the people of the Soviet Union and the Eastern Bloc by virtue primarily of the technological revolution, began to see the West for what it really was: the home of liberty and prosperity rather than the false vision that they had theretofore been fed. Perestroika played into a nascent desire for change, but economic collapse alone certainly does not fully explain the end of the Cold War or the dissolution of the Soviet empire.

The political earthquake attending Gorbachev's program of glasnost was also, I think, a very necessary ingredient. The intent of glasnost or "openness" was originally rather limited, and that was to provide a means to root out corruption from the Brezhnev era. After all, this corruption was an economic drag that the Soviet Union could no longer afford. But the effect of glasnost, however modest in design, really was enormous. In effect, it let the freedom genie

2. "Gosplan"—the Soviet state planning agency, responsible for setting prices and production throughout the Soviet economy.

out of the bottle. Perestroika and glasnost then fed into deeply rooted nationalist sentiments that had long been stifled by an artificial construct, which was the Soviet Union itself. The struggle for national self-determination first, of course, appeared in Eastern Europe and then it spread to the Baltics, to the Ukraine, and to Central Asia. The spread of political and intellectual freedom unleashed a centrifugal force that tore apart Moscow's empire, from Bucharest to East Berlin, and later tore apart the Soviet Union itself, from Tallinn to Tashkent.

The end of the Cold War reminds us once again of the enduring power of ideas and the resilience of the human spirit to think and act freely. But any examination of the end of the Cold War would be incomplete without consideration of the geostrategic contributing factors as well. In the end, Ambassador George Kennan, the father of containment, was proved prophetically right. As long as the West and the United States stood strong and united, the Communist bloc would eventually disintegrate, unraveling from internal contradictions. The nature of perestroika and glasnost and the sympathy that these reforms engendered among Western public opinion really allowed the United States and its allies to treat this former adversary, the Soviet Union, as a partner rather than as a defeated foe as the end approached.

In 1989, we in the Bush administration knew that we were not able to deliver reform to the Soviet Union. But we realized nonetheless that we could assist the process, and we could assist the Soviet leadership as well by fostering a supportive international environment. As President Bush told Chancellor Kohl in February 1990, "We are going to win but we must be clever while we are doing it." We wanted, frankly, for the Soviet Union to go out peacefully, and accordingly we focused on areas of mutual advantage. And when I say we wanted the Soviet Union to go out peacefully, I am not talking about the implosion of the Soviet Union. We wanted the course and direction that the Soviet Union had theretofore taken to end peacefully. Early in the Bush administration we identified a number of such areas of mutual cooperation. These included progress toward creation of a Europe whole and free, resolution of regional conflicts, expansion of arms control, institutionalization of glasnost and democratization, and the provision of technical assistance to support economic reform in the Soviet Union itself.

U.S.-Soviet cooperation began in real earnest on regional conflicts in 1989; it picked up speed in connection with the agreement of both countries to the "two plus four" process for German unification in February 1990, and reached its apex when the United States and the Soviet Union were able to look past their considerable past rivalries to stand together against Saddam Hussein in August 1990. But one thing we should never forget as we talk about this tremendous event over the course of the next two days is that the Cold War was colored by its potential for turning hot. So in a military sense many view the end of the Cold War as a victory for American and Western armed forces. While this view is not altogether wrong, I think it is important that it be clarified. The end of the Cold War really was a military victory of a different kind. It was one in which capabilities and technology, and not infantry and firepower or aircraft, were the crucial factors. The 1980s and the early 1990s witnessed a technical revolution in military warfare, one in which sophisticated technologies such as computers and stealth weaponry fundamentally changed strategy. Not insignificantly, high-technology projects like President Reagan's Strategic Defense Initiative stood as a concrete example to the Soviet army that it was falling behind in the technological arms race, and in this sense new thinking in Soviet foreign policy may have been an outgrowth of the recognition of the difficulty of competing in this era. In order to gain the intellectual and technological resources for modernization, the Soviet military initially supported many of the efforts to open Soviet society and supported many of the efforts to liberate its economy. For the Soviet Union to keep up strategically, scientists and technicians needed room to innovate. Later, when the Soviet military began to oppose reform, it had become too late. Ironically, then, the attempt to bring the Soviet Union into the twenty-first century strategically, economically, and politically through new thinking, through perestroika, through glasnost, fostered the very forces that caused the Soviet Union to implode. Indeed, I think that perhaps the grand irony of the twentieth century is that Mikhail Gorbachev sought to engineer neither the demise of communism, nor the breakup of the Soviet Union. Yet he will be credited— appropriately, I think—with having done both. This outcome is not just ironic, it is paradoxical.

Despite the trends I have outlined here, which suggested the eventual cessation of the Cold War in any event, I think it is important to remember that a range and a variety of outcomes were very definitely possible. The *peaceful* end of the Cold War was by no means a preordained event. It was contingent on a series of historical events, some of them rational, some irrational, some intended, some unintended, and this brings me to my final and perhaps most important point. And that is that the events we discuss here this weekend were above all shaped by people—many of the people at the tables on either side of me here. The peaceful end of the Cold War was brought about by the hard work and the brave actions of individuals like Ronald Reagan and George Bush and Mikhail Gorbachev and Helmut Kohl and Margaret Thatcher and François Mitterrand, among others. These leaders all made very tough but informed decisions, and they accepted their consequences. The Soviet Union went out with a whimper and not a bang because of the judgment and because of the choices of these leaders, and so in the final analysis, history remains very much manmade. Thank you.

Anatoly S. Chernyaev:[3] Secretary Baker, we very much appreciate the initiative to hold such a conference, because we believe that the memory and the knowledge of what happened during the years that we are discussing here must be preserved. Despite the many problems and even misfortunes and tragedies that happened afterward, we believe that what happened then was absolutely necessary, and we should remember it, and we should discuss how it happened.

I would like to make five brief remarks to follow up on what Secretary Baker has just said. First, in studies of perestroika it is very often said—with some truth—that Gorbachev's foreign policy was not the result of strategic thinking, but that it was based mostly on Gorbachev's domestic concerns. Ambassador Matlock demonstrated this brilliantly in his remarkable book. But even though this is true, it is not the whole truth, and it does not definitively capture Gorbachev's motives. The new foreign policy of Mikhail Gorbachev was also based on thinking autonomous from domestic concerns. There were a number of elements involved. For example, the understanding that a nuclear catastrophe was a real possibility. This differed from the view of the previous Soviet leaders, who still clung to the idea that if a nuclear war were to erupt one day, it would end in our victory. Gorbachev regarded a nuclear war as a total catastrophe, as a global disaster.

Another crucial element in the new foreign strategy is Gorbachev's conviction—which had not yet jelled in the first years of perestroika but took

3. Here and throughout the conference, Mr. Chernyaev's comments were translated by Pavel Palazchenko.

shape later—that we had lost the ideological war which we had been conducting for so many decades in the international arena. That ideological war had
been lost not just because of technological and economic inferiority, but
because the ideology itself that underlay it was wrong. Yet another important
element was that long before Gorbachev became the general secretary, he
became convinced that no one was going to attack us. And, a final element
that was very important in defining Gorbachev's foreign policy was his moral
principles. Those moral principles evolved over his entire life, and basically
they boiled down to the rejection of violence, to the rejection of the use of
force, not just in policy and politics, but generally in life, as a way of living in a
human society. And hence there really was a total lack in Gorbachev of undue
respect for the military or any kind of special fascination with military parades
and demonstrations of military power.

The second remark that I would like to make is about our attitude of
confidence and trust toward the U.S. administration. That was not born easily, but once it emerged, the development of this attitude of trust and confidence was a lot faster on our part than on the part of the U.S. administration
and on the part of the American establishment. So this process of the development of mutual trust was evolving at different speeds and in different ways.
There is something that can be explained here by the unique features of our
national character and probably of American national character, but there is
something paradoxical in the fact that we evolved trust faster than our
American counterparts. After all, particularly our generation was bred in the
spirit of anti-imperialism and anti-U.S. rhetoric. And of course there is also
the older Russian tradition of mistrust of the West and the feeling that the
West will never really love and trust us that goes back to [the Slavophiles]
Danilevsky and Dostoyevsky. So it is paradoxical that we evolved that trust
faster than our U.S. counterparts.

Third, in developing our relations we relied less on the art of diplomacy
and more on human relationships, more on building human contacts and
human rapport among the people who actually became involved in the development of the relationship. I think we can date it to the spring of 1987. As of
that moment, Gorbachev's relations with the United States no longer were a
zero-sum game of foreign policy where one side gives more and the other
yields more. For Gorbachev, the main goal, the overriding objective, was to
end the confrontation, to end the Cold War, and it was for that reason that he

accepted the kind of concessions that are still being criticized. Many in our country still cannot forgive him those concessions.

My fourth remark: the Cold War ended in Malta, it ended in 1989 rather than in 1991 when George Bush visited the Soviet Union or when the Soviet Union collapsed. If we don't accept that the Cold War virtually ended in 1989, then we will not be able to explain German unification, we would not be able to explain collaboration of the Soviet Union and the United States during the Gulf crisis. I think that diplomatic finesse can sometimes override historic truth, but it cannot cancel it. We certainly could draw perhaps a parallel with the history of the U.S. Civil War. It would be the same as saying that the Civil War in this country ended not in 1865 but in 1877 with Reconstruction. The elements of the Cold War were present afterward, and they are still present in international politics, but that does not mean that the Cold War is still there. It ended at Malta in 1989.

And my fifth remark. This is not a compliment but a statement of fact: the Bush-Baker administration played an enormous role in the process of building new international relations in 1989–91. The positions and the attitudes toward the Soviet Union as outlined by George Bush at Malta were things that we very much hoped we might hear, but still it was a surprise, still it was something that we very much welcomed when we heard them. It was only later that we, including Gorbachev, learned about the enormous work that was done by the administration during the so-called pause, or strategic review. Unfortunately, in 1989, we in Moscow were receiving a lot of information that was bent in a negative way in order to prevent the development of a more trustful attitude toward the United States. Even I as foreign policy assistant to Mr. Gorbachev was not at that time familiar with important and very crucial statements that Secretary Baker made on October 4 and October 16. I did not learn about that in a timely way, whereas in fact those were extremely important statements. And I must mention here the role that Mr. Baker played in the process of German unification. The way that process was concluded is the way that it ought to have concluded because anything otherwise would have been a tragedy. The Nine Points as outlined by Secretary Baker played an enormous role in making this process smooth and in the positive conclusion of that process.

And finally on a personal and emotional note, let me say now that we have met that I, like many people on the Gorbachev team, believe that Gorbachev, so to say, got from the West less than he deserved as compared to what other people got from the West—people who became possible only because of Gorbachev. Thank you.

Don Oberdorfer: We're going to turn to 1989 in a minute, but first Minister Bessmertnykh wanted to add something.

Aleksandr A. Bessmertnykh: May I just refer a little bit to the conceptual part which was raised about the demise of the Soviet Union and the end of the Cold War? There is a prevailing view in U.S. scholarly and political thinking that the demise of the Soviet Union and the end of the Cold War is almost the same thing, or at least the basic characteristic of the end of the Cold War is the end of the Soviet Union. I think that we have got to be clear on that, and I agree with Professor Greenstein and with Mr. Chernyaev and with the rest who said that these are two important historical events that developed on their own—influencing each other, of course, but they are *two* historical events, not just one historical event with two shadows. The Cold War was something that we tried to kill together—the United States and the Soviet Union. I wouldn't know whether it ended in 1989 or some other moment. I would agree that Malta was one of the most prominent events which proved that the Cold War had ended somewhat earlier. It doesn't matter—a matter of months is not important. But if the Cold War had not ended at that time, many things would have developed differently.

As for the Soviet Union, its self-destruction occurred for the reasons that Secretary Baker just mentioned. I think this is an absolutely correct and brilliant analysis, including the economic stagnation and glasnost and national strikes in the country, et cetera. But it has almost nothing to do with the end of the Cold War. So in the Cold War there were no winners, and the loser in the general competition between the two sides was the socialist system that existed in the Soviet Union. Hypothetically it was quite possible that we could have had the end of the Cold War, the end of the socialist system in the Soviet Union, and the Soviet Union still preserved.

Oberdorfer: Thank you. We'll return to the collapse of the Soviet Union in the final session. For now: 1989. As Mr. Chernyaev said, there was a great deal of progress in Soviet-American relationships in 1987 and in 1988. Mr. Gorbachev came to Washington in 1987 to sign the INF treaty. In 1988, there was the agreement for Soviet forces to leave Afghanistan; and President Reagan went to Moscow, met Mr. Gorbachev, and went into Red Square. At the end of 1988—and I remember this well because it happened at a luncheon at *The Washington Post*—Margaret Thatcher declared that the Cold War was over. In January 1989 President Bush took office. There was then a strategic review, sometimes called the pause, that lasted from January until May. In May, two fundamental things happened: Secretary Baker went to Moscow for the first time and met Mr. Gorbachev on his home ground, and President Bush went to Texas A&M University and in effect broke the near silence in the American government about his fundamental policies toward the Soviet Union, declaring that the United States wished to now move "beyond containment."

Later that year, Foreign Minister Shevardnadze came to Jackson Hole in a very important meeting with Baker and others on the State Department team. They had some important discussions that led up to the December meeting in Malta. That's the period that we are going to be discussing. In February 1989, Ambassador Matlock wrote a lengthy and interesting series of cables back to Washington giving his view of where Soviet-American relations stood at the outset of the Bush administration. I am just going to read the first paragraph of the first message, which really sets the context for this discussion: "We have an historic opportunity to test the degree to which the Soviet Union is willing to move into a new relationship with the rest of the world, and to strengthen those tendencies in the Soviet Union to 'civilianize' the economy and 'pluralize' the society. U.S. leverage, while certainly not unlimited, has never been greater. That leverage should be used not to 'help' Gorbachev or the Soviet Union but to promote U.S. interests. The most central of such interests is the long-term transformation of the Soviet Union into a society with effective organic constraints on the use of military force outside its borders."

That was Ambassador Matlock's take on what needed to be done as the Bush administration began its activities with Moscow. And I first would like to ask Secretary Baker and Mr. Scowcroft, in their opinion, how well was this done at the beginning? What were the difficulties in getting up to running speed in that period?

Baker: Don, I think you pinpointed the date on which things began to really move forward, and that was in May immediately following my first trip to Moscow, when I came back and reported on the results of that trip to President Bush. We had undergone the strategic review, the so-called pause, which really was not much of an exercise in terms of productivity. One of the problems that we had with it is that we entrusted the strategic review to bureau-crats who had been in place for some time, and many of whom had a vested interest in seeing to it that the policies did not change too much. But I think you have to remember that any administration to be effective has got to put its imprint upon foreign and security policy. Even though President Bush had been Ronald Reagan's vice president for eight years, it was important that he put his imprimatur upon the foreign and security policy of the Bush adminis-tration. That was the reason for the strategic review to begin with.

Furthermore, there were really two schools of thought in our adminis-tration. We had one school referred to as "the status quo plus" crowd, who had felt that the Soviet Union was disintegrating at a rapid rate and all we really had to do was wait for the apple to fall from the tree and pick it up. Others of us felt that there were things that we could do productively to encourage an international environment that would promote reform and openness in the Soviet Union. There was quite a bureaucratic struggle going on internally with respect to those two competing views. We ended up doing, in my view, many of the things that are mentioned in that cable from Jack, particularly testing the Soviet Union in various ways to determine if the new thinking was real, if some of the rhetoric we were hearing was more than just words. We talked about adopting a policy of seeking mutual advantage, and I laid out five areas in which we would seek to work with the Soviet Union to the mutual advantage of both countries. But it wasn't until May that this hap-pened—a delay that has been criticized by some, but which, in my view, was not an inordinate amount of time for a new administration and for a new pres-ident to put his imprint upon foreign and security policy. Let me say, I cer-tainly agree with Mr. Chernyaev's comments that there was greater trust developed earlier on the Soviet side than there was on the American side, but the reason for it was the strategic review and the fact that we had had a change of administrations. Even though it was a vice president succeeding his presi-dent, it nevertheless was a change of administration.

Oberdorfer: General Scowcroft, would you like to add something here?

Brent Scowcroft: Yes, just a little, starting with the strategic review. I agree completely with what Jim has said. Relying on the bureaucracy turned out to be a frail reed. We had another problem, though, and that is that for the first two and a half months it was really the President, Jim, and me. We had no secretary of defense, and that made it very difficult for us to sit down and plan a comprehensive strategy, so that helped to slow things down.[4] I also plead guilty to the slow buildup of trust, and probably me more than anyone else. In my formative years in national government, I had gone through the détente period, which I thought had left an aftermath of enervation in the United States—cuts in defense budgets, a reduction of a vibrant containment policy— bringing forth on the Soviet side discussions about the change in the "correla- tion of forces" and so on. I was not sure in 1988 and 1989 that we were seeing a sincere change on the part of President Gorbachev or whether this was a return to détente. The West was tired at this time, governments were looking for any way to cut back on defense budgets. Gorbachev's speech to the U.N. in December 1988 got great applause, and I wasn't sure it was for real, and so, as Jim [Baker] said, what we wanted to do is to go slow enough to see whether or not the Soviet side would follow up on these pronouncements that showed so much promise.

One other point. You cannot leave Eastern Europe out of a discussion of our initial days, because one of the things that Jim and I especially wanted to do was to play on the ferment in Eastern Europe in a way that would help get Soviet troops out. So initially we changed our focus on arms control from strategic nuclear arms control to the CFE [talks on Conventional Forces in Europe], and pushed through—with some internal resistance in our govern- ment—a proposal for a bilateral cut in U.S. and Soviet forces. That became the heart of one of our strategic initiatives during this period.

Oberdorfer: I would like to ask Minister Bessmertnykh about your per- ceptions of this time, as U.S. policy, which previously had gone so far so fast under President Reagan and his team, suddenly slows down to a crawl in the first months of the new Bush administration. Do you think in retrospect that it made much of a difference that it took four or five months, rather than tak- ing off from where you were before and moving right ahead?

Bessmertnykh: For the Soviet side the pause was a very important period of thinking and rethinking, of having a lot of doubts and hesitations, a lot of nervous discussions about what the new administration was up to. You have got to admit that, because there is something that you should understand. Gorbachev liked and very much respected President Bush, and their close relationship started when Bush was the vice president, including the meeting

4. Reference to the nomination of Texas senator John Tower as secretary of defense, whose confirmation was stalled in the Senate until it was defeated on March 9, 1990.

in December 1988 on Governor's Island when the two presidents were there, President Reagan and President Bush. So Gorbachev did not actually expect that Bush when he took office was going to be slow on the development of the relationship. Actually, President Bush told Gorbachev that he was for the further development of the relationship.[5] So when the pause started, there was a lot of nervousness in government circles and people were worried—What is happening? At that time I was the first deputy foreign minister, and I reported to Shevardnadze on a number of occasions that nothing terrible is happening. This is a new administration, in my view, which started that pause for domestic political reasons rather than for a strategic rethinking of the relationship, because we know that with the Reagan administration there was no threat to him and his administration from the right. With the Bush administration there was kind of a problem on the right side, and the Bush team wanted to show to its own people that they were not just inheriting a policy to carry it on as it was, but they were on their own: that even if they end up continuing that policy, it is just because they thought about it for several months and made up their minds.

But then something interesting started to happen. In 1989 Henry Kissinger suddenly came to Moscow, and the discussion was on Eastern Europe.[6] People in Moscow started to think that the Americans were turning their focus on something very, very delicate for the Russian side. Eastern Europe somehow became almost the centerpiece of the efforts and talk at that time. That was also kind of disturbing to the government. I don't know whether Gorbachev was disturbed about it at that time, but I know that there were many who were disturbed. And, of course, the right—the opposition people in the government—were trying to use this pause to pressure Gorbachev. They would be saying to him, "You see what has been happening, you have been telling us all that the Americans are the ones to work with. You have

---

5. For Gorbachev's own contemporary report of this conversation to the Politburo, see "Minutes of the Meeting of the Politburo of the Central Committee of the Communist Party of the Soviet Union (CPSU CC) 27–28 December 1988 (Excerpts)," *Cold War International History Bulletin*, no. 12/13 (fall/winter 2001): 24–29.

6. In January 1989, former Secretary of State Kissinger went to Moscow to deliver a letter of greeting from Bush to Gorbachev. He discussed with Gorbachev and Aleksandr Yakovlev a possible U.S.-Soviet dialogue on mutual restraint in Eastern Europe; in effect, to reassure the Soviets regarding their security interests in the area in order to encourage their maximum tolerance concerning the political liberalization under way there. Bush and Baker rejected the idea of such back-channel talks. The proposal, and the Bush administration's reaction to it, are discussed in more detail in Chapter 5. For Gorbachev's contemporary reactions, as reported in Politburo discussions, see Chapter 7, note 53.

changed your strategic view of the United States, you have declared that the United States should not be less secure than the Soviet Union." And "Now, you see, this pause showing that everything is not so simple." But then the whole thing ended with Jim's visit to Moscow. In looking back I would say that those concerns did not reflect at all on the further development of the relationship. The key difference that we would see in the American approach was in Malta. I mean the change of priorities presented in Malta was something that was really basically important for the Soviet side.

Oberdorfer: We are going to get to Malta in a little bit, but first on this period, one thing that I thought was very interesting that General Scowcroft said, apropos of your remarks about Eastern Europe, was that "we wanted to play on the ferment in Eastern Europe in a way that would bring about changes in the whole situation." Of course, the United States was not saying that publicly at the time, but this was a part of the whole buildup toward the NATO proposal on conventional arms control and so on. So this is an important strand that will go further in our discussions of Eastern Europe. Bob Zoellick has something he would like to add.

Robert B. Zoellick: I have several points related to that. First, what is useful to note on the strategic review is how there are formal processes and informal processes. While there was the strategic review that Brent and Secretary Baker talked about, that wasn't the whole picture. Basically our view was that we wanted to manage that process so it did not get in our way while we were developing our own policy, which Secretary Baker would develop further with the President and with Brent. For the reasons that people mentioned, no one expected those formal reviews to turn up much.

Second, it is amazing how within the space of five or six years one can forget the degree of suspicion and competition that was built into this relationship over forty-five years. I think it is important from a historical perspective not to forget that. I remember visiting a number of senators and congressmen with Secretary Baker before his confirmation hearings. The general tone that we got from Republicans and Democrats was "be careful, don't go too quickly." They never said that much in the following months, but there was a strong sense that Ronald Reagan was a romantic and wanted to secure his place in history. On the "new thinking" concept in foreign policy, I remember a document that President Bush had typed during the course of the transition that emphasized Central and Eastern Europe, and I think this fit into this competitive nature of the relationship. He was quite clear that Gorbachev was playing an active role in Germany and in Western Europe, and, in a sense, one way of testing the seriousness of the Soviet changes was to press ahead in Central and Eastern Europe. The administration moved quite promptly to do that. If you recall, there was the visit in Poland and Hungary in the early summer. Even those of us who were pushing to engage had to recognize that as honest analysts we saw very strong limits to where perestroika could go. Those from the economic side did not see that this was necessarily going to produce the results that Gorbachev wanted. That created potential dangers that you had to be aware of.

The May summit, I think, is telling here. We tried to stress regional conflicts as a way of moving away from the traditional monitor of U.S.-Soviet relations, which was arms control. Actually, we had a hard time doing that in that meeting, and I remember as we were leaving that Gorbachev actually trumped us by announcing some minimal reduction in short-range nuclear missiles that the press jumped on and that destroyed our effort to try to develop the story of regional conflicts. If part of the Soviet purpose was to develop trust, that wasn't a very good way to do it. However, it probably had another effect that was useful: it played to Secretary Baker and President Bush's competitive edge. When they came back, they were quite clear that before long, they were going to have to get ahead of this or else they were going to lose what might still be a propaganda process.

This related to how we explained issues. We struggled with how we would articulate both to the Soviets and to the American public what we were trying to do, and we first focused on this concept of "testing," which you saw in a number of documents. This again shows a sense of irony in history. Secretary Baker actually gave a major speech in the spring that was supposed to set this off; however, he gave it, it turned out, on the day that the Oliver North verdict came down, so it got absolutely no press. We also felt that it was too negative of a tone, and that's why you will see, as Mr. Chernyaev reported, in the September–October period, we consciously made three remarks. One of them was in testimony to the Senate Finance Committee on Economics, which was a conscious effort to show the Soviets that we understood what was happening in economics. We took advantage of Secretary Baker's past Treasury role to do that, and then there were the two speeches, one "The Points of Mutual Advantage," and the other the arms control speech.

The reason I emphasize the competitive relationship is that I think this switched—Secretary Baker and General Scowcroft would have a better sense of this—but my feeling was by the time of Malta, the competitive impulse had changed to one of more of a constructive working relationship. Sometime in that period I think perhaps the success of the NATO summit gave President Bush a feeling that he could move to that.

The last point I will make, which I think is critical in any discussion like this, is that you have to remember alliance relations, and, in fact, some administrations pay more attention to these than others. But I think our administration was very keenly aware of alliance relations during this period, and that both pushed us but also limited us, because during part of this early period we frankly had our hands full dealing with this SNF [short-range nuclear forces] issue with Germany, which basically was trumped with this summit.[7] It is also one explanation probably of why the United States started to shift some focus from Britain to Germany, because that was going to be the key player in this end-of-Cold-War period.

Oberdorfer: I would like to ask Sergei Tarasenko who, of course, was at the right hand of Eduard Shevardnadze during this period and throughout, to take up what Bob Zoellick has just mentioned: the slow change from a relationship at the beginning of the Bush administration which was very much centered on the competitive aspects throughout the year of 1989, ending with Malta, where more of the constructive side of things came out. What was it like in 1989 while the U.S. government, with which you had previously had these very warm relations, was going through this metamorphosis?

Sergei Tarasenko: Thank you, Don. Maybe we will take it in pieces, because that is too big an issue. I will go step by step, as diplomacy proved to be the right approach to the problem. Reading Secretary Baker's book, I was surprised to see the similarities in problems which Shevardnadze faced and the Secretary faced in forming their teams, and their broader approach to policies, and especially his conclusion that it is politics, the internal issues, that are bigger than foreign policy issues. You have to at first prove your approach inside

7. Reference is to U.S./NATO plans to modernize short-range nuclear missiles (those with ranges less than 300 kilometers) by replacing old Lance missiles with modern Lance-II missiles. These weapons would all be deployed and—if war ever came—used on German territory, thus "singling" that country out for a specific threat and generating a potential conflict of interest between Bonn and Washington. Some U.S. officials saw Gorbachev's proposals at the May summit regarding these missiles as an effort to exploit this contradiction. The matter is discussed further below.

with your friends and colleagues. The problem was that the process was not synchronized. The Soviet Union covered this period before Gorbachev formed his team and formed his approaches, and Shevardnadze formed his team and his approaches. The new administration came, and they faced a lot of problems: It's easy to *say* "hit the ground running.". . . I think even that had it not been President Bush, another president could have afforded a speedier approach on the issue. But by virtue of the fact that President Bush was a vice president before, my guess is that it would be especially difficult for him just to continue the previous policies as if nothing happened. He had as a new president to form his own image, his own approach, and that was the issue. I completely agree with Minister Bessmertnykh that at times this pause did cause problems. The problem for the embassy and the Foreign Ministry was what I would call "irritation control." We worked in that mode, trying to tell to the Politburo as a whole: "Be calm, it's internal, it will pass. Let them sort things out, and then everything will be on track. Don't hurry." But there were a lot of people inside the Soviet Union who played the other theme, saying, "Look at these Americans, they are plotting something."

Oberdorfer: General Scowcroft has something he would like to add.

Scowcroft: Just a couple of points. This was a very complicated period for us. I just want to raise two things. The first was to add something to what Sergei said. President Gorbachev had his team. You were in place, you were used to working together, you were all set. President Bush's team had two great characteristics: we all knew each other very, very well, we had worked together in one form or another, and in that sense we already had an inherent cohesion, but everybody had a little different perspective. We were all facing in the same direction, but the emphasis and the points of priority were not all the same, and during this period we were sorting all that out. The second point is that at the same time, we had a real crisis in U.S.-European relations with the short-range nuclear forces, and a call—sometimes formally, and sometimes under the table, so to speak—from the Soviet Union for a "third zero": that is, let's get rid of the short-range forces [SNF] just as we had the intermediate range forces. That was an *extremely* sensitive issue for us. The Germans were very sympathetic to that notion. Kohl had an election coming up, and there was a lot of resistance to the continued maintenance of short-range nuclear forces. On the other side, Mrs. Thatcher was saying, "We need a *strong* declaration; there's never going to be a third zero." And so we were

trying to sort this out all during this period at that same time, and I had forgotten about the famous statement that President Gorbachev made while Jim
Baker was in Moscow, a proposal for unilateral cuts in short-range nuclear
forces. So all this went on until the NATO conference, when thanks to the
combination of our CFE proposal, to which NATO was very attracted, and
some absolutely masterful negotiation by the Secretary of State about SNF,
we came out of it. But the SNF dispute sort of hung over this whole period
and made it very complicated.

Baker: Let me say something very quickly, Don, to add to what Brent
said. I haven't forgotten the initiative that President Gorbachev threw on the
table at the end of our first meeting. I had had one brief meeting with
Shevardnadze in March, I had a brief meeting in Vienna with Shevardnadze—
a very brief, sort of a formal meeting. I then had the meeting in Moscow with
President Gorbachev. This was my first meeting in Moscow with the leader of
the Soviet Union. I had been carrying an awful lot of water internally during
this period of trying to get organized, pushing for a proactive approach to the
Soviet Union, saying, in effect, we need to get going here. I think we can do
business with these people. But I want to tell you: I was almost a voice in the
wilderness taking that approach. The Defense Department, the CIA, many
people in the NSC including my buddy here [indicating Scowcroft], were all
somewhere else. Now, I had a thirty-five-year friendship with the President,
so I had a little bit of a leg up on that position, *but* then I go to Moscow and
Gorbachev cuts the legs right out from under me by throwing this wonderful
propaganda initiative on the table—they are going to eliminate five hundred
short-range nuclear weapons. Five hundred! That's great, they have thousands
of them, we had eighty-eight![8] We had eighty-eight, they had thousands, and
we were having great difficulty with the Western Europeans, so we saw that as
an effort to continue to try to drive a wedge between us and our Western
European allies, and frankly that set us back a little bit in terms of our being a
little bit more forthcoming and a little bit more trustful. I think we overcame
that in the next event, which was Wyoming. It was right after the Wyoming
meeting, Mr. Chernyaev, that I made the three speeches in October about

8. Baker here is referring to short-range ballistic *missiles* (those with ranges of less than 1,000 miles). The
United States had 88 Lance I launchers, as opposed to about 1,400 roughly comparable launchers for the
Soviets. Of course, the United States deployed thousands of other short-range nuclear *weapons* in Europe,
mainly for use on Air Force bombers. In addition, the Soviets always argued that short-range nuclear weapons
deployed on U.S. warships in the Mediterranean, North Atlantic, and Pacific would be available for use against
Soviet forces in the event of war.

what our approach to the Soviet Union should be leading up to Malta. I just wanted to clarify that.

Oberdorfer: I just want to mention one thing along those lines that on the plane coming out of Moscow after that first summit where Gorbachev gave you this wonderful sounding proposal, you told us reporters about it on the plane, and it was all the big story. On that plane in addition to the regular State Department press was Bob Novak, who is very generous toward all public officials, and he wrote in his column after that experience: "Baker's one of the foxiest of the inside operators dealing with Congress and American politics, but he is the new boy in the global high stakes game, and Gorbachev left him sprawled in the dust."

Baker: It was better than that. The headline was: "Gorbachev Rolls Baker." Here I was the foremost proponent within the administration for moving forward constructively with the Soviet Union!

Scowcroft: I loved it!

Baker: That's right. When I got back, a lot of people said, "You see, we told you so."

Oberdorfer: Ambassador Matlock, at the beginning of this session, I quoted your cable about what ought to be done. How do you evaluate this period?

Jack F. Matlock Jr.: First, let me just comment and endorse some of the things said earlier, because I think they are very important. It is very important that we not confuse the end of the Cold War with the end of the Soviet Union. Obviously some of the things that made the end of the Cold War happen created conditions that led first to the end of Communist rule in the Soviet Union, and then to the end of the Soviet Union. I don't think either of those second events, which I think were just as important in history, followed inevitably from the end of the Cold War. Quite the contrary. It did seem to me that ending the Cold War was a triumph for both countries, and I think it ended on fair terms for both countries. The problems later in the Soviet Union developed entirely for internal reasons and without, in many cases, any great encouragement from the West. So I think that this has been a problem both here and in Russia today: people tend to telescope these events and it is very important that we not do it.

Looking back at my own assessment at that time of the so-called pause, as the American ambassador in Moscow I certainly understood the reasons for the policy review. My feeling at the time was that if momentum had been restored about May, there would have been no real problem, maybe just short-term ones. But sitting in Moscow we were not as preoccupied with the short-range missile question. I guess my own feeling was these were not of that much military use and maybe it wasn't that big an issue. In any event, my feeling was that when we came out of the policy review, it was an appropriate time to come out with some forward-looking new proposals, not just in arms control but also on the regional talks, which had begun well before. We had started those back in 1984 and 1985 and had already begun to bear fruit in the Afghanistan withdrawal. It did seem to me that if we could have done maybe half of what we did at Malta by June, that would have created a certain momentum in the relationship, which would have been very helpful, helpful particularly in speeding up some internal reform decisions.

I may be wrong in this, but it seemed to me that to let some of the uncertainties drag through the summer did have a negative effect. I recall that despite our attempts to reassure Gorbachev that this did not reflect any lack of interest in moving the relationship ahead, by early July he was concerned enough to take me aside at a social function and say, "You know, please tell the President to be more considerate." He wouldn't tell me what he meant "be considerate" about. I inferred it was some of the statements that he [Bush] made about Eastern Europe, and it was very clear that he was very antsy about what was said publicly on Eastern Europe. I suspected that he realized that they were going to have a very turbulent period there, and if he was accused by others in the Politburo of in effect giving in to the Americans rather than being able to react to events in what he would consider a rational way, this would make it more difficult for him to handle. This was my inference. The nervousness probably continued longer than it needed to, but in the final analysis it would be hard for me to say that any real damage was done. I think things came out in the end probably about the way they would have in any event, except maybe regarding some of Gorbachev's internal decisions, and on that I cannot speak.

Oberdorfer: Mr. Chernyaev.

Chernyaev: I wanted to make a comment. It is my impression from what has just been said that probably at that time Gorbachev overestimated the powers of his interlocutors, Bush and Baker. He probably thought that they had the kind of powers that the general secretary of the CPSU Central Committee had. He really could not totally believe them when they said that there are certain things that we cannot do. For example, he was able to achieve as early as April 1989 a Politburo resolution which recorded and registered and codified all the principal elements of the new thinking, and I have the paper here with me. During the first years of the new thinking foreign policy, Gorbachev was not resisted by members of the Politburo on the major initiatives, such as disarmament, arms control, and improvement in U.S.-Soviet relations, et cetera. And so quite often in his discussions with very close friends, he was angry, he was irritated. He said, "Why can't the president of a superpower, the secretary of state, who hold the No. 1 and No. 2 positions in that country, cope with the resistance of those who are opposing those changes that we all believe are necessary in international affairs?" By the way, from the start Gorbachev trusted Bush and Baker in the sense that he never doubted their sincerity, he never put their words in question. And when we speak about Malta and beyond, I have notes that were taken during the discussions between Gorbachev and Bush, and Gorbachev and Baker, that really prove that there was a human rapport among them, that Gorbachev actually in a personal way trusted those people. And it was my impression that they reciprocated.

Baker: Well, I can confirm that we did. Following probably from the July meeting that I had with Shevardnadze in Paris on the margins of the Cambodian Peace Conference, from that time forward, including Wyoming and, of course, during the period of the speeches that I gave about moving forward with the relationship with the Soviet Union preparatory to the Malta conference, and I am quite sure that President Bush would confirm that as well.

Oberdorfer: Okay, Mr. Zoellick.

Zoellick: This is a very brief point but it's one that I think is an important challenge for historians, and that is, if you simply look at this as a bilateral relationship, you will be misled. We mentioned a little bit about alliance relations but remember that Secretary Baker and I in particular were spending a lot of time during our first months trying to refashion a policy toward Nicaragua, which was an extraordinarily divisive issue in U.S. politics. This was one of the first points that we tried to stress with the Soviet Union in terms of a regional relationship to raise to a new level. There is a book by Bob Kagan that basically takes the point of view that we were snookered by the Soviet Union on this.[9] So you have to look at that issue. And you have to look

9. Robert Kagan, *A Twilight Struggle: American Power and Nicaragua, 1977–1990* (New York: Free Press, 1996).

at alliance relations, which were critical to George Bush. So working out the relationships with the allies was the prerequisite to moving ahead with the Soviet Union. In some ways, the proposal that we came up with for conventional forces was a relatively quick proposal. It's not so easy, particularly without a secretary of defense, to do that. And it was much more than a military proposal, because, as Brent was suggesting, it was also a proposal that would start to send a signal that if troops left Central and Eastern Europe, that would have a political effect. So I think it is very hard if you don't look at all the different fields. This is one of the difficulties of an ambassador in the field—Jack's perspective—because there you are primarily looking at the bilateral relationship, and frankly there is no way you can have the same feel as you do when you are trying to manage the five or six different rings of the circus.

Oberdorfer: Okay, Minister Bessmertnykh.

Bessmertnykh: I just don't want to leave the audience with the feeling that Gorbachev was scheming against Jim when he came to Moscow for the first meeting. You know, when he suggested the reduction by five hundred short-range nuclear missiles, it was associated not so much with the idea of dividing European NATO members from the United States. You must remember, that was the time when Lance missile deployment was discussed.[10] When we were preparing the position for Gorbachev, it was basically designed to—let's use this word—to disrupt the plans of deploying the Lances in Europe. It was actually a military strategic idea, rather than a political one.

Baker: But it disrupted the plans of those of us who were trying to resolve the SNF problem in a way that would permit us to go forward constructively with the Soviet Union. I mean I think it may have backfired in that sense.

Pavel Palazchenko: The point was about that follow-on to Lance. It was extremely difficult to prove to anyone in the Soviet Union that that would not be the same missile in terms of range that the Soviet Union agreed to destroy under the previous INF treaty, and so it was a difficult domestic Soviet matter. You have your problems, domestic issues related to foreign and defense policy. We had our own domestic problems related to foreign and defense policy.

Baker: You didn't want to follow on to Lance, and neither did the Germans. We were . . .

10. That is, a possible replacement of old Lance missiles with modern "Lance-II" missiles.

Palazchenko: But the problem was not just that we didn't want the missile. It created a problem that Gorbachev began to be criticized for at that time . . .

Baker: I understand.

Palazchenko: . . . for being too soft on the INF treaty, for destroying a missile which the Americans would then be building, so I mean he was in the eyes of some people a softie by agreeing to that.

Bessmertnykh: There was a very important element that was very psychological for Gorbachev. As you may remember, he had agreed in his talks with Shultz to include the SS-23 in the range of weapons to be reduced.[11]

Palazchenko: Exactly. That was the second zero.

Bessmertnykh: So when Secretary Baker came to Gorbachev, Gorbachev mentioned that to you during that conversation because he was criticized, he was weakened by the agreement given to Shultz. So he needed the disruption of the Lance deployment.

Baker: I am not arguing that maybe he *needed* it, but what I am saying is it didn't move the relationship forward at that particular time.

Oberdorfer: We are talking about the situation leading up to the Malta meeting, which took place in December 1989. It really started with a letter that President Bush wrote in Paris, sitting on the steps of the American Embassy, I believe. General Scowcroft can tell us a little bit about how the Malta meeting came about.

Scowcroft: The issue of a summit had been an early subject of discussion within the administration. We came to the conclusion that U.S.-Soviet summits that were not tied to specific achievements and agreements that could be made were relatively detrimental to the United States and useful to the Soviet Union, because summits always created an atmosphere of euphoria, arising just from the fact of the two leaders getting together. That was okay if it was accompanied by things that we wanted to get done. We didn't really have any proposals to make. We had not plotted through the arms control issues, so we really didn't want to have an early summit. Then, I think two things happened. The President went to Eastern Europe and saw the ferment there and said,

---

11. Inclusion of the SS-23 "Oka" missile in the INF negotiations was strongly opposed by many in the military, defense-industrial, and arms-control communities in the Soviet Union, who argued that it was really a short-range missile. Indeed, to this day critics of Gorbachev cite this as one of his unforgivable concessions to the United States.

"This can be dangerous." And then he went to the NATO summit, and all of his European colleagues said, "You have to meet with Gorbachev." And he said: "I don't care whether we get anything done or not; we don't even have to call it a summit, but I think things are moving so fast it is dangerous for the two of us not to sit down and talk."

Then the question became, okay, where? And the President said, "Gorbachev came and addressed the U.N. last December, why doesn't he come and do that again and we can go up to Camp David for the weekend and just have some really good talks?" So he wrote the letter to Gorbachev from Paris proposing that. The answer we got was that President Gorbachev could not address the U.N. two years in a row; that wouldn't work. How about—I'll have to ask you, Aleksandr—maybe Spain? The President came back and said, "Well, I have to go to Alaska in September to look at the oil spill. How about Alaska?" And President Gorbachev came back and it was quite obvious he did not want to be on U.S. territory, and he says how about Spain? And the President said, "Look, I want to just meet with President Gorbachev. I don't want a third country where we have to go through all the protocol and arrival ceremonies and so on. I don't want to do that." So we were sort of at a stalemate when we found out that President Gorbachev was going to make a state visit to Italy. The President's brother had recently been to Malta and said what a lovely place it was! And we started talking. The President says, "Well, Malta is the same problem, I don't want a third-country host." So then we thought, well, President Roosevelt and Prime Minister Churchill had a meeting off Newfoundland on a U.S. and a British cruiser, and that's how Malta got born. And Aleksandr, you ought to tell it for your side, because you were one of the main messengers back and forth.

Bessmertnykh: I was sent by Gorbachev after the letter was received, and the whole thing was almost spoiled by the fact that it was not carried through Shevardnadze but through Marshal [Sergei] Akhromeev. And I don't know, Brent, was it your idea or not?

Scowcroft: He was there, and he was going back!

Bessmertnykh: Since it was handwritten, and delivered by a marshal, Gorbachev looked at that letter as very, very confidential, so he did not even inform Shevardnadze about it. He wrote about it by chance a little bit later. Then he sent me to Washington to work with you on where and when to get that summit, and it was declared that I was coming for some other reason—

Baker: Wyoming.

Bessmertnykh: . . . Wyoming, preparation for the Wyoming meeting. But actually Brent brought me from the State Department garage in his car to the White House, and nobody noticed, even Don Oberdorfer didn't know about it! We had an intensive talk in the presidential apartment on the second floor of the White House, and all the major advisers were there. You have completely correctly discussed talks on where and how the meeting was to be held. We discussed the Bering Straits, but it was December, the end of the year, and it was impossible. Then we came to this idea of having two ships. Gorbachev laughed a little bit about it but then it was agreed. But when we agreed on Malta that we should meet on two naval ships, we did not actually take into account the concerns of Libya. Suddenly when it was announced, Moscow was virtually bombarded by the leader of that country who suspected that the American and the Soviets and the naval ships were actually exercising a pressure game against him, which was absolutely impossible.

Baker: His name then, Sasha, was Qaddafi and it still is Qaddafi![12]

Bessmertnykh: Exactly, exactly. But I think what was important was when President Bush told me when I was sitting there with you, "No papers, no big proposals. We should just talk as two leaders, free of advisers, free of anyone. We are going there just to talk about the basics of the relationship." When we were preparing for Malta, of course there were some ideas that probably we should still carry something with Gorbachev. Then we decided not to do it. So Gorbachev went well prepared for general discussions, because by the time of Malta we already had some problems in Eastern and Central Europe and we had started to have problems in the Baltic. The German situation was also already noted. So Gorbachev realized that Malta would give him an excellent chance to discuss the basics of the relationship with the president of the United States for the first time without papers prepared so that they could really move the relationship to some good results in this time of turbulence.

Tarasenko: I would like to add a new handle to this Malta issue, and this is concerned with the ministerial meeting in Paris. When Shevardnadze learned about this Akhromeev channel, by chance Secretary Baker just mentioned it, expecting that the Minister knew about the content of this letter, but my Minister was furious, furious! And that was the first major crisis between

---

12. Here, Baker uses the diminutive form of Bessmertnykh's first name.

Mr. Baker and my boss, and we did have several mini-crises and some bigger crises. Again, I don't want to tell just that such crises happened, but that we found ways to solve them earlier, not to develop them. After all, these are tactics. But on a lighter side, I tried to explain to Shevardnadze why the Secretary did not inform him about this letter, and I said that the Secretary might have known that the embassy, the ambassador, is bugged by the French. So in a way . . .

Baker: I'm not going to answer that, Sergei, I won't answer that! But I will say that that little difference of opinion did not get in the way of our very fine personal relationship, and the reason it didn't is because I blamed the channel on Scowcroft!

Scowcroft: Well, I was guilty, but it was very innocent. The President had written a letter and he looked at me with those steely blue eyes, and he said, "I don't want this one to leak!" And I said, "Well, it just so happens that Marshal Akhromeev is in town. I can't imagine that that is not a secure channel." It had nothing to do with the normal ministerial channel, and I assumed that you thought that Shevardnadze knew about it.

Baker: I assumed he knew about it when I mentioned it.

Bessmertnykh: It was too secure a channel!

Oberdorfer: Right. Pavel, you were there at Malta, and you have written about its significance. In your view, what was it?

Palazchenko: We have some notes here from Malta, and Mr. Chernyaev has studied those notes, and I think he will speak about some of the points that were made by both sides, some very significant points of importance that went beyond the issues that were discussed at Malta.[13] So I think that I will want to delegate this to Mr. Chernyaev. In the meantime, I would just like to make a remark about the Soviet context of Malta, because not much has yet been said about that. The context was that at that time, on the one hand, the situation was becoming more and more tense and strained for Gorbachev every day. For example, when Minister Bessmertnykh called me from Moscow, I was on home leave at my mother's house near Moscow. He called me from Moscow and asked me to come very quickly to translate an important letter, and he sent his driver to pick me up, and I came to Minister Bessmertnykh's office in

13. Excerpts from Anatoly Chernyaev's notes of the Bush-Gorbachev discussions at Malta have been translated and published. See "At Historic Crossroads: Documents on the December 1989 Malta Summit," *Cold War International History Bulletin*, no. 12/13 (fall/winter 2001): 229–41.

Moscow. I translated the letter from Gorbachev that he had to carry about a meeting that eventually became the meeting in Malta. I was watching TV at that time when I received that call, and the program was about one of the first miners' strikes in the Soviet Union. Then, of course, the Baltic situation was also heating up at about the same time. The overall situation was beginning to be strained for Gorbachev, and domestic criticism by more traditionalist elements in the Politburo was still muted, but became more and more intense. Muted but intense—that's how I would characterize it.

On the other hand, another thing was happening: A tremendous movement within the country among the people, and particularly among the more politically active people—the intelligentsia in Moscow and in Leningrad. This was an enormous intellectual and mental breakthrough at that time, which I feel was not at that time recognized sufficiently in the United States. I feel that even in those remarkable cables from Ambassador Matlock, this movement was not sufficiently recognized. And the movement was that increasing numbers of people everyday were beginning to think that we must become a normal country. A normal country: it was as simple as that. It's not just that we wanted to live better, to have more sausage, as they say, and to have more consumer goods, and so forth. A normal country. At that time, I think Gorbachev and Shevardnadze were extremely sensitive to that change of mood, and that affected their preparation for the Malta summit. That's why they wanted to talk not so much about the bean counting, the missiles, and things like that, but about the overall setting. That was very, very important. That's just a little introduction that I wanted to make about the Soviet domestic setting that has to be recognized. Mr. Chernyaev spoke about trust developing at different speeds. Trust was developing at different speeds, and the understanding of the enormity of this mood change in the Soviet Union was also developing, perhaps at different speeds among different people in your country.

Oberdorfer: Now did Mr. Chernyaev want to add something here?

Chernyaev: First of all, it really looks a little funny today when we speak about preparations for Malta, and all of this being so top secret, being shrouded in so much secrecy and confidentiality. When was it announced? I think that it was finally announced in September?

Baker: The first of November, I think.

Chernyaev: But the understanding that there will be this kind of mini-summit was definitive in July. And it was a very timely meeting: that's the most important thing about it. Those who were there remember very well that the President and General Secretary were congratulating each other upon having been able to establish a different kind of relationship, having been able to start reinforcing and strengthening that new relationship exactly at a time when turmoil and unpredictable processes began, particularly in Eastern Europe and in Germany. It is amazing that even though there was that pause—and perhaps it was too long and it did some damage—by the time that Bush was writing that letter to Gorbachev on the plane, he was already saying that his attitude toward the Soviet Union had changed completely. And as we recall during the first meeting at the delegation level in Malta, this is what he said from the very start. But of course that delegation level meeting was preceded by a one-on-one talk between Gorbachev and Bush that covered briefly more or less all issues, and I feel that that was a breakthrough toward a candid and frank relationship. I would even use a Soviet word, a comradely, frank, and candid relationship. Of course, they had an argument about Cuba. Bush I don't think really understood the problem that Gorbachev faced with respect to Castro. Gorbachev could not understand why the administration was unwilling to engage perhaps in even very secret, very covert contacts with Castro. In that talk, Bush assumed that the Castro regime in Cuba was a puppet Soviet regime, and Gorbachev, I believe quite legitimately, argued that that was not so. They discussed the problem of Nicaragua, and that problem then was discussed at the delegation level meeting. And, of course, they discussed the problem of arms supply through Nicaragua to the Salvadoran rebels.

But what struck me was the assumption that I felt was present in the remarks of both the President and the Secretary of State that it was not Gorbachev who was deceiving the U.S. side. Rather it was that probably Gorbachev was being deceived, that probably some people on the Soviet side were not telling Gorbachev the truth. [The President and the Secretary of State] never suspected Gorbachev of being insincere. There was a funny little discussion also at that summit about the Philippines. As you recall, at that time there was a little rebellion and some major or colonel was even trying to bomb President Aquino's palace. And the United States responded to that, and in the Soviet press at that time, there were accusations of the United States interfering in the internal affairs of the Philippines, and Gorbachev picked up those accusations. And Bush, of course, said in response quite properly, "Look, this is against Aquino. This is someone who is actually trying to bomb the palace of a legitimately elected president of the Philippines. They are asking us for air cover to prevent that kind of bombing, and that is not interference, that's quite proper and legitimate." Now in response Gorbachev spoke of Eastern Europe. He said, "Well, in Eastern Europe you see what is happening there. You see the democratic forces, you see the various popular fronts, you see democratic people actually in rebellion against what we can say are legitimate governments of the Eastern European countries. So at some point, some colonel there might request Moscow's assistance in order to defend that legitimate government in some Eastern European country." And the President's answer was very concise and very substantive. He said, "I understand."

Scowcroft: You are being too gentle, though. President Gorbachev said, "I have ended the Brezhnev doctrine and you are creating the Bush doctrine."

Oberdorfer: I might say the thing that many of us who have written about this period find the most interesting and important in Malta, and the reason I think people say perhaps this was really the end of the Cold War, as opposed to the end of the Soviet Union or the end of Communism, is the following statement. After Bush had presented a number of things that the United States was prepared to do for the Soviet Union, especially in economic terms, Gorbachev returned to the table. He turned to the changes in Europe and their meaning for the Soviet-American relationship, and said, "We want you in Europe, you need to be in Europe. It's important for the future of Europe that you are in Europe, so we don't want to see you out of there." Then, Gorbachev went on to say, "We don't consider you an enemy anymore. Things have changed. We don't think of you in those terms." That was a profoundly important statement for the general secretary of the Communist Party of the Soviet Union to make to the president of the United States. We are no longer enemies, and that really in a way is the bookend on that particular chapter. Now: those in the audience, if you want to say something, please raise your hand.

Philip Zelikow: I am Philip Zelikow, and I have been involved in some of these events and studied some of the documents and written about them. Two comments only on this very interesting panel. The first is: For the panel and the audience you will have heard now three different definitions of when the Cold War ended. One is that it ended in November 1988. That's the definition of Margaret Thatcher; it's also essentially the definition of George Shultz. It is also, by the way, the view of the neoconservatives such as Perle,

Kirkpatrick, and Weinberger, who believe that they won the Cold War in a
story that basically had ended by 1988, and the rest was all just epilogue.[14]
Two: You have heard from Mr. Chernyaev that the Cold War ended at the
Malta meeting in December 1989. Three: You've heard from Mr. Baker, and
you would hear I think from others in the Bush administration, a view that the
Cold War ended in the late summer and fall of 1990. I simply ask both the
panel, but especially the audience, to reflect on the different definitions about
the Cold War and what it means to have ended the Cold War that is implicit
in these three different deadlines. Because if you understand the three different definitions of the Cold War and what it means to end it, you will unlock
the key to explaining a lot of the politics and dynamics of this period.[15]

The second comment is on the pause of 1989, and I think that the panel
has both underestimated the importance of this pause and overestimated it.
They have underestimated it in this sense: they have not fully discussed just
how hard the conceptual problem was in early 1989. The United States government was really trying to come up with an entirely new East-West agenda,
and the gravity of that conceptual challenge has not perhaps been fully discussed. One option of course was to make a linear projection of the Reagan
administration's agenda, and if you want to know what that leap forward would
have been, moving very quickly to sustain the momentum of what the Reagan
administration was doing, you get an excellent illustration of that agenda by
reading Ambassador Matlock's cable. Ambassador Matlock was very close to
the Reagan-Shultz policy on the Soviet Union when it was crafted during his
service in Washington, and that cable is an excellent illustration of what that
agenda looked like to folks who knew it well in February 1989. You will notice
the cable emphasizes Cuba and Central America; it does not mention CFE, it
does not mention Soviet policy in Eastern Europe, and it does not mention
Germany, of course. Indeed, it does not really mention Poland either,
although it is discussed in another cable. So you could go with that.

Alternatively, you could go with the Henry Kissinger agenda, which was
briefly alluded to in I think the comments of Minister Bessmertnykh and

14. For this view, see Beth A. Fischer, *The Reagan Reversal: Foreign Policy and the End of the Cold War*
(Columbia: University of Missouri Press, 1997), and Jay Winik, *On the Brink: The Dramatic Saga of How the
Reagan Administration Changed the Course of History and Won the Cold War* (New York: Simon & Schuster, 1996).

15. See, for further discussion, Philip Zelikow and Condoleezza Rice, *Germany Unified and Europe Transformed: A Study in Statecraft* (Cambridge: Harvard University Press, 1995), chap. 1; and Thomas S. Blanton,
"When Did the Cold War End?" *Cold War International History Project Bulletin* 10 (March 1998): 184–91.

which is discussed a little bit in my book and I think also perhaps in Mr. Baker's book and in Mr. Oberdorfer's book.[16] That alternative was quickly rejected at the outset of the Bush administration. That then left some other alternatives which were just not clear, and it took a few months to begin to come up with that alternative incrementally in April and May 1989.

But I think in a sense that that pause has been overestimated, because as far as I can tell reflecting on this period, I can find no policy consequences from this pause whatsoever. It was simply a factor in the public relations game because the press was making a great deal of this pause.

Oberdorfer: Thanks.

Baker: Don, can I just add something about what Phil has just said? I couldn't agree more with what he said in terms of the fact that, in my view, there were no enduring policy consequences of the fact that we took three to four months to put a Bush imprint upon policy toward the Soviet Union, at least no enduring policy consequences from the standpoint of the United States. Now Jack suggested that maybe there were some with respect to internal developments within the Soviet Union. I am not sure there were any, and he isn't sure there were any, but there weren't any as far as the United States is concerned. We came out at the right place in May, and we pursued it appropriately and in the right way, and beneficially from the standpoint of the overall relationship. Let me just quickly say why it is my view that the Cold War ended sometime in 1990, notwithstanding the importance of Malta—and it was extraordinarily important. Malta was where President Bush formed the close personal bond and relationship with President Gorbachev that frankly I had formed in September with Minister Shevardnadze, and there was no doubt in anybody's mind after Malta what the direction of the policies of the two countries was going to be. But I think you prove a fact by actions. The actions that I think were the real conclusive evidence of the end of the Cold War were the agreements we were able to reach on the most difficult issue of all, the unification of Germany in peace and freedom, and the fact that together we stood up against naked aggression by a country that had been a former client state of the Soviet Union. It was very difficult for you to do that, and we understand that, but those were two actions, real actions, that I think proved once and for all that the Cold War was over.

16. See note 6.

Oberdorfer: Mr. Chernyaev?

Chernyaev: Well, certainly if you consider the Cold War without the human element of leadership—the leaders of the Soviet Union and the United States—you can say that even after Malta certain things were continuing in the mold of the Cold War. But unless the Cold War had ended at Malta, how could we have achieved the kind of German unification that was accomplished, the war in the Persian Gulf? So what worried Gorbachev during the Persian Gulf crisis was how to make sure that new international relations were not thwarted, were not scuttled. He wanted to make sure that this does not actually destroy the post Cold War. The Persian Gulf crisis in this interpretation is post Cold War. He was worried about that being brought back to the Cold War. And that famous remark that was made by Gorbachev at Malta that we no longer regard you as an enemy is something that Gorbachev said in the beginning of the second talk with President Bush, and that second talk was also aboard a Soviet ship, the *Maksim Gorky*. Because of the weather we were not able to go to an American ship.

We have encountered that phrase that "after hearing the U.S. initiatives, the delighted Soviet leader told Bush 'we don't consider you an enemy anymore.'" But it's not that simple. Going to Malta Gorbachev was politically and emotionally already quite prepared to make that statement. For quite some time, even before Malta, he had not regarded the United States as an enemy, so it was not just a reaction of delight to some U.S. initiatives. And Gorbachev had said that actually several times on several occasions in somewhat different terms both to you Mr. Secretary and also to you Ambassador Matlock, including that remark at a social occasion at Spaso House when he talked to you and asked that the President be more considerate. But, indeed, Gorbachev had been saying for some time that we are waiting for the moment when our U.S. partners will start doing more than just saying rhetorically that they wish perestroika and Gorbachev good luck. When will they start actually doing something to facilitate that? So we were really quite amazed, we were really pleasantly surprised at Malta when Bush outlined a specific agenda of cooperation with the changing Soviet Union. That was a breakthrough. That was a real breakthrough. That was really a transition from word to deed.

Speaking about the atmosphere in relations between countries like our two countries, it is of fundamental importance. I would have very much welcomed it if there had been some kind of candid video camera that would have made footage of that lunch that Gorbachev had on that ship. At that lunch, Secretary Baker and President Bush said, "We are not speaking in terms of aid, in terms of help, what we would like to do is to create conditions to facilitate the process of perestroika and the reforms in the Soviet Union." That was the official line that they presented. But actually the atmosphere at that lunch table said a lot more than that. Secretary and President Bush were speaking about what they would suggest that Gorbachev do in order to resolve economic and social problems. They were actually showing themselves to be willing to recommend things that would be helpful, that would really help Gorbachev to extricate himself from the political and economic problems at that time in the Soviet Union. So the atmosphere was one actually of being helpful. And Secretary Baker had provided such helpful advice before. For example, at that meeting in May in 1989, he had said to Gorbachev that "you should have started price reform a lot earlier when you still could have blamed the previous leaders for those problems."

Baker: You should have!

Chernyaev: While Gorbachev at that time dismissed that suggestion, what he said was this: "The problem of price reform should have been handled by us twenty years ago." But now, he said, a year or two, well, we'll wait and we'll make it. But it is exactly those two years that he actually did not have.

Oberdorfer: Brent?

Scowcroft: This is probably a psychological point on the end of the Cold War. I agree with everything Mr. Chernyaev said about Malta. It established a personal relationship between the two leaders that made all of the subsequent events possible. It really did establish trust, but you used the word "atmosphere," and for us Malta was atmosphere. And for us the Cold War started in Central Europe, and therefore with the unification of Germany what had started the Cold War finished the Cold War, and for us it was kind of a neat package. I am inclined to agree that the Gulf Crisis was the first post–Cold War cooperation.

Oberdorfer: Mr. Bessmertnykh.

Bessmertnykh: It seems I have a very specific concept of the Cold War that is not shared by the majority of my colleagues. I think the Cold War is something different than just a long, intensive conflict between the states. If it were, then the Israeli-Arab conflict would be a cold war, which it is not. So the Cold War in my view is not an interstate or intergovernment tension and conflict, it's intersystem conflict, and the Cold War started in 1917 as conflict between the communist system and the democratic system. . . . The last chapter of the Cold War started in 1945. And I believe that the Cold War basically ended in Malta, but not because Gorbachev said you are no longer an enemy in our eyes. It was an important statement but it did not signify the end of the Cold War, because statements of that kind were uttered by both sides in the atmospherics of friendship before that. I think there was something more important than this said in Malta, and that is something that was said by Gorbachev and shared by Bush: "We recognize the freedom of choice for the countries of Eastern and Central Europe and we recognize their freedom to correct the initial decisions about their own systems." This was of *absolutely* enormous importance. So he actually said they have the right to change the initial decisions about going communist and to become free countries.[17] And the second part of his statement was when those countries develop themselves for the purpose of democratization, you should not interfere with that, you should not exploit that moment for the interests of the United States, and the American president agreed with that. That was a decision of paramount importance that signified the end of the Cold War, because that signified the end of intersystem conflict. This is my view of it.

17. Bessmertnykh addresses a rarely noted ambiguity in Gorbachev's proclamations of "freedom of choice" and "nonintervention" in his U.N. General Assembly speech of December 1988 and other speeches; namely, did Gorbachev still subscribe to the Soviet view that the East European peoples had exercised freedom of choice when communist regimes were imposed after World War II? And if so, did this mean that any effort to aid democracy movements constituted "intervention"?

2 The Unification of Germany

THE FALL OF the communist regimes in Eastern Europe in the second half of 1989 and the sudden breaching of the Berlin Wall in November marked the most fundamental shift in Europe since its division into opposing camps following World War II. In August 1989 the Solidarity labor group in Poland formed the first Eastern European government not led by communists since the Cold War's dawn in the late 1940s. In September, Hungary announced that it would no longer prevent East German citizens from crossing the border to Austria. In October, the ruling communist party of Hungary reconstituted itself as a socialist party. A few days later Gorbachev in Helsinki proclaimed what his spokesman called "the Sinatra doctrine" instead of the Brezhnev doctrine—countries could "do it their way." And on November 9, the East German government inadvertently made an announcement that effectively opened the Berlin Wall.[1]

The collapse of the Berlin Wall did not, however, resolve the future of Germany, the most powerful nation of central Europe and the source of two twentieth-century world wars. This session focused on the diplomacy that led to the unification of Germany and the realignment of Europe. In mid-February 1990, Baker persuaded the Soviet leaders as well as those of Britain and France to sponsor a "two-plus-four" mechanism to deal with the future of Germany. Thus began five months of intense diplomacy, including a U.S.-Soviet summit meeting in Washington, to persuade Moscow to accept the incorporation of the German Democratic Republic (East Germany) into the Federal Republic of Germany (West Germany), and to include the reunited Germany in NATO. This accord, sealed by West German chancellor Helmut Kohl in a meeting with Gorbachev in July, brought about intensified domestic criticism of Gorbachev as well as dramatic movement to unification.

Oberdorfer: The fall of communism in Eastern Europe came with a suddenness that very few people anticipated: that this great gash across Europe, which Winston Churchill in 1946 called an Iron Curtain, should suddenly end, and that Europe—to use President Bush's phrase—should become "whole and

---

1. See, in particular, Hans-Herman Hertle, "The Fall of the Wall: The Unintended Self-Dissolution of East Germany's Ruling Regime," *Cold War International History Bulletin*, no. 12/13 (fall/winter 2001): 131–40.

free." Tonight we are going to talk about how that happened. I also want to begin by reading three small excerpts from books by three of our panelists. Pavel Palazchenko writes: "The decision to 'release' Eastern Europe was made, and [the leadership] did not go back on it when the full implications became clear. Was that a victory for the West? Perhaps. But even more, it was a victory of Gorbachev and his supporters over themselves, over the past in themselves—the most difficult victory anyone can achieve. I do not believe that the coming generation of leaders will ever have to make decisions of such magnitude or such agonizing difficulty."[2]

The second excerpt is from Ambassador Matlock's book, *Autopsy on an Empire:*

German unification, which was as late as the summer of 1989 a remote goal, became a reality before the leaves fell from the Central European trees in 1990. It happened so quickly that many people in the West, once their initial surprise and disbelief passed, began to think of it as an inevitable, almost automatic process. Doubtless the artificial East German state could not have lasted forever. It was destined for eventual collapse. Nonetheless there was nothing inevitable about the timing, the shape, or the form of the settlements that reunited Germany and ended the artificial division of the European continent. I am confident that history will regard the negotiations that occurred between March and July of 1990 as a model of diplomacy and their outcome as one of the most notable achievements of statesmen ever.[3]

And finally from Secretary Baker's book, *The Politics of Diplomacy,* in which he wrote: "The story behind the creation of Two-plus-Four [the "two-plus-four" mechanism in dealing with Germany] on February 13, 1990, is a classic tale of "great power" diplomacy—and one in which I was reminded forcefully that, as location is to real estate, timing is to statecraft."[4] That is what we are going to be discussing tonight, and I can think of no better way to start this than to ask Secretary Baker to tell us something about what was on his mind as the Wall was opening, and one was faced with the real prospect of the reuniting of Germany for the first time since the Second World War.

2. Pavel Palazchenko, *My Years with Gorbachev and Shevardnadze: The Memoir of a Soviet Interpreter* (University Park: Pennsylvania State University Press, 1997), 145.

3. Jack F. Matlock Jr., *Autopsy on an Empire: The American Ambassador's Account of the Collapse of the Soviet Union* (New York: Random House, 1996), 386–87.

4. James A. Baker III, with Thomas M. DeFrank, *The Politics of Diplomacy: Revolution, War, and Peace, 1989–1992* (New York: G. P. Putnam's Sons, 1995), 195. Other indispensable sources on German unification include Philip Zelikow and Condoleezza Rice, *Germany Unified and Europe Transformed: A Study in Statecraft* (Cambridge: Harvard University Press, 1995); Angela E. Stent, *Russia and Germany Reborn: Unification, the Soviet Collapse, and the New Europe* (Princeton: Princeton University Press, 1999); and Hannes Adomeit, *Imperial Overstretch: Germany in Soviet Policy from Stalin to Gorbachev* (Baden Baden: Nomos Verlagsgesellschaft, 1998).

THE UNIFICATION OF GERMANY

Baker: The reunification of Germany is something that the North Atlantic Alliance had favored, but hadn't talked about much for a long time. It was a rather sensitive subject, particularly with some of our allies, specifically Britain and France, who had some serious reservations about seeing Germany reunified and were fearful that history might repeat itself. And, indeed, when we first began to address the issue, there were some reservations within our administration about whether we should begin to discuss publicly something that could be as divisive and difficult as reunification. In one of my early speeches on the subject, I think I used the word "normalization" rather than "reunification." But I remember on President Bush's trip to Eastern Europe in July 1989, we went to Hungary and met Prime Minister Németh, and he presented President Bush and me with some pieces of barbed wire, which were the first parts of the Iron Curtain that had been demolished. They had them mounted on some copperplate, and I still have those in my office in Houston. I remember also very vividly in April 1989 meeting with Shevardnadze in Paris on the margins of the Cambodian Peace Conference and talking to him for the first time about whether the Soviet Union would let Eastern Europe go or whether there would be any resort to the use of force, and he was very definite in saying that that would totally defeat the purposes of perestroika and glasnost and there would be no use of force. I remember reporting that to President Bush and being very pleased as things progressed to find that those assurances proved to be true, just as they did when President Gorbachev gave similar assurances to President Bush.

There were three types of proposals floating around out there when people talked about a mechanism for unifying Germany. One of them was the idea of a grand conference, maybe a CSCE [Conference on Security and Cooperation in Europe] conference, a meeting of all countries that were interested in affairs in Europe. That was a procedure that we felt was way too unwieldy. Others favored simply a Four Power conference—I think, Sasha [Bessmertnykh], that this may have been the preferred mechanism initially of the Soviet Union—where the four occupying powers would meet and take the steps necessary to release their occupation rights and effect a unification of Germany. The other solution that was kicked around was a German-only solution, where East and West Germany would get together and decide the questions involving unification. None of those really appeared to us to be a satisfactory approach, and—thanks in large part to a memorandum that came to me from Bob Zoellick and Dennis Ross, who was head of the Policy

Planning shop at the State Department—we came up with the idea of a "two-plus-four" mechanism, where the two Germanys would deal with the internal aspects of unification and the four occupying powers would then deal with the external elements of unification. We set about trying to sell that to the various parties involved, and ultimately we were successful in doing so. There were some initial reservations, on the part of the Soviet Union as well as on the part of Britain and France. But this permitted the Germans to deal with the internal aspects, it permitted the Four Powers to deal with the external aspects. Most importantly of all, it gave us a diplomatic process which would permit us to keep up with events as they took place on the ground, and events were taking place on the ground very, very rapidly.

Oberdorfer: What was the sense in Moscow?

Chernyaev: The question that is very often asked of me by reporters and researchers is when did Gorbachev decide to agree to the unification of Germany: The answer is that there is no such date. There was a certain evolution of his views. Almost from the start—as early as 1987—he said that it was the will of history that there are now two German states and history will eventually decide what is going to happen, and we will see—it may take a hundred years for it to decide, it may take ten years. We don't know. Let's wait and see. That was his initial formula. He said that to President Weiszäcker of Germany in 1987, and this was his position to which he was sticking. Of course, that position was innovative in a way, compared to the position of our foreign policy in the pre-Gorbachev period. That is to say, even then in principle he did not rule out the possibility of German unification. In private discussions among close friends even then he was saying that to force a great nation to remain indefinitely divided is wrong and we are not going to have a common European house while that situation persists.

The decisive moment that really persuaded him of the inevitability of that process was his visit to Germany in the summer of 1989. He saw a different country. He saw a new country. He shed the stereotypes that at that time still persisted among our leaders and also among our people with respect to Germany. Internally it was then that his resistance to the possibility [of unification] disappeared, but he understood very well that whereas this change of mind had happened to him, it may not necessarily have happened in the party and among the people, where there were still memories of what happened during World War II. What was particularly important was the psychological aspect, the understanding that emerged as a result of that visit, among the Germans, not only in West Germany but also in what was then the GDR, that Gorbachev would not resist by force the possibility of unification. That understanding now triggered the flight of East Germans across the border and helped to create an atmosphere that was conducive to a more rapid process of unification.

Of course, everyone knew even then that relations between Gorbachev and Honecker were not going well. Honecker did not like perestroika, he was prohibiting our magazines from being sold in Germany, he instructed his party organizations to criticize perestroika. Gorbachev was not concerned about that, he said that anyone can take the kind of attitude toward perestroika that he wants. So when he visited the GDR for the celebration of the fortieth anniversary of that country in early October 1989, he saw that, as he likes to put it—and this is a phrase that is very often still being ridiculed in our country—"the process is under way, the process is unfolding." He did not want to go. He said to me several times, "Tolya, I don't want to go. I will be in a spurious, embarrassing position. I don't want to go, but on the other hand I don't want to embarrass Honecker by just not turning up." So from a political and diplomatic standpoint, it was necessary for him to go; and once there he saw that it was the end.

And those words "the end" were used by Polish prime minister [Mieczisław] Rakowski when they were standing on the podium facing thousands and thousands of people who were marching in that parade to celebrate the anniversary of the GDR. They were marching past the podium where the entire GDR leadership was, and they were chanting "Gorby! Gorby! Gorby!" without even mentioning Honecker, who was embarrassed. Gorbachev very graphically described to the members of the Politburo what was happening then, and he said, "Rakowski came up to me and he leaned over to me and said, 'Mikhail, you don't understand German but I do. I cannot only hear those slogans chanted but I see what is written on the banners that people are carrying.'" And Rakowski said: "This is the end."[5]

And so when I am asked, and when Gorbachev is asked, "What was your reaction to the fall of the Berlin Wall? Was it panic?" Some people think that

---

5. According to reports, people were shouting "Gorbachev, help us! Save us!" When Rakowski translated this for Gorbachev, he is reported to have told the Soviet leader: "These are Party activists! This is the end!" Quoted in Stent, *Russia and Germany Reborn*, 88.

there was panic in Moscow. Some people think there were plans to use tanks, that there were plans to let the troops out of the barracks. This did not happen, there was no panic. He saw that that was inevitable. People say, although I don't know whether that is true, that Soviet troop commanders in Germany several times called Moscow and asked what they were supposed to do in this situation, but I know for a fact that Marshal [Dmitry] Yazov, who was defense minister at that time, never even asked Gorbachev that question. He couldn't afford to ask that question, because he knew what the answer would be, that Gorbachev would never allow any kind of use of Soviet troops that were at that time in Germany. Gorbachev is now sometimes accused of having two faces; that when he spoke to East German leaders such as [Hans] Modrow or [Egon] Krenz or [Grigor] Gysi, he promised them moral support, but when he spoke to, for example, Secretary Baker, he said different things. Well, from a purely formal standpoint that may be true, but you have to remember that at that time, two sovereign states still existed, and he thought that the best way would be a gradual rapprochement between those states.

And by the way, I must say, Jack, that there is something of an inaccuracy in your book about this in that the position of Genscher and Kohl is described somewhat inaccurately. That is to say, in the very beginning, Genscher and Kohl, too, agreed with Gorbachev that the most desirable option would be a gradual evolution and gradual rapprochement of the two states. It is not true that from the very outset Genscher and Kohl insisted on Article 23 and that Gorbachev until the very end insisted on gradual evolution.[6] It was not quite so. And since Gorbachev believed that there was a certain degree of understanding between him and Kohl on this, he was very angry when Kohl announced his famous "ten points" in the Bundestag, which aimed at a rapid confederation in Germany. So to understand Gorbachev's position during those rapid changes at the end of 1989 and early 1990, you have to understand that it was most important for Gorbachev to make sure that the European process continued, that the process of ending the Cold War and the division of Europe continued. He was worried that the rapid events in Germany might really undermine and destroy that European process. And the

6. Reference is to the Federal Republic of Germany's Basic Law, which contained two routes to unification: Article 23, which provided for the accession of additional states (*Länder*) to the Federal Republic (which would imply the dissolution of East German states and absorption of its states into West Germany); and Article 146, which provided for the replacement of the Basic Law with a constitution adopted by a national constitutional convention upon unification (a route implying the merger of two countries into a new Germany).

fact that he understood the inevitability of unification is attested by a phrase that he uttered in a conversation with President Bush at Malta in early December 1989. He said at that time, as though in passing, "Maybe a united Germany should be neutral." When you discuss whether a united Germany should be neutral, that means that you accept the possibility of a united Germany, and that was very early on. But the process, of course, then unfolded and expanded so rapidly, more rapidly than anyone had expected, that the important thing was to keep pace with the process and to make sure that it did not undermine the new relations that were beginning to take shape in Europe.

And it was at that time, on January 27, in Gorbachev's office at the Central Committee rather than in the Kremlin, that there was a meeting of Gorbachev's inner circle, so to speak, that I describe in my book.[7] So you can regard that date, the twenty-seventh of January, the date when a political decision was taken by the Soviet leadership that unification of Germany was inevitable and that our main task was to work together with the Americans in order to make sure that that process is a peaceful one.

At that meeting, Akhromeev was given an instruction to prepare the withdrawal of troops from Germany. And also at that meeting, the decision was taken how to handle the external aspects of unification, the famous "four-plus-two" or "two-plus-four," and even in the media there has been some indication of who has the copyright on that formula. So I hope you will not regard me as lacking modesty if I say that at that meeting I was the first to say that we need a mechanism of the Four Powers and the two German states, and I first used the word "six" and then "four-plus-two." And by the way, Eduard Shevardnadze at that meeting objected to that language. He said that formula would be dominated by NATO countries. On the other hand, I don't want to undermine Jim Baker's priority in putting forward that formula because, indeed, probably our thoughts were moving in the same direction at that time. He brought that formula to Moscow just ten days later. The only problem was whether it should be two-plus-four or four-plus-two. You understand the difference? Gorbachev was sort of indifferent, and he used it both ways, but for Germans this was very important. If it is two-plus-four, then the Germans solve their own problems, and the four victorious powers only consider external

---

7. For Chernyaev's summary of this meeting, see Anatoly S. Chernyaev, *My Six Years with Gorbachev*, ed. and trans. Robert D. English and Elizabeth Tucker (University Park: Pennsylvania State University Press, 2000), 271–72.

aspects of their own interests after unification. So as of that day, the really dramatic and difficult question was the problem of a united Germany in NATO. That problem was eventually resolved properly, naturally, and productively, and for that we have to thank in large measure Secretary of State Baker. It's my personal view—and some people, including Gorbachev, don't agree with me—that that problem for us was hopeless, and we shouldn't have raised it in those terms. But then, of course, the process began to unfold mostly between us and the Americans and of course the Germans, and that great historic undertaking was under way, and here I stop. In Washington, at the end of June, that decision was finally taken about NATO.

Oberdorfer: Sergei wants to say something.

Tarasenko: Just one short remark. It was a very interesting presentation, but I wonder whether we had at that time a Foreign Ministry in our country or was it only Gorbachev and no foreign minister at all. On the other side, we hear that it was President Bush, the Secretary of State, and diplomats; but on our side it looks like we had Gorbachev and nobody else. I reserve my right to continue.

Baker: That's a very interesting account that I had not heard before, and it may explain why when I first previewed two-plus-four to the Soviet Union on the seventh of February, Minister Shevardnadze was really a little bit less receptive to it. You had a very involved foreign minister, Sergei, who was playing a major role, but he was a little less receptive to the idea than was President Gorbachev when I surfaced it with him the next day or that afternoon. That was a departure from what my usual experience had been on my trips to the Soviet Union. But I remember specifically President Gorbachev saying at the end of our meeting, "Four-plus-two, two-plus-four, assuming it relies on an international legal basis is suitable for the situation." And I found that surprising at the time, particularly since Eduard really did not appear to think a lot of that idea initially.

Oberdorfer: Brent, do you have something you wanted to add?

Scowcroft: Yes, just a couple of quick points. As I indicated this afternoon, part of our strategy toward the Soviet Union was to shift focus and put Eastern Europe up front, which traditionally had not been the case with the United States. In doing that, we worried a lot about the liberalizing pace that could be sustained in Eastern European countries without bringing a sharp reaction either from the Soviet Union or from the governments of those states. We even worried about making the President's trip to Eastern Europe—that it might produce riots, demonstrations, or something that would produce a backlash. We were concerned *a lot* about that really until President Gorbachev went to Germany in October for the fortieth anniversary of the GDR. There it was quite clear that what Gorbachev had to do to stop the situation was to give powerful support to Honecker. If he didn't do that, this situation was hopeless, and we watched very carefully, and he didn't do that. Indeed, he made a few comments that were semi-critical, and then it became, I think, quite obvious that Gorbachev was going to let the situation in Eastern Europe go.

From then on, it started to accelerate sharply, and you are right about Kohl at one period talking about confederation, but his principal concern as the exodus from East Germany went on was that this was unsustainable from two standpoints. First of all, the East Germans could not be absorbed in West Germany, and second, he was afraid of the denuding of East Germany, so that when unification did take place, there would be such an imbalance between the countries. As the situation accelerated in January and in February, Kohl started to talk to President Bush about very, very rapid unification. And with the French, the British, and the Soviets not being enthusiastic about unification, if all three of them got together, the two-plus-four process could be a device for slowing down the situation and making it absolutely untenable. So those are the kinds of things we worried about all the way through this, and I am still surprised that the British, the French, and you all [Soviets] didn't get together earlier on and figure out a way to slow the process down, because the United States was the only one supporting Helmut Kohl in rapid movement.

Palazchenko: My own, personal feeling was that the two-plus-four process was basically a front and that it was rather skillfully played by both sides once it was decided that it would take place, but it was *not* the most important thing. Starting sometime in November, when Shevardnadze went to London and talked to Margaret Thatcher—and she clearly indicated that she didn't like the process of unification, and she certainly didn't like the rapidity of that process—perhaps there was at that time a possibility of, as you put it, getting together with them and trying to slow things down. My own impression at that time was that both Shevardnadze and Gorbachev understood pretty well that if that happened, any kind of slowdown would be at our expense. It would be *us* slowing the process down, and *them* basically looking on as if, but for us, they would not slow the train. We would just, you know, put ourselves on the rails. I mean that worried me mightily, and it is my impression that as early as November Gorbachev and Shevardnadze understood it, and basically my feeling was that the whole game was about that, rather than about the inevitability of reunification or about how to best handle two-plus-four. So I feel that this was the most important thing that was happening, and I think that was eventually played right with the exception, of course—here I agree with Mr. Chernyaev—of that unfortunate issue of NATO membership. Here I think it was probably not quite right for us to raise it so sharply. On the other hand, the West was not helping us to defuse, to devalue, that issue at that time and to make it just perhaps sound a little less noisily and dramatically in the international discussion.

Baker: We helped you . . .

Palazchenko: . . . I mean, not enough, . . . I saw that you were trying.

Baker: We helped you with our Nine Principles that we came forward with . . .

Palazchenko: Absolutely,

Baker: . . . which were very, very helpful.

Palazchenko: Exactly, the NATO Conference, the NATO decision . . .

Baker: And the London summit.

Palazchenko: Absolutely, absolutely, I agree.

Scowcroft: But much earlier, the issue quickly became not German unification but NATO.

Palazchenko: That's it. I thought that was unfortunate.

Scowcroft: People had given up, because German unification was out of anybody's control, it was moving so fast. The issue was, would it be inside NATO or not.

Baker: I think just as a sidebar, Don, we ought to take note of the fact that when Gorbachev went to Berlin, he made the famous statement that policy for the GDR would be made in Berlin and not in Moscow, and that was a fairly dramatic statement at the time. It was a clear indication of what the course was going to be.

Oberdorfer: Bob Zoellick has something to say.

Zoellick: I just have a couple of observations, and I also wanted to ask our Russian colleagues a question, if I could. I think one of the dimensions that makes this diplomatic process a very unusual one is that while it was very fast-paced—because of events on the ground and the fact that people were leaving

East Germany—and we were dealing with very immediate issues, we were able to take a long-term view. Perhaps because we saw this as such a historic turn of events, we did look at historical analogies, and we were particularly sensitive about trying to have the unification occur in a way that avoided planting the seeds of future problems. In particular, we wanted to avoid singling out Germany, having Germany unified in a way that some future generation of Germans would say, "We weren't treated fairly and we have objections we have to rectify." Second, the reason that we were so strong about linking Germany to NATO was because one of the successes of the past forty-five years had been to link this Central European power to this Western structure, and we felt that was an important point for the future that I think affected some of the Russian thinking eventually. But, third, we wanted to engage the Soviet Union so that they also did not feel that at the end of the day this was done without them.

The two-plus-four process was one of the few areas where there was a difference in the U.S. government in what otherwise was a very smooth cooperation. For those of us who favored the two-plus-four, we felt that while momentum was on our side because of the process in the inter-German relationship, that the Soviet Union had its own equities. It had its Four Power rights, it had 380,000 troops there, it had lots of ways to make trouble, and that we could create a process that would allow us to engage the Soviet Union while momentum was on our side. I think that the Nine Points was an effort on our part to ask, "What is it that the other side needs by way of explanation?" In fact, what is interesting is that those Nine Points were all out in the public realm as separate pieces. But we put them together as a set partly because we put ourselves in the shoes of our Soviet colleagues and asked, "What might they need to explain it on the home front?"

The question that I have is a variation of what Brent was asking, and that is not only why did not the Soviet Union perhaps work with Britain and France to slow down unification, but why at a given point did you not take one of the steps that you might have taken to separate Germany and the United States? For example, on NATO it could have created a very delicate situation that would have caused us a terrible difficulty if you had said, "All right, Germany can be in NATO but it has to be in NATO the way the French are in NATO—not part of the integrated military command." Or, "Germany can be in NATO but without any nuclear weapons." That would have caused a very difficult problem in U.S.-German relations, and perhaps the judgment was that wouldn't serve your interests, but I am curious as to how you saw that.

Oberdorfer: Mr. Bessmertnykh?

Bessmertnykh: Before answering that question, I would like to make a couple of comments. First of all, the story of reunification looks like it was very simple when you have heard everybody say something about it. In fact, it was not that simple, it was not that naïve, and it was not that placid. There were a lot of nerve-wracking situations in Moscow, and there was enormous anxiety in Gorbachev, and even more in Shevardnadze. The situation was really very tragic, because German reunification is one of the mysterious occurrences of the twentieth century, when an event of this magnitude just happened without a strategy, without joint efforts by someone, without planning. Actually, the whole reunification started with the people on the ground, and then their leaders started together to think about what to do. Kohl didn't have a plan. Of course, he wanted reunification, but he was taken by surprise at the velocity of the events. The British and the French, of course, didn't want reunification at all, but then events started to move so dramatically that they had to accept it. Gorbachev didn't want reunification of Germany, and of course, he was one of the most unhappy men when he faced this prospect. But the events were actually uncontrolled. They were developing uncontrolled by either the Great Powers or by the Germans themselves. So there was no strategy, there was only tactics. When we came to four-plus-two that was already the period of a more regulated process, but before that it was an ecological process, and an extremely emotional one.

I think one of the profound miscalculations by Gorbachev was that he didn't consider the German Democratic Republic as something different from other East European nations. When he equalized the situation by talking about East Europe *including* the GDR, he was making a *fantastic* conceptual mistake. All the other countries could move to democracy and a market economy, because they had their own histories, et cetera. East Germany did not have that option. East Germany had a *raison d'être* only by being different from West Germany. As soon as it was becoming similar to West Germany, it really was losing the grounds for its existence, and Gorbachev did not understand that at that time, because all of the socialist states were equal to him. He didn't like Honecker—actually nobody liked him in Moscow—but Honecker was the only one who realized that the only way to continue the existence of that country was to go a non-perestroika way. I do not agree with Mr. Chernyaev when he said that we were not pushing the East Europeans to the perestroika way. We were. The only country which was ahead of us in the perestroika way was Hungary, and a little bit later, Poland, but all the rest were behind us in developing reform in the country, so we were pushing them very hard. And along with Bulgarians, Czechs, Romanians, we pushed the GDR in the same way. So that's why we didn't do anything about the GDR, because we had already committed ourselves to let the people in Eastern Europe go, including the GDR. Gorbachev couldn't do anything already after Malta, because he unintentionally included the GDR in the list of the countries that will have to make their own choice. This is how I think it happened. It was a combination of natural forces, of people's involvement on the ground, and the unpreparedness of the leaders. This was a fantastic combination of things that made one of the most important events of the twentieth century happen.

Oberdorfer: I think it is a very good point that people were voting with their feet, as we like to say in this country, that no government was in control of them, at least in the initial phase when people were pouring out of Eastern Germany. Phil.

Zelikow: Thanks. I agree with Aleksandr Bessmertnykh that the issue is much more troubled and conflict-ridden than it is portrayed, although actually I think he does not give Gorbachev enough credit for having a plan. He makes Gorbachev, I'm afraid, seem a bit negligent and even witless, and that was not the case. Gorbachev is actually a formidable character, and he had a plan. Maybe it was a bad one, maybe there were misjudgments, although no one had plans that were notably better, but I think the main point is, were the two superpowers on parallel paths? No. I think there are three important things to understand. First, details here really matter a lot. Our recollections will impose a surface smoothness and coherence to these events that order a reality that was much more disordered than we make it appear when we summarize these things. This happens in our own memories. The most sincere and honest recollections will impose an order and coherence on these events that they did not have at that time. For example, Gorbachev did not equate the GDR with the rest of Eastern Europe; in fact, the notes we have from the January 27 meeting have Gorbachev saying, and I quote: "We definitely have to single the GDR out. It is a special case. The GDR is not Romania. The Communist

Party in the GDR is a serious matter. Czechoslovakia, Bulgaria, Hungary are interested in us; they will recover, but they cannot go too far away. Poland is a special case, but the most special case is the GDR."

And if you read Gorbachev's own account, as well as Chernyaev's account, and Kochemassov's memoirs, it's very plain that Gorbachev takes an intense interest in the GDR.[8] You see, he had a plan for the GDR. And the plan is revealed in its greatest detail in a meeting that he has with Egon Krenz on November 1, 1989, eight days before the Berlin Wall opens. Now keep in mind that Krenz has just been made the head of the GDR and Krenz is considered Moscow's man, he's considered that way even in the East German government. Finally Gorbachev has an East German leader he can really talk to, and they have a little meeting with nobody there but Gorbachev, Shakhazarov, Krenz, and the East German note taker who took practically verbatim notes, fifty-two pages' worth, which we have read.[9] Gorbachev has a plan. Of course, the plan is not that decisions are going to be made in Berlin. Good luck! Gorbachev is sitting there going over with him the selection of cadres, leadership decisions, he is taking an intense interest in every detail of what the East German government is going to do, because their notion is, "We have a problem of popular unrest and we should solve that problem by you imitating our example."

You see, in 1989, people thought Gorbachev was a success. They thought he was popular, and the idea was, "Let's have little Gorbachevs in Eastern Europe," and Krenz was the first nominee for "Little Gorbachev." Modrow would have been ideal, but Krenz would do, especially since he was Moscow's man. They go through very great detail about how Krenz is going to operate, how he is going to handle the West Germans, how they are going to handle the rest of the Europeans. They're thinking about these problems, even to the issues of travel regulations. Now the plan may involve some misjudgments, but we belittle the story when we accuse Gorbachev and the Soviet government of philosophical passivity about tidal events in Eastern Europe. That's not really the case. In part, these events are not tidal forces, people just kind of coming up

8. See Mikhail Sergeevich Gorbachev, *Memoirs*, trans. from the German edition by Wolf Jobst [which was translated into German from the Russian original by Georges Peronansky and Tatjana Varsavsky] (New York: Doubleday, 1995); Chernyaev, *My Six Years with Gorbachev*; and Wjascheslaw Kotschemassow, *Meine letzte Mission* (Berlin: Dietz, 1991).

9. See "Memorandum of Conversation between Egon Krenz, Secretary General of the Socialist Unity Party (SED), and Mikhail S. Gorbachev, Secretary General of the Communist Party of the Soviet Union (CPSU), 1 November 1989," *Cold War International History Bulletin*, no. 12/13 (fall/winter 2001): 140–51.

out of anyone's control, and that's because we often miss the detail of the relationship between international events and domestic events.

In fact, the West and the Soviets engaged in a deliberate battle to shape
the popular expectations of the East German people that began in earnest in
November 1989 and did not end until after the East German elections of
March 1990. The East Germans in November 1989 did not want unification.
That changed. It was changed in part by things that were happening on the
international scene, as well as things that were happening inside East Germany,
and they were the products of deliberate strategies adopted by both the West,
especially the United States and West Germany, and by the Soviet Union. Just
to offer one other final illustration of how details matter: Anatoly Chernyaev
recounted the January 27 crisis meeting, and he did so quite honestly and quite
correctly, but again when he says "we accepted unification on January twenty-
seventh," he is talking about unification in the form of a confederation, not
unification in the form of the *destruction* of the East German state. That was
the idea that they were considering on January 27, that was what Modrow was
proposing. When they say, "We sent Akhromeev to work on the withdrawal of
Soviet forces from Germany," that's in the context of Modrow's plan for
mutual withdrawal of *both* U.S. and Soviet forces, a plan which they allude to
in the notes that Anatoly refers to. So details matter a lot.

The second big point is that there are actually a lot of things that have to
be explained, and all of them were points of contention between the United
States and the Soviet Union at different times. The timing of unification, for
instance, which even in late January, Gorbachev and the Soviet leadership
think will take multiple years and their whole notion of how they are going to
manage this in their own country and internationally hinges on that estimate
of timing. The timing of unification is crucial, and the Americans and the
West Germans developed a deliberate strategy about that. Another point of
contention: the character of the new German state. Will it be the Bonn
Republic with the East German Republic liquidated or some new state?—
which was, by the way, the main plan for unification that had always been envi-
sioned from the 1950s. Will Germany be in NATO, including the NATO
integrated military command? If so, are United States and Soviet forces in
Germany going to be treated equally, or do Americans stay and Soviets go?
These are all different issues on which there were major points of contention,
as Aleksandr Bessmertnykh reveals.

And the final dimension on which again there are not parallel tracks working and which have to be comprehended are the interactions on the international scene, because this is not just a story about Germany. That story can't be intelligently understood without some comprehension of what's going on domestically inside the Soviet Union, whether it's in Baku, whether it's the fact that here in late 1989 while all these events are going on, Eduard Shevardnadze is offering his resignation, for reasons having nothing to do with events on the international scene but having to do with things that have happened in Georgia. That, of course, is a factor. You have to understand what's going on in Poland in August 1989, you have to understand what's going on in the CFE negotiations, which matter *enormously* to the Soviet military. You have to understand the role of the Lithuanian crisis, which is exceptionally important in 1990 and into early 1991, and you have to understand the reverberations all this is having with the whole transformation of the NATO alliance and the transformation of the European Community, which is vitally affected by all these developments. So when you hear these presentations, you hear one side saying, here's what we had in mind, and the other side saying here's what we had in mind, and it sounds like the philosophies can be reconciled, but you'll lose the tensions, the conflicts, and also the key policy deliberations that really make the policies turn out the way they do.

Oberdorfer: I think there was some confusion over here about the questions of Shevardnadze's resignation, and it is explained by the fact that he tried to resign at the end of 1989, and Gorbachev talked him out of it, and then he actually resigned at the end of 1990, saying that a dictatorship is coming. Pavel.

Palazchenko: I think Philip was saying many things that we would have to be taking into account in the analysis of those events. On the other hand, I think the whole assumption that within four months there was this bid for the shaping of the behavior of the East Germans that was won by the West is unproven. What is more, it's unprovable. I think it assumes a lot more in terms of the ability of any country or any entity such as the West to really shape the behavior and the expectations of huge masses of people. To say that the Germans did not want unification, let us say in November 1989, may be true. Maybe at that time, the East German intelligentsia, for example, some of them were indeed thinking in terms of confederation. But it was clear to Gorbachev— and he said so to Secretary Baker, I think in early February—that confederation might be a good option preferred by members of the intelligentsia. He mentioned, I think, Günter Grass or some German writers, he mentioned a conference in West Germany, et cetera, et cetera. But at that time, I think it was already clear to him that it would be a very rapid process, and to say that within just a couple of weeks or a couple of months the West was able to shape the expectations, to shape the behavior of the German people, is unprovable. What is provable, of course, is that the West by its very existence and by its greater economic success definitely over years and decades shaped the expectations and, in a way, the long-term behavior of people not just in the GDR but also in the Soviet Union. That's quite different.

Oberdorfer: Sergei.

Tarasenko: Certainly, timing is important when we are talking about these events. I will just recount the actual events as they happened. Before his speech in Brussels, Shevardnadze was to go to Europe on a trip and by necessity say something about East Germany. So the European Department people prepared a draft of this speech, and the basic premise of this speech was the words by Gorbachev that we will not allow the GDR to get into trouble. That was all they came out with, saying we better stick to the position announced by the General Secretary; there was no leeway on this issue. Then, in my presence Shevardnadze said, "Well, do you expect me to go to this meeting and repeat this silly position? I am the minister and I cannot say such things." And then the drafting was referred to his inner circle, and a coherent piece was prepared with certain, let us say, criteria for what was acceptable, what was not acceptable for the Soviet Union in the context of German unification. When that piece was shown to our *Germanisty* [German experts] inside the Ministry, they were in an uproar. All the top leaders from the department and the deputy foreign minister responsible for European affairs protested that it is impossible to come out with such a position. It's beyond all our principal lines, and so on. Well, they had to confront the Minister on this issue, and defend their position. In one-on-one meetings with three individuals from the German department, the Minister asked the same question: "Do you think that this position can be defended or supported and we can afford not to develop our line of argument?" So against strong objection, he went out and delivered this speech as it was prepared without clearing with anyone. So therefore I argued earlier that it would be mistaken to say that all the things done on this issue were done in one place, but they were done in several places. We should be aware of that. That's the truth.

The other issue I would like to draw your attention to is that the only person who publicly defended the Soviet position on unification was Shevardnadze and the Foreign Ministry. The success of our eventual, say, "getting away" with this decision largely can be explained by the fact that from the very beginning we were very open about what it was about, what was at stake, what the options were. Robert will certainly remember the role of [Aleksandr] Bonderenko, a war veteran who fought in World War II, and who was in charge of specific, detailed negotiation on the issue. I understand how hard it was to work with this guy, but Shevardnadze was specifically saying that we must involve this guy in this process. "If we have a war veteran on our side, then we will be on firm ground." And this clarity and openness in a position saved the day. If you remember those dramatic events at the party congress, when actually the Politburo was on the verge of collapsing, well the only guy who defended successfully the unification issue was Shevardnadze, and he won the argument against Ligachev, against military men, against hard-liners. It should be on the record. From the very start the most crucial issue for us was to get public support for our position, because the country may become divided. That would be extremely dangerous. Therefore we paid so much attention to enlisting public support and being as open as we could and really everything was on the table, nothing was under the table. That was very important.

Oberdorfer: Brent, you had something.

Scowcroft: I think Pavel is right about the United States not controlling all this process. We are overlooking one very important development in this period, the elections in East Germany in March. In early 1990 there was a lot of discussion about a confederation, a gradual assimilation that might go on for a long time. Even Helmut Kohl thought that the East German elections would be won by the Social Democrats, and in West Germany the Social Democrats wanted a confederation. What happened was that the Christian Democrats swept the elections in East Germany, and the East German government effectively dissolved. From that point on, unification of some kind was virtually inevitable. And then the issue became, would it be inside or outside NATO? But that election took the game away from all of us and from all the maneuvering everybody was doing.

Zelikow: Let me interject on that one point. Kohl, as an election tactic for March, trumpeted the results of the February meeting in Moscow as a green light for unification in order to signal to the East German people that the Soviets had given a green light. You will remember that the Moscow government was furious that Kohl had done this and then went to strenuous efforts to try to broadcast in every possible way that they had not given such a green light, because they saw how Kohl was using it. He then made the decisions to go all the way on Article 23, on monetary union, on one-to-one on the mark—all of which was designed to distinguish himself from the SPD so sharply that he would then present a plausible electoral alternative—meanwhile saying that the Soviets are willing to go along. So this now makes him and his platform a distinctive, plausible alternative to the SPD, which was the whole way Kohl was trying to shape up the March election fight in East Germany, so even in that case, it takes nothing away from the East German people to acknowledge that the most important players, like Helmut Kohl, were trying to use international events to shape that outcome.

Oberdorfer: Jack?

Matlock: It seems to me, as I can infer, that everyone around the table genuinely feels that the agreements that were eventually reached regarding Germany were in both the Western and the Soviet interests. That view, though, of course, is not shared by a lot of people, particularly in Russia today. I was struck, for example, by the comment in Ambassador Dobrynin's memoirs, which said that Gorbachev did not negotiate strongly enough and therefore got, in effect, a bad deal.[10] I think that's absolutely wrong, because when you think about it, a unified Germany in NATO, in fact, was more in the Soviet interest than other outcomes, including some of the outcomes that the Soviet leaders at times seemed to be insisting upon. And this I say in all sincerity. I think that the argument that Secretary Baker brought to Moscow when he met first with Shevardnadze on February 7 and with Gorbachev on the eighth was persuasive. He posed the question—obviously, I am paraphrasing—"Do you want a Germany unified without an anchor in NATO? Don't forget that NATO is also the only mechanism for an American presence in Europe. Do you want that? Or, do you want a Germany that will be anchored in NATO and all that that means, including an American presence in Europe?" What struck me was the fact that though Gorbachev did not immediately agree, you could tell that he found this a very telling argument. Probably he had been thinking about it before, because, if I recall, he said

10. Anatoly F. Dobrynin, *In Confidence: Moscow's Ambassador to America's Six Cold War Presidents (1962–1986)* (New York: Random House, 1995), chap. 33.

something like "These are very important points that you have raised. We must think about them." He wasn't quite prepared to commit himself.

Baker: Excuse me, Jack, but I do think he said at that time, we either hope or expect that you Americans will maintain your presence in Europe.

Matlock: Yes, he did.

Baker: He did say that.

Matlock: Oh, yes. That's right.

Baker: Which is fairly indicative.

Matlock: And he also said that he understood this reasoning. He wasn't ready to sign on to everything. My point is that it does seem—and it seemed to me at the time—that Gorbachev was genuinely convinced as he looked at this. And, yes, the position changed. People were thinking things through. I don't think either side had a grand design at any point until things began to move along. But it did seem to me that Gorbachev became genuinely convinced that this was in the interest of his country and his problem was therefore an internal political problem—how do you make it work? Because it was also apparent to us that probably the only person who agreed with him was Foreign Minister Shevardnadze at that point. And so I wanted to pose the question: Is this the way it was viewed on the Soviet side? Was this a matter of looking not only at the inevitability of unification, which everybody recognized, but also thinking about the implications for the Soviet Union and its national interests if a united Germany should not be in NATO but should be left to shift around in the hold of the ship of European politics in the future without that grounding? My impression was that he became genuinely convinced and from then on, it was a matter of crafting a way that he could make it possible politically. But I am asking a question.

Oberdorfer: Could we answer it briefly?

Bessmertnykh: This is a very short comment. First, I would like to respond to Philip about the fact that Gorbachev had a plan, because he was a great man. Of course, he was a great man, but he didn't have a plan! He is a man with whom I have been working and whom I admire tremendously, and he is my hero and a legend. But he didn't have a plan. And that's an unfortunate situation, because nobody had a good plan, neither Washington nor Moscow. On the second point, you said that he selected the GDR out of other countries. Yes, because it was so important, but not for the reasons I was talking about. He did not select the GDR in pushing the country toward reforms the same way as he did push the other countries. This is a different story, so the quotation does not apply to this. I would mention one fact. When actually things started to evolve, Gorbachev, Shevardnadze, and all of us realized, there was no way to stop reunification, so what we were trying to do is just to bargain from the situation the best we could. The events were just rushing out from us like wild horses and we were trying to catch them, and they were still running. So that was the situation, the real one, the factual one. When we were saying before, we would like to support one type of reunification, then another, it showed that we just couldn't make up our minds. Things were evolving so, so fast.

But there is something which was not mentioned today and which was a matter of great concern, and this is the borders. When the reunification of Germany started to be the problem on all of our minds, the basic issue on the mind of the Soviet leaders was what kind of influence it would have on the post–Second World War borders.[11] When we got the confidence that it was not going to lead to the change of the borders, that made the whole thing much easier. I was already the minister for foreign affairs when the reunification process came, and I had to defend all the agreements and treaties in the Parliament, and so everything that was done before me I had to protect. As some may remember, I asked for a closed session of the Parliament for the basic discussions of the documents regarding reunification, and one of the basic arguments I used at the closed session concerned the borders. I was frank with them. I said, "Yes, things were developing so fast. Maybe we should have gotten a better deal, but we just couldn't because we didn't have an ability to do it." And the main thing that facilitated reunification was the fact that the post–Second World War borders were going to be intact. This is something just to be taken note of. Another example of how things were rushing: You mentioned Modrow's three-stage plan. It was our plan; we gave it to Modrow to announce. It just shows how hectic it was, so unfortunately we didn't have a wonderful plan. But maybe it helped even to solve the issue, to improvise, rather than to have an ironclad plan that might have prevented us from being more adaptable to the situation.

---

11. The reference here is to the complex set of border changes in Eastern and Central Europe after the Second World War by which the Soviet Union acquired territory at the expense of Germany (including East Prussia/Königsberg—today's Russian Kaliningrad), Romania, and Poland, while Poland acquired a substantial swath of formerly German territory lying between Stettin and Breslau.

Oberdorfer: Now Mr. Chernyaev briefly, because we want to go to the audience.

Chernyaev: The most important thing for Gorbachev at that time on that issue was that he regarded the process of unification as a democratic national movement. From his standpoint it was quite legitimate, quite consistent with his new thinking, and therefore opposing that national movement, or interfering with it meant opposing himself and opposing his own philosophy for which he began perestroika. I agree with Jack Matlock's analysis in his memoirs, which is very sophisticated. At the end of one of the chapters, he asks whether Gorbachev could have interfered with the process of unification. He certainly could not preserve the puppet regime in the GDR. He could not close the border. He could not restore the Berlin Wall. But he could just refuse to withdraw the troops, and no force in the world would have made him do that. So you said that Gorbachev was someone who could be convinced, but why was that? Because he had a general concept that you could not prevent reunification, you can only channel it—and together with the Americans he tried to do it. You were persuading him, Baker was persuading him, Bush was persuading him, and eventually it was an interesting discussion in Moscow on May 18 when you visited, and also later in Washington.

Some people say Gorbachev quite unexpectedly agreed with Washington, to Bush's formula on NATO membership. That was not unexpected, it was a result of persuasion and evolution. I feel that some people here suggest that this was done by us, this was done by the Americans, Thatcher and Mitterrand were trying to hold up the process using Gorbachev, et cetera. I think that this was an objective process. Of course, there was politics. Aleksandr Bessmertnykh was right: Gorbachev had to change his behavior on the basis of the realities, and he did. Otherwise, he would have failed dismally.

Oberdorfer: Sergei?

Tarasenko: I have just one answer to Mr. Chernyaev on whether Gorbachev could keep armed forces in Germany and who would force him to get out. Money!

Oberdorfer: All right, we have a few minutes left for questions. This gentleman here.

Unknown: This is a question for the Russian side. I was just wondering when the Sinatra doctrine was adopted, was it viewed as a departure from previous Eastern European policy? Was it seen as a renunciation of the Warsaw

Pact? What type of political pressure from Communist hard-liners was brought upon Gorbachev?

Chernyaev: Well, the principle of freedom of choice was one of the main principles in the new thinking. In October 1988 Gorbachev made a speech, an address to the United Nations, and he enunciated that principle there. He said freedom of choice for all without exception, and those with ears heard. And the Americans, Secretary Baker and others, were watching to see whether Gorbachev acted consistently with that principle. Of course, we had a very special problem with the Baltics but that's unique. Now you are asking whether there was resistance on the Soviet side to that principle. I have mentioned that in April 1989 there was a Politburo decision where all the principles of the new thinking were spelled out. That principle of freedom of choice for all is in that decision as one of the first items. And Mr. Raymond Garthoff who is present here, analyzes this particular topic in great detail in his book, *The Great Transition.*[12] The book is really an encyclopedia of the new thinking, and it is extremely detailed and extremely well explained. And so it was not until resistance began to Gorbachev on all fronts—particularly domestic, but also foreign—that these kinds of objections began to appear. That was mostly 1991 when they started to accuse him of not only precipitating the collapse of the Socialist camp, but also precipitating the collapse of the Soviet Union by means of that new thinking.

Oberdorfer: All right. Next question.

Ralph Begleiter: I would just like to hear maybe a brief comment from any of you. You have all made a big point about how chaotic events were and how you policymakers were all being driven by the people on the ground and so on. Maybe a brief comment on to what extent the chaos was reinforcing itself through the media coverage of these events, and whether your own indecision and your own inability to confront these matters was being magnified by what appeared at that time to be fairly chaotic media coverage as well of what were the Russians going to do? It was as chaotic in the media as it seemed in reality. Was it all being magnified and was that a problem for you as policymakers?

Oberdorfer: Bob Zoellick wanted to take that one up.

Zoellick: I think, Ralph, it's important not to get a misimpression on this chaos theory here. At least in my view, this is what created the underlying

12. Raymond L. Garthoff, *The Great Transition: American-Soviet Relations and the End of the Cold War* (Washington, D.C.: The Brookings Institution, 1994).

momentum that allowed us to follow a plan. I mean, having worked in a lot of different areas, I honestly feel that this is one where we had as clear an objective from the start—a unified Germany, democratically in NATO—and we created a process for it, and we had a series of substantive proposals for it. What allowed us to have an advantage at each point in the diplomatic process was that the events on the ground were moving in our direction. So insofar as there was a media effect, I think it was moving in the direction of strengthening this momentum—for example, the pictures of Chancellor Kohl campaigning in the Eastern states.

I agree that perhaps the East Germans at one point didn't know what they wanted, but once they started to have a sense that they actually could choose—and remember, these are people that had a sense their whole lives they could never choose—it was pretty darn clear what they were going to choose. I had this sense even anecdotally when Baker and I were visiting Potsdam shortly after the Wall came down in December. We were talking with a number of the Lutheran leaders who were in a very idealistic group who had taken, at some risk to their lives, the lead in this process. They were sort of believers in a "third way," yet when you asked them what they thought was going to happen they were free to acknowledge that what most East Germans wanted was what they saw on television. They wanted what the West Germans had.

Oberdorfer: Pavel?

Palazchenko: I thought perhaps that the word "chaos" was used too much here, because mostly I think it's rather the pace of events, the rapidity of events that we meant when we spoke about this groundswell, rather than the chaos. It was not really chaotic if only because it was moving all in one direction extremely rapidly. But about the media, let me tell you I think there was one story that the media really did not cover and it was an important story, and I wanted to talk about that during our discussion, and that is the attitude of the Soviet people. My distinct impression during the whole development was that the attitude of most of the Soviet people, including even most of the older generation, was of acceptance and even support for German unification. That was not covered. I think that that was helpful. I don't know what the impression of the American Embassy and intelligence and the media was in the Soviet Union, whether you had the same impression. I would like to ask our American colleagues whether an effort was made on their part to understand what the attitude of most of the Soviet people was toward that.

Matlock: Obviously, certainly. I think our feeling was that most of the Soviet people would accept the decisions and would understand the need for

German unity and that this was not directed against them. However, we did feel that the military, many people in the party, and probably in the security organs, would be very concerned.

Palazchenko: That's right, in the establishment, there was, I think, a division.

Matlock: And that there was an emotional issue with the fruits of the war that would affect, particularly, the older generation. So I think we knew there would be opposition. It was a political problem, and I must say as of December 1989 I personally felt that it was an insoluble political problem for a united Germany to stay in NATO and be blessed by the Soviet leadership. I did feel that it would be in the Soviet interest if they could come to accept it, and that's why I was interested, because I saw the task as convincing Gorbachev and giving him enough support to explain to the people to get this through. But we did see the opposition coming mainly from hard-line party types, the military, and probably also the KGB.

Palazchenko: That is to say, members of the establishment. I was asking about the people, whether you tried basically to survey public opinion.

Matlock: Not in any systematic way, no.

Baker: No, but let me say that in every meeting that I had with Shevardnadze or with Gorbachev that was one of the central topics of discussion: The issue of how difficult this was in light of history and in light of the attitude of the Soviet people, particularly on the question of unification as a member of NATO. Let me say one other thing, and it's in response to Ralph's question and I just want to echo what Bob Zoellick has said. There may have been a little chaos in terms of what was happening on the ground, but that didn't do anything but help us achieve unification of Germany within NATO, which is what we thought was the right approach and which I frankly think, based on the discussions with President Gorbachev, he also understood the benefits of. I mean, two-plus-four was surfaced in February 1990, and Germany was unified in July, so I think we had a plan, I think we pursued the plan, and everybody ultimately was on board with it, it happened, it happened peacefully, and Germany was unified within the alliance.

Oberdorfer: And it happened very rapidly.

Baker: And it happened rapidly, and there wasn't any chaos in the way we approached it diplomatically. Maybe there was some chaos on the ground, but if there was, it helped drive the process.

Oberdorfer: Bob?

Zoellick: Just one other point, Ralph, on your question, and I think it's an important one. Most of the attention on two-plus-four is in the statecraft and diplomacy. At the time, one of the thoughts that was in our mind—I have actually discussed this with Phil, who has a different perception—was that it was also a device of public diplomacy, and the Germans were keenly aware of this. The moment that announcement came out of Ottawa that there was going to be a creation of a two-plus-four process to work on German unification, the signal to the Germans was, "it's happening, it's going to get done."

Oberdorfer: Okay, we have time for one more question.

Unknown: I am curious as to whether the Russian leadership anticipated in advance the symbolic, perhaps media-enhanced impact of the actual, physical dismantling of the Berlin Wall. Did they recognize in advance that it would resonate in a context far larger than that of Germany alone? And, as an aside to that, I am just curious as to how that symbol played out in Russian public opinion, how the Soviet people interpreted this image on the TV sets of this wall coming down.

Oberdorfer: Sergei?

Tarasenko: I would return to my previous point about how openly we approached this issue, and the argument our leadership posed to the public. Actually, we said, we will be in a better position. Look, now our forces are confronting NATO forces directly. After the unification, the NATO forces will not be moved to the east, and there will be actually a demilitarized zone and the possibility of some conflict of some incident then becomes lesser. Then, if you recall, we agreed that there will be a reduction of Bundeswehr, and then NATO was extremely forthcoming in the London summit, creating at least a changed perception of what kind of organization it was. So with all these arguments, we managed to at least come across to our public, it seems to me, with the idea that we have got if not the best deal, at least a decent deal which under the circumstances may be the best we could hope to get. My personal view is that indeed that strategically, tactically, and politically, the position of the Soviet Union improved after the unification of Germany, and the security of the country grew and became more stable and stronger.

Oberdorfer: General Scowcroft?

Scowcroft: To answer that question specifically, we definitely had the impression that the collapse of the Wall had special significance for the Soviet Union, because up until that point Gorbachev had reacted with equanimity to everything that had happened in Eastern Europe, no concern at all. But right after the Wall fell, he sent a letter to Bush and Thatcher and maybe to Mitterrand, warning against events, that they were getting dangerous and we had to be very careful.

Oberdorfer: I think that the case of Germany and its unification is really an incredible example of the importance of timing. Had it happened earlier than Gorbachev and Gorbachev's full perestroika, it would have been a devastating problem in Europe. If it happened a year later when Gorbachev was much weaker, it probably could not have happened without tremendous consequences far beyond anything that we saw so far. That it was able to happen so rapidly and so peacefully was really an extraordinary historical moment, and that was due in no small part to the people who you see here in front of you dealing with each other in a moment of history in which nobody was really in charge.

3 The Persian Gulf War

IRAQ'S INVASION OF Kuwait on August 2, 1990, brought the United States into conflict with a Persian Gulf state that was close to the Soviet Union geographically and had been a Soviet arms recipient. In the past, Moscow almost certainly would have defended its client and strongly opposed U.S. armed intervention near the Soviet borders. This time, in an important test of the new relationship between the superpowers, Baker and Shevardnadze issued a joint statement condemning the Iraqi action and calling for an arms embargo against Iraq. While not without misgivings and internal opposition, the Soviet posture was a major asset in the U.S. drive to line up a powerful and inclusive coalition to drive Iraq from Kuwait. In the following discussion, the conferees address how the United States elicited Moscow's cooperation against the Iraqi aggression against Kuwait and analyze Gorbachev's frantic diplomatic efforts during the crisis.

Oberdorfer: This morning we are going to focus on the cooperation between the United States and the Soviet Union following the Iraqi invasion of Kuwait on August first of 1990, a cooperative arrangement that led to the restarting of the Middle East peace process after the war against Iraq. Yesterday we had a debate about when the Cold War really ended. Chapter 1 of Secretary Baker's memoir is titled "The Day the Cold War Ended," which in his definition was the day he and Minister Shevardnadze issued in Moscow a joint declaration opposing the Iraqi invasion of Kuwait, calling for an arms embargo, and agreeing to take practical measures to oppose this aggression. I'd like to start by asking Secretary Baker a little about the significance in his mind of these two former antagonists standing together against an action taken by Iraq.

Baker: Don, as we began to move from confrontation to cooperation, certainly in Malta and maybe even a little before that, the words coming from each side were clearly consonant with the idea that the Cold War was over. But the action really began with the unification of Germany and particularly what happened on August 3, 1990. That's why I say that as far as I'm concerned, that's clearly the day the Cold War ended. It was quite remarkable for the American secretary of state and the foreign minister of the Soviet Union to stand shoulder to shoulder and condemn the actions of Iraq, which had been, after all, a Soviet client state. It would have been unthinkable and unheard of in an earlier time. I begin the book flashing back to the day in late January 1981 when I was walking across West Executive Avenue with Ronald Reagan to conduct his first press conference as the newly elected president of the United States. That's where he made reference to the Soviet Union in a very, very negative way, and here, scarcely nine years later, we're standing side by side, not only condemning the action, but agreeing that we would join together in implementing an arms embargo against Iraq.[1] This was not an easy action for the Soviet Union to take. Shevardnadze told me later, in fact, that while he had the approval of President Gorbachev to jointly condemn the action, he did not have specific or express approval to join with us in an arms embargo or at least that portion of the statement that called for an arms embargo.

It would be interesting to hear from our Russian colleagues what was actually happening back in Moscow at that time. I think one reason that Shevardnadze was so forward leaning in this case was because we had been meeting a few days before in Irkutsk and we got reports from back home that Iraqi troops were beginning to mass. I raised it in a meeting with Shevard-nadze—Sergei was there—and I said: "We have some very disturbing reports. I wish you would check into it and perhaps you can restrain Iraq." They came back and said, "There's nothing to it. We've checked with our intelligence sources; it would be completely irrational for Saddam Hussein to do this. It's not going to happen, don't worry about it." Two days later, of course, Iraq invaded Kuwait. One reason I think Eduard was so forward leaning in this instance was because he felt embarrassed and in a sense betrayed by the erroneous intelligence that he had received.

Whether that's the case or not, this was a very, very important and signal event in terms of the international community's response to Iraq's invasion of Kuwait. We really had not at that point consciously concluded that we wanted to build an international coalition to eject Iraq from Kuwait. I spent most of the evening of the second of August in Ulan Bator, Mongolia, on the phone with Brent and the President back in Washington and with Dennis Ross and

---

1. At his first news conference, President Reagan stated in answer to a reporter's question that Soviet leaders "reserve unto themselves the right to commit any crime, to lie, to cheat, in order to attain [their goals]." Quoted in Lou Cannon, *President Reagan: The Role of a Lifetime* (New York: Simon & Schuster, 1991), 282.

Bob Zoellick in Moscow. We decided that if there was any chance of getting a joint statement with the Soviets, it would be very meaningful and therefore instead of coming back more directly from Mongolia to Washington, I should go through Moscow. This was when the idea of responding to the invasion in a very broad way and through the mechanism of an international coalition was really born. Save for Mongolia, which joined with us immediately in con- demning the action, the Soviet Union was one of the first countries that joined with us in condemning the action. We all voted together in the United Nations to condemn it, and it was the beginning of building an international coalition. Of course, the Soviet Union was the most important member of that coalition.

We were, therefore, able, all of us, to deal with this aggression in ways that would not have been possible during the Cold War. There was never any certainty as we moved along that the joint efforts of the Soviet Union and the United States would continue. There were many efforts on the Soviet side to try to reason with Saddam to get him to withdraw from Kuwait. There were efforts in advance of our moving in the United Nations Security Council for a resolution embargoing naval traffic from Iraq. There was a particular instance where an Iraqi ship was sailing in the Gulf after we had established an embargo and there was a lot of pressure within our government. The Chairman of the Joint Chiefs, the Secretary of Defense, Brent himself, and many others were saying, "We have to take out that ship or we will lose credibility. We can't establish an embargo like this and then fail to act." Mrs. Thatcher was aggres- sively pushing the President. On the other hand, Shevardnadze was saying, "Give us just a few more days. We think maybe we can do something about this." I was pleading with the President for a few more days. Fortunately, we got a few more days and therefore the coalition didn't break up right after it had been formed with the Soviet side leaving the reservation. Those are some of the things that quickly come to mind, Don.

Oberdorfer: Bob Zoellick, you were in Ulan Bator (what a place to be dealing with this!). You [Baker] note in your book that there were nine tele- phone lines in the whole country.

Baker: That's right but Bob Zoellick was not in Ulan Bator; I was in Ulan Bator! I want to say something about that for a minute. This shows you how little things and personal matters can sometimes substantially affect poli- cies. We'd been in Irkutsk meeting with the Soviet Union and conducting some very serious business. I was going to Mongolia because here was a tiny, little country sandwiched in between the giant Soviet Union and the giant People's Republic of China that had been communist for a long, long time and wanted to reform economically and politically. We thought it was really a symbolic situation. So I went up there. We'd been traveling an awful lot. Zoellick and Ross conned me into believing that it might be important for them to go to Moscow and have some policy discussions with Tarasenko, but the truth of the matter is it would get them home to their families two days earlier. So they didn't go to Mongolia and how lucky and fortunate for us, and I would say for the world, that they happened to be in Moscow. As I write in my book, a more prudent despot than Saddam would have chosen a different time than August second of 1990 to attack Kuwait because he launched his attack on the very day that the president of the United States was meeting with Margaret Thatcher in Aspen. Right at the same time that the American secretary of the state was meeting with the Soviet foreign minister, just as it so happened some of my principal policy assistants were in Moscow. So it was not a very good choice of dates as far as Saddam was concerned.

Oberdorfer: While you were in Ulan Bator, Zoellick was in Moscow and getting the news of this and talking to you, along with Dennis Ross. So, Bob, what happened?

Zoellick: I mentioned yesterday how I thought that in 1989 until Malta there was a certain competition that pushed the parties. In contrast, this was a classic period of cooperation. We had gone through German unification together. The final treaty hadn't been signed, but the spirit of working relations was quite extraordinary. I share the Secretary's view that part of our ability to work with Minister Shevardnadze in that very early period was the sense of near embarrassment that he had from the incident in Irkutsk. I'd be very interested to see whether the Russians and Sergei share that view. We were on our way to some policy planning talks. For any of you who know Dennis Ross, you'll realize how difficult this was. Dennis was so looking forward to these policy planning talks which we were going to have with Sergei, that when we got off the plane and saw Ambassador Matlock and found out the scale of the invasion, it was really hard to pull Dennis away from those talks.

Another little piece of public diplomacy here is that we flew back on Minister Shevardnadze's plane, which was an extraordinary plane, much better than we had ever had. With us was Ralph Begleiter who was interviewing

Shevardnadze; so there was a news person who picked the exact right moment. After we stopped at the Embassy and we contacted Sergei and said we were going to have to deal with this issue and I'm afraid we'd have to push off the policy planning talks. We met Sergei in his office and he said that we would have to get an immediate update. We all agreed and we thought that he was going to contact somebody in his intelligence service, but instead he turned on CNN!

There are a few conceptual lessons here. First, we were quite focused on the possibility of how this announcement of the United States and the Soviet Union at an early point in a crisis could set a whole different stage. I continue to think that this is one of the points that is overlooked in all the drama that followed. Given the conflict between the United States and the Soviet Union for forty-five years, the fact that from the very start, almost before France and others had lined up, the United States and the Soviet Union were physically in a picture, making a common statement, was quite important. This leads to a second point. I was surprised upon leaving government that people sometimes felt the U.N. could do this and the U.N. could do that because people often forget that the United Nations is still a united group of nations. If the United Nations is going to do anything, it depends on the most powerful nations and whether they decide to do something. This was the start of using that forum effectively. It was also the start of a massive coalition effort and the reason I draw that out is again I think from the side of U.S. policy there's a temptation to talk about unilateralism and multilateralism as if they are opposites. In my view, the real test of the United States is how to use its leadership to try to build coalitions, and that's the most challenging task of all.

Sergei would have the most interesting insights on the drafting. We prepared a number of drafts. Every time Sergei came back, it came back in pretty bad shape. He very calmly would go back again and again. I think there may be some interesting insights as to what was going on within the Soviet government at this point. Not only did Minister Shevardnadze and Sergei have to contend with those within the Foreign Ministry who had very long-standing commitments to Iraq, but I'm very curious about what was happening with the Soviet military, for example. Not only did the Soviet Union have eight thousand people there, but it obviously also had a very long-standing military commitment. At one point, we tried to wave Secretary Baker off because we were so concerned about the statement. This is one of the challenges: If you are going to put yourself on the line for a public diplomacy statement, you'd better make sure it works. We were quite concerned that we were going to come out with something that was such oatmeal that it would be counterproductive. The questions that I'd be interested in concern what was going on within the Soviet government at this time.

Baker: They did try and wave me off at the time when it didn't look like we could get a statement that was anything more than a reaffirmation of the actions that each country had already taken condemning the action—in other words, when we couldn't get a statement that also went to an arms embargo. But they couldn't reach me because when the Secretary of State travels there's a communications satellite that's devoted to maintaining communications, particularly when you travel to Ulan Bator. Things were happening so fast and furiously on the ground in Iraq that Washington had concluded that that satellite could be better used to help us determine exactly what was happening on the ground. So there wasn't any way that they could reach me to tell me, "Hold off, don't come, we don't have the statement." So I was under way and they were saying all the while to Sergei, if you can't do better than this, we're going to tell Secretary Baker not to come. They couldn't have reached me anyway.

Zoellick: But we still used it.

Oberdorfer: Sergei?

Tarasenko: I don't see any sense in giving the known facts. There are a lot of things written specifically in Secretary Baker's book—a very detailed account of what transpired over these days. So I'd better dwell on the inside story from my point of view as I saw the situation there. Another piece of luck was that at that time Gorbachev was out of Moscow, not because Gorbachev would interfere and be less eager to proceed along these lines, but because his absence from Moscow prevented the military and the other agencies from reaching him and interfering in this affair. Shevardnadze was basically in charge of the situation, and the other guys did not know what was going on. That maybe was the important factor in a broader sense

Baker: Sometimes that's very important from the standpoint of a Foreign Ministry.

Tarasenko: It's so true. Then there is the internal Foreign Ministry situation. Shevardnadze convened a broad meeting of all heads of department. To be short, I'll say that nobody supported his position. Yes, [some were ready to support him] with some reservation, but basically, everyone present was against the idea of going out with a joint statement with the United States. Then, after all that encouraging support, the Minister decided to proceed.

There was another bit of historical luck, when Secretary Baker's plane blew a tire in Irkutsk, so we got two more hours for our decision-making process. I'll try to re-create the situation. When we received the news that the Secretary was delayed and we had some extra time, I was with the Minister in his office. We ran through the lists, so to say, checking things, and we were very much concerned at that time about the fate of the nine thousand Soviet citizens in Iraq. Suppose tomorrow a school bus carrying Soviet children will be attacked in Baghdad by an angry mob, who will be responsible for that? I recall that the Chief of the Middle East Department took me by the lapels, and pushed me in the corner and said, "Sergei, tomorrow if that happens, I will give your telephone number and you will explain to the parents what happened to their kids." So, we sat in the office of the Minister. We had some time so we went over this checklist, and then we came to the issue of what we would do if something really goes wrong in Baghdad.

I remember that I said, "For me it's clear. I will say that I gave you bad advice; I am responsible for this advice and I take responsibility for myself and resign." I said, "I think that the same is true for you." Shevardnadze was not the guy to hide something behind my back—it's too small a back to hide for such a person. So, he said, "Yes, I understand that I'd have to resign immediately in that case." Again, the issue was how high the risk is. I said, "Look, we took several risks already introducing unilateral actions condemning the action of Saddam. So far we were lucky, Saddam didn't react to our steps. Let's take another risk. It doesn't increase much the general level of risk." Shevardnadze fell silent, certainly I was silent as well, waiting for the Chief to say something, and we sat in his office in complete silence over forty minutes, maybe an hour. I saw that he was thinking the situation over. You know that there was a bracketed phrase and much depended upon this phrase.[2] Not a single word was said during this forty minutes or hour. Then Shevardnadze's secretary came in and said, "[Secretary Baker's] plane is coming in, you have to go to Sheremetevo [airport]. Let's go." The rest is history. That's one part of it. There is the human cost of diplomacy as well. It looks like you are taking decision. When you have nine thousand lives and you have to assume responsibility—even for a single life—it is not easy, believe me.

I'd like to recall another episode. I cannot place it in time, but it was on the verge of the major decision to use force, passing the resolution in the U.N.

---

2. The bracketed phrase concerned an immediate arms embargo on Iraq.

about applying "all necessary means." I was in Shevardnadze's office at this time. A call came from Gorbachev, and I was present during the talk; usually I would leave the room but Shevardnadze said, "Stay." I stood. I heard one side of the conversation. It was, as far as I can guess, a tough conversation. Shevardnadze told me the substance of it. He said that Gorbachev told him that "you are being duped by the Americans. They have been talking about cooperation and partnership, but I have reliable information from reliable sources that the American side will attack Baghdad at 3:00 P.M. Moscow time." It was around one o'clock in the afternoon on that very date. Shevardnadze, in my presence said, "I don't believe that. I trust Secretary Baker. I trust his promise that they will inform us. They will consult with us before using force in the Gulf. So, I cannot accept that. I think that we will have to proceed with our plan." Then again we sat for a couple of hours waiting for this three-hour deadline, listening to the radio, asking people in the cipher room to report to us as soon as they got any news whether the U.S. side will start an offensive or not. When this deadline passed, it was such a relief. So, this is an episode from a very dramatic story—a prolonged dramatic period in our relationship and in Gulf policy as well.

Baker: When we met in the airport, it was my feeling that Shevardnadze had really not decided whether he was going to remove those brackets or not remove those brackets. I remember we talked for over an hour before we went down and met with the press before he finally concluded he would remove the brackets and we would go for an arms embargo together. He talked very emotionally about the nine thousand Soviet citizens that were in Iraq, but I was able to remind him that we had thousands of Americans there as well. The one promise that he wanted me to make to him was that we had no plans to launch an attack on Baghdad and, of course, we did not and I was able to make that promise. We went forward from that point on and cooperated. You mention the word "trust," and I have to tell you that I think the fact that trust by that time had developed on both sides—certainly between me and Eduard Shevardnadze, but I think also between President Bush and President Gorbachev—was largely responsible for what we were able to accomplish.

Oberdorfer: General Scowcroft wanted to add something.

Scowcroft: The fact that when the conflict broke out Jim was in Ulan Bator and Bob Zoellick was on his way to Moscow may be one of those fortuitous accidents in history. I think what might have happened had Jim been in

Washington when this started. Then we would have had to say, all right, "Should we send him to Moscow?" The answer is no, you couldn't send him to Moscow from Washington unless you had the outlines of an agreement. Would that have been possible if everybody had not been there ready to go? So it may have been one of those lucky accidents. I think it is hard to overestimate the significance of that joint declaration. Whether or not this was the end of the Cold War, this was one of the most concrete manifestations that the Cold War was over because one of the hallmarks of the Cold War for decades had been that any time there was a big international crisis, the United States was on one side and the Soviet Union was on the other. That sort of defined the Cold War. Here we were standing shoulder to shoulder. That spawned on our side the hope for what we began to call the New World Order, with the United States and the Soviet Union standing shoulder to shoulder. Through the U.N. we could deal with one of the age-old scourges of mankind, unprovoked aggression against one's neighbor. I think it was really a momentous event.

One interesting point on this oil tanker that was sailing from Iraq and the debate about whether or not [to take action]. An embargo had been in place, but there was no enforcement mechanism. We had a heated debate, both within the administration and with the British. It was not really about the Soviet Union, it was about enforcement. Prime Minister Thatcher was a strong believer in Article 51. She said, "We don't need and we don't want to go to the Security Council for additional authorization. We might not get it." So that was the issue, and I was very concerned that this was the first time we were being forced to put up, if you will, when challenged on it. Would we stand up to the challenge, or would it look like we were backing away? Jim, I think, was all alone in urging the President to give Gorbachev a couple more days. The President sided with Jim, wisely so. Then we called Margaret Thatcher, and she said, "Well, all right, George, but this is no time to go wobbly."

Oberdorfer: Bob?

Zoellick: I just want to draw a lesson here. The development of trust, credibility, or a sense that the country's word was good and that its leader's word was good, is highly important—particularly for the United States, which is most effective as an alliance or coalition leader. This is one of the things that is very hard to explain because it doesn't lend itself to natural daily press coverage. But you can see from this episode that other people who were making uncomfortable decisions often need to rely on trust. I think this is one of the dilemmas the State Department is often put in because the State Department is often the part of the government that does have these personal relations. So it often is being accused of being wobbly in its own regard because it's trying to manage these relationships. But I think we were well served because George Bush had his own set of personal relationships and was very cognizant of their importance. The weakness that it always creates, and this is one of the other dilemmas in history, is then people start to say, "Well, are personal relations taking over for national interests? Are the relations among the leaders guiding the national interest?" This was obviously the case later on with the question of whether President Bush was too tied to President Gorbachev. My own view of this is that it's a misstatement. I don't think the United States ever lost sight of its national interest, but, on the other hand, as you can see, you can't ignore the people you're dealing with, not only because that's not the way human beings interact but because if you do, then you lose the opportunity to get the advantages of the sort of situation we just talked about. I suspect this is going to be true today with the current different set of leaders.

Oberdorfer: I'd like to turn to the Russian side. Various things that have been written, including Secretary Baker's book, have sometimes identified the people who opposed the U.S.-Soviet joint action as "Arabists." And then Sergei's rendition suggests that President Gorbachev was receiving misinformation—the word "disinformation" sometimes is used—from whom I don't know. What were the forces inside the Soviet Union that really did not want this kind of joint action to take place, and what was their motivation?

Chernyaev: I will try to speak to that, but first let me make a few remarks from the Gorbachev angle, so to speak. I agree that in the beginning and when the cooperation with the Americans was being organized initially, Shevardnadze was the point man. Gorbachev received information from him and worked out specific steps with him. On a few occasions, indeed, Shevardnadze first took the decision and then informed Gorbachev on what he had done. I do not recall any occasion that Gorbachev objected to those decisions by Shevardnadze. Once he even said, "Good for him. In situations like this, this is the way to act." On August 2 Gorbachev and I were at that ill-fated Crimean residence in Foros which a year later became the site of what turned out to be a tragedy for Gorbachev.[3] When the cable was brought to him on that day describing what

---

3. Reference is to the August 1991 coup attempt against Gorbachev, during which he was forcefully detained in this presidential dacha.

had happened, the Iraqi invasion of Kuwait, he responded with words that are unquotable, particularly for those who understand Russian. He said: "This paranoid man thinks that I will cover for him, that I will protect him from the Americans and from the entire U.N." He said, "You know, Tolya, this is something that could undermine all that we've been doing since Malta. So, let's be very careful and we should know that the most important thing today is our cooperation with the Americans." He also added, parenthetically as it were: "Well, the almost 1.5 billion dollars that Iraq owes us can now be written off." As to the joint statement, yes, indeed, this was discussed between Gorbachev and Shevardnadze. Initially, Shevardnadze himself said that perhaps we should object to the inclusion of the mentioning of the arms embargo in the joint statement because we have already unilaterally embargoed arms to Iraq, and have already suspended arms shipments to Iraq. This is our own unilateral decision, why include it in a joint statement?

Now concerning objections to a policy of cooperation with the United States, and who had those objections: I don't know what was happening in the minds and heads of our generals, of the people from the military-industrial complex who had long-term arms contracts with the Iraqis, but I do not recall any single, formal approach from them to Gorbachev with any protest against our policies.

Until the very last moment, until the beginning of the ground forces' operation against Iraq in the Gulf, Gorbachev still believed that he would be able to persuade the Iraqis, or perhaps to intimidate the Iraqis into ending their occupation and withdrawing from Kuwait. He wanted to prevent the use of force, if at all possible. He wanted to prevent the kind of attack that was mentioned here by General Scowcroft because he felt that the use of force might undermine the new thinking and the new international relations that we were trying to build. So that was the basis for Gorbachev's own diplomacy.

I have here transcripts of Gorbachev's three meetings with [Iraqi foreign minister] Tariq Aziz: one on September 5 and two in February prior to the beginning of the land operation. And I would just like to read out some excerpts from those transcripts to show you what Gorbachev was saying to Tariq Aziz. This is all unpublished material, and the meetings were attended by very few people, perhaps five individuals on either side. On September 5 Gorbachev said to Tariq Aziz: "Internationally, the calls for tough measures against Iraq are beginning, and becoming more widespread. You understand what it means? Do you want this? I cannot believe that the Iraqi leadership would want to submit its nation to such a cruel fate." He spoke about the actual possibility of the use of force against Iraq. "We do not want a military solution and we will speak in Helsinki to Bush and will tell him that it is dangerous. But in order to avoid a military solution, your own position has to be constructive and realistic. We need realistic steps on your part."

Aziz replied:

I can say in full responsibility that the Iraqi leadership and the Iraqi people are not afraid of confrontation. The potential of hatred and anger that has accumulated for many years in Iraq and in the entire Arab world against the United States, against the pro-Israeli policy of the United States, is at a boiling point. All Arabs are ready for confrontation. We understand that the confrontation can result in a head-on collision and the consequences of that collision will affect not only the Arab region but the entire world. But we are not afraid of this prospect. The Americans are mistaken if they think that they would be able to take us out by a surgical operation. If they try it, then it will be a long and bitter conflict that might turn things totally upside down in this region of the world. We as revolutionaries are not afraid of this outcome; we are ready to sacrifice.

Baker: He was right—it took a hundred hours!

Chernyaev: [continuing Aziz quotation] "In Iraq, all of us have always believed that Kuwait is part of our territory. This fact is there, and it cannot be avoided." Gorbachev said: "Following the five resolutions of the U.N. Security Council, following the sending of a large U.S. military contingent to the Persian Gulf, it's totally unrealistic for you to speak of negotiations. You have to show readiness to withdraw Iraqi troops from Kuwait. If you say that Kuwait is part of Iraqi territory, then there is nothing to talk about. Nothing. What can we talk about if you say this?" Now, Aziz objected: "Kuwait is to blame for these problems in many ways. It was flooding the international oil market with oil and as a result the OPEC established price of $18 per barrel was driven down to $11 per barrel. That could have meant a loss to Iraq of $7 to $8 billion a year with such prices. So, what we have done is also caused by this reason." Most probably this was one of the main causes why they struck exactly at that time. Gorbachev answered, "We are familiar with this position. I would have much preferred to hear something new. As regards to the Persian Gulf, the world is speaking just about the same language to you." Aziz had accused Gorbachev of "speaking American," speaking in an American language about the Persian Gulf. "Frankly, you have not left us any other choice. We would much prefer the Iraqi side to take a new approach. What you have told me was just an outline of well-known positions; and therefore, we definitely have taken a different attitude toward this meeting, but we are not rejecting further contacts with you. This is the conclusion of this talk."

Oberdorfer: Fascinating. You will recall that in October, Gorbachev sent Yevgeny Primakov down to Iraq to try to do some negotiations with the Iraqis that did not prove to be successful. Then several points along the way that fall and winter, Gorbachev interceded with the United States to try to stave off first bombing and then the land attack on Iraq. My question for the U.S. side is, what did you think was going on with Gorbachev and the Russians? Did you perceive this as Gorbachev attempting to be an honest broker? Or, was Gorbachev attempting to stave off a military action which might be destructive of the Soviet position in the Middle East? Or did you think that Gorbachev was trying for the record to be able to say that he had tried to head off this situation?

Baker: First of all, Don, it is important to recognize that Eduard Shevardnadze, who had leaned so far forward to be a part of the international coalition to eject Iraq from Kuwait, had taken a lot of hits as a consequence. He ended up, as you remember, resigning in December 1990. This was after we had talked almost daily for weeks because there had been a series of further U.N. resolutions that had passed with respect to which the United States and Soviet Union voted together. I think that President Gorbachev was motivated in the right way in terms of his entreaties to us to try to find a way to solve the problem without the use of force, although the first Primakov mission was deeply resented by the Foreign Minister (this was just before he resigned) because, in effect, the President had designated someone else to play in his sandbox in a very substantial way. That was a real problem for Shevardnadze.

I think that Gorbachev was motivated by a number of concerns. First, he wanted to see if he could produce peace, a political solution that did not require the use of force. Second, he was concerned that the war would be a far bloodier and longer conflict than it turned out to be. As a side comment here I would like to mention the fact that during the course of those weekly and daily conversations I was having with Shevardnadze leading up to Resolution 678 authorizing the use of force to eject Iraq from Kuwait, we did something unprecedented: We had our military, General Howard Graves, who was traveling with me as the representative of the Joint Chiefs of Staff, give the foreign minister of the Soviet Union a *detailed* military briefing of our capabilities, and what we were going to do if it came to it in Kuwait. That's how far the relationship had come.

But I think the motivation was very well intentioned. The problem was having gone to the United Nations Security Council together and with many other nations for resolutions requiring the *unconditional* withdrawal from Kuwait, there was no way we were ever going to agree to any sort of negotiation. There was a lot of talk about giving Saddam something that would permit him to save face. Our view was we could never and would never negotiate down from a U.N. Security Council Resolution that says "get out and get out unconditionally." We were not going to tie it to the Palestinian problem; we were not going to tie it to issues in the Middle East; we were not going to tie it to oil wells on the border; we were not going to tie it to access to the Gulf or anything else. "You get out and you get out unconditionally"—there really was no room for a negotiation.

Oberdorfer: Minister Bessmertnykh, you were one of those who on behalf of President Gorbachev intervened with the United States on the eve of the military action. What do you think Gorbachev had in mind? Was he really sincerely trying to stop it, or what?

Bessmertnykh: Before coming to this point, may I add something to help understand why we had been cooperating with each other so eagerly from the very start? You see, there was an interesting situation just before the Iraqi aggression as far as the diplomacy of the Soviet Union and the United States was concerned. If you don't mention it, you won't be able to completely understand some of the motives behind the cooperative actions by the two superpowers. The interesting part of the time before the aggression was that both the United States and the Soviet Union were playing to recruit Iraq into the ranks of better friends. Our intelligence was reporting to us about the U.S. attempts to work with Iraq, and we were trying to balance that through our attempts to work with Saddam Hussein. Saddam probably felt like he was courted by the two superpowers and probably that increased his crazy notion that since he's been courted, he could do anything in this situation. It was one of his basic mistakes. The feeling of betrayal, I think, was felt both in Washington and in Moscow. I met Saddam Hussein twice before that (and, of course, numerous meetings with Tariq Aziz, but I was not the minister at that time, but the first deputy foreign minister), and he was trying to impress on us that he would like to make the relationship between Iraq and the Soviet Union an exemplary one—the best relationship in the world. But at the same time we knew that he was already working with the U.S. on improving their relationship. So that psychological fact should be counted when we talk about how eager we all were to act against Saddam who betrayed both of us. It's an element just to be remembered.

There is another thing I would like to add as a psychological element. You can't analyze things without introducing human ethics and diplomacy. Shevardnadze was from the small country of Georgia. He was the leader of that country for years and decades. Now a small country of Kuwait was attacked and occupied. You know, people sometimes rarely mentioned Kuwait at this time. But to Shevardnadze himself, it was a huge psychological shock that a small country just could be a victim of a larger neighbor; and he felt that someone should do something to protect this small country. It was also a part of his thinking, not only his thinking but of his emotions. I talked about that with him when he came to the General Assembly of the United Nations; I was the ambassador at that time in Washington. We went to New York and we talked about that. He told me about how much he was concerned about the fate of Kuwait, a small country, so ruthlessly attacked. I just wanted to add these psychological elements that were very important in understanding the many things that were done.

Shevardnadze was making enormous efforts, understanding that it could cost him a lot in his political life and in his life as a foreign minister. In September 1990, he had already felt that he might resign because of the pressure that resulted from the unification of Germany. The pressures that resulted from what was happening in the Persian Gulf were enormous for him. He was a different man, and I think, Jim, you may remember how he looked and how he behaved in that month. He was a completely changed person. He was suffering internally. He knew that what he was doing was correct, but he knew it would cost him a lot. As for the general attitude about the military part of the situation, I would like to say the following. I'm sure that both Gorbachev and Shevardnadze, by supporting the threat of a military action against Iraq, were actually not really prepared for the attack itself. They hoped very much that it could be avoided. They thought that this joint intention to repulse aggression with military force would affect any reasonable man in the world. They hoped for this to the very last moment. But the moment when we realized that it would not work was when Secretary Baker met Tariq Aziz in Geneva just about six days before the military action. I was in Washington when we heard the information about this failed negotiation. It was clear to me and they had reported to me and reported immediately to Gorbachev that the military action could not be avoided. Again, when Jim called me when I was a minister already late at night and said, in about an hour or two military action will occur, I awakened Gorbachev and said that this is going to happen. Gorbachev said, "Why don't you call back Jim and maybe we shall have some more time and we will make a last effort to impress Saddam Hussein that things are really coming."

Baker: For four weeks, we had given him a date of January 15.

Bessmertnykh: Yes, I know. But Jim said it's just impossible because the B-52s are already airborne, you can't stop them or recall them. They could have been recalled, but I think the action at that time absolutely unavoidable and necessary.

As for Primakov's missions, I agree with what you have said. Shevardnadze didn't like it because the situation was very delicate and he was in control of it. He didn't want someone getting into it and spoiling the whole delicate game with the United States against Iraq. It was Primakov's idea; it was not Gorbachev's idea to send Primakov to Baghdad. It was Primakov who imposed himself on Gorbachev by saying: "I have known Saddam Hussein for twenty years, we were friends from the very beginning, we are still friends and the only man in the Soviet Union whom he trusts is me." And Gorbachev said, "Yevgeny, okay, let's try it." So, that was how it all happened. After he went to Baghdad, Gorbachev somehow liked Primakov's report because there was some hope in the report that Saddam may be ready to do something if the Americans would accept some of the conditions. Then he sent Primakov to Washington and he was meeting with President Bush. Jim and I were at that meeting, and I remember that it was not the warmest meeting I was ever present at. Primakov reported back that the United States was not forthcoming with accepting the conditions. He said that probably we should go on trying with some with some face-savers for Saddam, because Primakov was confident that if he could design a face-saving gesture or action, Saddam would withdraw. He felt that Saddam was reasonable, but it was the wrong conclusion.

Oberdorfer: General Scowcroft.

Scowcroft: Just very briefly, let me be slightly less diplomatic than our Secretary of State. I think we saw many of these events leading up to the actual attack as a struggle for the mind of Gorbachev between Shevardnadze and Primakov. I do agree with Sasha that before the war we were both trying to make Saddam into a more respectable member of the community. Our sense was that for the Soviet Union, Iraq represented one of the pillars of its Middle East policy, both militarily and industrially, and that Primakov represented that. After all, he was a Middle East expert, and he was speaking for the system in saying we have an enormous stake in Iraq and we can't just throw it aside for cooperation with the United States. In Helsinki, for example, the first meeting we had was one on one with the two leaders. Jim Baker and Eduard Shevardnadze met separately. In that meeting Gorbachev's presentation to me was a vintage Primakov presentation because it was, "We'll get the Iraqis out of Kuwait *in exchange* for a conference on Palestine" and so on. Then when the ministers came back and we all met together, we found that Jim and Eduard had worked out a communiqué that was very much along the lines that we had started our cooperation with. After a little back and forth struggle, President Gorbachev said, "Okay, we'll go with the communiqué." But that seemed to us to be the pattern, and we noticed, maybe for the reasons that you suggest, after Shevardnadze resigned a great increase in the activity by Gorbachev to try to pull back and avoid a conflict.

Oberdorfer: Bob Zoellick wants to add one point.

Zoellick: I just want to add one other observation on what was going on here, and that is that on the U.S. side you'll hear a lot of discussion about the coordination of state, defense, the military. This is obviously the official function of the NSC. But notice what's happened on the Soviet side. Gorbachev has gone from general secretary of the party to president and what he has left behind in that process are the Soviet coordinating mechanisms, because those were linked in part to the general secretary's position, in part to the Politburo and in part to the Communist Party organs. So when he is moved to president, what you see time and time again in this period is that he and Mr. Chernyaev are doing a lot of the coordination themselves. It is a combination of Foreign Ministry and Gorbachev. So when we ask questions about what the military is doing on this, you don't hear about them. But that doesn't mean they're not thinking, it means there's no formal process that draws them in. I think in its own way, as Brent said, Primakov became an entrepreneur of that part of the Soviet system that was no longer part of a policy network. At least, that's one hypothesis; part of what you're dealing with here is a transition in organizational systems.

Chernyaev: I feel that the whole Primakov story is overblown; it's overblown both by the media and in the political community. Let me say that

I feel the entire story of that Primakov mission should be looked at in the context of Helsinki. The Helsinki meeting between Presidents Gorbachev and Bush was not just the place where they issued the joint communiqué against Saddam Hussein's aggression. It was the beginning of a major new phase in the relationship. It was in Helsinki that George Bush said that what is happening will actually decide whether we will be able to build a new international order. That was his very first phrase, and Gorbachev agreed. One little detail: it was in Helsinki that Gorbachev and Bush started to work on a first-name basis. All that happened after that happened in a totally different context. It was the context of a new relationship. Gorbachev wanted to prevent the use of force, he wanted to prevent, if possible, the land operation, but he was not playing games, he was not maneuvering, he was not intriguing. That was absolutely out of the question for him.

It is true that Primakov is an ambitious man. He thought that he was a major expert on the Arab world; and therefore, he had so many friends there and he could make his words count. By the way, the first time Primakov's name was mentioned in Helsinki was not by Gorbachev, it was mentioned by President Bush. He did that in the following context. He said, "Well, I don't want to use force but I'm asking you if I have to use force, will you be able to support me if that becomes absolutely inevitable? Mikhail, can you say so?" Then he suggested that perhaps Primakov could be sent there to impress upon Saddam Hussein the gravity of the situation and that force would be used. Primakov certainly did not have any mandate to conduct his own policy there. He certainly did not represent the military or the military-industrial complex. He represented himself; he represented his own ambition, and his own intention to try to have an impact on the situation. The only negative thing that I see about that mission by Primakov is that Primakov was trying to maintain in Gorbachev a kind of illusion that Saddam Hussein could be impressed, that you could have an impact on Saddam Hussein. Primakov published a book very quickly after those events, and the main theme of that book was that had he been given perhaps seven days, perhaps ten days, he would have worked things out and the war wouldn't have taken place.[4]

Oberdorfer: The Helsinki meeting was in September, and the Primakov mission was in October. Do you all remember this being brought up at the Helsinki meeting?

4. See E. M. Primakov, *Missions à Bagdad: Histoire d'une négociation secrète,* trans. Fabienne Mariengof and François Olivier (Paris: Éditions du Seuil, 1991).

Baker: This is the first time I've ever known that President Bush was responsible for sending Primakov to Baghdad!

Scowcroft: I don't think so.

Palazchenko: We have a record of the conversation, we have a transcript.

Baker: I'll tell you this, by the time he got to Washington, it was a different story.

Oberdorfer: I would like to turn at this point to a perhaps unintended consequence of the activities we've been talking about this morning regarding the restart of the Middle East peace process. It's been said already that there was a meeting in September 1990 in Helsinki at which Mr. Gorbachev asked that as part of the arrangements for the U.S. and Soviet joint efforts to oppose the Iraqi invasion of Kuwait the two should agree that this would be the restart of the Middle East peace process, which had been fairly dormant for a number of years. The U.S. side disagreed with this as a condition, but in fact I think that was the germ of the impetus that did take place after the Gulf War. How did the Iraqi invasion of Kuwait and U.S.-Soviet cooperation then lead to restarting the Middle East peace process, which nobody contemplated being restarted at that particular point and which had its own achievements in the years to come? I think Secretary Baker would be the first person to ask.

Baker: A number of the efforts of President Gorbachev and others to avoid a hot war and get Iraq out through the means of a political solution revolved around the idea of some sort of linkage to the Middle East peace process or to dealing with the Arab-Israeli issues. It had been the position of a number of the Arab countries for some time that there should be a large international conference sponsored by the United Nations to deal with problems of the Middle East peace. The Soviet Union had supported this. The United States never had supported this because our close ally, Israel, had always taken the position that what she wanted was face-to-face direct negotiations with her Arab neighbors and not something that was sponsored by the U.N., which had historically been rather negative toward the Israeli position. We made it clear in all of our discussions with President Gorbachev, Eduard Shevardnadze, and Sasha Bessmertnykh that in our view there could be no linkage. We had resolutions of the United Nations Security Council calling for the unconditional withdrawal of Iraq. And in any sort of agreement with respect to the holding of an international conference or dealing with the problems of the Palestinians or anything like that that we might give Saddam Hussein to "save face" would be a mistake because it would really mean that he would reap some benefits from his unprovoked aggression and we would be negotiating downward from the United Nations Security Council resolutions.

So we were never willing to agree to that, but we made some commitments to our Soviet friends that we would be interested in addressing the problems of the Middle East in the aftermath of Iraq's withdrawal from Kuwait, however that withdrawal took place. Following the war, I felt—and it wasn't uniform within our administration but the President also felt this way and his vote was the only one that really mattered—that there was a window of opportunity here to maybe break an old taboo between Arabs and Israelis, the old taboo being that they would never sit down face to face and negotiate peace, save for the single exception of Egypt. You can't get to peace if parties are unwilling to talk to each other. We felt there was a window of opportunity, and we talked to the Soviet leadership in the immediate aftermath of the war about the possibility of an approach that would involve a regional conference sponsored by the Soviet Union or ultimately Russia and the United States at which Israel and her Arab neighbors would sit down face to face. This is what ultimately led to the Madrid conference in September 1991.

Discussions and negotiations between Israel and Syria, a warm peace between Israel and her neighbor Jordan, progress toward peace between Israel and the Palestinians, the turning over of a significant proportion of the occupied territories to Palestinian self-government or self-rule—all those things flowed from the Madrid conference. Madrid was made possible in large part because of the change in the geopolitical situation. The Cold War was over. No longer did you have a situation where the United States was supporting Israel and the Soviet Union was supporting some of Israel's more implacable Arab enemies. Together, the United States and the Soviet Union, or the international community if you will, had defeated Arab rejectionism in the Gulf in the form of Iraq, and the circumstances were very propitious for our being able to convince moderate Arab states that they should abandon the forty-year-old policy of refusing to talk to Israel and come to Madrid and begin a serious and substantive peace conference. That's of course what happened.

Oberdorfer: Mr. Bessmertnykh, you were very much involved in the restart of this. Do you want to give your ideas about it?

Bessmertnykh: I agree with what Jim just said. There was a feeling at the very beginning of 1991 that the United States and the Soviet Union could push the idea of bringing Arabs and Israel together. The situation in the Persian

Gulf, however tragic, gave a certain chance to work on the Middle East settlement because everyone was in the same camp. The Arabs—except for the Palestinians and, to a certain extent, the Jordanians—were in one boat as far as the Iraqi negotiation was concerned. I personally believed it could help to start the movement to direct talks between Arabs and Israelis. I remember that I participated as a minister in the Soviet Embassy in Washington in working out the joint statement of 1976 or 1977 in the Middle East, which concerned the American relationship. We made an effort at that time to have a joint statement on working on the Middle East. This statement didn't work well because it was immediately received with a negative reaction from many quarters, including important quarters in the United States.

So it took many years and those tragic events in the Persian Gulf gave us another chance to start working on it again. Jim is completely correct that in previous administrations we both were always trying to do something but it didn't work very well because of the animosity between the Arabs and Israelis and because the Soviet Union was not yet very forthcoming. So in 1991 we thought it could be a good occasion and it was a good occasion and it did work. The statement Secretary Baker and I made was very cautious but it was very positive; we said it's possible to start working for a Middle East settlement. The conference that we suggested was a "regional conference." The first position of the United States was that it should not be a conference, it should be only bilateral talks. Then we came to the idea of regional conference, and then we worked with the Arabs and the Israelis. It was actually the first time in history that a Soviet foreign minister ever visited Israel. We went not only to Tel Aviv but to Jerusalem, where we met Prime Minister [Yitzhak] Shamir. They were very cautious about United Nations involvement and European involvement.

We were talking not only about cosponsoring the conference, but also cochairing the conference, which was an important development in the discussions. When Shamir said, "We are against an international conference, even regional conferences," I said, "All right, if two foreign leaders meet, it's already an international conference. It is not a domestic conference." So we were playing a kind of a game a little bit between the two of us, the U.S. and us. We both understood that it was definitely not going to be the conference that was proposed years ago. It would be a new conference but it was still international. I think it was a great thing that was done because it brought about those talks. I remember the most difficult elements were [President

Hafez al-] Assad of Syria and of course [Yasir] Arafat. The two of them were the most adamant oppositionists to this idea. So we both worked on them. Jim would meet us and he didn't meet Arafat, and I would also meet with Assad. Once we went together to the Middle East and met in Cairo and then we started working again on those people. Slowly, slowly, just drop by drop, we moved them to the idea that they can see each other and they can start talking. The most important thing, in my view, in breaking down the barrier was my word with Arafat. Arafat was adamant against any kind of conference in the first place, but then slowly he started to understand that he might find himself outside the crowd. I met him in Geneva, and we talked through the whole night. He didn't say yes, but what's important is that he didn't say no. So we both, the two superpowers, created an atmosphere in which the Arabs and the Israelis started to talk, and I think we were correct. History has proved that we were correct by using the opportunity, and not losing the opportunity, to bring these sides together, and the results are evident today. There are problems but they have already come through a lot of difficulties and now they try to live side by side. The whole geopolitical situation in the Middle East has dramatically changed.

Oberdorfer: Sergei, you wanted to add something?

Tarasenko: Just some recollections, mostly personal. I started my career in 1961 in Cairo, so I'm partially an Arabist as well. By the time the process was started in the Middle East, I was, I wouldn't say in comfort but in exile [at the Foreign Policy Association's Moscow office] near the Kursk railway station after the minister's resignation; so I was outside of the scope of this process. But I still feel a little bit proud of my large contribution to the Middle East process. Sometimes in life, in diplomatic life specifically, it's useful when your Xerox does not work. We happened to produce the only copy of the statement for the Helsinki meeting. I arrogantly entered the room and gave this piece just to Gorbachev. The other guys in the room—Primakov was there and certainly would have liked to see what it is about. But there were no copies! And, you know, it's after all a summit, top officials are everywhere, so the President looked through the paper and then we withdrew it quickly because someone needed to retype it and so on. That was my last contribution.

Baker: That was a very important contribution because the whole argument there had been whether or not the communiqué coming out of Helsinki with respect to our joint efforts to get Iraq out of Kuwait would have some linkage to the Middle East problem. In this particular communiqué—in that one copy—there was no linkage, and that was extraordinarily important.

Zoellick: I just want to underscore Sergei's role here in a number of different dimensions. Sergei worked very closely with Dennis Ross and with me, and what was a particular bond between Sergei and Dennis was their great love of Middle Eastern affairs. I think that this is something that drew them together early on, and it had an effect, in particular, on Dennis's thinking, in that one of the hardest challenges when a country faces a war is what will be the end of the war and what will be the peace arrangements, because there is an incredible intensity in a government about winning the war. Indeed, as people may recall, there were some who argued that one reason the United States should not fight a war in the Gulf would be that it would kill all chances for peace with Arabs, that if Americans killed Arabs that would end it for all our lifetimes. And not at all being a specialist, I remember Dennis's comment that he thought this was exactly wrong, that he thought that Arabs would go with winners and that, in fact, at the end of the Gulf War we had a special opportunity, not only because the sense of incredible American power but also because of the end of the Cold War and the end of the competition that Secretary Baker talked about. I think the last element of this was that within the U.S. government there was a very strong natural reaction not to have the Soviet Union in the Middle East because this had been a point of competition and for years the United States has been successful in keeping it out. I think to Dennis's credit he saw an opportunity for the Soviet Union and part of it grew from his experience with Sergei. So here is a combination of both personal relations but also a strategic concept.

Chernyaev: The idea of an international conference mentioned here was an old idea, and by the way, it was mentioned at Malta. As for how this idea worked during the Gulf crisis, it is true that in Helsinki there was a rather tough discussion between the two presidents about that. Gorbachev was indeed saying that we should not drive Saddam Hussein into a corner, that we should give him perhaps a minimum of opportunity to save a little political face, otherwise he might do a totally reckless thing and destroy his own country and a lot of other places. Gorbachev said something that looked to me like an improvisation; maybe the Foreign Ministry people will correct me but I thought that this was not in his briefing books when he was going to Helsinki, so it looked like an improvisation. The idea was we could speak to Saddam Hussein about an international conference but we would at the same time say that the withdrawal of the Iraqi troops from Kuwait has to be unconditional. But we will declare that we will convene an international peace conference with the five permanent members of the Security Council present and some Arab countries as well. I must give credit to President Bush that he stood very firm as regards that idea. He said we must not give even the slightest hint to Saddam Hussein that he might derive any benefit from his aggression. If we do, then our credibility would be totally shattered and in three or five years we could face a much worse situation. Because the situation would look like this, he said: for decades people tried to solve the Middle East conflict and could not succeed, but once Saddam Hussein struck Kuwait, things started to fall into place. At Helsinki, this was mentioned at least three times, first in a one-on-one talk, then with delegations present. Gorbachev tried to see whether there was any way to give Saddam Hussein some kind of face-saving opportunity in order to solve the problem without the use of force. Nothing came out of this. Eventually, they did come in Helsinki to a friendly understanding and the joint communiqué was extremely important, and it went far beyond the conflict itself.

Here I'd like to recall what Jack Matlock said: that you can persuade Gorbachev. Later, when Gorbachev met with Tariq Aziz several times, he made sure that there shouldn't be any hint of any kind of linkage or precondition, that the withdrawal has to be unconditional. "Linkages," said Gorbachev, "are not acceptable."

Oberdorfer: Secretary Baker.

Baker: I just want to say that the regional conference was really not a conference. It was a construct that we developed that would permit the Israelis to say that they were for the first time going to have the direct face-to-face negotiations that they'd always wanted and that would give the Arab side the ability to argue that it indeed was an international conference. The ground rules were that immediately after the opening session the parties would meet within the next two weeks in face-to-face discussions. But the fact of the matter is that it could not and cannot today reconvene under the ground rules except with the express consent of each and every party there. So it was a construct that we used and I think used effectively.

Oberdorfer: A diplomatic nicety, if you will. . . . Perhaps this is a time for those in the audience who have some questions to raise them. This gentleman here is first.

David Schwartzbach: I'm a graduate student here at the Woodrow Wilson School. I was curious to know how both sides felt that this legacy of cooperation affected the point of friction with Iran today.

Baker: I'll take a shot at that. There wasn't any cooperation on Iran that I'm aware of. I had a number of discussions about Iran with Shevardnadze specifically that I can recall, conversations that related primarily to Iran's state sponsorship of terrorism and Iran's opposition to any meaningful progress toward peace. I think we agreed to disagree about whether or not there could be an effective effort to isolate Iran. I remember on one occasion meeting with Shevardnadze when he had come back from a trip to Iran and tried to reason with the Iranian leadership regarding the death warrant on Rushdie and had been unsuccessful. But I'm not aware of any specific areas of cooperation on Iran and I think we probably just agreed to disagree.

Oberdorfer: General Scowcroft wanted to add to that.

Scowcroft: That is certainly my recollection that we didn't have extensive discussions on Iran, and indeed my feeling is that the Russian side saw Iran as a good market, both civilian and military. I know we had a deep discussion about selling submarines to Iran, which we lost, and I think we simply went our separate ways on Iran.

Oberdorfer: Anybody on this side?

Bessmertnykh: There was not any kind of cooperation on the Iranian affairs because the Soviet Union had its own policy on Iran. Of course we discussed some negative parts of their behavior, including terrorism and these kinds of things. But for Russia, Iran had its individual role and a certain interest, especially when we were involved in the war in Afghanistan. The fact is that Iranians controlled about nine or ten mujahedin groups that were pretty dangerous for the Soviet army in Afghanistan and they were able to strike in the back of our troops there. So this angle brought Iran into the area of our interest. We were to neutralize Iran enough so that they would not do any harm to us in Afghanistan, especially when we were removing troops from Afghanistan. We—Shevardnadze and I—had come to the conclusion that we should do something about improving the relationship with Iran. I went to Tehran and met with [Ali Akbar Hashemi] Rafsanjani, who was at that time not yet the president of Iran but was becoming the president of Iran. And, as you may remember, it was followed later with Rafsanjani's visit to Moscow.

But before that, there was nothing important between Russia and Iran because it was not even considered as a good market. You should not forget one important thing: there was an eight-year war between Iraq and Iran during which Iraq was our ally. So, Iran for eight years was not in the area of our interest, but as soon as the war stopped, we felt freer to deal with Iran. I think the Americans knew about our moves in Iran, and we still believe that it was a correct course because it would neutralize Iran in Afghanistan. It would also save our future relationship as far as this area is concerned. I think Russia now is actually maintaining improved relations with Iran just because of the turmoil in the area of the Caspian Sea, which was always considered a Russian-Iranian Sea. Now, of course, Azerbaijan is claiming a part of it, as are some other countries. So, Iran was a Russian game and not a Russian-American venture.

Oberdorfer: On this side, Dick.

Richard Ullman: I'm Richard Ullman on the faculty of the Woodrow Wilson School. The conversation thus far has focused on the early stages of the war. I'd like to learn the views of the Russian participants regarding the aftermath of the war. In retrospect, how do you feel the aftermath of the war affected relations between the two superpowers? But also, how did it impinge upon the dissolution of the Soviet Union? What was the view of the military establishment in your country regarding the conduct of the war, the aftermath of the war, and the relationships between the two powers?

Oberdorfer: Somebody on the Russian side?

Tarasenko: I was in exile!

Bessmertnykh: I will make just a couple of comments on that. When the military action was on, a slight difference appeared in our viewing the scale of the military actions. We were pressured by many friends of ours in the Middle East and by some people in Moscow as well to raise the issue with the U.S. administration on the scale of military actions. We thought that the United Nations resolutions did not allow attacks on Baghdad and civilian targets. We thought the U.N. resolutions provided only for striking Saddam's troops in Kuwait.

Baker: "All necessary means."

Bessmertnykh: All necessary means, yes. This is how it was interpreted by the two sides. There was a discussion on that problem, but it didn't spoil their relationship because the military actions were fast enough. If they had continued for months, then probably it would have grown into a problem between the two countries, but it didn't because the war stopped very quickly. This is something, as I remember, that had a certain element of misunderstanding for a while but when the whole thing was over, we both considered it a great achievement. The aggression was stopped, and the Arabs actually didn't raise hell as some suspected. So the Arabists, as you call them, were quieted by the facts because they had been trying to frighten Gorbachev with the notion that the more we support the Americans, the more problems we shall get from the Arabs in the area. But the Syrians, who had not been the best friends of the United States for years, were the ones who participated more actively in the joint action in the Persian Gulf than anybody else. They sent their tanks—actually those were Soviet tanks—and they proved better than the American tanks!

Baker: He has just pointed out a significant disagreement.

Bessmertnykh: [The tanks were superior only] in the sense of that area. So I don't think there was a negative result of that joint cooperative action. I think it really strengthened their relationship. But it spoiled and weakened the position of Gorbachev within the country. I remember a plenary session of the Central Committee—I think it was April 1991. The plenary session was going all right but unexpectedly we noticed that almost everyone was criticizing Gorbachev on the Persian Gulf involvement, and the morning session was influenced by all those outcries from the leaders of the Communist regions, et cetera. Then during lunchtime Gorbachev asked me what should we do about this plenary session because it was really going to be ruined and it would cause great damage to Gorbachev because all the materials of the plenary session were to be published. He said, "You should speak on that." I didn't have any time to prepare myself, but then I spoke at the plenary session in defense of what had happened. Among other arguments, I used this argument against those critics. When they said, "You used force against an Arab country, you participated in an action against an Arab country, so you really departed from the basic policy and strategy of the Soviet Union. That's an error. You will lose the Middle East, you will lose everything there." This was the thrust of the criticism. I said, "All right, don't forget who we were defending. We were defending a small Arab country—Kuwait. So our actions are in defense of the Arabs, not in defense of anything else." So this helped somehow to quiet down

the discussion. In general, of course, the consequences, the political consequences for Gorbachev and Shevardnadze, of course, were pretty tragic.

Chernyaev: I agree with what Mr. Bessmertnykh just said. I'd like to add
a few words about how Gorbachev later described his actions and his behavior
during the crisis. He felt that he had done everything he could do in order to
prevent a war that was very destructive for Iraq and for the Iraqi people. Many
lives were lost and there was a lot of destruction. Indeed he was doing everything. He had one final meeting with Tariq Aziz on February 23—you know
what that date means.[5] That started after midnight. He came especially for
that meeting and that meeting lasted four hours into the morning. This was
not a diplomatic meeting. Gorbachev really banged his fist on the table. He
said, "What are you doing, don't you understand what's going to happen to
your people, to your country, to your capital? Don't you understand that?
After more than a month of air war, in which you've already lost 80,000 people,
don't you understand what a land war will mean?" He proposed two options
of a statement that could be made and that perhaps left a chance for Saddam
Hussein to find a way out of that situation without land war. Both were strictly
within the logic that I mentioned. No linkage with an overall Middle East settlement, unconditional withdrawal, unconditional end to the occupation.
They did discuss some possible concessions in terms of the timing of the withdrawal, a somewhat longer time of the withdrawal, and also they discussed the
possibility of ending the embargo. At the end Tariq Aziz, in a rather Oriental
way, praised Gorbachev, thanked the leader, as he put it, of a great power,
which was doing so much in order to save human lives, et cetera, et cetera.
Then he went back home to Baghdad and at 12:00 noon he called Gorbachev
from Baghdad.

Let me read out what was said. This was after Tariq Aziz had talked to
Saddam Hussein: "The Iraqi leadership praises the efforts of the President of
the USSR. It will work with Gorbachev, both on the peaceful settlement of
the current problem and on the development of bilateral relations between
our two countries and positive changes in the region." So, it was a polite
refusal. Thank you for your efforts, but there will be no unconditional withdrawal. This is how it all ended following enormous efforts by Gorbachev. For
three days Gorbachev had been trying to do something. Here is a list of his

5. The ground assault on Iraqi positions in Kuwait was scheduled for the following day.

telephone conversations with just about everyone, starting with President Bush, and including Japanese leaders, et cetera, et cetera. He had been working for three days to try to do something to prevent a military solution. He wanted to use every opportunity through every channel, the international channel, the U.N. channel, to try to put pressure on Saddam Hussein. And also he made one final effort to try to persuade the President of the United States to postpone somewhat the ultimate measure of using ground forces. This means that in the framework of the New Thinking, Gorbachev indeed had done everything in order to make sure that the overall, global peace process, the global improvement in international relations, was not undermined by this crisis. But at the same time he did recognize, and in private, candid discussions with us, he did say that the United States had to do it, the United States had to bear this burden, had to use force—to use means reminiscent of the Cold War in order to save the overall global peace process.

Even though the crisis was tragic, I don't think it had a negative impact on U.S.-Soviet relations. You recall that this was happening in January and February 1991 when it was the beginning of the last year of the Soviet Union. The situation was very dramatic, and Gorbachev needed good relations with the United States and support for that. He felt that partnership with the United States could be a factor in saving our country, in saving the Union.

Oberdorfer: We'll get to that part this afternoon for sure. Minister Bessmertnykh wanted to say something. One of my American participants also wonders, and I wonder if you could answer this question. You mention that it was the Soviet view that the U.N. resolution did not extend to U.S. entry or occupation of Baghdad. Suppose the war had continued, and, of course, you know this was a controversial question in this country, whether the forces should have continued into Baghdad to topple Saddam Hussein. Had the war continued into Baghdad, what would have been the Soviet reaction?

Bessmertnykh: Well, this is a very hypothetical situation, of course. I think we deal with a somewhat different interpretation of one of the U.N. resolutions on that, and I have mentioned the difference of interpretation. I just wanted to add a footnote to that meeting with Tariq Aziz, because in my view it was a very important moment. I was in Spain at the time on a visit and I found that Tariq was flying to Moscow, so I canceled all my meetings and rushed back to Moscow. I came there early in the morning and asked for the documents of the conversation between Gorbachev and Tariq Aziz, and I was given those documents; it was about 5:00 A.M. or 6:00 A.M. When I looked at the plan, which was presented by Gorbachev to Tariq Aziz, I was completely dumbfounded because it was something, in my view, which would ruin the whole thing. I immediately suspected the author of the plan, because it was only Gorbachev and Primakov who were present at the meeting. I called Primakov early in the morning and said, "Please come to the Foreign Ministry. Let's have a discussion because I don't accept the document you have presented to Tariq Aziz." It gave the Iraqis a free way, almost too much and it was completely unacceptable to the coalition, to the Americans, and to us.

He rushed to the Foreign Ministry, and so he made it at about 7:00 A.M., and I said: "You've got to renegotiate with Tariq Aziz." He said, "It's impossible. Gorbachev has already done it." I said, "No, if we don't renegotiate this point with Tariq, we are going to face a tremendous crisis in this area." But it was early in the morning, and of course, we didn't have a chance to consult Gorbachev. So on my own, I invited Tariq Aziz to the Foreign Ministry, and we said that the plan that he received after midnight was not exactly the plan that we were going to give to him. We presented him with a more balanced plan, with stricter demands on the Iraqis. Maybe that was the reason why Iraq immediately responded, "Thank you, no help is needed." I just wanted to tell you that it was something that just was unbalanced. It very often happens that in critical situations, critical decisions are taken under pressure, and it's always a coincidence of events that may either help it or ruin it. I just wanted to add this as a footnote for historians.

Oberdorfer: Sergei, then Pavel.

Tarasenko: A footnote to a footnote! It seems to me that if we had not exerted that much effort to save Saddam, we might have had a chance to save the Soviet Union.

Palazchenko: May I say something? I'm not sure that it can be proven, that what Sergei has said can be proven. It's very difficult to argue that.

So far as the hypothetical question that was asked, I would like to answer it. What would have happened had the United States gone all the way and actually occupied Baghdad, perhaps established an occupation regime there? My own feeling is that it would have created a terribly tough situation for Gorbachev. There would have been a tremendous outcry by people who had already started to criticize his policy on this crisis. You remember there was that article by [former deputy foreign minister Georgy] Kornienko against

Shevardnadze, ostensibly, and his policy on the Middle East. Certainly Shevardnadze was targeted, but Gorbachev was targeted, too. So had the United States gone all the way to Baghdad, I think that would have created an extremely tough situation for Gorbachev and the Soviet Union. I remember Secretary Baker, once he came to Moscow in March, talked to Eduard Shevardnadze, who was at that time already a private person, and I remember Shevardnadze saying that "you did the right thing by stopping exactly where you did in your land war against Iraq." Frankly, that was my feeling, too, that what the United States did was exactly right.

Baker: Don, I can't let that go by without commenting further because the question has been raised in an area that doesn't have anything to do with the relationship between the United States and the Soviet Union or the United States and Russia. The very people who were so reluctant to support President Bush in ejecting Iraq from Kuwait in the first place—and you recall it was a very unpopular position in this country until the international coalition was built and public support was generated both by resolution of the Congress and among the American people—are the ones saying, "Hey, you really screwed it up because you didn't go to Baghdad." There are many reasons for not going to Baghdad that don't relate to our relationship with the Soviet Union, or the effect it might have had on events in the Soviet Union, not the least of which, of course, is the people who say you should have gone to Baghdad [but] don't give any consideration to the number of American lives that would have been lost if we had done that. They don't give any consideration to the consequences of occupying a huge Arab country like that. We might still be bogged down in a guerrilla war in Iraq. They don't give any consideration to how tough it might have been to find Saddam Hussein in a big country like that. I recall when we went into Panama, it took us two weeks to find [Panamanian president Manuel] Noriega in a little old country like that where we had military bases. So who's to say we could have been successful?

But one thing I do know, and it's similar to the effect it would have had in the Soviet Union: We wouldn't have a Middle East process today if we had gone beyond the United Nations Security Council resolutions under which we were acting. We had made commitments to many countries that we were going to perform those resolutions, and that was going to be it. I had personally, I know, given assurances to both you, Sasha, to Eduard Shevardnadze, and to President Gorbachev, but beyond that we had given a lot of assurances to members of the coalition, and we would have lost the Arab members of the coalition immediately. We wouldn't have a peace process today, and it was clearly the right thing to do to end it when we had fully performed the substance of the Security Council resolutions. I just had to say that since the subject has been brought up, because it is something that is debated quite frequently in this country.

Oberdorfer: About an hour or two ago I was about to recognize Vlad Zubok.

Vladislav Zubok: My question is about a sideshow in Lithuania. We have in the chronology of this briefing book that on January 13 Soviet soldiers killed fifteen civilians in Vilnius. That could have been a major crisis had there not been a larger crisis in the Middle East, and it reminds me of the situation in 1956 when the Soviets attacked Hungary in expectation that Western attention would be drawn elsewhere to the Suez. At the same time, it's clear now on the basis of new documents that the Gulf War and the crisis that was brewing before the Gulf War became a rallying point for Gorbachev's opponents, and we have documents that indicate already in December in 1990 the KGB leadership started to plot a coup against Gorbachev. Also General [Valentin] Varennikov now does not hide that he personally participated in the crackdown in Vilnius in January 1991. So my question to the Russian participants is to what extent do you see the Gulf crisis as a starting point for a coup against Gorbachev and therefore a very important step toward the demise of the Soviet Union? That is bridging the gap between this session and the next session.

Tarasenko: Though I was a private person at this moment, it so happens that I know General Varennikov personally quite well. I express only deep surprise at the ability of these guys to perform any meaningful task. If you compare the Gulf War with this operation, the coalition lost less than two hundred people, while we managed to kill twenty people without achieving any object, only hurting ourselves. If you want this TV tower out of order, there is a way just to cut the cable and that's it. Why use tanks against it?

Baker: Why use Syrian tanks!

Oberdorfer: Rob English has a question.

Robert English: I also have a question about the legacy of this war in the psychological dimension. This was an amazing demonstration of high-tech weaponry, of NATO's military prowess. I use the word "demonstration" knowingly because it was televised, not only in the West but also in Russia. By design, by accident, or by the ingenuity of many ordinary Russians, it was just about this time in late 1990 that suddenly a lot of people were watching CNN, Sky Net, and the British Network. Many ordinary Russians saw the same round-the-clock coverage of these amazing high-tech munitions. I'm curious about the long-term impact of this humiliation of their one-time ally they trained and supported on both hard-liners' and military people's thinking, and also on ordinary Russians. And all this is occurring the same time that the Warsaw Pact is dissolving and NATO is taking its first small step eastward. Here was a dramatic demonstration of how overwhelmingly superior the West was in this new arena of high-tech, computer-controlled, laser-guided weapons, something like Star Wars, and it seemed to be working. And it was seen by many, many Russians.

Palazchenko: As far as the effect of what you call the demonstration of military might and high technology on our people's idea of the West's superiority, I would say that at that time most people were so aware of that superiority and they were so aware of the economic inferiority of the old Soviet system that any additional proof, even given in this spectacular war on television, was only adding to the attitude and to the mind-set that was already there. It was actually one of the main factors in radicalizing public opinion. People at that time were very aware of the bankruptcy of the old system in all respects, including military technology. These things tend to go in pendulum swings. Today, many people say, we still have military technologies that are second to none and some are even superior to American technology. At that time the swing of the pendulum was toward awareness of the inferiority, so I don't think that this kind of display was of any particular importance. I know that many people were watching that. Many Russians were, on the one hand, of course, admiring the technology; on the other hand, I know that many people, including those who understood the need for the use of force, understood the need for the air warfare and the land warfare, were also saying, look this is coming at tremendous cost in human lives. This is something that perhaps should have been avoided. So it's not as simple and as straightforward as some people think.

Oberdorfer: Mr. Bessmertnykh.

Bessmertnykh: Just a couple of words about that. This is a very interesting question that was asked. I wouldn't completely agree that the Russians immediately recognized the superiority of the United States's technology. Yes, there were people who did that, but the majority of the people realized that the best of Russian strategic potential was not sold to Saddam Hussein. He was not in possession of the best of Soviet arms, so there was no question of comparing the two potentials. But the performance of the U.S. technology was enormously effective and impressive, no question about it. I remember Gorbachev in my presence asked the Minister of Defense Yazov, "Why did it so happen that the Americans destroyed the antiaircraft defenses so easily? Is there something wrong with the system?" And Yazov said, "No, there's nothing wrong with the system, but there is something wrong with the people who handle those systems." But we should also have in mind the fact that the United States intelligence and armed forces had about six months of opportunity to prepare for the military actions with no one interfering with that—no one—and the whole world was helping to prepare that military action. It was a unique situation in world history, and it will never be repeated. So it was also a fact that helped very much. A small element for the Foreign Ministry people, when they saw "SLCMs"—that means sea-launched cruise missiles—used against land-based targets, they said, "Ah ha! We were always right telling our American counterparts that the SLCMs should be the part of the strategic reduction of weapons. The Americans would always say, "no it's just an antiship weapon. They will not reach land-based targets." So, by using the SLCMs in the Persian Gulf, they destroyed their negotiating position on the SLCMs in the arms control of strategic weapons.

Baker: By that time it was too late, though.

Oberdorfer: Bob Jervis.

Robert Jervis: I'd like to ask a question to probe where the limits of the cooperation of the Gulf War were in two ways. First, to what extent did the two sides share information about Saddam, what his intentions were, what the capabilities were? Did the U.S. ask for, and did the Russians supply, information on Russian military systems in Iraq and those related areas? Second, in the last-minute diplomacy before the ground war started that was discussed so interestingly by the Soviet side, to what extent was there communication between the American leaders and Gorbachev about what deal he was trying to broker and what deal he was trying to accept? Because we have just learned, and correctly, that if certain proposals had been accepted by Iraq, it would have created a great deal of friction between the U.S. and the Soviet Union, and I wonder about the extent of the communication on that at the time.

Baker: There was a lot of communication on that at the time. It's all detailed in my book. It's not a pitch for the book, it's just that it would take me longer to go through all of it chapter and verse right here, but there were telephone calls from President Gorbachev to President Bush. There was one call in particular I remember where President Bush had been having a meeting in the Oval Office and the call came through. President Bush had to swear in Lynn Martin as labor secretary if I'm not mistaken. I took the call and talked to President Gorbachev for quite some time, and I think this was the proposal that resulted from the exchanges you had with Tariq Aziz there toward the end, a proposal that we found unacceptable and we expressed the fact that we found it unacceptable.

With respect to weaponry, the only thing I recall is the fact that we briefed Shevardnadze in quite some detail about the capabilities of our weaponry. We did a lot of that with the Iraqis also in the January 9 meeting with Tariq Aziz in Geneva. We painted a pretty grim picture for them about what was going to happen if they didn't leave unconditionally. I remember in the course of General Howard Graves's briefing of Shevardnadze, Shevardnadze saying, "Aren't you concerned about the SCUD missiles," and General Graves said, "Not at all." He said that we think those missiles are very, very inaccurate and they do not represent a threat to our military. They could very well represent some sort of a threat to civilian populations in urban areas and that sort of thing. That's what I remember with reference to your question.

Oberdorfer: Brent, did you want to add something?

Scowcroft: I would just say, we did ask a lot of questions about Iraqi military capability, about military equipment factories that the Soviet engineers had built, about Soviet weapons capabilities, and so on. I would have to say that I think the cooperation was okay. Did they give us everything we would have liked to know about Soviet weapons capability? No. We probably wouldn't have done any more than they did. But the cooperation was, I think, okay.

James Hershberg: I'm Jim Hershberg, director of the Cold War International History Project at the Woodrow Wilson Center in Washington, D.C. Another word that has not come up but which is relevant to this session is Yugoslavia. I'd like both sides to address the issue of why after this spectacular albeit difficult example of cooperation between the two sides to counter aggression in the Persian Gulf in late 1990 and early 1991, there was such an acute failure to forge effective cooperation just a few months later to prevent a conflict in Yugoslavia from turning as violent as it did. Was Milošević's timing as good as Saddam's timing was bad? Was it a factor of domestic situations on the two sides? What other issues prevented that kind of cooperation in Yugoslavia that had worked and had supposedly set an example for the post–Cold War era in the Persian Gulf?

Oberdorfer: Okay, let's get this question, too.

Betty Glad: I'm Betty Glad of the University of South Carolina, and I have a question about this very neat war. Did you really think the casualties would be that low? Remember, Admiral Crowe was indicating his congressional testimony that it would be a bloody war. You had General Powell, according to some accounts, being somewhat concerned about going into the war, initially at least. The CIA, according to some reports, was saying that it would be a fairly bloody exchange. In a sense, did you take account of these and how did you deal with them? I'm asking on the American side.

Baker: There were a lot of things said in congressional testimony by virtue of President Bush's willingness to take this matter to the Congress and ask for a vote of support. I'm confident that he knew that he had the constitutional authority to take the action that we took in the Persian Gulf, whether he got Congress's support or not, but as a matter of consensus-building and public diplomacy and support he took it to the Congress. That, of course, gave the opportunity for a lot of testimony, such as Admiral Crowe's testimony to the effect: "How can you consider doing this? This is going to be extraordinarily bloody." I remember a congressman pressing me when I was testifying before the House, "What's it worth, Secretary? How many Americans is it worth? How many lives is it worth? Is it worth 250,000? Is it worth 100,000? Is it worth 50,000?" So we got a lot of that kind of stuff, and that's really, in my view, what Admiral Crowe was doing up there before the Senate in Sam Nunn's hearings. The casualty estimates that I saw, and Brent should speak to this as well, never approximated those kinds of numbers. On the other hand, we did see some casualty estimates that were in excess of the numbers that actually resulted. We saw estimates of loss of aircraft, for instance, in the first raid that far outstripped the fact that all the planes came back safely. So to answer your question as succinctly as I know how, we were pleasantly surprised—I know I was—by the low number of casualties and by the effectiveness and efficiency of the manner in which our military performed the task.

Oberdorfer: General Scowcroft, do you want to add anything to that?

Scowcroft: No, I think that's exactly right. Estimating casualties in a war against the fourth-largest military power in the world at that time, which had battle-seasoned troops and so on and so forth, is a pretty chancy thing, and the Pentagon was very, very cautious about doing it. Some of the estimates were that they would be as high as 50,000, and we never thought they would be in that range at all. Maybe 5,000, maybe at the outside 10,000. But we were pleasantly surprised.

Oberdorfer: All right. Now the final question before we break for lunch. Jim Hershberg's question, why, with cooperation as it was in the Gulf and in the Middle East, was there an inability to cooperate with regard to Yugoslavia to head off the disastrous things that happened there later? Secretary Baker, do you want to take that on?

Baker: I think that the two cases are not really comparable. In Kuwait you had a case of unprovoked aggression by a large country against another; in Yugoslavia you had a civil war breaking out. The fact of the matter is in Yugoslavia there are no boy scouts. There were no boy scouts when it started, there still are no boy scouts. Everybody has committed atrocities. Perhaps the Serbians have done the most egregious things there and done more of them, but it's happened on all sides. And the other thing at least as far as the United States is concerned is that it was the view of President Bush, myself, and I think everybody in our government that the national interest of the United States did not rise to the stature of putting American men and women on the ground in the former Yugoslavia to prevent that civil war from happening. We would have lost quite a few if we tried to prevent it. I think we would lose quite a few today if indeed we tried to reverse it. We're not reversing it today. We are accepting the de facto partition of Bosnia that has taken place. Our view was we just fought a major war in the Persian Gulf, we fought three wars in this century in Europe—two hot ones and a cold one—and everybody should not be looking to Uncle Sam to solve every conflict that breaks out around the world. We cannot be, and should not be asked to be, the policeman for the world. So if you say you had an obligation to stop this because of the nature of the humanitarian nightmare, I ask you why didn't we cooperate with Russia to stop what's happened in Rwanda, which is every bit as bad, if not worse. I think that's the main reason that you did not see the kind of action in Yugoslavia that you saw in the Gulf. One major reason is our national interests were not as impacted and not as involved, and they still aren't today.

Oberdorfer: Someone on this side want to add anything?

Bessmertnykh: I agree with that analysis, but I would also like to add that the United States, and the Soviet Union, and the European countries had been trying to forestall that tragedy in Yugoslavia and at the foreign ministers' meeting in Berlin in June 1991. We tried hard, Jim and myself and [Hans-Dietrich] Genscher and some other ministers, to do something. But the truth of the matter is that it was a different situation. Second, some of the allies of the United States had their own policy vis-à-vis Yugoslavia. The Germans were playing their own game in Yugoslavia, and what they have done actually prompted many things in Yugoslavia. Third, we tried to revive the system of CSCE as far as Yugoslavia is concerned but the system didn't work. It was too fresh, too young. It couldn't do it, and NATO didn't want to get involved. Fourth, the Yugoslavians themselves were not sure what they wanted. We asked them, "What would you like us to do to help you?" And the Yugoslavians didn't have the answer. So that was the situation we were in when the Yugoslavian tragedy was evolving.

4 Countdown to the Collapse of the Soviet Union

THE FINAL SESSION directly addressed the crucial backdrop to all the preceding diplomacy of the Cold War's end: Soviet domestic politics and the mounting dual crises of the communist system and the Soviet empire. The conferees discussed efforts by Bush, Baker, and Matlock to warn Gorbachev of an impending coup. The discussants also explored the collapse of Gorbachev's support and the final crisis and dissolution of the Soviet Union. They addressed the extent to which the policies and actions of the United States and its allies played a part in these events. There was a sharp debate on the question of whether the Soviet Union could have been saved in some form, and whether U.S. policy could have done more to support Soviet reforms.

Oberdorfer: I have three questions about this whole period which I hope in the course of things will get addressed this afternoon. First, could the Soviet Union have been saved in something like the form in which it was taking shape the last year of Gorbachev? Second, should it have been saved? Would the people of Russia and the other constituent elements be better off? Would the international community and the United States be better off if it had been saved? And, third, is there anything the United States and its allies should have done which they did not do to influence the outcome as it eventually took place in the former Soviet Union? I think perhaps a good way to start is to ask Ambassador Matlock to tell us about his meeting with [Moscow] Mayor [Gavril] Popov and what happened then.

Matlock: The meeting was in June—Thursday, June 20. Part of the meeting, at least, has been recorded in Mr. Chernyaev's notes.[1] I think that our perceptions of what precisely was said may differ in a few particulars, but in essence what happened was that Popov came to me—he had been invited to lunch, and I had gotten word that he couldn't come but he'd like to call on me because I had already announced that I would be departing in a few weeks. Politically, this was a strange week in Moscow because on Monday the prime minister Mr. [Valentin] Pavlov had made a proposal to the Supreme Soviet

1. See Anatoly S. Chernyaev, *My Six Years with Gorbachev*, ed. and trans. Robert D. English and Elizabeth Tucker (University Park: Pennsylvania State University Press, 2000), 352–58.

that he be granted extensive powers. It was in a closed session at which the head of the KGB, Mr. [Vladimir] Kryuchkov, and the minister of defense, Marshal Yazov, had spoken strongly in favor of that. That, of course, was a closed session, but they were getting as leaky as Washington is, and I think by Wednesday morning summaries of what they said had already been leaked to the press. Also, Gorbachev then announced that he had not approved this proposal and so everybody was abuzz: What the heck is going on? How can the prime minister, who is subordinate to the president and named by the president, without his knowledge go to the Parliament and ask for the transfer of some of the president's rights to him? And then how can this be supported before the Parliament by other subordinates of the president?

Okay, that was the political background in Moscow. Popov came in, and we went through social niceties, and as we chatted when nobody else was in the room, he wrote me a note saying we need to get a message to "Nikolayevich," meaning Yeltsin. Yeltsin was that week in Washington, and he was due to meet with President Bush that very morning. Of course, that was a few hours later because this was about 12 o'clock noon Moscow time. He said we need to get word to him because there is a conspiracy to remove Gorbachev. His words in Russian were "snyat' Gorbacheva." He didn't say when, but obviously he thought the matter was urgent because they had to get the word to Yeltsin. I simply wrote on it, "I'll send a message but who is behind this?" And he took the piece of paper and wrote four names on it. The names were Kryuchkov, Pavlov, Yazov, and [Anatoly] Lukyanov. Pavlov was the prime minister, the one who had made the proposal that week; Kryuchkov, the head of the KGB; Yazov, the minister of defense; Lukyanov was chairman of Parliament. I, of course, noted in my mind those names, and he took the paper back, tore it up, and put it in his pocket.

We continued to chat, not a word, of course, was uttered about this aloud, and after an appropriate time, twenty-five or thirty minutes, he left, and I was expecting guests for lunch so I immediately did a handwritten report and sent it by courier to the embassy to transmit to Washington as rapidly as possible for transmittal to the President and the Secretary, with the request that it be passed on to Yeltsin. Notice that Popov didn't come to inform us. He came to use us as a communications channel to Yeltsin because it was the only one he had. In any event, that was the report. Later, I got instructions to go and warn Gorbachev, and I said (this was on secured telephone line) all right. I agreed we should give him some warning, but I said I don't think it's appropriate to name these people because it will seem like a provocation if I go in and tell the President (that is, the American ambassador tells the [Russian] president) that his prime minister, minister of defense, the head of his police, and the head of his Parliament are conspiring against him. And, I said, besides, with what's going on this week, he should be able to put two and two together. And the person who called me agreed, yes, that's appropriate and I said, at all costs, there must not be any mention of the source. And that was certainly agreed.

So, I telephoned Chernyaev, and he got an immediate appointment, probably as a result of a conversation that Secretary Baker had had with Bessmertnykh in Berlin. I went immediately, of course, and I thought very carefully how I am going to word this because it would be natural to assume that we had some special intelligence information, and I didn't want to leave the impression that it was an intelligence report. And I recall that I used the phrase that we had a report that was "more than a rumor but less than confirmed information of sufficiently serious import that the President considered it necessary to pass on." Apparently, I didn't do this very well because Anatoly writes that he thought I said intelligence information and also he drew the conclusion I didn't believe in it. Actually, I thought *very* likely it was accurate, again given the shenanigans that were going on in Parliament. A conversation ensued more or less along the lines of what you can read in Chernyaev's notes.[2] I would say the only point that I would differ from this account was that I tried to make clear that it was not intelligence; obviously I was not successful. And, second, I apparently inadvertently left the impression that I myself didn't believe in it. I did say, we can't confirm the information but it is more than a rumor. In other words, I kept trying to encourage them to take a closer look at it. He protested that everything was okay, and we would see tomorrow—actually he did go before the Parliament the next day and get the motion voted down.

Oberdorfer: Now, that was passed on back to Washington and in due course, modern communications being what they are except when they move by satellites, Secretary Baker was informed about it, and you dealt with Bessmertnykh.

---

2. Ibid.

Baker: That's right. Well, we first told the acting secretary, who was Bob Kimmitt at the time, to get back in touch with Jack and tell Jack to go see Gorbachev. So that's where his instructions came from, from me, and I think I was in Berlin. And I talked to the President on the secure phone, and we discussed the importance of letting Gorbachev know about this. It was easy to let Yeltsin know because he was right there in Washington seeing the President. We concluded that the best way to get the message to Gorbachev was for Jack to go in, for me to tell Sasha in Berlin and suggest to him that he find a way to encourage Gorbachev or Chernyaev to receive Matlock when Matlock applied for an appointment—that the matter was important and that they should receive the American ambassador and that's basically what I did in Berlin with Bessmertnykh, although I never told Sasha who the source of the rumor was and he didn't find that out, as I understand it, until he got back to Moscow.

Bessmertnykh: Gorbachev told me. I think it was a very important moment, and I think the U.S. side did the best they could, as it was a completely correct action to instruct the Ambassador and to talk with me. When Jim Baker told me, I immediately realized that I just couldn't get in touch with Gorbachev from Berlin because I didn't use my individual channels. I could go only through the KGB channels, and I told Jim that what I shall do, I shall call Mr. Chernyaev and ask him to immediately receive Ambassador Matlock when he applied. I think it is good luck that when you requested an appointment Anatoly had arranged it immediately, but usually it may take hours, if not days. So I called Chernyaev when I went back to the Embassy, and he said, "He was just here." And I think the reaction was that the message was not very serious, or something like that, because we couldn't discuss the details, actually we were using just general phrases. I said, I am aware of the substance of the Ambassador's message, and Anatoly said, yes, he delivered it to Gorbachev.

The next day I flew back to Moscow, and I asked Gorbachev to give me an audience so that I could talk with him following that conversation with the Secretary. That morning there was a ceremony of the laying of flowers on the Tomb of the Unknown Soldier because it was the twenty-second of June. After that, we walked to the Kremlin from Red Square, and it so happened that when I was walking with Gorbachev Pavlov was always next to him on the other side. I had to maneuver Gorbachev to his office so that we could walk there together without Pavlov because I knew that Pavlov could be part of what we have been discussing. So when we were in the office I asked Gorbachev,

"Have you got the complete message from the Ambassador?" He said, "Yes, I've got it and I talked to with Popov, who delivered that information for the American side. I asked Popov, why he did it, why he informed the American president instead of informing the Soviet president against whom the coup was being prepared? Why didn't you rush to see me and tell me there is a danger for you, Mr. President? Why did you rush to the U.S. Embassy instead?" Popov, according to the description by Gorbachev, felt very uneasy, and later in 1994 there was a public discussion between Anatoly Chernyaev and Popov about that incident in the press. They exchanged three or four articles against each other. And Popov denied in his articles the fact that he informed the American side. But in the last article under enormous pressure from Chernyaev, he accepted it. He recognized that he did it. So I think Gorbachev didn't take the warning very seriously at the moment, because he thought—and I think correctly—that that message was based on that action that was undertaken by Pavlov and Yazov and Kryuchkov in the Supreme Soviet. I think he should have listened to that report more seriously, but that is how it was.

Oberdorfer: Before asking Mr. Chernyaev, I just want to raise one point with General Scowcroft. Ambassador Matlock says in his book that he believes that Bush inadvertently told Gorbachev on the telephone that Popov was the originator of this information. Is this correct?

Matlock: I was told that. When I was briefed on the phone call, the person who briefed me on the secure line said, "Unfortunately the President let slip who your source was." At that time, I thought "How can this happen?" And yet Popov later told me that Gorbachev knew, he knew that he could have only known through us and he was furious.

Bessmertnykh: May I ask a question, because there is one point which is missing in the story. It was a message from Popov to Yeltsin. We are talking about the reaction of Bush and Baker to that message. What was the talk between someone and Yeltsin? Who delivered it to Yeltsin, and what was his reaction? Why didn't *he* call Gorbachev?

Oberdorfer: Brent.

Scowcroft: When we got the word about it, as a matter of fact, the President was meeting with Yeltsin. So the President explained what the message was, and turned to Yeltsin and said, "What do we do?" Yeltsin said, "Let's call Gorbachev." So we put in a call to Gorbachev and never did get him. I have no idea what the problem was, but he did not return the President's call until the next day. Whether the President used Popov's name, I have no idea. I don't remember that. But Gorbachev sort of pooh-poohed the notion, and I must say that in the discussion between the President and Yeltsin about what it might be, they came to the conclusion that it was really the Pavlov maneuver in the Parliament. And, in fact, that would constitute a coup, so I don't think it was invested with dramatic importance by either the President or Yeltsin.

Oberdorfer: Maybe the incident is not that vital but it happened to involve almost all the participants here so it seemed like a good one to address.

Matlock: Could I add just one note? In the spring of 1992 after the Soviet Union had already collapsed, I asked Popov if he had any objection if I wrote about this, because although some things had been published, I didn't want to say anything about it without his permission, and he said, "You have my permission." And then he said, "You know, I was furious when Gorbachev found out who had given the message." But he said, "In the long run, this may have been helpful because Kryuchkov learned that he had a leak in his circle. He so constricted the number of people involved in his plot that this was probably one of the causes of its failure." So he said paradoxically maybe this whole thing contributed to the failure.

Oberdorfer: I'd like to ask Mr. Chernyaev to address not only this but the general situation at that time in the spring and summer of 1991: rumors of a coup, the weakening of Gorbachev, the sense that things were not being well handled and well organized. To what degree do you think that Gorbachev had a sense that there was really a lot going on underground in an effort to bring him down?

Chernyaev: Let me first speak to the main question that you asked first. My answer to that is that Union of Soviet Socialist Republics could not have been saved and should not have been saved, because in that form it was not just a symbol but it was a form of existence of a totalitarian and totally unitary state even though it was called a federation, a union. The democratic market reforms as contemplated by Gorbachev inevitably condemned that kind of USSR to extinction. And therefore he started to reform and to transform that state. Unfortunately, he came much too late to understand the need for such a transformation into a new kind of union, and he himself regards that as one of his major mistakes during his years in power. So the question then is whether that state could have been reformed. And my answer is that after the attempted coup that was no longer possible, even a reform at that stage was no longer possible.

And now back to the episode that you have been discussing.

Oberdorfer: Wait a minute. Just before you do that, could you explain why you think the attempted coup . . .

Chernyaev: I will answer, but first will go back to the fact that at the very highest level the United States of America thought it possible, indeed thought it its duty, to warn Gorbachev and to express their concern really shows the kind of relations of trust, not only of personal trust, but also of political trust. It shows that Mr. Matlock, Mr. Baker, Mr. Scowcroft, President Bush, all wanted, in a way, to save Gorbachev and in this way to save the state of which Gorbachev was president, the state which was reforming itself and transforming itself and trying to move toward [becoming] a democratic country.

About the plot, whether there was a plot, my position is that there was no real conspiracy because real conspiracies are really done differently. There were rumors, there was talk and speculation, rather alarming speculation in the press. Among people in very high-ranking positions in the government, there were people who were at that time very much against Gorbachev. So those ideas and those opinions of those people who were against much of what he was doing were quite well known to Gorbachev. But he said, "Well, this is pluralism." Sometimes he said with a smile, "We started it and we must now learn to cope with a situation when opinions differ." So when those four—Pavlov, Kryuchkov, Yazov, and Lukyanov—spoke in the Supreme Soviet asking for special powers, even though it was done in closed session, it was kind of sensational, and I called Gorbachev. There were others who called Gorbachev, saying to him, "Look, what is happening?"[Gorbachev's press secretary Vitaly] Ignatenko called Gorbachev, . . . and said, "Look, what is happening?" And he [Gorbachev] said, "Whatever they are saying in the Supreme Soviet, we have the Novo-Ogarevo process of creating a new Union in place, so whatever they say really cannot affect that."[3]

Chronologically, I think, Mr. Ambassador, you are right and I was wrong because it was after your talk with Gorbachev that he berated Pavlov, and strongly criticized him. He said, "Look at what you are doing. How are you behaving? Now even in Washington, people know the kind of scandal, the kind of thing that you are doing in the Supreme Soviet." Pavlov tried to justify himself, tried to apologize. He claimed that he had not even asked for any kind of emergency powers, that all of that was just a distortion of what he had actually said in the Supreme Soviet.

3. Reference is to the negotiations on a new Union treaty that were conducted among Gorbachev and the leaders of nine Soviet republics in a dacha in Novo Ogarevo, outside Moscow.

About the conspiracy itself [that is, the conspiracy that resulted in the August 1991 putsch], yes, there were meetings of those people in Moscow and outside of Moscow. They came together, they vented their anger at Gorbachev. They said, "Look, the country is going down but he is acting irresponsibly by not putting an end to it. Something needs to be done." But the actual beginning of their plot was when they met on August 4, which was after Gorbachev had left Moscow and went to the Crimea, right after his talks with President Bush ended in Moscow. So when they met on August 4, what they thought and what they discussed was this: How to take advantage of Gorbachev's absence in order to go to him? They thought: let's go to him and present him with a demand; let's scare him a little bit; scare him not with some threats, but actually, they said, let's show him what the situation is. Let's scare him a little bit and then he will either sign a decree imposing a state of emergency or he will temporarily step back, give us his powers, and then we will restore order and later he will return on a white horse, so to speak, and start all over again.

They thought that was a plan that could work, but a conspiracy is when you think about the first step, the second step, the third step, and the fifth step. They did not think through even their second step. They did not think through what would happen if Gorbachev refused to follow their demands. I will not recount all that dramatic conversation; I was at that time at Foros [Gorbachev's presidential dacha at the Crimean coast] and you will need another conference to really go into all those details. But Gorbachev said no. And when Gorbachev said no, the whole thing was lost. Even though they brought tanks into Moscow, they did not dare to use weapons against the people of Moscow. And Yazov was forced almost the very next day to give an order for the troops to withdraw from Moscow. I saw Yazov when he came to Foros following the failure of the coup expecting that Gorbachev might perhaps give him an audience, might see him, and he was not given that audience. Anyway he was sitting in a small room downstairs. I saw him taking his cap and throwing down his military cap and swearing and saying, "Oh, I'm a real old fool, a real old idiot for having worked with those other idiots." And it was afterward when they were put in that prison in Lefortovo and accused of high treason that they changed their line and started to present themselves as though they were really the potential saviors of the country, almost like the Decembrists of the nineteenth century. That was not the case in August following the failure of the coup. At that time Yazov looked so pathetic, and Kryuchkov wrote an extremely apologetic and pathetic letter to Gorbachev apologizing and saying, "I am guilty of having committed an offense against you and against your family and against Raisa Maksimovna" and all of that.

But the fact that in the very center of Moscow things like that could happen was the key negative factor in the failure of the process of reforming the Soviet Union and transforming our federation. Right after the coup, the republics used that occasion to really start running away from the center. The parade of declarations of independence started two or three days after failure of the coup, so it was an enormous negative influence. Suddenly, following the coup, Gorbachev had no leverage that he could use in order to stop that process, because there was no morale in the army, in the state security, in the interior ministry, in the party, and Gorbachev did not have any kind of social movement or social force to try to remanage the situation. Certainly even after the coup, Gorbachev tried to save the Novo-Ogarevo process of drafting a new Union treaty, and two new drafts were prepared and discussed, but all of us who were present there saw that as an agony. No attempt to save the union, to save the process could have succeeded after the coup really destroyed that process.

Finally, my answer to one of the key questions, the last, the final question that you put to us, What could the United States have done to help Gorbachev in that situation? I must say that after the coup, the ministers of finance, the ministers of the economy of Western countries started to come to Moscow very often. After the coup, they talked to leaders of the republics, they talked to the leaders in Moscow, and then they came back to Gorbachev and they asked him, "Whom do we talk to? The republics?" A pathetic moment came on December 1, 1991. The ambassador of Great Britain, Sir Roderick Braithewaite, came to see Gorbachev with a letter from John Major about a G-7 loan worth $14 billion but even that money, which was not much in terms of the country's needs, came just a week before the agreement at Belovezh forest between Yeltsin and two other leaders to dissolve the Soviet Union.[4] So at that time really there was no state to give that G-7 assistance; it was too late.

I'll finish with a question to Secretary Baker. You remember at your very first meeting with Mr. Gorbachev, you spoke about the need for economic aid. Despite all your arguments and all that you were saying, until the very end he

---

4. Belovezh ("Bison") forest is in Belarus; the agreement (sometimes called the "Minsk" agreement/treaty) was to create the "Commonwealth of Independent States," and thereby to dissolve the USSR. The other two leaders were Leonid Kravchuk of Ukraine and Stanislav Shushkevich of Belarus.

could not understand that you didn't have money in your pocket that you could just take out and put on the table—that there are laws, legislation, Congress, the business community, et cetera. And you remember a particularly dramatic discussion with Gorbachev when you came in May 1990 prior to the Washington summit, when Gorbachev said, "I am beginning real, radical, dramatic, market oriented reforms in our country and in order to support those reforms, we need perhaps $15–$20 billion dollars. We understand that the United States perhaps does not have all that money to give us alone, but you can work with other countries." And you, Mr. Secretary, said that you would talk to the President, you would talk to members of Congress, and you would talk to G-7. My feeling is that eventually that the Group of 7 did not come through, and it did not help Gorbachev the way it could have helped Gorbachev at a crucial moment. So my question is, did you believe that Gorbachev really wanted to implement market-oriented reforms, or did you have doubts until the very end whether he wanted such reforms?

Baker: I think that he wanted to implement the market-oriented reforms and that he knew that the free market model was the one that worked and he'd seen it work in the West. But I don't think that there was any *real* knowledge on the part of the people that worked for him or really on his part about what it took to get to a free market economy. In that first meeting with him in May 1989 that you referred to yesterday, I remember specifically talking at some length as a former treasury secretary of the United States about some of the steps that needed to be taken to get to a free market model and particularly the importance of instituting price reform. And a year later, in the May 1990 meeting you're talking about, no steps had been taken at all, and we frankly felt that the spirit was willing but the flesh was weak. We thought you wanted to get to a free market, but you weren't willing to make the really hard decisions that were required to get there. That's what we felt. In our view *all* the economic aid in the world would not have changed the result unless there had been a satisfactory reform program going.

I got $5 billion for you from the Saudis if you remember. We ought to at least put that in the record. It's not $15 billion but it's 33 percent of it, and it's a nice piece of change. In the first place, it would have been impossible for us to cobble together $20 billion, given particularly the legislative restraints we were under. But in the absence of real fundamental reform and evidence that that was going forward, it wouldn't have worked anyway.

Let me answer your three questions. Could the Soviet Union been saved? No. Should it have been saved? No. Is there anything that we could have done that we didn't do? No.

Oberdorfer: It's a good one-word answer but . . .

Baker: I am glad our Russian friends agree with me that the Soviet Union should not have been saved.

Tarasenko: But Mr. Chernyaev qualified it, the Soviet Union, the USSR in that form, as it stood as symbol of totalitarian . . . [cross conversation]

Baker: That's what I'm saying.

Oberdorfer: Beyond the no, Jim, can you explain a little bit why you think that, or what is your reasoning in the answer to those questions?

Baker: The reasoning why it shouldn't be saved is because in that form it was a union that was imposed by force and by totalitarian rule, and it denied freedom of self-determination, of speech, of a whole host of other freedoms that we think are important. Therefore, I don't think it should have been preserved in that form. The other noes are pretty obvious. Could we have saved it at that point? The answer is no. Even if we had thought it should be saved, and we didn't think it should be saved.

I want to put to rest one other canard that floats around out there, and that's the idea that we stuck with Gorbachev too long. We still get a lot of criticism for sticking too long with Gorbachev. In fact, there's even a suggestion of it in Jack Matlock's book, believe it or not.

Matlock: Not really, I'll clarify that.

Baker: And maybe that's because he left in 1991. But in any event, let me explain why that simply is not the case. We knew, there was trust, as you pointed out, we trusted your leadership, you trusted us. We were moving toward a peaceful resolution of the most terrifying confrontation in this century and one that had the potential of annihilating mankind. Why in the world wouldn't we stick with someone who was taking those kinds of steps? I say all the time in speeches that the personal and political courage of Shevardnadze and Gorbachev was absolutely remarkable. Can you imagine taking a country like the Soviet Union and trying to turn it around 180 degrees socially, politically, economically? That took extraordinary personal and political courage, and we were going to dance with the one who brought us to the dance, and we were going to stick with Gorbachev and we did. I was I think the last high-level visitor you had in December 1991, or at least I was close to it. And when

I came in there I was really saddened. I was saddened to see the way Boris Yeltsin was treating Mikhail Gorbachev, just in human terms, how he insisted on receiving me in St. Catherine's Hall, how he talked to me at length about who controlled the nuclear button, and how in that last meeting I had with Gorbachev, where only you and Shevardnadze and Yakovlev were still there and still supporting him, it was quite obvious what had already happened, or what was certainly going to happen within two weeks. So people criticize us for staying too long with you. What did we lose by doing that? Absolutely nothing. Nothing because the minute the situation changed, the minute Yeltsin became president of Russia and the Soviet Union imploded and all the rest of it, he wanted to get close to the United States and he did, and we developed a very close relationship with President Yeltsin, and we moved forward on the same fronts that we had been moving forward with you on Start II and a whole host of other things. So when people keep repeating, "You have stayed too long with Gorbachev," and now they are criticizing Clinton for staying too long with Yeltsin. Baloney! Baloney! Yeltsin has been a reformer as well, and he has continued to move Russia in the same general direction in terms of its relationship with the United States. I wanted to speak to that issue because we hear it all the time.

Oberdorfer: Well, Mr. Zoellick and Ambassador Matlock are both entitled to have their say. Zoellick because he's been wanting to, Matlock because you brought up his book and so it is only fair. But I must say, Mr. Secretary, in my mind there is some contradiction between the idea that here Gorbachev and Shevardnadze are these courageous people, trying desperately to turn this country around, and the idea that they don't deserve our support because they haven't become democratic yet.

Baker: That's not what I said.

Oberdorfer: I know that, but I'm just saying that in my mind, here on the one hand these guys are doing the things that they were doing, both internationally and internally, but the fact is they started from a base that is, you know, Andropov, Brezhnev, Chernenko, and so forth. So they've moved a long way, and yet you're saying that this system didn't deserve to be saved because it wasn't really democratic, it was still totalitarian. Well, you can't really expect it to become more democratic overnight. Right?

Baker: No, but you're talking about saving the Soviet Union as it existed at the time it expired, and I'm saying it should not have been saved. I'm saying the same thing that Mr. Chernyaev said, for crying out loud, and he was the national security adviser to the president of the Soviet Union. How can you quarrel with that?

Oberdorfer: All right, Bob Zoellick.

Zoellick: Actually, the way that I was going to try to address your three questions was to focus on economics and nationalities, because those are at the heart of the questions about whether it was going to be transformed and whether it would survive. What was striking was that in all the other sessions we were talking about basically the foreign policy, and yet I know what was an undercurrent of our internal discussions and our discussions with the Soviets was how were they going to deal with these economic and nationalities issues. I think the key answer to your question is, we couldn't do that for them. There is just no way in the world that the United States could solve those problems for them. Now, on economics I believe to this day that Gorbachev did not really understand the nature of the market economic reforms. I sat through a lot of meetings with him, and I sat through a lot of meetings with his advisers on this subject, and it was quite clear that the longer he delayed, the harder it was going to be to achieve. Remember, Secretary Baker and I had just seen the struggles of Latin American market economies trying to go through this in the course of the 1980s. Those were regular market economies, and so this was going to be a problem that was much worse. We had our own limits obviously because while the Soviet Union was having problems in the Baltics, while they were supporting Cuba, it would be hard to get real economic aid.

My view was that we could do it once. You could amass the $24 to $40 billion, whatever the sum would be to help a program once, so you had to make sure that it was a true economic reform program. We actually tried to find the people, and one of the people was actually Grigory Yavlinsky, who relatively early on we thought had a chance to do this. In the summer of 1991 we maneuvered to get [Grigory] Yavlinsky to come to Washington in advance of the economic summit because we wanted to try to signal to Gorbachev that if you are going to follow some plan this is the guy who would try to do it. And just to add ironies to the earlier discussion, the person who pops back up here is Primakov. So Primakov comes with Yavlinsky and with a lot of these other characters (who were the economic advisers), and Primakov kept trying to make the point that somehow you could blend these two styles, you could blend reform of a command economy with the [introduction of a] market economy, which just was impossible. So one of the sad things about this was, for example, you couldn't even communicate clearly. The example that I always come back to is stabilization. For a market economist, stabilization has a certain meaning in terms of dealing with deficits, money supply, inflation, and it's related to prices. Now when you talked about stabilization to some of the command economy people, they liked it. But they had a very different idea of what stabilization meant. It meant basically re-controlling the economy. So part of the problem here was finding a group of people that Gorbachev would support to make the economic reforms. Frankly, I personally think that he, himself, knew how difficult it would be, and he hesitated, in part, because he wasn't comfortable with it.

Now the other issue is nationalities. This is very interesting, and Sergei would be able to comment on this. We had a special window to this because remember Shevardnadze was a Georgian, and as I recall he may have been one of the only members of the Politburo who was a non-Russian. Gorbachev himself probably had less experience than prior general secretaries with the nationalities issue. So as early as 1989 going out to Wyoming, I remember a very thoughtful discussion on the plane about the problems of the nationality issues. I remember as well that we would try various formulas, and Baker tried this a number of times with the Baltics early on. Let the Baltics go, this would be a vehicle that you might be able to reconstitute others, give them various ideas. And I remember actually on this trip when the Gulf War started that this was one of the subjects that we were talking about with Sergei, which is how do you deal with this question of nationalities. One of the tragedies of this was that some of the reform movement we could see would be split as the republics split, so there was a mixed feeling here because some of the reformers would channel their own efforts into nationalism and you would lose the overall efforts to try to reform the country. But again, the real problem here is that at the end of the day the Soviet Union would have to work it out, and recognizing that it wasn't, we frankly started to open ties, as Mr. Chernyaev said, to other republic leaders simply to prepare for that possibility. The one thing here that we have to be careful about in terms of the U.S. or Western role is a little bit of humility of what is possible for one country to do to another. I mean, the size of the Soviet Union, its history of its own economic structure, meant that, fundamentally, while we could help, we could only help if they were willing to make the changes.

Oberdorfer: I wonder if Ambassador Matlock would say whatever he wants to say in response to Secretary Baker but also address the questions which we have been talking about: should the Soviet Union, could the Soviet Union have been saved? Could or should the United States have done anything fundamentally different than what it did in the last year of the Soviet Union?

Matlock: Let me take the second one first. Actually I agree with everything Secretary Baker said except the implication that I didn't agree. But first of all, I think that it was impossible to save the Soviet Union as it was constituted, and the Soviet Union as it was constituted should not have been saved. I think that what was being talked about by late 1990 and 1991 as the Union treaty was being negotiated, that is, a union of sovereign states—if that could have been achieved, it would have been advantageous from a number of points of view. It may have had certain disadvantages, but it would have greatly simplified a number of the issues that we and they had to deal with. That's assuming that that union was going to allow the Baltic states to go free. My assumption is that since they weren't participating, that when the Union treaty was signed, there would be sort of an automatic allowing the Baltic states to go free. Whether that was ever possible, we will never know. I think, in theory, to the degree it was possible, it would have been desirable if it was voluntary, because it would have provided the mechanism for a more uniform reform. Actually the reform has been more difficult in many of the republics than it has been in Russia. Since then a number of other problems have had to be faced, such as control over nuclear weapons, and so on, and so far reasonably successfully, but these problems would not have been presented in the same form if you had had a follow-on union of a voluntary nature. So it seems to me the answer is different if you asked about that union.

Now on the question whether we stuck with Gorbachev too long, I fully agree with Secretary Baker, no we did not. We had very good reasons. The only nuance in my own approach was that in 1989 and 1990—between the period when Yeltsin was in Washington the first time and made such a bad impression, and when finally we were authorized to tell him in April 1991 that if he came to Washington under other auspices, the President would receive him—that we should have been more open to dealing with him, not instead of Gorbachev, goodness knows not, but as a putative opposition leader, explaining to Gorbachev this is the way democracies work. And furthermore, I thought we could have done more to encourage Gorbachev to try to reach a deal when he still could, because frankly to those of us who were observing the situation, I would say certainly by early 1990 but even by late 1989, it was quite clear that perestroika wasn't going to work if Yeltsin and Gorbachev continued at loggerheads. Gorbachev needed Yeltsin. Maybe Yeltsin was a rival all along, maybe he never could have cooperated—he had always been a problem to manage—but he would have been much easier sort of in the camp than he was outside. Probably those of us on the spot saw much earlier than Gorbachev himself the dangers that Yeltsin presented to Gorbachev's position. Our simply refusing to deal with him almost in any form, even as president of Russia (not that we totally refused, but it was a gradual thing), yes during that period I thought that we should have done a little more, but in no way in exclusion to Gorbachev. Gorbachev was the president; we were right to stick with him as long as he remained the president.

Is there anything we could have done that we didn't do? Maybe not. Certainly, the solution was not to throw a lot of money at the problem. Our reaction there was absolutely right. I think that the [real problem was the] whole bungling of the economic reforms throughout on the Soviet side, such as the rejection of the Shatalin Plan, which certainly wasn't perfect, but it would have moved them in the right direction, and then later the total bollix-up when Yavlinsky was trying to develop something and Primakov and others came in and in effect derailed that in the spring of 1991. It was probably already too late by the spring of 1991. In 1990 I think things could have been done. If there was any failing, and this is an "if," we could perhaps have given more attention to ways that we could have helped Gorbachev put together some sort of advisory body that would have included his own people and outsiders to find them a way and to indicate that if this seems to make sense, we would do our best to support it. To give him some assurance that, for example, if he accepted the Shatalin Plan and he needed some money at some point, that we would try to find it to back that Plan. I do think we could have done probably more along those lines. Whether it would have worked, well frankly, probably not. But the time to have tried was between 1989 and 1990. It was not in 1991. By 1991 it was probably already too late.

Oberdorfer: General Scowcroft, you have something you want to say?

Scowcroft: This horse has been pretty badly beaten already. Could the Soviet Union have been saved? History never reveals its alternatives. But let me make just a couple of points. On Ambassador Matlock's comment about a different kind of a voluntary union, indeed it was my impression that Gorbachev was moving in the end quite dramatically toward something which would have been more a British commonwealth type of sovereign states and that that was a distinct possibility. But in my view, two things happened. First of all, when Gorbachev came back from the Ukraine [after the August 1991 coup], instead of supporting him and undergirding him, Yeltsin humiliated him in brutal fashion and withdrew from him what little authority was left as the result of the coup against him. And then when the Soviet Union in fact was dissolved, it was not dissolved by Gorbachev, he wasn't even a participant. The agreement in Minsk was among three of the republic presidents. And, indeed, President Yeltsin called President Bush before he called Gorbachev, even to tell him about it. Let's just suppose for example that Yeltsin had said, "The Soviet Union needs to be saved, the president right now is President Gorbachev, I would like to be it some day, but I'm not right now," and had put his shoulder behind Gorbachev and pushed for a weak Union treaty, which would have given a lot of the national sentiment free rein in the republics, I'm not sure it could have not have been saved. But that's just a personal opinion. Should it have been? I'm agnostic. I don't think it's up to Americans to say whether or not the Soviet Union should have been saved. I think for a military man having all those missiles divided up a little more didn't break my heart. Should we have done anything differently? I think we are so far out on the margins of what was going on inside the Soviet Union, I think the answer is almost certainly no.

Palazchenko: Just a few words about the economy and whether Gorbachev understood market economy or whether he was totally in the dark about what it meant. I think that probably starting sometime in 1989, judging from your conversations with him, he started to understand a lot more. He didn't know how to get there. Some say he didn't have the courage to take the steps to get there. But he had a pretty good idea that a market economy is an economy where the prices are not all set from the center, that also you have to address other problems. He didn't know really how to get there, and I would say that it was very difficult at that time to know how to get there. I remember, Mr. Secretary, you talked to him, to Shevardnadze in 1989, I think on the plane to Wyoming, and you raised three things: the budget deficit that needed to be closed, price liberalization, and bankruptcy. And look what is happening today.

Baker: The ruble overhang.

Palazchenko: The ruble overhang, right. Look what is happening today. Price liberalization has been done. But look, for example, at the budgetary situation, even today it is terrible. Those were difficult problems, not just whether you understand those problems or not. Look at bankruptcy. You asked Shevardnadze point-blank. "You are looking at what you call a socialist market economy: will there be bankruptcies in that socialist market economy?" Shevardnadze said, yes. Now today we have ostensibly a capitalist market economy in Russia. Are there bankruptcies? This is a very difficult question, and we still do not have a proper mechanism for bankruptcies. We don't have a proper working mechanism that had been working in real market economies for centuries. So I am not saying Gorbachev understood everything, but those were things that were extremely difficult to implement.

Baker: Oh yes, we understand that.

Palazchenko: Even today, many of them are still hanging in the air.

Oberdorfer: Sergei and then Minister Bessmertnykh.

Tarasenko: I'd like to remind the audience that you are looking at four communists, four members of the Communist Party in good standing with a lot of mileage behind us. We defended the system. Those who worked at the U.S. Embassy in Moscow and dealt with me, . . . can say that I served the system. Aleksandr Aleksandrovich worked in Washington for many years. People who knew him then know he was capably defending the interests of the state, that's for sure.

So how does it happen that we honest believers, so to speak, communists, oversaw the collapse of communism? I joined the Communist Party at the age nineteen, that's the earliest possible age. So all my life I was a member of the party. I never canceled my membership. I am talking about that to draw your attention to a human dimension of this problem. It's been a very interesting highbrow discussion on technical issues, on the economy, on market reforms, everything. But there are we people, living creatures, living under certain conditions, and any state, any organism, will live as long as the constituent members want it to live—continue to have this will to live—and a lot of people within the party, and even more within this society as a whole, lost faith in the system completely.

And if you measure it on a historical scale, my mother was born before the Revolution. She died a year ago waiting for the elections, for a chance to vote for [Communist Party presidential candidate Gennady] Zyuganov. She was a true believer. She made her career under the Soviet power. I was a communist of another color, so to say. I saw the world, and I had a lot of quarrels with my mother on ideological issues. I will not go into details. My son, who was born in 1961, was completely indifferent to communist ideology, to Communist Party membership, to anything of this type. So we are talking of a phenomenon. My mother survived the Soviet Union, my mother survived communism. So the whole thing occurred within a generation.

I would say that maybe we are dealing here, not with a kind of big political system, but a kind of cult, you know, with crazy ideas and maybe some high-minded ideas, but society took a wrong turn. It's not after all . . . an animal herd that will proceed in any direction. The better part of society found that we were heading in the wrong direction. When that happened, the Soviet Union was doomed and communism was doomed, because if we good communists did contribute in our modest way to the collapse of this system, and we did, I hope, then that society cannot live. Society consists of people, and if it loses the support of people, it's doomed and has no right to continue to slip and slide.

Chernyaev: My friend, Sergei, said he was speaking on behalf of all of us. It is true that all of us were members of the Communist Party, two of us were even members of the Central Committee of the Communist Party, but our lives were very different even though I agree with your final conclusion. I joined the party in 1942 during World War II when I had the rank of junior lieutenant. For me, joining the party was not an ideological action, it was not an action that signified my belief in communism. It was a patriotic action. I spent half a century practically as a member of the Communist Party. I was never a communist believer. I was never a communist believer even when I was a member of the Soviet Central Committee, but you are right that unless any one of us wanted to become a dissident or an emigrant, if we wanted to serve our country, we have to serve that country within the system that the country had at that time. And therefore the breakup of the Soviet Union is not in and of itself a tragedy to me. The tragedy is what I see happening today to our country. The tragedy is that when Gorbachev and we started perestroika, we had in mind something different from what we see today. We wanted to see our country become a normal democratic country, a country much like all the others, perhaps a big country but without any special purported rights, without any unique messianic ideas. I am quite sure that Russia will become a normal democratic country, respected throughout the world when it finally divests itself of that chauvinistic syndrome. That has to be done not just politically but also psychologically, in the mind-set. And that will take several generations perhaps.

Oberdorfer: Minister Bessmertnykh?

Bessmertnykh: I think we should go back to those times from today. In those times Gorbachev and the people with him didn't want the destruction of the Soviet Union, they didn't want the demise of the country. He was eager to change the system, and he was at a later stage prepared to destroy that system, but he was never planning and he was never willing to destroy this state. Here it is very important again to differentiate the two concepts of a state and of a system. Because when communism came to Russia it actually took residence in the same state of the same Russian Empire. The Empire didn't go to pieces when communism came into that empire. So communism might have left the country without disrupting it, and democracy might have taken residence in the same country. And that was exactly the scenario that Gorbachev was following. He was trying to remove communism from the Soviet Union, and he is unhappy about the demise of the Soviet Union. His latest book is called *The Union Could Have Been Preserved.*[5] So we should not mix those two things. When we are strongly criticizing communism; that's all right. This is a complete belief of all the people who were with Gorbachev. But Gorbachev is an unhappy person, like many other people in Russia, including Yeltsin, about the fact that the Soviet Union was dismembered. I just wanted to put this truth on record.

I want to look back. What could have been done? I think that the Union of the Soviet Socialist Republics could not have been preserved as a Union of Soviet *Socialist* Republics. It could have been preserved as a Union of Democratic Republics. But in a practical sense, I think, what we should have done, and the American leaders were hinting at this in private conversations, we could have preserved the Soviet Union without the Baltic republics. If we had listened to the Baltic players when they first asked for special status within the Soviet Union. They were not asking for separation from the Soviet Union. They were asking for a special status within the Soviet Union. We missed that.

---

5. See Mikhail Sergeevich Gorbachev, *Gorbachev—On My Country and the World*, trans. George Shriver (New York: Columbia University Press, 2000).

As leaders of the country we had an enormous opportunity to preserve this situation. Even at a later stage, when they were claiming and demanding independence, we should have accorded that independence to the Baltic states and the rest would have stayed.

My impression, feeling, almost a confidence, was that the United States leaders did not want the destruction of the Soviet Union, and actually they were doing their best to preserve it. The only thing they were strongly demanding was the freedom for the Baltic republics. That's true. But they were saying to us in privacy: "Let the Baltics go and as for the rest of the Union you should install good control of it. You can use even force for that." The truth should be always the same whether it was the truth of that time or the truth of today.

Was it good for Russia, for the Soviet Union that some of the countries went? I think, now that it's happened, it's all right. A large part of the public opinion in Russia doesn't want re-creation of the Union. They don't want many of the republics to become their neighbors again, their sisters and brothers. They just believe it would be a great economic burden for Russia to accept them. Even Byelorussia [Belarus], which is spiritually and nationally very close to the Russians, is not very much welcome by the Russian public opinion.

As for the West, and whether it could help or not. I think the whole question, the concept of someone helping to preserve another country is an erroneous one. I think in a certain way it is even kind of a humiliating one for the country we are discussing. Actually when Gorbachev was asking for money and was asking for support and for the credits, he was not asking that in terms of preserving the nation or the country, he was just trying to bridge the economic problems he was facing every day. He was just trying to improve the everyday economic situation of the nation. So it shouldn't be considered as an attempt to preserve something. The Americans, like the rest of the West, were correct enough to tell everyone to think it is up to the Russians either to preserve their country or to lose it, and they were correct in that.

Baker: I just want to say that while I do not think it should have been preserved certainly as a Union of Soviet *Socialist* Republics, which is what we were confronted with, that doesn't deny the fact that we were quite surprised at the rapidity of the implosion, at the agreement in Minsk, and how rapidly the devolution took place, and how many of the republics were quite prepared to go an independent route.

Just one final thing. While flying to Wyoming in September 1989 Eduard Shevardnadze and I had a long discussion. We had two or three other discussions—I think one even with Gorbachev—about the importance of trying to set up a mechanism whereby the Baltics could go. I remember talking about how it seemed to us that it would be so much better if you had three more little Finlands up there because that was the biggest irritant. They were the ones pushing the hardest for independence—an independence that we continued to recognize (we never recognized their incorporation, as you know). But somehow that never seemed to be accepted. I remember particularly Shevardnadze telling me that if that happened that it would mean the end of the Union. I didn't agree with that at the time, and I'm really not sure that I agree with it now. It seems to me that a referendum would have been the way to go. Let the people of the Baltics vote; give them the opportunity. The answer that always came back was, "We're working on a mechanism, we're working on a Union treaty, we'll have that Union treaty very shortly." And I think if you could have found a way early on, Sasha, and I really agree with you, to cut the Baltics loose, it might have diminished some of the impetus, although maybe not, because you had the Ukraine and the others.

Tarasenko: Mr. Secretary, may I ask in this connection if you remember in these talks about making the Baltics a separate case, Shevardnadze told you that "I'm a Georgian virtually and I know my people and Georgia will immediately ask for independence. You cannot separate the Baltics from the others."

Baker: That's right, absolutely.

Tarasenko: That was his position.

Baker: Sergei, the first trip—apart from the April meeting in 1989 in Paris—where I began to develop the really close, personal relationship of trust and friendship with Eduard Shevardnadze was in his apartment where he and Anuli entertained Susan and myself for dinner on that May 1989 trip. I was struck and continue to be struck by the comments of the wife of the foreign minister of the Soviet Union when she was talking about her home republic of Georgia, and she was talking in the language of a true Georgian nationalist. She was talking in the language of independence. So I understand how he felt quite clearly, that you couldn't provide that mechanism for the Baltics and not for the rest of them.

Unknown: Some of us who have worked with Texas had a similar experience! [laughter]

Baker: Hey, listen, what we need to make clear about Texas for our Russian friends particularly is that it is one of only two states of the United States of America that was an independent country *before* it became a state of the United States. Does anyone know what the other state is?

Zoellick: Vermont. You can tell I heard this one before.

Baker: The only reason he knew it, too.

Oberdorfer: Bob, did you have something you wanted to add?

Zoellick: Just as a personal observation I want to note that while I think for our side dealing with these major issues was obviously very demanding, stressful, and difficult, I remember feeling again and again how many of our Soviet counterparts were truly courageous people because dealing with these problems under the stresses that they were under was just inconceivable. The foreign policy problems were difficult in and of themselves, but on top of that the strains that they must have been feeling in their own system as well as their country were enormous. Frankly, there were a number of historic decisions that were quite critical, at least in my view, toward resolving issues like German unification and others that I can only ascribe to great personal courage.

PART II
Analysis

5 Once Burned, Twice Shy? The Pause of 1989

Derek H. Chollet and James M. Goldgeier

"WHEN THE BUSH administration came into office," recalls President George H. W. Bush's national security adviser Brent Scowcroft, "there was already a lot of talk that the Cold War was over. . . . But to me, you know, my life spent in the Cold War, the structures of the Cold War were still in place. The rhetoric was different, but almost nothing else was different. And having been in the Reagan and Ford administrations and through détente, I thought, you know, once burned, twice shy." Worried that the Gorbachev agenda was simply designed to lull the West to sleep while the Soviet Union revived itself and created an even bigger threat to American national security, President Bush and his national security adviser were on heightened alert as they came into office in January 1989.[1]

Meanwhile, for many other observers, it was obvious at the end of 1988 that the world was on the brink of a great transformation. In less than three years, Soviet president Mikhail Gorbachev had placed his country on a course few thought possible. The Soviet economy was sputtering, its society opening, and its military power, in Kennan's terms, mellowing. In dismantling the world as we had known it, Gorbachev had found an unlikely partner in Ronald Reagan. To Reagan, the evil empire was of "another time, another era."[2] He and Gorbachev had done more to curtail superpower arsenals than ever before, or ever expected. As the Reagan-Gorbachev era came to a close, some were even claiming that the Cold War was already over. Although that point could be debated, what was certain was that U.S.-Soviet relations were better than ever before.[3]

---

1. Keynote address by Brent Scowcroft at a Brookings Institution National Issues Forum, "The End of the Cold War and What's Happened in the Ten Years Since," December 2, 1999, available at www.brook.edu (December 1999). See also George Bush and Brent Scowcroft, *A World Transformed* (New York: Alfred A. Knopf, 1998), 11–12.

2. Quoted in Don Oberdorfer, *The Turn: From the Cold War to a New Era: The United States and the Soviet Union, 1983–1990* (New York: Poseidon Press, 1991), 299.

3. For overviews of the Reagan-Gorbachev era in U.S.-Soviet relations, see Raymond L. Garthoff, *The Great Transition: American-Soviet Relations and the End of the Cold War* (Washington, D.C.: The Brookings Institution, 1994), 1–374; Oberdorfer, *The Turn*, 1–326; and Henry Kissinger, *Diplomacy* (New York: Simon & Schuster, 1994), 762–803. For an interesting argument that Reagan was more responsible for Gorbachev's foreign policy reorientation than commonly understood, see Beth Fischer, "Toeing the Hardline? The Reagan Administration and Ending the Cold War," *Political Science Quarterly* 112, no. 3 (fall 1997): 477–96.

Thus, the initially cautious approach of the Bush administration toward the Soviet Union during 1989 has been the target of considerable criticism from policymakers and academics alike. As the new administration came into office, many hoped that President Bush and his team would stay the course and vigorously support Gorbachev. Yet as Reagan's secretary of state George Shultz left office in early 1989, he worried that his successors "did not understand or accept that the Cold War was over. . . . President Reagan and I were handing over real momentum. I hoped it would not be squandered." In the view of many observers, this is precisely what happened—as one has quipped, the Bush administration "fumbled."[4] Critics thought that the new president seemed disoriented and wasted valuable time, not really engaging Gorbachev constructively until the autumn 1989, just when the revolution in Eastern Europe was under way.

Therein lie two puzzles. Why, after all of the goodwill of the late Reagan years, did the Bush administration eye Gorbachev with concern and skepticism? Why didn't Scowcroft "get it" if Shultz already did? And why, after initial suspicion about Soviet motives, did the Bush administration's support begin to develop, and as it turned out, at different times for different individuals?

When scholars study "mistakes" in international relations, they often focus on the failure to identify threats, since the inability to balance rising powers adequately often has such harsh consequences. The buck-passing of the 1930s, for example, is widely disparaged for allowing Hitler to unleash a military force that the West might have checked at far lower cost several years before the attack on Poland. The pause of 1989 raises a different theoretical issue, one whose implications are admittedly less clear: the failure to take advantage of opportunities that arise when countries that have formerly posed threats now seem open to accommodation. These missed opportunities are interesting because they pit different theoretical issues against one another—

---

4. George P. Shultz, *Turmoil and Triumph: My Years as Secretary of State* (New York: Charles Scribner's Sons, 1993), 1138; Jack F. Matlock, Jr., *Autopsy on an Empire: The American Ambassador's Account of the Collapse of the Soviet Union* (New York: Random House, 1996), 177–200. In 1989 Matlock, who had served as the senior NSC official on the Soviet Union during the Reagan administration, was the U.S. ambassador to Moscow. For a representative academic argument about the Bush administration's missed opportunity, see Robert Legvold, "Lessons from the Soviet Past," in C. Richard Nelson and Kenneth Weisbrode, eds., *Reversing Relations with Former Adversaries: U.S. Foreign Policy after the Cold War* (Gainesville: University Press of Florida, 1998), 17–43. Deborah Larson argues that because the Bush administration was suspicious of Gorbachev's intentions, it "wasted an entire year" and "lost an opportunity" to develop relations. See Deborah Welch Larson, *Anatomy of Mistrust: U.S.-Soviet Relations During the Cold War* (Ithaca: Cornell University Press, 1997), 191 and 225.

for example, the psychological constraints on processing new information correctly versus the structural constraints on responding to conciliatory behavior. Their implications are not as obvious, however, because unlike cases where threats are misperceived, it is not always so easy to explain what tangible benefits would in fact have occurred if only decision makers had figured out their new and improved environment sooner.

From a theoretical standpoint, the skepticism of Bush administration officials is easier to explain than the acceptance over the course of the year by different officials that in fact Gorbachev was "for real." To explain the former, one has at least three choices. First, one can argue that the Scowcrofts fell prey to two typical psychological biases: the common problem of reading evidence to fit prior expectations and the "fundamental attribution error." In terms of prior expectations, as Scowcroft said, "Once burned, twice shy." The consensus in the Republican Party was that the Soviet Union had forged agreements with the United States in the 1970s only to subvert them by taking hostile actions throughout the Third World. It was easy to seize upon any Gorbachev propaganda to argue for trickery. For those who had seen détente crash and burn, absent a declaration from the Soviets that they had conceded defeat and would pull out of every regional hot spot, Gorbachev's actions could always be explained away as spurious indicators of change. Meanwhile, the fundamental attribution error leads individuals to assume that any conciliatory behavior by an adversary is situationally induced, and is not an indication that the adversary has fundamentally changed his disposition. In other words, it is easy to argue that an adversary is taking a conciliatory action because he has to rather than because he really is different from his predecessors.[5]

To argue that Bush, Scowcroft, and others were simply prisoners of their Cold War mentality, however, would miss two other possible explanations. In an international system that lacks a central authority, states that fail to take care of themselves can suffer real damage, particularly from a nuclear-capable adversary. The fundamental attribution error may be neither fundamental nor

5. On these errors, see Robert Jervis, *Perception and Misperception in International Politics* (Princeton: Princeton University Press, 1976), and Philip E. Tetlock, "Social Psychology and World Politics," in S. Fiske, D. Gilbert, and G. Lindzey, eds., *Handbook of Social Psychology*, 4th ed. (New York: McGraw-Hill, 1998), 867–912. On formative experiences, see Jervis, *Perception and Misperception*, 283–87; Deborah Welch Larson, *Origins of Containment* (Princeton: Princeton University Press, 1985); James M. Goldgeier, *Leadership Style and Soviet Foreign Policy: Stalin, Khrushchev, Brezhnev, Gorbachev* (Baltimore: Johns Hopkins University Press, 1994); and Christopher Hemmer, *Which Lessons Matter? American Foreign Policy Decisionmaking in the Middle East, 1979–1987* (Albany: SUNY Press, 2000).

erroneous, since in foreign policy, accepting too easily that an adversary has changed his stripes can have such high costs. Therefore, being slow to accept change in the harsh Hobbesian world of international politics may be an "adaptive" error of intelligent decision makers.[6]

Finally, costs are not always international. As a Republican president not as confident of the backing of his conservative base as Ronald Reagan, George Bush needed to make sure that his credentials as being tough on the Soviet Union could not be questioned. With preconceptions about Soviet behavior, concerns that being wrong could severely damage U.S. national interests, and not wanting to alienate their shaky conservative base, Bush, Scowcroft, and company had plenty of reason to disappoint George Shultz and others. Why then did they come around over the course of the year, some sooner, others later?

This seems the most challenging puzzle, but a close look at 1989 offers a plausible answer: the development of interpersonal trust. This is an issue that decision makers intuitively understand—when they refer back to the period, Bush, Scowcroft, former Secretary of State James A. Baker III, and others, whether in their memoirs or in the transcripts in this volume, constantly refer to trust. So do Gorbachev, Shevardnadze, and their advisers Anatoly Chernyaev and Sergei Tarasenko. And yet, trust is difficult to achieve in a realm, in which, as discussed above, intentions are often unclear and penalties often so severe. When we look at how trust actually developed, and particularly as we see Baker's evolution in comparison with his colleagues, one factor stands out as producing change: the degree of personal contact among the leaders. Bush administration officials did not support the Soviet Union until, just like their immediate predecessors, they came to trust Gorbachev personally. The evidence reveals that as personal relations developed, the U.S. policymakers' perceptions of Soviet intentions changed for the better, thus enabling them to pursue a strategy based on cooperation and conciliation.

Although foreign policy leaders typically strive to form "good relations" with their counterparts, the influence of such relationships has remained virtually ignored by scholarly analysts. Such "first image" explanations are often passed over for more elegant explanations that focus on state institutions or the international system. Of course, personal relationships alone do not sufficiently explain how leaders overcome mistrust and facilitate cooperation. For

6. This issue is raised in Philip E. Tetlock and James M. Goldgeier, "Human Nature and World Politics: Cognition, Identity, and Influence," *International Journal of Psychology* 35, no. 2 (2000): 90.

example, if fundamental interests remain conflictual, then it is often hard to build trust. But when interests are becoming convergent (when opportunities should not be missed), or in times of great change (where interests are being transformed), personal relations can—and often do—play a key role.[7]

To explain how personal relations and trust influenced the course of U.S.-Soviet relations during 1989, this chapter proceeds as follows. First, we briefly discuss the concept of trust in interpersonal and international relations. Second, to set the context for decision making in 1989, we review the policy priorities the Bush team brought into office. Third, by focusing on the "strategic review" period during the spring of 1989, we describe the prevailing policymaker beliefs about the Soviet Union, exploring how these influenced the Administration's perceptions of Soviet behavior, and thus its policy decisions. Fourth, we will assess how these beliefs changed. In particular, we will examine the evolution of personal relations between senior U.S. and Soviet leaders, and how this influenced the Bush team's prevailing beliefs about Gorbachev's intentions and the image of the USSR as the enemy. Finally, the chapter will conclude with an assessment of this case in terms of international relations theory.

Trust

Whenever we talk about decision making, we have to remember one key fact that academics often ignore: decision making is hard. As Gary Klein has argued in his wonderful exposition on this subject, to define problems and then to generate a new course of action requires that one make many judgments: about goals, about possible anomalies, about urgency, about the merit of the opportunity, about proper analogues, about "solvability." One has to be able to use intuition and make mental simulations to figure out a problem and to gauge where things are headed.[8]

Add to the general problem the typical one faced by new administrations: they have to get their own acts together. We often mistakenly assume that the Bush administration was merely a continuation of the Reagan administration. But like any new administration, it wanted to stake out its own identity and agenda. As Scowcroft stated at the Cold War Endgame conference, "President Gorbachev had his team. You were in place, you were used to

7. For a parallel account of the importance of personal relations in revising Soviet perceptions of Reagan, see William D. Jackson, "Soviet Reassessment of Ronald Reagan, 1985–1988," *Political Science Quarterly* 113, no. 4 (winter 1998–99): 617–44.

8. Gary Klein, *Sources of Power: How People Make Decisions* (Cambridge: MIT Press, 1998), 141.

working together, you were all set. President Bush's team had two great characteristics: we all knew each other very, very well, we had worked together in one form or another, and in that sense we already had an inherent cohesion, but everybody had a little different perspective. We were all facing in the same direction, but the emphasis and the points of priority were not all the same, and during this period we were sorting all that out."[9]

Combine the inherent difficulties of decision making in uncertain environments with the challenge for a new team wanting to make its mark and function smoothly, and it is easy to see why the development of trust would take time. Trust, after all, involves predictability and credibility. You have to feel comfortable that the other side can keep its word, that it is not looking to undermine or embarrass you. Not only does this take time, but it also usually takes repeated interactions. And if you are starting out with a preconception that a person is saying and doing things to set you up for a fall later on, building trust will be even more difficult.[10]

Trust typically evolves in several phases. First comes simple rational calculation. You are figuring out risk and gauging the shadow of the future. You keep your guard up and try to minimize the costs of being wrong. If you are wrong, you can just go back to where you were before. So, trust begins with simple cost-benefit calculations that take into account the reputational costs to each side of breaking up. After an initial "feeling out" period, trust can actually become internalized and become separate from short-term interest-based calculations as the parties come to know one another. This happens through personal experience and direct communication. Only through better information about the other side can this "knowledge-based" trust get built.[11]

Some might counter that relationships between states are always built on interest alone, and what might seem like "trust" is merely a reflection of rational calculation based on external conditions. But for leaders in the real world, the ability to believe that the other side desires and is able to deliver on a commitment becomes crucially important both personally and politically. Leaders want to know that their counterpart's word is good.

9. Chapter 1, p. 31.

10. This section is heavily based on Roderick M. Kramer and Tom R. Tyler, eds., *Trust in Organizations: Frontiers of Theory and Research* (Thousand Oaks, Calif.: Sage Books, 1996). See also Larson, *Anatomy of Mistrust*, 19.

11. Roy J. Lewicki and Barbara Benedict Bunker, "Developing and Maintaining Trust in Work Relationships," in Kramer and Tyler, *Trust in Organizations*, 120.

Interestingly, for trust to develop, it may be better to be a novice than to be experienced. It is harder to overcome existing beliefs than it is to establish new ones. Someone like Scowcroft, with deep and negative experience dealing with the Soviets, had a set of intuitions that made it harder for him to believe what he was seeing. An experienced policymaker might need even *more* personal contact to create a new set of experiences to lead to a new set of intuitions. Baker, on the other hand, with much less Cold War involvement, could come to the table with fewer blinders, and that may have made it easier for him to see earlier that in fact Gorbachev and Shevardnadze were not their predecessors.

When interests are highly conflictual, building trust is less relevant to understanding a relationship, whether interpersonal or international. But when they become convergent, confidence that the other side will respond in predictable ways to accommodation can be crucial to further cooperation. The Bush team was highly skeptical about Gorbachev's motives initially, and the cooperation of the Reagan years halted. But as 1989 proceeded, that skepticism gave way to growing acceptance that concessions were real, and a new world order was at hand. What began as typical cost-benefit calculations that sought to minimize the risk of being wrong did give way to a knowledge-based understanding that Gorbachev and Shevardnadze were offering real concessions in predictable and credible ways. Bush and Scowcroft may have begun the year twice shy, but they ended it with much greater confidence that the Soviet side could be trusted; they had, in fact, finally internalized the idea that this was no mere détente. And while events like the fall of the Berlin Wall in November 1989 left a dramatic imprint on how decision makers were viewing their changing environment, it was the change in beliefs wrought by increasing personal contacts that was largely responsible for ending the pause that had begun in January.

Rethinking Priorities for U.S. Foreign Policy

When the Bush administration entered office in January 1989, it did so with three major foreign policy priorities. The first, interestingly enough, was domestic. President Bush aimed to reestablish a bipartisan political consensus for foreign policy at home. Although bipartisanship is a recurring goal of U.S. presidents, particularly new ones, it was particularly important for President Bush. The Reagan administration's battles with the Democratically controlled Congress over such issues as Central America and the Strategic Defense

Initiative had soured relations considerably. Bush and Secretary of State Baker, neither of whom were amateurs when it came to domestic politics, believed that bipartisanship was the essential element to a successful foreign policy. They believed that they had to clear this obstacle away before they could move forward on other items on the diplomatic agenda. It is for this reason that they chose as their first "diplomatic" initiative to reach an agreement with the Congress over U.S. policy in Central America.[12] But they also believed that building bipartisanship meant not moving too fast in U.S.-Soviet relations, given the mood on Capitol Hill. Baker aide Robert Zoellick recalls that prior to Baker's confirmation hearings, both sides of the aisle were saying, "Be careful, don't go too quickly." As he put it, "They never said that much in the following months, but there was a strong sense that Ronald Reagan was a romantic and wanted to secure his place in history."[13]

President Bush's second priority was to improve and reenergize relations within the Western alliance. Gorbachev's popular initiatives to reorient Soviet security policy—such as his dramatic unilateral cut in conventional forces announced in his December 1988 U.N. speech—had rattled transatlantic relations. NATO seemed to lack leadership and purpose; in the words of one analyst at the time, the Alliance was in the midst of a "mid-life crisis," knowing it had to change but uncertain about how. Alliance relations had been a major foreign policy issue of Bush's 1988 presidential campaign, and he had called for an early NATO summit to set a deadline for decisions. Divisive issues loomed, such as how to react to Gorbachev's conventional force cut and what to do about U.S. short-range nuclear forces (SNF) that were scheduled for deployment in West Germany. To begin consultations on these issues and to signal U.S. determination to revitalize Alliance cohesion, Baker's first trip abroad as secretary of state was a whirlwind tour of NATO capitals.[14]

Satisfying these first two priorities was in many ways a prerequisite for the third—rethinking the U.S. approach toward the Soviet Union. Once the Administration had rebuilt a bipartisan consensus for policy and reestablished U.S. leadership in the Western Alliance, it would be better equipped to shape

12. See James A. Baker III, with Thomas M. DeFrank, *The Politics of Diplomacy: Revolution, War, and Peace, 1989–1992* (New York: G. P. Putnam's Sons, 1995), 47–60.

13. Chapter 1, p. 28.

14. The NATO summit occurred in May 1989. See Baker, *Politics of Diplomacy,* 43–45; Robert L. Hutchings, *American Diplomacy and the End of the Cold War: An Insider's Account of U.S. Policy in Europe, 1989–92* (Baltimore: Johns Hopkins University Press, 1997), 27–31; and Richard Betts, "NATO's Mid-Life Crisis," *Foreign Affairs* 68, no. 2 (spring 1989): 37–52.

relations with the Soviets. With Soviet power waning, administration officials understood their task to be finding a way to manage its decline. In doing so they wanted to inject a sense of "realism" in the U.S. approach. Despite the dramatic improvement in U.S.-Soviet relations, the Bush team believed that there were many issues left on the table—the resolution of regional conflicts and the future of Eastern Europe, for example. Although the Cold War rhetoric had subsided, the Bush administration still saw a Soviet Union with a force structure and policies that threatened U.S. interests. Given these disparities, President Bush and his team wanted to put the spotlight on Gorbachev's deeds, not words.[15]

In this sense, it seemed to many of them that their predecessors' claims about the end of the Cold War were premature. And the primary testing ground for gauging Soviet intentions would be Eastern Europe. As Scowcroft recalls, "If we were to end the Cold War, Eastern Europe had to be a key part of it, because that's where it began and that's where the structures of the Cold War still existed. So that's the first thing we did. We put arms control on the back burner. We didn't want to talk about it, and we didn't for six months or so, and elevated instead what was happening in Eastern Europe, which always had been an asterisk or a footnote to our policy with the Soviet Union."[16]

In laying out a new set of priorities, President Bush and his team sought to make their own distinct diplomatic mark and do more than to implement simply "Reagan-plus." This meant changes in both personnel and policy. It was in this spirit that President Bush launched an across-the-board strategic review of foreign policy, a review that aimed to reassess U.S. interests, objectives, and strategies for diplomacy.[17]

The Strategic Review and Perceptions of the Soviet Union

The formal process of reevaluating U.S. policy toward the Soviet Union began in January 1989. A full review of strategy appeared to be a prudent

---

15. Injecting "realism" into the approach toward the Soviet Union was one of the core themes of Baker's confirmation hearings in January 1989. See "Nomination of James A. Baker III," *Hearings Before the Committee of Foreign Relations, U.S. Senate,* January 17 and 18, 1989 (S. Hrg. 101-9), especially 16–18.

16. Scowcroft's remarks at the Brookings Institution National Issues Forum, December 2, 1999. See also Michael Beschloss and Strobe Talbott, *At the Highest Levels: The Inside Story of the End of the Cold War* (New York: Little, Brown, 1993), 3–42, and Baker, *Politics of Diplomacy,* 41.

17. By all accounts, the transition from Reagan to Bush was much more abrupt than expected, creating shifts in policy that were quite different from public expectations of continuity. As Robert Hutchings of the NSC staff recalled, "There was no such thing as a 'Reagan-Bush' foreign policy. Before 1989 there was Reagan; afterwards there was Bush." See Hutchings, *American Diplomacy,* 6, and Matlock, *Autopsy on an*

idea—in an era of dramatic change, it seemed sensible to reassess old assumptions. Furthermore, the Administration did want to make it clear that it was
different from its predecessor. "Even though President Bush had been Ronald
Reagan's vice president for eight years," argues Baker, "it was important that
he put his imprimatur upon the foreign and security policy of the Bush administration. That was the reason for the strategic review to begin with."[18]

Unfortunately, as an attempt to prod the bureaucracy to think creatively
about managing the relationship with the Soviet Union, this idea proved disappointing; as Baker put it, the effort was "neither truly strategic nor a proper
review."[19] Rather than spark bold thinking, the decision set in motion a
tedious, time-consuming bureaucratic process that produced nothing but
"mush." Bush had alerted Gorbachev to expect this "pause" during a phone
call the day he took office, and the Soviet president seemed to understand. But
as months went by, the Soviet leadership, along with just about everyone else,
became anxious for some announcement of a decision. Even those within the
Administration were disappointed with both the process and the product.
Finally, President Bush put an end to this misery, announcing the review's
highlight—moving U.S.-Soviet relations "beyond containment"—in a May 12
speech at Texas A&M University.[20]

However disappointing the results of the review, a look back at that
period gives one a picture of the Bush administration's initial beliefs about its
policies for dealing with the Soviet Union. Understanding these prevailing
beliefs helps illuminate how policymakers perceived Gorbachev's behavior, as
well as the rationale behind the Administration's policy priorities.

Two beliefs dominated senior policymakers' thinking. First, Bush administration officials believed that the prospects for Soviet reform were tenuous
and thus reversible. In early 1989, there appeared to be little reason to doubt
that Gorbachev's position was dangerously unstable. Some likened the Soviet
leader to a pilot who had taken off but had no idea where to land—and a crash

Empire, 182–185. For an account of the large shoes Reagan left to fill, see John Lewis Gaddis, "The
Unexpected Ronald Reagan," in *The United States and the End of the Cold War* (New York: Oxford University
Press, 1993), 119–32.

18. Chapter 1, p. 25.

19. Baker, *Politics of Diplomacy*, 68.

20. For details on the review, and explanations for why it proved unsatisfying, see Baker, *Politics of
Diplomacy*, 68–70; Hutchings, *American Diplomacy*, 21–47; Beschloss and Talbott, *At the Highest Levels*, 19–68;
Oberdorfer, *The Turn*, 328–34; and Philip Zelikow and Condoleezza Rice, *Germany Unified and Europe
Transformed: A Study in Statecraft* (Cambridge: Harvard University Press, 1995), 24–27.

seemed imminent. The President and his advisers feared the backlash and upheaval if Gorbachev were removed from power, and remained leery of identifying themselves too closely with him. As internal tensions escalated in the Soviet Union (such as a violent crackdown in Georgia and a wide-scale coal miners' strike), U.S. officials became even more concerned about the future of reform. Therefore, the Bush administration initially was careful to tie its approach to perestroika's success, rather than Gorbachev's personal survival.

That Gorbachev and reform were vulnerable was the common assessment of intelligence reports prepared for policymakers. Gorbachev's chances for survival emerged as the primary question Soviet specialists at the Central Intelligence Agency grappled with during 1989. The answers were almost uniformly pessimistic. One April assessment explained that the situation was more unstable than at any time since the Great Purge era, and that Gorbachev's economic program was a "near disaster." The nationalities tensions could "unleash centrifugal forces that will pull the Soviet Union apart," or at least "create tensions that . . . will undermine Gorbachev's reforms." By September, the prevailing view had only become even more grim. Placing the blame on Gorbachev's "domestic gambles," one report explained that the Soviet leader "had brought Soviet internal policy to a fateful crossroads, seriously reducing the chances that his rule—if it survives—will take that path toward long-term stability." As for the future, the main concern was that "conditions are likely to lead . . . to continuing crises and instability on an even larger scale." The CIA believed that Gorbachev's ability to control the events he had turned loose were "doubtful at best."[21]

The private and public comments of several senior officials reflected these concerns. Privately, aides like Scowcroft recommended that the President focus on perestroika the policy rather than on Gorbachev the man. Scowcroft's deputy, Robert Gates, warned that "Gorbachev might be succeeded not by another Gorbachev but by another Stalin." At the State Department, the Policy Planning Staff (which was extremely influential under Baker) began to review

21. See Directorate of Intelligence (CIA), "Rising Political Instability Under Gorbachev: Understanding the Problem and Prospects for Resolution, An Intelligence Assessment" (April 1989), quoted in Kirsten Lundberg, "CIA and the Fall of the Soviet Empire: The Politics of 'Getting It Right,'" Kennedy School of Government Case Program, C16-94-1251.0 (Harvard, 1994); idem, "Gorbachev's Domestic Gambles and Instability in the USSR, An Intelligence Assessment" (September 1989), reprinted in briefing book for the conference on the "Cold War Endgame" at Princeton University, March 29–30, 1996; and Douglas MacEachin, *CIA Assessments of the Soviet Union: The Record Versus the Charges*, Center for the Study of Intelligence Monograph, 1996, available at www.cia.gov/csi/monograph/russia/3496toc.html.

the probabilities for an "impending crisis" in the Soviet Union, and possible
scenarios if one were to develop. On occasion, such pessimism leaked out publicly. For example, in an April 1989 interview on CNN, Defense Secretary
Richard Cheney admitted that he suspected Gorbachev would "ultimately fail."
Several months later, Gates had prepared a speech with a similarly grim assessment, but was forbidden to give it after the personal intervention of Baker. The
Secretary of State did not disagree with the assessment, but did not think it
should be aired openly. "[Gates] had made a fundamental mistake by failing to
distinguish between what the administration thought privately and what we
said publicly," Baker recalled. "While that [pessimistic] view was shared by
most of us, highlighting it in our public comments would have had the effect of
pulling the rug out from under the President's statements that we supported
perestroika."[22] Thus, even if the team had "trusted" Gorbachev, there would
have been reason for them to move cautiously, and as Baker argues, "maximize
our diplomatic gains while minimizing risks."[23]

However, since the pessimism about Gorbachev's future would continue
whereas the approach did change as the year went along, a second initial belief
must have been even more important as a basis for policy from January
through May 1989: that competition remained the driving principle of U.S.-
Soviet relations. Bush had been uneasy with Reagan's conciliatory approach.
He had said as much publicly during the 1988 presidential campaign, and the
"pause" gave the new administration a way to slow the runaway train of Reagan's
idealism.[24] The Soviets might be weak, the logic went, but they were still trying to maximize interests at a cost to the United States. Senior officials were
skeptical of Moscow's true intentions, and believed that Gorbachev's actions
were motivated to expose U.S. weaknesses. From this perspective, Gorbachev's
dramatic announcements—such as his December 1988 U.N. speech—were
not part of an overall strategy to end the Cold War, but to seize the initiative
from the United States and set the global agenda to reflect Soviet interests.

22. See Beschloss and Talbott, *At the Highest Levels*, 17–25, 54–55, 99–100, and Baker, *Politics of Diplomacy*, 70, 156–58. Gates, a Soviet specialist who had served as deputy director of the CIA during the Reagan administration, had been in a similar situation with Secretary of State Shultz a year earlier. In this case, Gates delivered his speech and became the focus of Shultz's considerable ire. See Robert M. Gates, *In from the Shadows: The Ultimate Insider's Story of Five Presidents and How They Won the Cold War* (New York: Simon & Schuster, 1996), 443–47, 473–75, 480–81.

23. Baker, *Politics of Diplomacy*, 69.

24. See David Hoffman, "Bush Doubts Soviets Have Changed: Vice President Disagrees with Reagan's Assessments at Summit," *Washington Post*, June 8, 1988, and David Broder, "Cold War 'Not Over' Bush Warns: Slackening Buildup Called a Mistake," *Washington Post*, June 29, 1988.

Baker explains that "Gorbachev's strategy was to weaken Western cohesion through high-profile, publicly attractive proposals and thus to gain economic benefits from the West."[25] Ambassador Jack Matlock in Moscow called this the "Soviet smile."[26]

Such views of Soviet behavior were not unlike Henry Kissinger's characterization of détente during the 1970s: the Soviets were deploying tactics of cooperation within a strategy of competition. Again, Scowcroft himself has explained how his prior experiences were an obstacle to trust:

I also plead guilty to the slow buildup of trust, and probably me more than anyone else. In my formative years in national government, I had gone through the détente period, which I thought had left an aftermath of enervation in the United States—cuts in defense budgets, a reduction of a vibrant containment policy—bringing forth on the Soviet side discussions about the change in the "correlation of forces" and so on. I was not sure in 1988 and 1989 that we were seeing a sincere change on the part of President Gorbachev or whether this was a return to détente. The West was tired at this time, governments were looking for any way to cut back on defense budgets. Gorbachev's speech to the U.N. in December 1988 got great applause, and I wasn't sure it was for real, and so, as Jim [Baker] said, what we wanted to do is to go slow enough to see whether or not the Soviet side would follow up on these pronouncements that showed so much promise.[27]

Within this perceived framework of competition, Gorbachev was on quite a winning streak. Even before entering office, the new administration found itself only able to react to the Soviet leader's bold moves. The cuts in Soviet conventional forces announced at the December U.N. speech threw the United States back on its heels. Gorbachev's evident warmth and energetic

25. Baker, *Politics of Diplomacy*, 45.

26. In three cables sent to Washington during February 1989, Matlock outlined his thoughts on the Soviet transformation and the goals for U.S. policy. In one, he explained that Soviet "diplomacy is likely to feature the smile, and its speech the language of compromise and conciliation." Although Matlock agreed that the Soviet smile was "creating problems for our alliances and driv[ing] wedges," his perception of Gorbachev's intentions differed greatly from the prevailing view in Washington. To Matlock, Soviet leaders were making a "virtue of necessity. They are covering their retrenchment with a hyperactive diplomacy in an attempt to preserve their great power position . . . on a diminished base of military power. The bottom line for the Soviet leadership will be whether they can cloak—and thus make politically acceptable at home—a diminished use of military force in their foreign policy." See "The Soviet Union Over the Next Four Years," Cable, Moscow 2962, February 3, 1989; "Soviet Foreign Policy Over the Next Four Years," Cable, Moscow 3850, February 13, 1989; and "U.S.-Soviet Relations: Policy Opportunities," Cable, Moscow 4648, February 22, 1989. These cables are reprinted in briefing book for the conference "Cold War Endgame" at Princeton University, March 29–30, 1996.

27. Chapter 1, p. 26. See also Fred Greenstein and William Wohlforth, eds., *Cold War Endgame: Report of a Conference Sponsored by the John Foster Dulles Program for the Study of Leadership in International Affairs, Princeton University, and the James A. Baker III Institute for Public Policy, Rice University*, Center of International Studies Monograph Series, no. 10 (Princeton: Princeton University Center of International Studies, 1997), 4.

personality—simultaneously described and derided as "Gorbymania"—won public plaudits in both Europe and the United States. Because President Bush and his advisers believed that the reality of Soviet power remained (in terms of force posture and assistance to regional conflicts, for example), they were concerned that the perception of threat was diminishing ahead of any actual decline.[28] Increasingly frustrated by what they saw as a widening disparity between Gorbachev's words and deeds, they struggled to get out ahead of the public relations curve. "I'll be damned if Mr. Gorbachev should dominate world public opinion forever," Bush wrote to a friend in March 1989.[29]

Once more, these views were reinforced by intelligence assessments. In three major reports that landed on policymakers' desks during February and April 1989, the intelligence community argued that Gorbachev's strategy was straight out of the "Leninist tradition: it calls for weakening the main enemy— the United States—by exploiting 'contradictions' between it and other centers of capitalist power in Western Europe, East Asia and the developing world." What had changed was the tactic: cooperation rather than confrontation. Although these estimates understood this shift as mainly a product of the Soviet Union's weakness, the CIA cautioned that "it also has an offensive intent." Gorbachev was playing nice, not because he really meant it, but because he needed to buy time. Moscow's leaders "appreciate that they can score gains far more quickly on the foreign policy front. In effect, new strategies toward the West are a means for Moscow to improve its competitive position in the short run through political means while waiting for domestic reforms to take effect." Gorbachev would seek room for maneuver with "surprise tactics [of] bold proposals or unilateral moves"—such as the cuts in Soviet conventional forces announced in his December 1988 U.N. speech—to put "the onus for reciprocal actions on the United States or [put] the United States on the defensive." Overall, the intelligence community warned that Gorbachev sought "political credit that he does not have to share with Washington."[30]

28. In public testimony, Pentagon planners repeatedly stressed the realities of Soviet force capabilities. See, for example, Secretary of Defense Cheney's April 25, 1989, hearing before the House Armed Services Committee. Excerpts appear in "Not the Time to Reduce Defense Capabilities," *American Foreign Policy Current Documents 1989* [hereafter cited as *AFPCD 1989*] (Washington: Department of State, 1990), 356.

29. George H. W. Bush to Sadruddin Aga Khan, March 13, 1989, reprinted in *All the Best, George Bush* (New York: Scribner's, 1999), 416. Such frustrations did lead to some public indiscretions, such as White House Press Secretary Marlin Fitzwater's May 1989 description of Gorbachev as a "Drugstore Cowboy," which he later admitted was a more colorful way of making the "deeds, not words" point. See Marlin Fitzwater, *Call the Briefing* (Holbrook, Mass.: Adams Media, 1995), 229–43, and Beschloss and Talbott, *At the Highest Levels*, 72–73.

30. These three reports, totaling over eighty pages, were the main intelligence products about Gorbachev's goals during this period. They are all now declassified. See the two Directorate for Intelligence

Understanding this mind-set about Gorbachev's intentions helps explain much of the Bush administration's policy direction during early 1989. Officials focused on arenas to test the Soviet leader's willingness to match his words with deeds.

Soviet behavior in Eastern Europe seemed an ideal venue. Bush had stressed the need to address the region during the 1988 campaign, explaining that Gorbachev's policies there would be a true test of his commitment to reform. Moreover, issues relating to Eastern Europe had not been the main focus of the Reagan-Gorbachev agenda, which concentrated primarily on nuclear arms control, tensions in the Third World, and human rights. In this sense, then, pressing the Soviets on Eastern Europe also had the added value of being a distinct foreign policy issue President Bush could make his own.[31]

An example of the Administration's willingness to use Eastern Europe as the arena to test Gorbachev came in December 1988 during the presidential transition, and former secretary of state Henry Kissinger played a leading role. Kissinger approached Bush and Baker with a proposal to open a dialogue with Gorbachev to put Eastern Europe front and center on the agenda. Although things seemed to be leaning toward liberalization in the region, Kissinger believed that since there were no guarantees, the United States should take the initiative and engage the Soviets on the issue. One idea, for instance, was to give the Soviets security guarantees in exchange for permitting East European self-determination.[32]

When Kissinger met with Gorbachev during a private visit to Moscow during January 1989, the Soviet leader signaled willingness to move forward with the proposal. Secretary Baker thought the idea had merit, although he believed it too close to a "Yalta II." He and his aides did, however, agree that

(CIA) products: "Moscow's 1989 Agenda for U.S.-Soviet Relations," CIASOV 89-10012X, February 1989, and "Gorbachev's Foreign Policy," CIASOV 89-10014X, February 1989, which are available on the CD-ROM, *CIA's Analysis of the Soviet Union, 1947–1991, Volume II*, available from the CIA's Center for the Study of Intelligence. The third report was a National Intelligence Estimate, "Soviet Policy Toward the West: The Gorbachev Challenge," NIE 11-4-89, April 1989, reprinted in Benjamin Fischer, ed., *At Cold War's End: US Intelligence on the Soviet Union and Eastern Europe, 1989–1991* (Washington, D.C.: Center for the Study of Intelligence, 1999).

31. See Hutchings, *American Diplomacy*, 25–40. Zelikow and Rice, *Germany Unified*, 18–20, make the point that to the Reagan administration, the postwar realities in East Europe "remained fixed, and they sought a renewal of détente—this time a genuine and lasting détente—as the best way to moderate the effects of Europe's tragic division." It was President Bush, they argue, who decided to make Eastern Europe the primary arena to test Gorbachev. Scowcroft echoes this point, explaining that "part of our strategy toward the Soviet Union was to shift focus and put Eastern Europe up front, which traditionally had not been the case for the United States." See Scowcroft's comments in Greenstein and Wohlforth, *Cold War Endgame*, 4, 11.

32. Predictably, Kissinger recommended that he serve as the channel. For details, see Hutchings, *American Diplomacy*, 35–37; Zelikow and Rice, *Germany Unified*, 27–28; Beschloss and Talbott, *At the Highest Levels*, 13–17; and Walter Isaacson, *Kissinger* (New York: Simon & Schuster, 1992), 727–29.

Soviet policy in Eastern Europe should be emphasized.[33] Although Baker
(with Bush's support) eventually quashed the proposal publicly, both he and
the President acted on its underlying premise: to press Gorbachev on Eastern
Europe. This decision is evident in Baker's public assessment of Kissinger's
plan in the *New York Times* in March 1989, his private conversations that
spring with Shevardnadze in Vienna and Moscow, and both his and President
Bush's speeches throughout the spring. Symbolically, the shift in emphasis was
important. "George Bush became the first Western leader to say plainly that
the Cold War would not be over until the division of Europe had ended and
Europe was 'whole and free,'" Zelikow and Rice observe. Perhaps tenden-
tious, the statement does reveal a fundamental point—Bush did make Soviet
policy in Europe his highest priority, and this was a conscious shift from the
Reagan approach. Substantively, this focus led to some real policy decisions, as
seen in Bush's announcement at the May 1989 NATO summit to cut U.S.
forces in Europe.[34]

The perception that the Soviets were only cooperating to compete also
sheds light on the priority of revitalizing cohesion within the Western
Alliance. In a January 1989 television interview, Scowcroft explained that
Gorbachev was "interested in making trouble within the Western Alliance.
And I think he believes that the best way to do it is through a peace offensive,
rather than bluster, the way some of his predecessors have." Baker described
the Soviet strategy as "premised on splitting the Alliance and undercutting us
in Western Europe, by appealing past Western governments to Western
publics."[35]

To blunt Gorbachev's perceived offensive to divide the West, the Bush
team set out to strengthen the Alliance by reestablishing U.S. leadership. "The
road to success with the Kremlin," Baker recalls, "began not in Moscow, but
in the capitals of Western Europe and Canada . . . the success of our East-
West policy depend[ed] on our West-West policy—the ability of the U.S. and
its allies to work together." Starting with the Secretary of State's tour of

33. Baker, *Politics of Diplomacy*, 40–41.

34. See Thomas Friedman, "Baker, Outlining World View, Assesses Plan for Soviet Bloc," *New York Times*, March 28, 1989; Zelikow and Rice, *Germany Unified*, 24–25; Hutchings, *American Diplomacy*, 39–47; Beschloss and Talbott, *At the Highest Levels*, 45–46, 79–81; and Oberdorfer, *The Turn*, 341–42. The key Baker speech outlining this view was delivered March 6 in Vienna; see "Our Purpose Is to Improve the Security of Europe," in *AFPCD 1989*, 269–74; Bush's most important speech was delivered in Mainz, Germany, on May 31, see "Positive Steps by the Soviets Would Be Met by Steps of Our Own," in *AFPCD 1989*, 293–96.

35. Baker, *Politics of Diplomacy*, 70; Beschloss and Talbott, *At the Highest Levels*, 17.

NATO capitals in February, the Administration spent a great deal of energy trying to solidify this West-West link.[36] It worked to solve the most contentious issue on the Alliance agenda, the scheduled redeployment of short-range nuclear forces (SNF) in Europe—indeed, Baker and his senior aides likely spent more time on this issue during the spring of 1989 than anything directly related to the Soviet Union. The Administration also used most of that spring to craft a troop-cut proposal for the President to announce at the May NATO summit, which would be Bush's debut as leader of the Western Alliance. The result was a decision calling for 15 percent cuts in NATO and Warsaw Pact conventional arms and 20 percent cuts in U.S. and Soviet troops in Europe. This announcement, which aimed to jump-start the Conventional Forces in Europe (CFE) negotiations, received rave reviews. It also proved critical to solving the SNF issue.[37]

Finally, the prevailing beliefs of instability and strategic competition help explain some policy roads not taken. For example, Ambassador Matlock's ideas for dealing with the Soviets, such as engaging them on economic reform or holding an early summit, were scarcely given a hearing. After raising these ideas with Bush, Baker, and Scowcroft both by cable and in person, Matlock recalls he encountered "heavy resistance." When understood in the context of the perceptions of instability and mistrust, however, Matlock's problems make sense. Given such uncertainty about the Soviet future, it seemed prudent to take a wait-and-see attitude. Policymakers were loath to do anything bold while the verdict on Gorbachev's future was out. Moreover, since the President and his closest advisers remained skeptical of Gorbachev's intentions, and were supported by the prevailing judgments of the intelligence community, they saw an early summit as nothing more than providing the Soviet leader another opportunity to upstage the United States with a peace offensive. In terms of trusting the Soviets, Matlock—who had experience and strong personal relations with Moscow—was already well ahead of Washington.[38]

36. Baker, *Politics of Diplomacy*, 90–92. Baker had made this West-West point a public theme, see "Power for Good: American Foreign Policy in the New Era," April 14, 1989, address before the American Society of Newspaper Editors, in *AFPCD 1989*, 5–10.

37. SNF and conventional force cuts were linked because the strategic purpose of SNF was to balance the Soviet advantage in conventional forces in Europe. Thus, once the President decided to cut the number of troops in Europe, it became easier to compromise on the SNF issue. For accounts of these decisions, see Baker, *Politics of Diplomacy*, 84–96; Gates, *In from the Shadows*, 461–64; Beschloss and Talbott, *At the Highest Levels*, 34–42, 74–80; and Zelikow and Rice, *Germany Unified*, 29–32.

38. Matlock may have undermined his proposals further through his vigorous opposition to the core of Bush's strategy, emphasizing Eastern Europe. Moreover, he clearly identified himself with the Reagan

U.S. Beliefs Evolve

If President Bush and his senior aides were influenced by beliefs of instability and strategic competition, then how and why did they turn to embrace the Soviets by the end of the year? Particularly when we consider the mistrust with which the Americans viewed Gorbachev during the spring of 1989, the about-face seems puzzling, especially as it occurred for different individuals at different times. In searching for an answer for this turnaround, one trend appears clear: the Bush administration's level of trust toward Gorbachev improved as personal relations with the senior Soviet leadership developed. Although trust evolved throughout the summer and fall—most notably between Baker and Shevardnadze—the culminating point was the December 1989 Malta summit.

That it took so long for experienced Bush administration officials to get comfortable with their counterparts may seem odd. However, despite the impressive government resumes of the President and his top advisers, few had had much interaction with senior Soviet leaders like Gorbachev and Shevardnadze. As Reagan's vice president, Bush himself perhaps had had the most exposure, most recently at the December 1988 Governor's Island summit. Yet even these experiences appeared too modest for Bush's famous reliance on personal relations. As for other officials, the only senior Reagan holdover was former treasury secretary James Baker, who had met Gorbachev and Shevardnadze each only once before as part of a larger group. This is even true of the relevant sub-cabinet officials—like Dennis Ross and Robert Zoellick at State, and Robert Blackwill and Condoleezza Rice of the NSC staff—who while knowledgeable about the Soviet Union, were personally unfamiliar with senior Kremlin leaders. Thus, it is clear that the incoming Bush team had a great distance to travel to equal the strong personal relationships enjoyed between Shultz and Shevardnadze and Reagan and Gorbachev.

Although President Bush reassured Gorbachev that he wished to establish strong personal relations shortly after taking office in January, it was not until March that a senior U.S. and Soviet official got together. Gathered in Vienna to launch the Conventional Forces in Europe negotiations, Baker and Shevardnadze met briefly. They discussed a wide range of topics, but given

---

approach to the Soviets, which did not endear him to Bush, Baker, or Scowcroft. For his cables from Moscow, see note 26.

Washington's ongoing policy review, the meeting was short on substance. Shevardnadze reassured Baker about Moscow's commitment to perestroika and positive U.S. relations. Nevertheless, the Secretary of State still seemed inhibited by skepticism. Shevardnadze used his speech in Vienna to announce another set of initiatives to shape the CFE negotiations, which had overshadowed the Secretary of State's own address. This ruffled Baker. Briefing President Bush on the Vienna meeting, he explained that Gorbachev and Shevardnadze were "leaders in a great hurry, possessing a sense of urgency but lacking a plan." He emphasized that the United States had to continue to test Soviet new thinking, and be prepared for present and future Soviet initiatives—such as the ones Shevardnadze had unveiled in Vienna—which "were having a real effect in Europe."[39]

After Vienna, senior U.S. and Soviet leaders did not meet for another two months. In May 1989 the main interlocutor was again Baker, this time in Moscow. As the first occasion for extensive discussions between the two sides since Bush took office, many looked to Baker's trip as a bellwether. The Secretary of State's primary objective was to continue the effort to test the Soviets, mainly by pressing them on Central America and transnational issues such as weapons proliferation and the environment. Although the results of these meetings were substantively promising, they did not change the dominant perceptions of U.S. policymakers. Indeed, if anything, what Baker saw in Moscow confirmed that Gorbachev was trying to upstage the United States and undermine Western consensus.[40]

The Secretary of State's meetings during May 10–11—his first visit ever to the Soviet capital—were, for the most part, substantive and candid.[41] Both sides reassured the other during formal presentations, Baker in stating Bush's wish to support perestroika and the Soviets in affirming their commitment to it.[42] Yet Gorbachev ended the visit with a surprise announcement, one that

---

39. Baker, *Politics of Diplomacy*, 63–68; Beschloss and Talbott, *At the Highest Levels*, 39–40. The Soviets were apparently unsure why Baker's speech was so "imperious[ly]"demanding. The consensus was that this was not a bad first meeting, but not a particularly auspicious beginning. See Pavel Palazchenko, *My Years with Gorbachev and Shevardnadze: The Memoir of a Soviet Interpreter* (University Park: Pennsylvania State University Press, 1997), 127–29.

40. Baker, *Politics of Diplomacy*, 70–72; Beschloss and Talbott, *At the Highest Levels*, 59–61; Oberdorfer, *The Turn*, 336–38.

41. For details on these meetings, see Baker, *Politics of Diplomacy*, 72–83; Beschloss and Talbott, *At the Highest Levels*, 65–67; Oberdorfer, *The Turn*, 341–45; and Garthoff, *Great Transition*, 378–79.

42. During an informal dinner at Shevardnadze's home, Baker started to learn about the extent of the Soviet nationalities problem. The Secretary of State left impressed by the Foreign Minister's passion and

left the Secretary of State sour. The proposal seemed constructive enough: the Soviets would unilaterally withdraw five hundred tactical nuclear weapons from Europe. However, since the USSR already had an overwhelming advantage in such weapons, Baker considered the proposal "strategically insignificant" and just another effort to "score points with European publics." The Secretary of State had been heavily involved in contentious negotiations with the Europeans over short-range nuclear forces, and Gorbachev's announcement only complicated the issue. He curtly told the Soviet leader that he saw the "political appeal" of such ideas and reminded him that "we should not let suspicions arise that one side was seeking advantage of the other."[43]

Baker returned to Washington convinced that Gorbachev was still playing games: "He [cut] the legs right out from under me by throwing this wonderful propaganda initiative on the table." This seemed to confirm the prevailing belief that Gorbachev's true intention was to one-up the United States and "drive a wedge between us and our European allies." It was exactly the sort of surprise the intelligence agencies had warned about earlier that spring. Not only did it shake Baker's confidence about Soviet trustworthiness, but it also gave ammunition to those at home who were criticizing Baker for being played as a sucker. As he recalls about later arguing that these were people the United States could do business with: "I want to tell you: I was almost a voice in the wilderness taking that approach. The Defense Department, the CIA, many people in the NSC including my buddy here [indicating Scowcroft], were all somewhere else." And the public ploy "set us back a little bit in terms of our being a little bit more forthcoming and a little bit more trustful." It would take the next event in Wyoming, says Baker, to overcome this setback.[44]

---

sensibility on the issue; he was struck how Shevardnadze and his wife, both ethnic Georgians, were proudly—if not defiantly—loyal to their nationality. In *Politics of Diplomacy*, 78, Baker recalls: "There I was in the Moscow apartment of the Soviet Foreign Minister, meeting with his intelligent and articulate wife who didn't have to be provoked into revealing that at heart she was truly a Georgian nationalist. I remember thinking that if a Politburo member's wife can be so passionate about her nationality, what is the proverbial man in the street thinking—and doing?"

43. This sentiment of mistrust also had been expressed in a letter from Bush that Baker handed to Gorbachev. The letter pointed out that in his 1988 U.N. speech, Gorbachev had said that the purpose of perestroika was "to make the Soviet Union a stronger power." Bush conceded that while such a position was sensible, "equally understandable is our concern that a stronger Soviet Union could translate into a more assertive military power." Recalling the letter, Gorbachev observed that "the Americans were apparently still influenced by obsolete stereotypes. We obviously had no intentions of that sort." See Beschloss and Talbott, *At the Highest Levels*, 60, and Mikhail Gorbachev, *Memoirs*, trans. from the German edition by Wolf Jobst [which was translated into German from the Russian original by Georges Peronansky and Tatjana Varsavsky] (New York: Doubleday, 1995), 501.

44. Chapter 1, p. 32.

Events in Moscow did, however, help produce some positive results. Gorbachev's actions seemed to push the Administration to assert itself; the way to deal with this "public diplomacy blitzkrieg" was to answer in kind. After Baker's trip, the President and his advisers were even more motivated to craft a bold initiative for the upcoming NATO summit. The result was Bush's proposed reduction in conventional forces.[45] Baker also advised the President to begin thinking about a summit with Gorbachev. By mid-July, with the SNF debate behind them and Bush's leadership within NATO affirmed, the Secretary of State felt the time was right. Bush apparently needed little convincing and began to lay the groundwork with the Soviets secretly for an informal summit.[46]

These decisions placed U.S.-Soviet relations on firmer ground. Bush gained confidence to meet Gorbachev on his own terms, trading proposal for proposal. This is the point in which the perception of mistrust started to break down. Starting in the summer of 1989, relations between the Bush administration and the Soviets improved dramatically with each personal interaction. Over time, the dominating belief of strategic competition evolved into one of cooperation—and again, the area where this occurred first was Baker's relationship with Shevardnadze.

The two met for the third time in Paris on July 29, on the margins of Cambodian peace talks. We now know that this meeting was a major turning point in Baker's perception of Soviet intentions. Building on their discussions over two months before in Moscow, Baker and Shevardnadze had a remarkably candid conversation about a wide range of Soviet problems, such as the miners' strike, ethnic tensions, and Eastern Europe.[47] Shevardnadze's statements on the core issues—the direction of perestroika, the Soviet Union's economic and social ills, and the commitment not to use force to solve problems either internally or in Europe—struck Baker emotionally as well as intellectually. "These were not the words of a government minister reading off a prepared briefing paper," the Secretary of State later recalled. "They were the words of a man involved in a historic struggle." It was clear that the Soviets were primarily

45. Baker comments in Greenstein and Wohlforth, *Cold War Endgame*, 9; Baker, *Politics of Diplomacy*, 92–96; Beschloss and Talbott, *At the Highest Levels*, 77–80.

46. Baker, *Politics of Diplomacy*, 168; Bush and Scowcroft, *A World Transformed*, 71–74; Beschloss and Talbott, *At the Highest Levels*, 93–94; Oberdorfer, *The Turn*, 366–69.

47. The summer months had been very difficult for the Soviet leadership. Over 150,000 coal miners had gone on strike, forcing Gorbachev into a corner and causing many to worry that a crackdown loomed. This unrest, combined with simmering ethnic strife, brought rumors of a major leadership shake-up. Given these concerns, Baker was anxious to hear from Shevardnadze and outline U.S. views directly.

focused on domestic questions, and that their behavior toward the outside world would be shaped by what proved most beneficial toward solving their internal problems. Baker understood, and informed President Bush as such, that Gorbachev and Shevardnadze needed the United States to convey support and confidence in their efforts, and show evidence of progress in relations.

The Paris meeting changed the tenor of the Baker-Shevardnadze relationship fundamentally. On a personal level, the Secretary of State started to feel an affinity for Shevardnadze similar to that shared by his predecessor, George Shultz. Reflecting on Paris, Baker later recalled that "[at] the more critical, informal level—centered around discussions of the domestic transformation of the Soviet Union and, by implication, its relationship to Eastern Europe—we were not so much foreign ministers as social commentators, sharing private worries and thoughts. . . . it became my role to comment on [Shevardnadze's] observations, hoping that my arguments would influence his views, however marginally, so as to help avoid the potential catastrophe that was so worrisome to him—and to me."[48]

If Paris started the process of dismantling American mistrust, then the Baker-Shevardnadze meetings in Jackson Hole, Wyoming, during September 21–23, accelerated it dramatically. For example, the Bush administration still believed the Soviet predicament was fundamentally unstable—indeed, by September there was plenty of confirming evidence.[49] But while instability and suspicion had worked together to breed inaction during the spring, Administration officials began to take a different approach as their level of trust evolved. Some U.S. officials now believed that Gorbachev was acting to implement real reform and not, as they had suspected earlier, attempting to undermine U.S. interests or split the Western Alliance. Therefore, they aimed to deal with instability by embracing the Soviets, forging agreements with them to "lock-in" permanent reform. In this way, members of the Bush team looked to Wyoming to bring progress on issues like arms control and to set the stage for the Bush-Gorbachev summit.

The most important substantive decisions emerging out of Jackson Hole concerned the negotiations on a treaty to reduce strategic nuclear weapons, or

48. See Baker, *Politics of Diplomacy*, 135–42, and Beschloss and Talbott, *At the Highest Levels*, 95–99. For Shultz's view of Shevardnadze, see Shultz, *Turmoil and Triumph*, 744–45.

49. Since July, the Soviet internal situation had only complicated further. Ethnic unrest erupted in the Baltic states, and Gorbachev had purged several hard-line leaders from the Politburo. The pace of change in Eastern Europe also marched forward: in late August, Gorbachev allowed a Solidarity-dominated Polish

START. Shevardnadze made the two most significant concessions—delinking START negotiations from an accompanying agreement on space-based defense systems, and pledging to dismantle the Krasnoyarsk radar, a system that the United States had long claimed was a violation of the ABM treaty.[50] Significantly, these proposals were not dismissed as evidence of insincere Soviet grandstanding as similar initiatives had been earlier that year; at least in the Baker State Department, officials perceived them as genuine efforts to make peace. Put simply, those who were beginning to trust Gorbachev and Shevardnadze's intentions no longer viewed this Soviet behavior as automatically suspect.

In this sense, the meaning of Jackson Hole is as much about the improvement in personal relations and the breakdown in mistrust as any negotiating accomplishment. Baker and Shevardnadze made an effort to spend as much informal time together as possible—a more relaxed atmosphere was precisely the point of going to Wyoming. For example, on the airplane to Jackson, they had a remarkably frank discussion on the nationalities question and Eastern Europe. Their discussions at the ranch were frequently conducted during walks in the woods, western-style barbeques, and long (but unsuccessful) fishing trips. This was a far cry from the staged atmosphere of most U.S.-Soviet interactions during the Cold War. It was much closer to a freewheeling interaction between peers, even friends. "Wyoming ushered in a new tone in our personal relations," Baker recalled. The Soviets shared this view. Shevardnadze's interpreter, Pavel Palazchenko, reflects that after Jackson Hole, Baker and Shevardnadze "were in agreement about the basic course of the relationship—from confrontation . . . to mutual understanding and cooperation, and eventually to partnership. And between the two of them it looked increasingly like friendship."[51]

In the weeks after Jackson Hole, Baker began to express publicly the trust and support for the Soviet Union that had been developing privately. In a series of three statements during October 1989, he outlined the core principle of

government to form, which was the first replacement of a communist regime in the Warsaw Pact. See Garthoff, *Great Transition*, 398–400.

50. Although these two were the most significant, Shevardnadze also conceded a third issue related to START: to delink the negotiations from an agreement on sea-launched cruise missiles, as the United States insisted. As for the Americans, Baker made one surprise offer: to reduce chemical weapons stockpiles by 80 percent, while continuing negotiations for a global chemical weapons treaty. See Beschloss and Talbott, *At the Highest Levels*, 110–21, and Garthoff, *Great Transition*, 384–85.

51. For details on Jackson Hole and its importance for the Baker-Shevardnadze relationship, see Baker, *Politics of Diplomacy*, 144–52; Beschloss and Talbott, *At the Highest Levels*, 109–12; Oberdorfer, *The Turn*, 371–74; Gates, *In from the Shadows*, 478–80; Palazchenko, *My Years with Gorbachev and Shevardnadze*, 145–50; and Carolyn McGiffert Ekedahl and Melvin A. Goodman, *The Wars of Eduard Shevardnadze* (University Park: Pennsylvania State University Press, 1997), 118–22.

U.S.-Soviet relations, to find "points of mutual advantage." His statements' tone and substance conveyed enthusiasm for joining with the Soviets to reshape superpower relations—reflecting the evolution of beliefs about Gorbachev's intentions and thus the perceptions of Soviet behavior. The statements made clear, however, that the belief of instability still prevailed. But many now saw uncertainty as more, not less reason to work with the Soviets to implement lasting change. With greater trust, they set out to "lock-in" as much as possible.[52]

Despite such statements, the belief that the U.S.-Soviet relationship was less about strategic competition than cooperation was still not as strong in some areas of the Administration as others. Far and away, Baker and the State Department took the lead in espousing this belief. The Secretary of State had been the main American interlocutor with the Soviets and had come to see first-hand that they could be trusted. President Bush leaned in this direction (no doubt influenced by Baker, his closest adviser and friend), but had not been as publicly outspoken. Other officials—such as Scowcroft, Gates, and Vice President Dan Quayle—had not quite caught the spirit of Jackson Hole.

Scowcroft reflects that "Baker appeared to me the most optimistic concerning [Gorbachev's] sincerity about reform. He may have been influenced by his relationship with Shevardnadze. . . . I still believed that Gorbachev remained a communist, [quite] prepared to take advantage of us whenever the opportunity arose." Although these divisions were largely hidden inside the bureaucracy, on occasion they were aired publicly. The day after Baker's October 16 "Points of Mutual Advantage" address, Quayle used a speech to stress the "darker side" of Soviet policy, explaining that improvements in superpower relations were "neither inevitable nor irreversible."[53] Clearly, an internal consensus needed to be built. Since the most important signal would come from the President, all eyes turned to Malta.

The Bush-Gorbachev shipboard summit off Malta during December 1989 was, despite the horrible weather that nearly capsized it, a resounding

52. Baker, *Politics of Diplomacy*, 155–56; Beschloss and Talbott, *At the Highest Levels*, 121–23. For Baker's speeches, see "Statement before Senate Finance Committee," October 4, 1989, in *AFPCD 1989*, 374–78; "Points of Mutual Advantage," October 16, 1989, ibid., 378–85; and "Prerequisites and Principles for Arms Control," October 23, 1989, ibid., 73–78. For a press account, see Thomas Friedman, "U.S. Offers to Aid Gorbachev's Plan to Revamp System," *New York Times*, October 27, 1989.

53. For the Scowcroft quotation, see Bush and Scowcroft, *A World Transformed*, 154. A discussion of Quayle's speech is in Ann Devroy, "Despite Speeches, Quayle and Baker Agree on Soviets, Aides Say," *Washington Post*, October 19, 1989; Beschloss and Talbott, *At the Highest Levels*, 122–23. Quayle's speech was not cleared by either the White House or the State Department.

success.[54] In terms of the signal it sent about superpower trust and cooperation, it should be seen as the capstone to the evolution of the Bush administration's beliefs. President Bush was determined to take a dramatic stroke; he
came to Malta with a list of seventeen initiatives, ranging from U.S. technical
assistance for the Soviet Union to specific goals on START. More cosmetic
than substantial, these proposals were a clear indication of the more supportive U.S. attitude. In this sense, the most important accomplishment at Malta
was less tangible than any policy. Malta did for George Bush what Paris and
Jackson Hole had done for Baker: it enabled him to interpret Soviet behavior
in personal terms. As Baker says, "Malta was where President Bush formed
the close personal bond and relationship with President Gorbachev that frankly
I had formed in September with Minister Shevardnadze, and there was no
doubt in anybody's mind after Malta what the direction I think of the policies
of the two countries were going to be." Even Scowcroft admits that the Malta
meeting worked far better than he had hoped. It established a personal relationship between the two leaders that made all of the subsequent events possible.[55]

Bush had come to the Malta meeting open to seeing Gorbachev in this
new light, even if some of his advisers were still cautious. As Bush said to
Gorbachev in their first meeting of the summit, "When I was editing the draft
of my letter to you about this meeting . . . I took stock of the fact that it meant a
180 degree turnaround from my previous position. The American people support this change."[56] And in both tone and content, the discussions off Malta
convinced Bush that Gorbachev was committed to fundamental reform and
would be a reliable partner in recasting superpower relations. Gorbachev felt
the same way. When Bush told him that his administration would "avoid doing
anything that would damage your position in the world," Gorbachev responded,
"I welcome your words. I regard them as a manifestation of political will. It is
important to me."[57] And after Malta, Bush characterized his relationship with

54. The accounts of the Malta summit are voluminous. For the best details on the summit as well as its
impact on personal relations, see Bush and Scowcroft, *A World Transformed*, 161–74; Bush, *All the Best*,
445–48; Beschloss and Talbott, *At the Highest Levels*, 153–71; Oberdorfer, *The Turn*, 374–86; Zelikow and
Rice, *Germany Unified*, 125–31; Gorbachev, *Memoirs*, 510–16; and Baker, *Politics of Diplomacy*, 168–71.

55. Chapter 1, p. 47; Bush and Scowcroft, *A World Transformed*, 173–74.

56. Anatoly S. Chernyaev, *My Six Years with Gorbachev*, ed. and trans. Robert D. English and Elizabeth
Tucker (University Park: Pennsylvania State University Press, 2000), 233.

57. Excerpts from the Soviet Record from December 2, 1989, on the Malta summit. In *The End of the
Cold War in Europe, 1989, New Thinking and New Evidence*, A Critical Oral History Conference Organized by
the National Security Archive, George Washington University, May 1998. See also Chernyaev's discussion in
My Six Years with Gorbachev, 233–35, for the importance of the Malta meetings to his boss.

the Soviet leader as "very personal." "I'll find ways to contact him in a very quiet fashion," he observed to a journalist at the time. "I can write him. I can call him . . . we can communicate."[58] Eleven months after taking office, Bush had finally picked up where Reagan left off—he trusted the Soviets.

Conclusions

The story of the Bush administration's approach toward the Soviet Union during 1989 reveals the power of policymakers' beliefs in shaping foreign policy. It also supports the argument that beliefs are a critical factor in whether both sides perceive mutual interests and can establish trust.[59] Suspicions about Soviet intentions and instability—suspicions that were supported by the intelligence community—made it difficult for President Bush and his senior advisers to trust Gorbachev throughout most of 1989, and they designed policy accordingly. During the first half of the year, the Bush team's belief that the superpower relationship remained strategically competitive influenced not only such initial policy priorities as unifying the NATO alliance or emphasizing Eastern Europe, but also the way they interpreted Gorbachev's behavior. Officials believed that the Soviets were merely cooperating to compete, and therefore perceived Gorbachev's concessions as part of a "public diplomacy blitzkrieg" to undermine U.S. interests. And we know from work in psychology that individuals tend to downplay disconfirming evidence or to make evidence fit preconceptions.[60] In addition, suspicion worked alongside another belief: policymakers saw the Soviet situation as inherently unstable. The fact that Gorbachev's prospects for success seemed in doubt exacerbated the Bush administration's caution. Particularly during the first six months of 1989, officials were reluctant to work with the Soviets until the future of reform became more clear.

Given such beliefs, how did trust develop? The history of this period shows that over the course of the year, the Bush administration's perceptions of Soviet intentions improved. In this process, the development of personal relationships with Soviet leaders was indispensable. As personal relations grew, the prevailing beliefs of suspicion and competition gave way to empathy and

---

58. As quoted in Beschloss and Talbott, *At the Highest Levels*, 167.
59. See Larson, *Anatomy of Mistrust*, 237–40, and Jervis, *Perception and Misperception*.
60. Philip E. Tetlock, "Theory-Driven Reasoning about Plausible Pasts and Probable Futures in World Politics: Are We Prisoners of Our Preconceptions?" *American Journal of Political Science* 43, no. 2 (April 1999): 335–66.

cooperation. Led by Secretary of State Baker, U.S. officials began to see first-hand that the Soviet leadership was sincere. They began to understand Soviet leaders' motives and empathize with their predicament. They believed Soviet promises were credible—that their deeds would match their words. And they not only trusted Soviet leaders as official counterparts, but in some cases, began to consider them genuine friends.[61] Such developments helped lead to the public reorientation of U.S. policy toward "points of mutual advantage," and gave policymakers confidence to pursue a strategy based on trust. Finally, the strength of personal ties reached full bloom at Malta, where Bush and Gorbachev's discussions codified the new direction in superpower relations.[62]

Strong personal relations also influenced the way the Bush team approached its other key concern—Soviet instability. By the end of 1989, President Bush and his advisers were no more certain whether or not Gorbachev would succeed or even survive. Indeed, with such rapid change under way in Eastern Europe, Gorbachev's ability to control the situation seemed even weaker. But rather than continuing their initial wait-and-see policy, they embraced Gorbachev symbolically and substantively. Bush and his inner circle came to trust the Soviets to reduce instability in ways consistent with U.S. interests, and thus decided to help. They did so in two ways: by locking-in mutually advantageous reforms wherever possible (such as arms control), and working with the Soviets to prevent unrest (in Eastern Europe, for example).[63]

Reflecting on how beliefs, perceptions, and leaders' relationships shape political outcomes has helped us solve the puzzle of the Bush administration's

61. The Baker-Shevardnadze relationship, in particular, bloomed into friendship. For example, in a letter to Shevardnadze after he had resigned as Soviet foreign minister in December 1990, Baker wrote: "[In] all of our dealings, I came to know you as a man of conviction and principle. Your word has always been good. And true to your convictions and values, you took a courageous and difficult step. It was in keeping with what you believe in and represent. . . . I consider it one of the privileges of my life to have been able to work with you and to be able to call you my friend." See Baker to Shevardnadze, February 20, 1991, reprinted in briefing book for the conference "Cold War Endgame" at Princeton University, March 29–30, 1996.

62. For an argument that stresses the value of face-to-face interactions in understanding another leader's goals and resolve, see Robert Jervis, *The Logic of Images in International Relations* (Princeton: Princeton University Press, 1970), 32–34.

63. This might help explain the overture the State Department made toward the Soviets in late December 1989 concerning possible Soviet intervention in Romania. With the Ceaușescu regime in the process of being overthrown, Ambassador Matlock reportedly approached Kremlin officials about the possibility of Soviet involvement to support the rebels. According to the Soviet account of the meeting, Matlock said that the United States would not view Soviet intervention to calm the crisis as a return to the Brezhnev Doctrine. Although the Kremlin dismissed this idea out of hand, the fact that it was raised helps illuminate the Bush administration's concern about instability—even to the point of welcoming the prospect of Soviet military intervention to contain it. See Thomas Blanton, "When Did the Cold War End?" *Cold War International History Project Bulletin* 10 (March 1998): 184–91.

initial approach toward the Soviet Union, and why it was slow in recognizing the opportunities to transform the superpower relationship that the Reagan administration understood so clearly. The discussion does raise several conceptual issues. First, the story presented here needs to address competing explanations, such as the argument that the developments that brought superpower comity were the result of external pressures—because the Soviet Union was weakening vis-à-vis the United States, it had to change to survive, and had no choice but to cooperate. In this view, leaders' beliefs and personalities would not drive outcomes, but merely be the result of the changing power distribution in the international system.

Although such arguments cannot be entirely dismissed, the history of 1989 seems to throw them in doubt. For example, they shed little light on why the U.S. approach toward the USSR changed from cooperation under Reagan during 1988, to competition under Bush during early 1989, and back to cooperation under Bush during the latter part of 1989. Soviet behavior remained consistent during this period; if anything, Gorbachev became more conciliatory. Yet with the transition from Reagan to Bush, U.S. behavior changed. The Bush administration's abrupt interruption of its predecessor's policy— only to return to it later—leaves evidence that outcomes were not determined by external circumstances alone. Something else had to be at work.

That being said, structural factors cannot be entirely ignored. The international environment establishes the conditions under which factors like beliefs and personalities can make a difference. As Fred Greenstein points out, political actors are not "unmoved movers"—without environments which allow for human intervention, "even the most gifted leader can make no mark."[64] Accordingly, the redirection of East-West relations could not have taken place without such structural preconditions as the economic and military decline of the Soviet Union and the relative strength of the United States. It is hard to imagine beliefs and personality having the same impact in 1959 as they did in 1989. But as argued above, seeing the international environment as permissive for the way the superpower relationship unfolded during 1989 does not help us with many of the specifics—for example, why the Bush team put East-West relations on hold for half the year, how they eventually came to

64. See Fred Greenstein, "Reagan, Gorbachev, and the End of the Cold War," in William C. Wohlforth, ed., *Witnesses to the End of the Cold War* (Baltimore: Johns Hopkins University Press, 1997), 190–219, and idem, "The Impact of Personality on the End of the Cold War," *Political Psychology* 19, no. 1 (March 1998): 1–16.

trust Gorbachev, and why events occurred peacefully. Thus, for a more complete explanation, one must consider the interaction between structural conditions and leaders' beliefs and personalities.[65]

The second conceptual issue is determining the independent influence of personal relations on trust. Could other factors account for the evolution of trust? For example, some might assert that it was not personal relations that mattered, but the type of Soviet concessions offered. This is essentially the "deeds, not words" argument that the Bush administration peddled in early 1989. Initial Soviet moves were written off, to use Baker's terms, as "strategically insignificant"; only when Gorbachev offered "significant" concessions did the Bush administration's perceptions of Soviet intentions evolve.[66]

The facts of this story do not support such an assertion. If the Bush team only needed evidence of strategically significant concessions to trust Soviet intentions, it is curious how they perceived Gorbachev's 1988 U.N. speech announcing unilateral cuts of conventional forces in Europe. In one dramatic sweep, the Soviet leader announced a reduction of 500,000 troops, 10,000 tanks, 8,500 artillery pieces, and 800 combat aircraft. Former NATO commander General Andrew Goodpaster called this "the most significant step since NATO was founded," and George Shultz hailed the speech as further proof that Gorbachev was willing "to engage." Arms control veteran Raymond Garthoff summarized the moment as one of "general recognition that the Soviet Union was now talking with 'deeds, not words' and was serious."[67] Yet as explained above, while others interpreted such moves as evidence of cooperative intentions, the Bush administration remained deeply suspicious of the Soviets, writing off such concessions as nothing more than public relations gambits. It was not until the summer and autumn of 1989—when strong personal relations

---

65. See James M. Goldgeier, "Psychology and Security," *Security Studies* 6, no. 3 (summer 1997): 137–66, and J. M. Goldgeier and P. E. Tetlock, "Psychology and International Relations Theory," *Annual Review of Political Science* 4 (2001): 67–92. See also Charles Kupchan, *The Vulnerabilty of Empire* (Ithaca: Cornell University Press, 1994); William Wohlforth, *The Elusive Balance: Power and Perceptions During the Cold War* (Ithaca: Cornell University Press, 1993); and idem, "Realism and the End of the Cold War," *International Security* 19, no. 3 (winter 1994/95): 91–129.

66. For the argument that actions speak louder than words, see Thomas Schelling, *Arms and Influence* (New Haven: Yale University Press, 1966), 150. For the point that by sacrificing one's ability to harm the other, one can increase the chances of mutually beneficial cooperation, see Robert Jervis, "Cooperation Under the Security Dilemma," *World Politics* 28, no. 2 (January 1978): 179–80. For a discussion on the problems of distinguishing between "cheap talk" and "costly signals," see Robert Jervis, "Drawing Inferences and Projecting Images" (paper prepared for delivery to the Security Studies Section of the International Studies Association, April 1996).

67. See Oberdorfer, *The Turn*, 319; Shultz, *Turmoil and Triumph*, 1108; and Garthoff, *Great Transition*, 367.

started to develop—that such key officials as Secretary of State Baker began to trust Soviet intentions. Significantly, the turning point for Baker in particular was his July 1989 meeting with Shevardnadze, an occasion in which the discussion centered around Soviet internal problems, resulting in nothing close to "strategically significant" concessions.

Another example of "significant" concessions by the Soviets that some argue were more important than personal relations was the cascade of events throughout the Soviet Bloc in the spring and summer 1989 that showed that Gorbachev was sincere.[68] From the Polish roundtable negotiations in early 1989 to the Hungarian border openings in May, the seating of a Solidarity-dominated government in Warsaw in late August, and the events that led to the fall of the Berlin Wall in November, Gorbachev repudiated Soviet imperial behavior and showed the world that he was truly a different leader. While in retrospect these remarkable events make the improvement in U.S.-Soviet relations seem obvious—even "overdetermined"—what's interesting is that both at the time and upon reflection, policymakers like Bush, Baker, and Scowcroft rarely cited such events as the reasons for their changing perceptions of Soviet behavior. They stress their personal relationships.

This leads us, finally, to a third and most fundamental conceptual issue: determining the influence of individuals on outcomes. One way of getting at an answer is the use of counterfactuals. If another leader had been in the same position under the same circumstances, would he or she have acted differently?[69] In terms of the story above, one only needs to think of how things would have been different had Ronald Reagan, like FDR, been allowed to hold a third term in office. Or if in the 1988 presidential election, a Democrat like Michael Dukakis or Gary Hart had prevailed.[70] To take a slightly more realistic scenario, what might have changed if Bush had asked Shultz to continue on as secretary of state, or Jack Matlock to return to his old job as the senior Soviet specialist on the NSC? It seems no great stretch to say that if the players had been shuffled, the outcome would have been different—it might not have taken U.S. leaders most of the year to come to realize that they could

68. We are grateful to Tom Blanton for discussions on this point.

69. See Greenstein, "Impact of Personality," and *Personality and Politics* (Chicago: Markham, 1969), 40–58.

70. For one of the more dramatic might-have-beens: in the 1988 presidential campaign, Gary Hart had decided that if elected president, he would invite Gorbachev to the inaugural and immediately negotiate an arms control treaty on strategic arms and nuclear testing. See David Remnick, "Winter on the Mountain," *The Devil Problem and Other Stories* (New York: Vintage, 1997), 15.

trust the Soviets. If this had occurred, perhaps the Cold War might have ended sooner, with greater benefits for both sides. In short, this case shows that leaders do make a difference.[71]

On the other hand, while we can show that individual beliefs and the development of trust were crucial to the ways in which the relationship with the Soviet Union developed in 1989, the question of how important the pause was historically remains an open question. Deborah Larson argues that the "delays and caution" cost Gorbachev a big success, particularly on the economic front, that might have made it likelier for the Soviets to achieve a successful transition to a market economy. Jack Matlock argues that the pause delayed negotiations on strategic weapons, "even though the issue had been studied during the entire eight years of the Reagan administration and Bush's appointees were thoroughly familiar with it," as well as squandered opportunities for "activating the economic relationship." On the other side, Bush administration NSC staffer Philip Zelikow says that there was no real cost to the pause. Baker perhaps splits the difference between the two opinions by saying that the pause left no "enduring policy consequences," at least from the U.S. side.[72] And after all, in the years to come, the United States did conclude strategic arms reduction agreements, ensured that a unified Germany remained a full member of NATO, and helped to manage a peaceful transition to a post-Soviet world.[73]

A Future Agenda

Just as scholars have revealed the importance of personality and beliefs in shaping U.S. policy at the beginning of the Cold War, more must be done to understand the influence of these factors on the Cold War's end.[74] The links between international structure and beliefs need to be parsed further. Under what conditions do beliefs and personality matter? Also, as in almost all of the

71. For a renewed call for scholarship that assesses the impact of personalities in politics, see Daniel L. Byman and Kenneth M. Pollack, "Let Us Now Praise Great Men: Bringing the Statesman Back In," *International Security* 25, no. 4 (spring 2001); and Alexander George and Juliette George, *Presidential Personality and Performance* (Boulder, Colo.: Westview Press, 1998). For a great example of a study that traces leadership to policy outcomes, see Valerie Bunce, *Do New Leaders Make a Difference?* (Princeton: Princeton University Press, 1980).

72. Larson, *Anatomy of Mistrust*, 224–25, 232; Matlock, *Autopsy on an Empire*, 200; Chapter 1, p. 45.

73. Tetlock and Goldgeier, "Human Nature and World Politics," 90.

74. For representative works on the influence of beliefs at the beginning of the Cold War, see Larson, *Origins of Containment*, and Melvyn Leffler, *A Preponderance of Power: National Security, the Truman Administration, and the Cold War* (Stanford: Stanford University Press, 1992).

scholarship on ideas or beliefs, more work needs to be done to explain their sources. Where do beliefs come from? What shapes them? Why and how can they change? This chapter has offered a rather simple, yet frequently over-looked response: personal relationships between leaders can be very influential in shaping beliefs about intentions and motives. Therefore, personal relation-ships can prove critical to overcoming mistrust.

Policymakers have long valued this point. Certainly the Bush adminis-tration officials all talk about how important key meetings were to their think-ing; as the president himself has remarked, "I liked the personal contact with Mikhail—I liked *him*."[75] These officials are certainly not alone. "Even in this era of computers and cyberspace," former secretary of state Warren Christopher has observed, "personal relationships continue to play a central role in the world of diplomacy and, in my judgment, always will." Strobe Talbott, the Clinton administration's "point man" on Russia policy, emphasizes in his memoir the personal relationship between Bill Clinton and Boris Yeltsin. And more than a decade after the events described in this chapter, George W. Bush used his first meeting with Russian president Vladimir Putin in June 2001 to stress the importance of "trust" in their relationship. Indeed, one of the first challenges any leader faces in foreign policy is his ability to interact construc-tively with diplomatic counterparts. Sour personal relations, Harold Nicolson noted long ago, diminish the chances for cooperation even when mutual inter-ests are at stake.[76]

However unexceptionable such observations may seem to those in policy circles, the influence of personal relations in foreign policy has been virtually ignored by academic analysts. Scholars certainly understand the importance of personality and personal relationships when it comes to decision making within their own departments; it is odd that they do not place the same importance on these factors when trying to explain how policymakers interact and make deci-sions. Perhaps this is because for scholars, the analysis of personality in politics is invariably difficult and particularly messy, causing some to regard such research as incompatible with producing valid, rigorous, and generalizable insights. Or perhaps such neglect merely reflects one of the fundamental ten-

75. Bush and Scowcroft, *A World Transformed*, 9.

76. Warren Christopher, *In the Stream of History* (Stanford: Stanford University Press, 1998), 453; Strobe Talbott, *The Russia Hand: A Memoir of Presidential Diplomacy* (New York: Random House, 2002); Harold Nicolson, *Diplomacy* (New York: Harcourt, Brace, 1939), 123.

sions in social science, between those who argue that outcomes derive from larger structures, processes, or institutions versus those who weigh the power of human agency. But when thinking about foreign policy outcomes, this chapter reveals the value of considering the latter. The evolution of the Bush administration's approach toward the Soviet Union during 1989 serves as a case in point of why individuals play such an important role in the development of interstate relations.

6 Trust Bursting Out All Over: The Soviet Side of German Unification

Andrew O. Bennett

> There is something paradoxical
> in the fact that we evolved trust
> faster than our American counterparts.
> —*Anatoly Chernyaev*

THE TRANSCRIPTS OF the Cold War Endgame conference throw into sharp relief many of the theoretical and historical puzzles of the end of the Cold War. Why did the Soviet Union fail to use force in 1989 to keep together the Warsaw Pact, as it had in Hungary in 1956 and Czechoslovakia in 1968? Why did the Soviet bureaucracy fail even to come up with a coherent option for using force in 1989? Why did Gorbachev fail to exact a higher price for German unification in 1990? Why did his acceptance of a unified Germany within NATO survive opposition from his foreign and defense ministries, which in this case did propose and push for alternatives?

These central puzzles have rightly been the focus of considerable research and theorizing, as they are here, but underlying them is the central paradox pointed out by Gorbachev's foreign policy adviser Anatoly Chernyaev. As William Wohlforth has noted, "What is striking about the whole story is how many unprecedented signals and gestures were needed to reduce American uncertainty about Soviet intentions (and how few such signals the Americans had to send to reduce Gorbachev's uncertainty concerning their intentions)."[1] The preceding chapter by Derek Chollet and James Goldgeier addresses the first half of this puzzle; the present chapter addresses the second. In doing so, it builds on Vladislav Zubok's account of Gorbachev's personal trust of the West and Robert English's account of the "new ideas" that Gorbachev and others introduced on foreign policy, and it integrates the material factors,

---

1. William C. Wohlforth, "Scholars, Policy Makers, and the End of the Cold War," in Wohlforth, ed., *Witnesses to the End of the Cold War* (Baltimore: Johns Hopkins University Press, 1996), 263. Scholarly debates over the end of the Cold War have focused to an unusual extent on the role of individuals, particularly Gorbachev, and the issue of trust. On Gorbachev, see, in addition to Vladislav Zubok's chapter, Archie Brown, *The Gorbachev Factor* (New York: Oxford University Press, 1996), and Janice Gross Stein, "Political Learning by Doing: Gorbachev as Uncommitted Thinker and Motivated Learner," *International Organization* 48, no. 2 (spring 1994): 155–84. On the issue of trust, see Deborah Larson, *Anatomy of Mistrust: U.S.-Soviet Relations During the Cold War* (Ithaca: Cornell University Press, 1997).

political conditions, and shared ideas that allowed Gorbachev's initiatives to prevail in Soviet foreign policy in 1989–90. The resulting mix of explanatory variables leans more on ideas and less on material incentives than Stephen Brooks and William Wohlforth's account does (Chapter 9 herein). Our two accounts agree that ideas and material constraints were both important, however, and we are not far apart on key counterfactual questions regarding when changes in the material balance of power would have allowed Soviet foreign policy change and when they would have compelled it, and regarding the range of alternative policies that the material balance might have accommodated.

This chapter outlines four of the principal theoretical approaches to the puzzles of 1989 and 1990 and the underlying paradox of Soviet trustfulness, and it uses each approach to illuminate not only the Endgame transcripts but also the substantial documentary and interview material that has become available in recent years. First, the "realist" approach, exemplified by Brooks and Wohlforth, emphasizes the material balance of power and argues that Soviet leaders refrained from using force and made most of the concessions in 1989 and 1990 because Soviet economic decline and Eastern European indebtedness left them little choice. Trust and personal interactions, in this view, played a very small role: only repeated "costly signaling" by the Soviet Union convinced the United States that the Soviet Union had indeed scaled back its ambitions to fit its resources. A second view, based on Jürgen Habermas's theory of "communicative action," maintains that U.S. and Soviet leaders engaged in a deliberative process in which leaders on each side allowed their interests, ideas, and even identities to be influenced by persuasive communications from the other side. This approach suggests that personal interactions and the trust they developed are central to explaining the Cold War's end. A third school of thought, drawing on theories of cognitive and social psychology, focuses on leaders' perceptions of the balance of power and their beliefs on the dynamics through which power can be exercised. This school emphasizes not just interactions among leaders but personal and shared experiences more generally as the sources of beliefs about international politics. Here, trust is not only affected by costly signaling but is also mediated by cognitively constructed beliefs and identities and the individual and social psychological dynamics through which these beliefs change. In a fourth view, domestic political constraints limit the options available to leaders, regardless of whether they trust their counterparts on the other side, and leaders play off domestic and international actors against one another.

Most experts agree that a combination of these four approaches is necessary to explain the end of the Cold War but debates remain about their interactions and relative weight and about the counterfactual "might have beens" they justify. This chapter assesses the strengths and limits of each approach, and the role each accords to personal interactions and trust. It also assesses whether each approach is consistent with the process-tracing evidence that has emerged as archival materials, interviews, and memoirs have become available. Throughout, but particularly in the section on Soviet domestic politics, the chapter brings in the views of those who later attempted a coup against Gorbachev, including Defense Minister Dmitry Yazov and head of the KGB Vladimir Kryuchkov, who are not represented in the Endgame transcripts.[2] The chapter concludes with a brief sketch of how the four approaches can be integrated into a single historical explanation of the Soviet side of 1989 and 1990; and as a guide to continued scholarly debate, it attempts to define as precisely as possible the relevant counterfactual claims this integrated explanation makes.

Realist Explanations for Soviet Concessions in Europe, 1989–1990

Realist explanations focus on changes in the balance of military and economic power as the source of changes in international politics. In the last several years international relations theorists have introduced many variants of "realism." Fortunately, it is not necessary for present purposes to delve into the theoretical differences among them, since leading realists and experts on the

---

2. It is important to note here several biases in the information available to Western scholars. First, we have far more information on the thinking of political leaders and officials in the Ministry of Foreign Affairs than on that of officials in the military and the KGB. The latter two organizations and their archives have remained relatively inaccessible. Second, we have more information on the new thinkers than on the conservatives. Westerners have engaged the reformers more frequently than the conservatives in conferences and interviews. Third, research and interviews have focused on the very top leaders, and we know much less about the views and behavior of midlevel officials. The top leaders had an outsized impact in the highly centralized Soviet system, but midlevel officials often have sharper and more candid recollections on policies within their more narrow issue areas, and these officials and their organizations shaped the information to which top leaders were exposed and the ways in which decisions were implemented. The actual fall of the Berlin Wall, for example, was the result of a comedy of errors and miscommunications between East German security organizations rather than a conscious decision by leaders. See Jacques Lévesque, *The Enigma of 1989: The USSR and the Liberation of Eastern Europe,* trans. Keith Martin (Berkeley and Los Angeles: University of California Press, 1997), 158–59; Angela Stent, *Russia and Germany Reborn: Unification, the Soviet Collapse, and the New Europe* (Princeton: Princeton University Press, 1999); and Hans-Hermann Hertle, "The Fall of the Wall: The Unintended Self-Dissolution of East Germany's Ruling Regime," *Cold War International History Bulletin,* no. 12/13 (fall/winter 2001): 131–40.

Soviet Union have themselves offered realist explanations for the transformation of Soviet foreign policy and the end of the Cold War.[3] Kenneth Oye, for
example, has argued that because of continuing relative economic decline the
Soviet Union chose to shed its overextended imperial commitments, including its subsidized allies in Eastern Europe. Because Soviet security was ultimately guaranteed by a Soviet nuclear force sufficiently large and secure to
absorb a U.S. first strike and still deliver a devastating retaliatory blow, the
Soviet Union faced an essentially "benign" international environment and
could afford to let go of contiguous territories no longer essential to its security and divert resources from the military back to the civilian economy.[4]
Similarly, Kenneth Waltz has argued that relative economic decline and imperial overextension created pressures for retrenchment in Soviet foreign policy,
and stable nuclear deterrence allowed the Soviet Union and later Russia to
withdraw from ambitious foreign policy and defense commitments without
risking direct great power challenges to their vital security interests.[5]

William Wohlforth has offered the most comprehensive realist explanation for Soviet retrenchment thus far, building on a close reading of primary
sources. Like other realists, Wohlforth draws on theories of hegemonic rivalry
and power transition to argue that Soviet economic decline led to Soviet foreign policy retrenchment. Brooks and Wohlforth argue herein that, contrary
to earlier estimates of modest growth, the Soviet economy was stagnant in

3. For analyses of "offensive," "defensive," "neoclassical," "contingent," and other variants of realism, see
Stephen G. Brooks, "Dueling Realisms," *International Organization* 51, no. 3 (summer 1997): 445–77; Robert
Jervis, "Realism, Neoliberalism, and Cooperation: Understanding the Debate," *International Security* 24, no. 1
(summer 1999): 42–63; Charles L. Glaser, "Realists as Optimists: Cooperation as Self-Help," *International
Security* 19, no. 3 (winter 1994/95): 50–90; Randall Schweller, "Neorealism's Status-Quo Bias: What Security
Dilemma?" *Security Studies* 5, no. 3 (spring 1996): 90–121; and Jeffrey W. Legro and Andrew Moravcsik, "Is
Anybody Still a Realist?" *International Security* 24, no. 2 (fall 1999): 5–55. For debates on whether "realism,"
as opposed to specific theories that fall under the rubric of realism, is even sufficiently specified to be tested
in the case of the end of the Cold War, see William C. Wohlforth, "Realism and the End of the Cold War,"
International Security 19, no. 3 (winter 1994/95): 91–129; idem, "Reality Check: Revising Theories of
International Politics in Response to the End of the Cold War," *World Politics* 50, no. 4 (July 1998); and Colin
Elman, "Horses for Courses: Why *Not* Neorealist Theories of Foreign Policy?" *Security Studies* 6, no. 1
(autumn 1996): 7–53.

4. Kenneth A. Oye, "Explaining the End of the Cold War: Morphological and Behavior Adaptations to
the Nuclear Peace?" in Richard Ned Lebow and Thomas Risse-Kappen, eds., *International Relations Theory
and the End of the Cold War* (New York: Columbia University Press, 1995). Like other power transition explanations, Oye builds on Robert Gilpin's theory of hegemonic power transitions. See Gilpin, *War and Change in
World Politics* (New York: Cambridge University Press, 1981). Oye does not rely exclusively on material
factors, but argues that institutional inertia and ideology help explain why Soviet retrenchment happened
only fifteen years after the Soviet Union attained nuclear parity with the United States.

5. Kenneth N. Waltz, "The Emerging Structure of International Politics," *International Security* 18, no. 2
(fall 1993): 44–79. See also Coit D. Blacker, *Hostage to Revolution: Gorbachev and Soviet Security Policy,
1985–1991* (New York: Council on Foreign Relations Press, 1993).

absolute terms and declining dramatically in relative terms in the 1980s. In Wohlforth's account nuclear weapons guaranteed Soviet security despite Soviet economic decline, and nuclear deterrence allowed greater Soviet risk-taking in terms of foreign policy concessions.[6] Such concessions were necessary because by the late 1980s, Soviet leaders knew their policies faced opposition from every other great power in the world, including not only the United States and the NATO countries but also Japan and China. While acknowledging that other policy options were open to Soviet leaders, Wohlforth argues that states that unsuccessfully challenge the dominant state in the international system are likely to retrench rather than seek preventive war, in contrast to dominant states facing decline.[7]

Moreover, in Wohlforth's view, Soviet leaders emphasized that security must be mutual because they had come to understand what Western political scientists call the "security dilemma." The security dilemma refers to the fact that because states' intentions are hard to discern, a state that seeks security by building more military forces can make other states feel less secure, leading them to increase their military forces. This can lead to an arms race that diverts economic resources and leaves both states less secure. Recognition of this fact reinforced a new Soviet belief that "balancing" behavior predominates in international relations, so that states rising in power or assertiveness face a growing coalition of adversaries, while declining or retrenching states encounter less opposition and more potential allies. These beliefs, combined with the security assurance afforded by possession of nuclear weapons, allowed Soviet leaders to make policy concessions in the expectation that this would reduce other states' fear of a Soviet threat and thereby dissipate the de facto anti-Soviet coalition. Continued domestic failures, however, forced deeper concessions than Soviet leaders had anticipated. In particular, the withdrawal from Eastern Europe was not planned but was the unintended consequence of failed efforts to revitalize the Soviet economy and stimulate political and economic reform in Eastern Europe while reducing subsidies to the region. By the fall of 1989, these policies had set in motion such widespread mobilized opposition to Soviet-backed governments in Eastern Europe that Soviet military intervention would have

---

6. Wohlforth, "Realism and the End of the Cold War."

7. This is also consistent with the psychological phenomenon known as prospect theory, whereby actors will take greater risks to avoid a perceived loss than to achieve a perceived gain. See Jack Levy, "Prospect Theory and International Relations: Theoretical Applications and Analytical Problems," *Political Psychology* 13, no. 2 (June 1992): 283–307.

led to unacceptable military casualties and expenditures, direct economic costs, and indirect economic costs from assuming the enormous international debts of Eastern Europe and dealing with Western economic sanctions.[8]

A fourth realist account, by Andrew Kydd, focuses more directly on the issue of trust and the role of "costly signaling." In this view, the security dilemma that arises from the difficulty of knowing other states' intentions can be ameliorated when a state takes actions that would be unacceptably costly or risky for a state harboring aggressive intentions. For example, a status quo state can focus on building defensive military forces, such as ground fortifications, whereas a revisionist state would be unwilling to eschew mobile military forces that could be used to seize territory. Thus, the Soviet Union had by the late 1980s built up such a revisionist reputation, in particular through its military buildup in Europe and its interventions in Afghanistan and elsewhere, that the West would not trust rhetorical Soviet commitments until the Soviet Union undertook costly signals demonstrating its credible commitment to less aggressive foreign policies. In Kydd's view, the Soviet Union did exactly this by agreeing in 1987 to the U.S. "zero option" proposal for removing all intermediate-range nuclear forces (INF) from Europe (which required removal of a much higher number of Soviet than American missiles), withdrawing Soviet forces from Afghanistan in 1988–89 even without a firm U.S. commitment to stop aiding the anti-Soviet Afghan rebels, announcing substantial unilateral cuts in Soviet offensive conventional forces in Europe in December 1988, and refraining from the use of force in Europe in 1989. Kydd concludes that Soviet concessions were also inspired by Soviet material weakness and ideational change, but he argues that the Soviet Union could afford "a few unrequited cooperative gestures" because of the robustness of nuclear deterrence.[9]

These realist accounts share many common points: Soviet relative economic decline as a motive for Soviet foreign policy change and cost-cutting on the periphery, nuclear weapons as a guarantor of Soviet security and an enabling factor in Soviet concessions, security dilemma dynamics as a source of

8. Wohlforth, "Realism and the End of the Cold War." Notably, Wohlforth's emphasis on *perceptions* of the balance of power and of the dynamics of balancing and the security dilemma bring him closer to the ideational accounts discussed below than most other realist arguments.

9. Andrew Kydd, "Trust, Reassurance, and Cooperation," *International Organization* 54, no. 2 (spring 2000): 343. Like Wohlforth, Kydd acknowledges a role for autonomous changes in Soviet ideas as well, stating that costly signaling complements theories on Soviet ideational change (327).

mistrust, and costly signaling as a means to address the security dilemma. All share as well a very rationalist view of "trust": trust is based on costly signaling and has very little to do with personal encounters or psychological dynamics.[10] In contrast to the Endgame transcripts and the memoirs of top officials, there is no mention of personal encounters at Malta or of the meetings between Foreign Minister Shevardnadze and Secretary of State Baker in Wyoming that the participants themselves view as important in establishing trust.[11]

These realist interpretations unquestionably explain a great deal of Soviet and American behavior toward the events of 1989 and the subsequent unification of Germany, and they are supported by substantial evidence from the Endgame transcripts and other documentary sources. Soviet leaders were indeed focused intensely on the problem of relative economic decline, and convinced that they could only address this problem if they attained better relations with the West.[12] They believed, most clearly in the cases of the INF agreement and the December 1988 conventional force reductions, that lopsided Soviet concessions were necessary to establish Western trust in Soviet new thinking.[13] As Chollet and Goldgeier argue (Chapter 5 herein), these moves were instrumental in inspiring American confidence that the Soviet leadership's commitment to new thinking was genuine. Recent evidence also indicates that Soviet leaders were aware in 1989 of the problem of Eastern European debts to the West, particularly those of Poland and East Germany, and that these leaders were concerned that any military intervention would force them to assume these debts.[14] As Tarasenko states (with evident exaggeration) in the Endgame

10. Kydd briefly discusses a "psychological strand" of theories of trust or reassurance, but most of the works he cites, with the exception of Robert Jervis's *Perception and Misperception in International Politics*, focus narrowly on unilateral cooperative gestures rather than personal interactions or other sources of psychological perceptions of trust or mistrust. Kydd, "Trust," 328. Accordingly, Kydd does not use or cite the memoirs of Gorbachev, Shevardnadze, or other Soviet leaders, nor those of Baker, Bush, or Scowcroft (the only memoir he references is that of Secretary of State George Shultz). Almost all of his process-tracing references on when trust actually emerged are to journalists, academics, and secondary accounts, rather than to actual policymakers.

11. James A. Baker III, with Thomas M. DeFrank, *The Politics of Diplomacy: Revolution, War, and Peace, 1989–1992* (New York: G. P. Putnam's Sons, 1995); Eduard A. Shevardnadze, *The Future Belongs to Freedom*, trans. Catherine A. Fitzpatrick (New York: Free Press, 1991).

12. William Wohlforth, *The Elusive Balance: Power and Perceptions During the Cold War* (Ithaca: Cornell University Press, 1993).

13. The Soviet withdrawal from Afghanistan and non-use of force in 1989 were inspired more directly by new thinking than by any Soviet plan to inspire trust. See Andrew Bennett, *Condemned to Repetition? The Rise, Fall, and Reprise of Soviet Russian Military Interventionism, 1973–1996* (Cambridge: MIT Press, 1999).

14. See Chapter 9 in the present volume; see also Vladislav Zubok, "New Evidence on the 'Soviet Factor' in the Peaceful Revolutions of 1989," *Cold War International History Bulletin*, no. 12/13 (fall/winter 2001): 10, 11, 13.

transcripts, one word explains why Gorbachev was forced to remove Soviet troops from the German Democratic Republic: "Money!"[15]

Realist explanations of Soviet foreign policy change suffer from important limitations, however. First, these accounts are not very attuned to Soviet domestic politics and the differences between Gorbachev and his opposition. Wohlforth gives some attention to this factor but he notes that "moderates and even conservatives . . . all wanted to get their hands on the human and material resources of the defense sector."[16] What this overlooks is that the defense sector wanted these resources too, and that for decades this claim on resources had not been challenged. This begs the question of why the entrenched military-party-industrial coalition that had dominated Soviet politics for decades lost out under Gorbachev to a seemingly weak coalition of intellectuals, consumers, and reformers. Explanations of Soviet foreign policy based on the bureaucratic or sectoral material interests of Soviet leaders face the same explanatory challenge. Similarly, Kydd's discussion of costly signaling omits the issue of signals that demonstrate actors are paying high domestic costs in addition to taking international risks. The December 1988 Soviet arms reductions, for example, were in part a credible costly signal because Chief of the General Staff Akhromeev opposed these reductions and resigned when they were announced. This same example shows that domestically costly signals can be a double-edged sword: they indicate that a leader is acting despite paying a domestic price but they also indicate that the policy may change if the opposition comes to power. Akhromeev, in fact, sympathized with the top officials who attempted a coup against Gorbachev in August 1991, and he hanged himself when the coup failed. Thus, in order to put trust in Gorbachev, U.S. officials had to be convinced not only that Gorbachev was

15. Chapter 2, p. 70. Tarasenko leaves unclear whether this refers to the potential costs of assuming the GDR's debts, the approximately DM 20 billion that West Germany paid to the Soviet Union to compensate for the troop withdrawal, or both. His emphasis on Soviet financial incentives alone is insufficient to explain the non-use of force in 1989, however. As late as October 31, 1989, by which time the Soviet Union had allowed substantial liberalization in Eastern Europe, Gorbachev was "astonished" to be informed by GDR leader Egon Krenz that the GDR owed the West $26.5 billion, $12.1 billion of which had accrued in 1989. Philip Zelikow and Condoleezza Rice, *Germany Unified and Europe Transformed: A Study in Statecraft* (Cambridge: Harvard University Press, 1995), 87. By this time, however, Gorbachev had already allowed independence movements in Eastern Europe to gather such momentum that they could be stopped only by a forceful crackdown. Financial pressures may offer a stronger explanation for why Gorbachev accepted German unification largely on Western terms, as the Soviet economy was in worse condition by mid-1990. Still, most of Gorbachev's advisers and many Western officials as well felt that Gorbachev could have demanded more policy concessions from the West as a condition of the withdrawal of Soviet troops from Eastern Germany.

16. Wohlforth, "Realism and the End of the Cold War," 112.

sincere in his stated intentions to reform Soviet domestic and foreign policies but also that he could succeed in maintaining his policies despite domestic opposition.

A second limitation is that arguments relying on costly signaling better explain changes in U.S. policies than those in Soviet policies. It is clear, from both Kydd's analysis and Chapter 5 herein (Chollet and Goldgeier), that numerous costly Soviet signals eventually convinced U.S. leaders that they could be confident of lasting Soviet policy changes. The prior emergence of Soviet trust in the United States is much harder to explain, however. The Soviet Union made more than "a few" unrequited cooperative gestures— Soviet concessions on INF and unilateral Soviet reductions in conventional forces came well before any comparable concessions by the United States. Soviet concessions began, in fact, at a time when U.S. leaders were using harsh rhetoric regarding the Soviet Union and funding anti-Soviet rebels in Afghanistan, Angola, and Cambodia. Moreover, in the talks on German unification, the Soviet Union assented to German unification on the basis of essentially unenforceable U.S. promises not to exploit Soviet weakness (and indeed some Russian leaders later felt that the NATO alliance violated these promises when it admitted new members in the late 1990s). Officials in the United States and Germany were in fact surprised that the Soviet Union did not bargain harder to keep Germany out of NATO, as Gorbachev's bureaucracy urged.[17] Because Soviet trust of the United States cannot be explained by costly signaling by the United States, the full weight of realist explanations falls on realist arguments that Soviet material decline forced policy concessions or, as in Kydd's account, on some combination of material decline and ideational change.

A third limitation of realist accounts is that they suggest several counterfactual claims that are not entirely convincing. Wohlforth's explanation implies that the Soviet Union might have used force to keep the Warsaw Pact

17. For example, the Endgame transcript in Chapter 2, p. 60, shows that Robert Zoellick asked Soviet officials, "Why at a given point did you not take one of the steps that you might have taken to separate Germany and the United States? For example, on NATO it could have been a very delicate position that would have caused us terrible difficulty if you had said, 'All right, Germany can be in NATO but . . . not part of the integrated military command' . . . that would have caused a very difficult problem in U.S.-German relations." Brooks and Wohlforth argue that this option could have been trumped by Western contingency plans to withdraw unilaterally from occupation rights in Western Germany. It is possible that economic pressures and Western unity (if maintained) would have forced other Soviet leaders to come around to Gorbachev's accommodating view of unification, but it is clear that almost no Soviet leaders were as forthcoming as Gorbachev at the time that he made key concessions.

together in 1989 if the Soviet economy had not been declining. It is plausible, however, that Soviet leaders would have refrained from force even if their economy had been growing. As discussed below, Soviet restraint was a function not only of economic decline but also of Soviet leaders' growing belief, in part from their experiences in Afghanistan, that the use of force was not an effective way to achieve political goals.[18] In addition, many Soviet leaders only belatedly came to believe that subsidies to Eastern Europe made the region a net drain on the Soviet economy. More convincing is the realist argument that nuclear weapons made control of Eastern Europe less important to Soviet security. Yet this raises a further counterfactual question: if material factors fully or greatly explained Soviet restraint in 1989, why didn't the Soviet Union abandon the Warsaw Pact in the mid-to-late 1970s when the Soviet Union already had nuclear parity and high oil prices made Soviet energy subsidies to Eastern Europe a "serious problem"?[19] Conversely, couldn't the Soviet Union have muddled through for another five or ten years in the late 1980s and early 1990s while sustaining Brezhnev's and Andropov's policies, since the sharpest Soviet economic declines arose after Gorbachev initiated reforms?[20]

Despite plausible evidence presented in Brooks and Wohlforth's chapter that Soviet economic decline started earlier in the 1980s than previously suspected, it is by no means clear that the material conditions Gorbachev faced were so different from those confronting Andropov or Chernenko a few years earlier that they compelled changes in foreign policy as radical as those that Gorbachev introduced. Moreover, it is clear that the greatest drag on the Soviet economy was the inefficiency of central planning; the defense burden (even at 20 percent or more of GNP) was a distant second, and the costs of subsidies to the empire were a distant third. Thus Gorbachev could have pursued economic reform at home while cutting the military modestly and maintaining the empire. More generally, decline can lead to various outcomes, including stagnation or lashing out, as well as retrenchment.[21] Some realists have agreed that their theories are indeterminate on the timing and nature of changes in Soviet policies, while still arguing that Soviet decline was a neces-

18. Bennett, *Condemned to Repetition?*

19. Brooks-Wohlforth chapter, citing Randall Stone, *Satellites and Commissars: Strategy and Conflict in the Politics of Soviet-Bloc Trade* (Princeton: Princeton University Press, 1996), 134.

20. Richard Ned Lebow and John Mueller, "Realism and the End of the Cold War," *International Security* 20, no. 2 (fall 1995): 185–86.

21. Ibid.

sary condition for Soviet retrenchment even if it was not a sufficient condition.[22] However, changes in the very factors that realists emphasize—the nuclear balance and the world economy—make it unclear whether decline was even a necessary condition for retrenchment, and they leave open a window of some fifteen to twenty years within which dramatic changes in Soviet foreign policies could have taken place.

Communicative Action and Soviet Foreign Policy Change

A second explanation of Soviet foreign policy change falls under what has been termed the "constructivist" approach to international relations. Unlike realists, who tend to assume that actors' preferences are relatively fixed and emphasize material constraints on these actors' behavior, constructivists argue that both material structures and ideational structures, or norms and shared ideas about causal relationships, constrain behavior. Constructivists maintain that actors and material structures are "mutually constituted," or that each shapes the other, and that actors' identities, preferences, and ideas are socially constructed through interactions with other actors as well as the material world (hence the label "constructivist"). Constructivists are thus interested in the processes through which actors' identities and preferences evolve, and in how actors create norms and how these in turn constrain actors' subsequent behavior.[23]

Thomas Risse has used one variant of constructivism, drawing on Jürgen Habermas's theory of communicative action, to explain the Soviet Union's surprisingly easy acceptance of German unification. Risse maintains that Soviet negotiations with the United States and Germany involved not only power-based strategic bargaining but also "mutual truth seeking with the aim of reaching a mutual understanding based on a reasoned consensus." This required that actors "be prepared to change their own views of the world, their interests, and sometimes even their identities."[24] In this view, Soviet and Western leaders directed their arguments toward testing whether their understandings of causal

---

22. Wohlforth, "Reality Check," 661.
23. Alexander Wendt, "Anarchy Is What States Make of It: The Social Construction of Power Politics," *International Organization* 46, no. 2 (spring 1992): 391–425; Peter J. Katzenstein, ed., *The Culture of National Security: Norms and Identity in World Politics* (New York: Columbia University Press, 1996).
24. Thomas Risse, "'Let's Argue!' Communicative Action in World Politics," *International Organization* 54, no. 1 (winter 2000): 1–2. See also Thomas Risse, "The Cold War's Endgame and German Unification," *International Security* 21, no. 4 (spring 1997): 158–85.

relationships were correct and determining which norms should apply to the issues under consideration. This kind of "argumentative rationality," Risse states, "implies that the participants in a discourse are open to being persuaded by the better argument and that relationships of power and social hierarchies recede into the background."[25]

Unlike the realist perspective, this interpretation echoes the Endgame conference participants in placing great weight on personal interactions and deliberations between leaders as a means of building trust and mutual understanding. Risse gives two primary examples from the negotiations on reunification that he interprets as reflecting argumentative rationality. In the first, Secretary of State Baker's arguments, together with his assurances that NATO would not extend its jurisdiction eastward, appear to have convinced Gorbachev that Soviet interests would be better served by a Germany anchored in NATO than by a united Germany outside NATO without the reassuring and restraining presence of U.S. troops on its soil. In the second, President Bush invoked the norm of self-determination to argue that a united Germany should have the right to decide which alliance to join, and Gorbachev agreed. This seemingly off-the-cuff concession created "a palpable feeling . . . among Gorbachev's advisers of almost physically distancing themselves from their leaders' words."[26] This suggests, consistent with both Risse's argument and Zubok's evidence on Gorbachev's susceptibility to ideational appeals, that Gorbachev was far more willing than his advisers to make concessions on German unification.[27]

Risse's interpretation is indeed consistent with considerable evidence on the unification process. Soviet leaders clearly did change their views on German unification in the course of the negotiations, with Gorbachev and Shevardnadze leading the way. This fits the expectation that those with the greatest personal contacts in a deliberative process should have changed their views the most, and it is consistent with additional process-tracing evidence, such as complaints by individuals not personally involved in the negotiations that their leaders had "gone soft" in the face of the other side's

---

25. Risse, "Let's Argue," 6–7.
26. Ibid., 27, quoting Zelikow and Rice, *Germany Unified*, 276–78.
27. Brooks and Wohlforth's argument, in contrast, suggests that any Soviet leader would have ultimately been pushed into similar concessions. This is possible, though it is also likely that either West Germany would have succumbed to Soviet pressure or that a new crisis in East Germany would have been necessary to convince other Soviet leaders of the need to back down. The fact remains that at the outset Gorbachev was far more willing to compromise on unification than any other top Soviet leader, including Shevardnadze.

arguments.[28] Risse is also persuasive in arguing that on power considerations alone, despite their economic crisis and the high costs of using force directly, Soviet leaders had several realistic options for bargaining harder. These included pushing Germany to choose between unification or NATO membership, insisting on the Soviet Union's legal rights as an Allied power, and using the 300,000 Soviet troops in the GDR as leverage. As Risse notes, these options were in fact raised by the Soviet bureaucracy, and as Robert Zoellick recounts in the Endgame conference, these options, particularly the first, would have put the United States in a "terrible difficulty," but Gorbachev did not pursue them.[29] By forgoing these options, Gorbachev set in motion a considerable domestic political backlash for having allowed the unification on relatively easy terms of a former adversary that the Soviet public, the Communist Party, and the foreign policy bureaucracy still vividly associated with Nazi aggression in World War II.

Risse's argument is also consistent with the fact that Soviet leaders managed to wring difficult concessions from the West, getting Germany to reaffirm existing borders and accept restrictions on NATO forces in the former GDR, and eliciting commitments from the United States to transform NATO from an anti-Soviet alliance to a European security organization with ties to the Soviet Union. Finally, Risse rightly notes that the FRG's commitment of DM 20 billion to facilitate the withdrawal of Soviet troops took place in September 1990, after Soviet leaders had already agreed to the basic outlines of unification, so it was more of a sweetener than a critical inducement in the unification agreement.

The use of communicative action theory to explain Soviet concessions on German unification faces several sharp limitations, however. Foremost among these is that it sets aside the balance of power between the actors involved. As Risse acknowledges, but does not sufficiently take into account, the theory's assumption of equal power was clearly not met in the negotiations on unification. The United States and Western Germany held such a preponderance of economic and military power that they did not need to wield this power ostentatiously. The Western leaders' conscious decision to avoid gloating

28. Several Soviet analysts interviewed by this author in Moscow in the spring of 1992, for example, complained that Soviet leaders had made unnecessary and unreciprocated concessions to the United States on Afghanistan.

29. Risse, "Let's Argue," 24; see also Zoellick's remarks on this point in the second session of the Endgame transcripts, Chapter 2.

in public over Soviet concessions, which Risse emphasizes, hardly constitutes evidence of equal power or equal treatment. Risse does note that Baker at one point threatened that the Western allies might unilaterally waive their rights in Germany as Allied powers if the Soviet Union did not go along, but more generally, he overlooks the issue of the GDR's debts to the West and the constraints these placed on the Soviet Union. As William Wohlforth has argued, such considerations make possible a very different interpretation of Gorbachev's concession to Bush. Gorbachev may have realized the potential economic and other benefits of cooperation and the "massive costs" of resisting the firm and united position of Bonn and Washington, and he may have consequently conceded preemptively. The balance of power was likely to become even more unfavorable over time, and the Soviet Union would eventually have had to concede at perhaps even greater international and domestic costs.[30]

The overall outcome—that Soviet preferences changed dramatically while U.S. preferences changed very little—was thus more consistent with realism than with communicative action theory. Contrary to the counterintuitive prediction of communicative action theory, as outlined by Risse, the materially weaker side was not disproportionately empowered by the process of mutual deliberation.[31] Not only were Soviet concessions of greater magnitude, they were essentially irrevocable. In contrast, the U.S. commitment not to extend NATO to the east was inherently difficult to enforce and in fact did not withstand the dissolution of the Soviet Union and the change of presidential administrations in the United States. Gorbachev had traded the bird in his own hand for one in the hands of Bush's then unknown successors. Overall, the process appears to have more in common with the "Stockholm syndrome," whereby individuals lacking any alternative come to trust those who hold power over them, than with a Habermasian dialogue of argumentative rationality.

A second limitation of Risse's approach is that it underemphasizes the cognitive processes through which individuals change their ideas, preferences, and identities. Risse rejects the view that "the elementary unit of social life is the individual human action," which he equates with rational choice theory. He embraces instead the argument that "human agents do not exist independently from their social environment and its collectively shared systems of meanings" and that there are "properties of structures and of agents that can-

30. Wohlforth, "Reality Check," 667.
31. Risse, "Let's Argue," 18.

not be reduced to or collapsed into each other."[32] This ignores a third view, based on developments in cognitive and social psychology, which focuses on the beliefs and social attributions of individuals and the *cognitive* rather than "rational" processes through which these beliefs change. Cognitive dynamics in this view form one set of causal mechanisms linking individuals to social and material structures.[33] For example, theories of social psychology and cognition suggest that we should have expected Soviet leaders' views to be more influenced by their own direct experiences and by interlocutors seen as being friendly toward the Soviet Union, such as European socialist leaders, than by adversaries, and there is some evidence that this was indeed the case.[34]

This point has empirical as well as theoretical and epistemological importance, for it shapes Risse's interpretation of the emergence of Soviet trust. For example, Risse notes the experimental finding from cognitive research that "the trustworthiness of the communicator as unbiased increases the persuasiveness of an argument during communication," but he does not point out the paradox that Soviet leaders apparently put trust in arguments made by the leaders of their long-term adversary. In addition, Risse does not offer any explanation for why Western arguments found a strikingly different reception from Gorbachev and Shevardnadze than from many other Soviet officials, including those who also participated personally in the negotiations. Both these puzzles might be explained through cognitive dynamics: we should expect the persuasiveness of communications to depend not only on the communicator but on preexisting variations in the individual beliefs of those receiving the message, and we should not expect a few hours of negotiations to have a stronger effect on beliefs than a lifetime of experience. These observations bring us to a third explanation of the emergence of Soviet trust that focuses on cognitive dynamics.

---

32. Ibid., 5. Yet if individual beliefs and shared beliefs cannot be spatially or temporally separated, as Risse seems to be suggesting, then endogeneity problems are insurmountable and traditional causal theorizing becomes impossible. On these issues, Risse cites Emanuel Adler, "Seizing the Middle Ground: Constructivism in World Politics," *European Journal of International Relations* 3, no. 3 (1997): 319–63, but my own reading of Adler's work is that he is calling for bringing in cognitive dynamics to constructivist theory. The middle ground of which Adler writes is not a blurring between individual beliefs and social structures, but a set of middle-ground hypotheses on causal mechanisms relating individuals to structures, and structures to individuals, but sequentially, rather than simultaneously. For a similar view on the need for constructivist theorists to focus on causal mechanisms, see Jeffrey Checkel, "The Constructivist Turn in International Relations Theory," *World Politics* 50, no. 2 (January 1998): 324–48.

33. One example of a noncognitive mechanism linking actors to structures is evolutionary selection. Other mechanisms, such as collective action dynamics, involve both individual beliefs and social norms.

34. Archie Brown notes that two of the most important of Gorbachev's foreign interlocutors were Willy Brandt and Felipe Gonzalez, both socialists. Brown, *Gorbachev Factor*, 116.

Cognitive Dynamics and the Puzzles of 1989–1990

Like Risse's interpretation, cognitive explanations fall under the broad ambit of constructivism because they focus on the formation and change of identities, beliefs, and preferences. Cognitive accounts also critique realism for treating preferences as structurally determined and relatively fixed.[35] Yet cognitive theories also critique communicative action theory for its relative neglect of cognitive dynamics as the causal mechanisms through which ideas change. For cognitive theorists, overlapping interests, costly signaling, and reasoned argument are insufficient to establish trust. Instead, "states often fail to cooperate even when their preferences overlap, because policymakers draw incorrect inferences about the motives and intentions of others."[36] In this view, because belief systems are resistant to change, the emergence of trust requires either more costly signaling than a rational actor account would suggest or an autonomous change in worldview that revises the image of another state as an adversary.[37] The slow emergence of U.S. trust in the Soviet Union fits the former pattern, while the more sudden and dramatic outbreak of Soviet trust in the United States fits the latter.

Three cognitive dynamics, drawn from experimental research in personality and social psychology, are particularly important to the emergence of trust and to Soviet decisions on the non-use of force in 1989.[38] First, according to

35. Cognitive explanations are particularly useful at explaining interpersonal differences in beliefs and "lessons learned" based on prior beliefs and the information to which individuals are exposed. They can also address intertemporal variations in beliefs, whether these beliefs are individual and idiosyncratic or widely shared, if changes in beliefs were out of proportion to those in material indicators and in the views of disinterested experts. Thus, Wohlforth's argument that Soviet leaders in the late 1980s widely agreed on the "fact" of economic decline does not eliminate an explanatory role for cognitive theory, since the consensus of just a few years earlier was quite different, and since there was limited consensus on the policy implications of Soviet economic decline.

36. Larson, *Anatomy of Mistrust*, 3. Misperceptions can also bolster cooperation and trust. Gorbachev, for example, wrongly expected up until late 1989 that reformist socialist governments, much like his own, would emerge and achieve legitimacy and stability throughout Eastern Europe. This gave him the confidence to make concessions he might not have made otherwise. See Philip Zelikow's statement in the Endgame transcripts, Chapter 2, pp. 61–64; see also Lévesque, *Enigma of 1989*, 3. Zubok, citing similar evidence, terms Gorbachev the "inadvertent liberator." Zubok, "New Evidence," 11, 13, 14.

37. Larson, *Anatomy of Mistrust*. Larson's theory, which emphasizes the necessity of repeated costly signals for the emergence of trust, fits the slow emergence of U.S. trust in the Soviet Union in the late 1980s, but it makes the emergence of Soviet trust in the United States harder to explain (Larson's case studies do not include the end of the Cold War, so she does not frame or address the puzzle of the emergence of Soviet trust of the United States under Gorbachev).

38. Robert Jervis, *Perception and Misperception in International Politics* (Princeton: Princeton University Press, 1976); Yaacov Y.I. Vertzberger, *The World in Their Minds: Information Processing, Cognition, and Perception in Foreign Policy Decision Making* (Stanford: Stanford University Press, 1990); Richard Nisbett and Lee Ross, *Human Inference: Strategies and Shortcomings of Social Judgment* (Englewood Cliffs, N.J.: Prentice-Hall, 1980); Larson, *Anatomy of Mistrust*; and Bennett, *Condemned to Repetition?*

attribution theory, individuals tend to view the negative or threatening behavior of perceived adversaries as reflecting these actors' inherent natures or dispositions, while they interpret the positive or accommodating behavior of
adversaries as being motivated or forced by situational pressures. Thus, when
one actor undertakes a costly signal in order to demonstrate trustworthiness,
that signal might be misinterpreted as a trick, an attempt to create a respite to
build up toward future aggression, or a concession forced by unfavorable
material circumstances. As Goldgeier and Chollet demonstrate, U.S. observers
commonly applied all three of these interpretations to early concessions by
Gorbachev, so repeated costly signals were necessary to convince U.S. leaders
of Gorbachev's sincerity. At the same time, attribution theory deepens the
puzzle of how Soviet leaders came to trust the United States at the very time
that the Reagan administration was pursuing hard-line policies vis-à-vis the
Soviet Union.

Second, both formative experiences and recent, vivid experiences shape
individuals' causal beliefs and their views of other actors. The lasting influence
of formative experiences can lead to similar views among a generation of individuals sharing experiences of a dramatic event early in their lives, such as a
war or revolution. In Soviet politics, for example, analysts have differentiated
the cohorts of the revolutionary generation, the World War II generation, and
the post-Stalinist generation (which has been variously labeled the generation
of 1956, the date of Khrushchev's "secret speech" denouncing Stalinism, or
the 1960s generation, reflecting the reformist currents that led to the 1968
uprising in Czechoslovakia). This does not imply unanimity within generational cohorts, however, as individuals' prior beliefs and personal experiences
vary greatly, just as some American college students "missed" the radicalism of
campus life in the 1960s. In addition, individuals' beliefs are influenced by
experiences that are direct, recent, and vivid, or evocative of some emotional
content. Depending on their content, such recent experiences can reinforce or
change beliefs derived from formative experiences. Cognitive theories thus
give some weight to both personal interactions, like those between leaders at
the Malta summit, and to the filtering effects of formative experiences and
their attendant beliefs.

Third, individuals' belief systems resist change in the face of discrepant
information but at the same time individuals seek "cognitive consistency"
among their beliefs. Because belief systems are hierarchically organized, central

beliefs are the most resistant to change; but when such beliefs do change, many subordinate beliefs are likely to change with them. This provides a limiting case for attribution theory: if sufficient costly signals or other discrepant information eventually changes the view of another actor as an adversary, then a rapid, gestalt-like change in beliefs and increase in trust is possible.

Drawing upon these dynamics, the cognitive explanation for the emergence of Soviet trust is as follows.[39] Gorbachev, Shevardnadze, and other "new thinkers" had indirect but formative experiences—particularly their witnessing the events in Hungary in 1956 and in Czechoslovakia in 1968—that made them skeptical of the efficacy and morality of using force. This aversion to force was reinforced in the 1980s by the ongoing and costly failure of Soviet and Soviet-backed military interventions in Afghanistan, Angola, and Cambodia and the mixed results of the internal crackdown in Poland in 1980–81. At the same time, the international reactions to these Soviet interventions led new thinkers to believe that the predominant response to the use or threat of force would not be bandwagoning, or acquiescence to the demands of the actor threatening force, but balancing, or concerted resistance to and alliance formation against the threatening actor. New thinkers also became convinced that the economic and security costs of Soviet allies in the Third World and even the Warsaw Pact outweighed the benefits these allies provided to the Soviet Union.

Changes in these tactical beliefs could not allow the Soviet Union to disentangle itself from its costly and failing foreign policies, however, until Gorbachev and others changed their core beliefs on the incompatibility of U.S. and Soviet interests and the centrality of class struggle in world politics. Gorbachev's key conceptual innovation was that he changed his view of the United States as an immutable adversary despite ongoing U.S. behavior—the Reagan doctrine, a massive military buildup, and harsh rhetoric regarding the Soviet Union—that seemingly validated this adversarial image. Gorbachev justified this change by arguing that security must be mutual, which constituted recognition of the security dilemma described above. This allowed him to portray U.S. policies as a reaction to the Soviet Union's aggressive policies

---

39. This draws on Bennett, *Condemned to Repetition?* 248–49. For other cognitive accounts of the change in Soviet foreign policy thinking, see Stein, "Political Learning by Doing"; Robert G. Herman, "Identity, Norms, and National Security: The Soviet Foreign Policy Revolution and the End of the Cold War," in Katzenstein, *The Culture of National Security;* and Jeffrey Checkel, *Ideas and International Political Change: Soviet/Russian Behavior and the End of the Cold War* (New Haven: Yale University Press, 1997).

in the late 1970s and early 1980s, rather than a reflection of the inherently aggressive nature of capitalism. In this view, U.S. intransigence provided an argument in favor of easing the security dilemma through costly signaling, rather than a confirmation of Soviet hard-liners' views of the United States. In other words, in this case cognitive consistency trumped attribution theory. This allowed Gorbachev to sustain a policy of essentially unrequited concessions, despite considerable opposition to the new thinking, until about the time of the Malta summit, when U.S. responses became more reciprocal. Soviet leaders viewed Bush's personal assurances at Malta that he wanted Gorbachev and per-estroika to succeed as a long-awaited vindication of their strategy.

This interpretation has the advantage of fitting considerable process-tracing evidence on the emergence of new thinking. Peripheral or tactical Soviet beliefs on balancing versus bandwagoning and the efficacy of force changed first. More central beliefs on the nature of world politics and that of the United States changed only later, starting in about 1986, after changes in tactical beliefs alone failed to bring the Soviet Union out of its intellectual and foreign policy cul-de-sac. This fits the predictions of cognitive theory on how change takes place in hierarchical belief systems. Moreover, Soviet officials' statements at the Endgame conference and in memoirs and interviews indi-cate, as cognitive theory predicts, the frequent use of personal and historical analogies in decision making. To take one example from the Endgame tran-scripts, Bessmertnykh reports that Shevardnadze favored a tough response to Iraq's invasion of Kuwait because he drew an analogy between Kuwait's vul-nerability to aggression and the vulnerability of his native republic of Georgia, which like Kuwait was small, relatively defenseless, and historically subject to invasion and domination.

Individuals' beliefs also appear to have varied as much by their personal experiences and the information to which they were exposed as by their mate-rial or bureaucratic interests. Defense Minister Yazov, for example, shared Gorbachev's conviction that the use of force against demonstrators in Eastern Europe could neither reverse the collapse of governments there nor serve Soviet interests at acceptable cost, and as the Endgame transcripts indicate, he never requested authorization to use force.[40] The fact that new thinking penetrated

40. See also the interview of Yazov in RFE/RL Newsline, vol. 4, no. 6, January 10, 2000, where he states that "there was nothing else that could be done in 1989 . . . we had to return home some day. The time had come."

across Soviet institutions, even against the apparent material interests of some of these institutions, helps explain why a rag-tag coalition of Soviet intellectuals and party reformers won out against the entrenched military-industrial-party (MIP) complex that had dominated Soviet politics since Stalin's time. Finally, the cognitive explanation fits the timing of changes in Soviet policy. It is hard to imagine the peaceful dissolution of the Warsaw Pact taking place when Yury Andropov was the top Soviet leader, for example. As Georgy Arbatov recounts,

The tragic events in Hungary in late October and early November of 1956 made a deep impression on Andropov, for he found himself at their epicenter. . . . He received a flow of reports about the activities of the rebels, about how mercilessly they settled scores with Communists, Party workers, and civil servants. He suffered a number of attacks himself. I knew that the events had caused the serious, life-long illness of his wife . . . and Andropov came under fire as he headed to the airport to meet Mikoyan. . . . the historic events created in him what people who know Andropov later called the Hungarian syndrome. This they defined as a guarded attitude toward domestic difficulties in the socialist countries. I interpret that to mean an excessive readiness to make very radical decisions to prevent these tensions from escalating into a severe crisis.[41]

As members of the "1956 generation" who viewed the Hungarian conflict from afar and with quite different emotions, Gorbachev, Shevardnadze, and other new thinkers were more averse to force and amenable to compromise.[42] Three top-level internal reports on mounting unrest in Eastern Europe in early 1989, for example, all ruled out the use of force.[43]

While the cognitive explanation resolves much of the indeterminacy of the realist explanation and adds explanatory power to other constructivist accounts, a focus on cognitive factors alone is incomplete. Cognitive arguments must necessarily be supplemented by organizational and governmental models that help identify how ideas are transmitted, why some ideas win out over others, and whose ideas matter.[44] In addition, more traditional material-

---

41. Georgy Arbatov, *The System: An Insider's Life in Soviet Politics* (New York: Times Books, 1992), 265–66.

42. Shevardnadze recounted in his memoirs that his formative views on the use of force were also shaped by the violent suppression of a demonstration in the Georgian capital of Tbilisi in 1956. *The Future Belongs to Freedom*, 20, 21. He also states that his father's short-term imprisonment by the NKVD was the "first and greatest shock" of his childhood (12).

43. See Jacques Lévesque, "Soviet Approaches to Eastern Europe at the Beginning of 1989," *Cold War International History Bulletin*, no. 12/13 (fall/winter 2001): 49–52. A fourth report, by the KGB, remains unavailable.

44. Jack Levy raises this point in his critique of learning theory. "Learning and Foreign Policy: Sweeping a Conceptual Minefield," *International Organization* 48, no. 2 (spring 1994): 287–89 and 299–302. See also Bennett, *Condemned to Repetition?* 98–112, and Sarah Mendelson, *Changing Course: Ideas, Politics, and the Soviet Withdrawal from Afghanistan* (Princeton: Princeton University Press, 1998), for an account that emphasizes domestic politics with a secondary role for cognitive theory.

ist models of domestic politics were not always wrong in the Soviet case: sometimes policy stands did follow from bureaucratic roles or positions. In the Endgame transcripts, for example, Tarasenko recounts how Shevardnadze had to fight against opposition by his German experts, European bureaus, and the military on the issue of liberalizing Soviet policies in Eastern Europe. Tarasenko also notes that Shevardnadze had to overcome the resistance of his Middle Eastern bureau, which had long ties to Iraq, to be able to help the United States confront Saddam Hussein.

Finally, the Soviet development of trust in the United States is still rather puzzling without taking Soviet material decline into account. It is hard to see how Gorbachev's conversion to new thinking could have forestalled stronger opposition from the MIP complex if the officials in this complex had not been convinced that change was necessary to reverse the Soviet Union's material decline. It is even possible that to some extent the development of trust in the United States was a psychological defense mechanism to reduce anxiety over policy changes forced upon Soviet leaders by material necessity. Similarly, a belief that balancing behavior would prevail was perhaps to some extent a convenient and anxiety-reducing way of believing that Soviet foreign policy retrenchment would undermine the anti-Soviet coalition and allow greater security at a lower cost.[45]

Soviet Domestic Politics and Soviet Foreign Policy Change

Because realist theorists failed to anticipate the dramatic changes in Soviet foreign policy and because realist theories appear indeterminate even as after-the-fact explanations of these events, scholars have proposed explanations based on developments in Soviet domestic politics. In some senses, a focus on Soviet domestic politics deepens the puzzle of how Soviet trust emerged despite the presence of a powerful Soviet MIP complex with a material interest in perpetuating the Cold War. In other respects, evidence on what individuals in this complex actually thought about the events of 1989 and 1990 helps illuminate the relative importance of material and ideational factors in explaining why this potential opposition coalition was not more mobilized or successful. Four models merit consideration here: Matthew Evangelista's model of domestic-international interactions, Jack Snyder's modernization theory, the

45. Wohlforth, *Elusive Balance*.

bureaucratic politics model, and the two-level games model.[46] I discuss each in turn, followed by an analysis of the views of Gorbachev's key opponents.

Domestic explanations all start from the assumption that international factors are indeterminate in many contexts. Matthew Evangelista argues that, depending on its domestic politics, a state experiencing relative decline but at the same time facing high threats abroad can seek allies, engage in a policy of appeasement, divert its dwindling resources to an arms race, or wage preemptive war (the last option, he notes, is neither acceptable nor necessary for states having and facing nuclear weapons).[47] Applying this observation to U.S.-Soviet relations, he suggests a model in which Soviet "moderates" believe that U.S. hostility is contingent on Soviet behavior, while "hard-liners" argue that U.S. hostility is inherent in the nature of the United States as a capitalist country. For moderates to prevail they have to demonstrate U.S. reciprocation of Soviet concessions. Consistent with costly signaling theory, Evangelista argues that U.S. concessions would have the strongest effect if they took place when the Soviet Union was economically weak. In this circumstance, concessions by the United States could not be attributed to Soviet strength or American weakness, and Soviet moderates would want to cut defense spending while Soviet hard-liners would agree on the need for a breathing space to rebuild the defense industrial base. The difficulty with this model, Evangelista notes, is that it is hard to test because historically "at those critical junctures when moderates managed to initiate gestures of moderation in Soviet foreign policy against the resistance of hard-liners, the United States declined to reciprocate" (though arguably the Malta summit is the clearest exception to this pattern).[48]

Similarly, Jack Snyder has argued that hard-line U.S. policies help Soviet doves when Soviet hawks are in power, and they help Soviet hawks when Soviet doves are in power. Both authors face the problem of explaining how

46. A fifth domestic politics model argues that the Soviet Union was better able to trust the United States than vice-versa because the United States was a liberal democracy with a more transparent government. Daniel Deudney and G. John Ikenberry, "The International Sources of Soviet Change," *International Security* 16, no. 3 (winter 1991/92): 78. This may have been a factor, but it does not explain why Soviet trust did not emerge earlier, since the United States was always democratic, and it overlooks the existence of hard-line factions prominent in the Reagan administration at the very time that the Soviet Union became more trusting.

47. Matthew Evangelista, "Internal and External Constraints on Grand Strategy: The Soviet Case," in Richard Rosecrance and Arthur Stein, eds., *The Domestic Bases of Grand Strategy* (Ithaca: Cornell University Press, 1993), 163–64.

48. Ibid., 173. On this point, Evangelista cites Jack Snyder, "International Leverage on Soviet Domestic Change," *World Politics* 42 (October 1989): 15, but it is worth noting that Snyder expressed this view prior to the Malta summit.

Gorbachev was able to sustain domestic support for a policy of repeated Soviet concessions up through 1989 despite limited reciprocation by the United States. Snyder argues that, contrary to his generalization, firm U.S. policies in 1987–88 helped Soviet doves because U.S. policies were viewed as a reaction to earlier Soviet aggression. This presupposes the kind of cognitive change discussed above, however, since a change in beliefs was first necessary for Soviet leaders, despite the tendencies predicted by attribution theory, to view U.S. behavior as a reaction to Soviet transgressions rather than an indication of American intransigence.[49]

Jack Snyder has also proposed a second domestic model, based on modernization theory, to help explain changes in Soviet foreign policy. In this view, the evolution of the Soviet economy from extensive development (building more of the same basic industrial goods) to intensive development (building more sophisticated and information-intensive goods) required a shift in the dominant Soviet coalition from the MIP complex to light industry and the intelligentsia. This economic transition also required better relations with the West, both to allow high-technology trade and to permit resources to be diverted from military production.

This explanation fits much of Gorbachev's thinking on economic reform, but it begs three questions. First, how did a rag-tag coalition of the intelligentsia and light industry win out over the powerful MIP coalition that had dominated Soviet politics for four decades? Second, why couldn't Gorbachev have built a stronger coalition by pursuing economic reform at home while appeasing the MIP coalition with a continuation of hard-line foreign policies, as Khrushchev attempted in the 1950s and China has done in the 1980s and 1990s? Snyder suggests that one answer is that Gorbachev learned from Khrushchev's fall from power but this brings learned ideas back in. Third, why was the MIP coalition unable to regain power in the face of limited U.S. reciprocation of Soviet concessions? In fact, Snyder, writing in 1987, predicted that the resurgence of the MIP coalition was more likely if Gorbachev's reforms did not improve economic performance and if a hostile international environment persisted, including U.S. efforts to deploy missile defenses, Eastern European demands for autonomy, and losses by Soviet allies in counterinsurgency wars in Afghanistan, Angola, and Ethiopia. As it turned out,

49. Jack Snyder, "The Gorbachev Revolution: A Waning of Soviet Expansionism?" *International Security* 12, no. 3 (winter 1987/88): 93–131.

these conditions were overfulfilled within two years, but the MIP coalition rebounded only moderately in 1990–91 as it pushed Gorbachev to scale back his reform efforts. The MIP coalition also subsequently failed to win power in its feeble coup attempt in August 1991.[50]

Similar puzzles bedevil more traditional bureaucratic politics models, which do not draw on modernization theory but which point to essentially the same MIP coalition members as likely opponents of Gorbachev's foreign policy concessions. There is indeed evidence in the Endgame transcripts and elsewhere that the military, the KGB, and elements of the foreign ministry were skeptical of Gorbachev's foreign policy concessions. On the basis of the bureaucratic politics model alone, however, it remains unclear why the seemingly powerful MIP coalition did not constrain Gorbachev more tightly.[51]

A fourth model, focusing on the "two-level games" that statespersons play in balancing domestic and international pressures, somewhat alleviates the puzzle of Soviet trust. The two-level game model argues that leaders often use domestic constraints to win concessions from international audiences ("I'd like to accommodate you, Mikhail, but the Congress won't let me"), and international constraints to win concessions from domestic audiences ("I agree with you, Senator, but the Russians will never go for that").[52] This allows leaders to discount rhetoric by their foreign counterparts that is intended for domestic consumption. Thus, when Bush met privately with Gorbachev just before the election year of 1988 began, he told Gorbachev that he wanted to improve relations but that Gorbachev would have to discount the harsh public statements that he would have to make to win the support of conservatives in his party and get elected. Gorbachev later called this "the most important talk Bush and I ever had," and he frequently referred to the conversation to assuage his colleagues when they complained of Bush's antagonistic public statements.[53]

Still, the overall puzzle remains: why wasn't Gorbachev's conservative opposition more mobilized and successful? Four factors are relevant here: the

50. Ibid. For a more detailed analysis of Snyder's argument, see Bennett, *Condemned to Repetition?* 54–58.

51. For additional evidence that fits the bureaucratic politics model, see Carolyn McGiffert Ekedahl and Melvin A. Goodman, *The Wars of Eduard Shevardnadze* (University Park: Pennsylvania State University Press, 1997), 77, 93, 159.

52. Robert Putnam, "Diplomacy and Domestic Politics: The Logic of Two-Level Games," *International Organization* 42, no. 3 (summer 1988): 427–60.

53. Michael Beschloss and Strobe Talbott, *At the Highest Levels: The Inside Story of the End of the Cold War* (Boston: Little, Brown, 1993), 3–4.

power of the office of the general secretary, Gorbachev's skill as a political entrepreneur, the fact that key leaders of the MIP coalition recognized the depth of the Soviet Union's material decline, and the fact that MIP coalition leaders shared many of the same lessons that new thinkers had drawn from recent and formative experiences regarding the limitations of using military force. The latter two variables demonstrate how the potential opposition coalition was divided internally, and not greatly opposed to much of the new thinking, rather than being either vehemently opposed to or forcefully overcome by the materially weak coalition of new thinkers.

There is considerable debate over what Gorbachev learned and when he learned it, but there is a strong consensus that the position of general secretary gave him enormous power over personnel and policies and that he concealed his agenda and presented it in different terms to different audiences to achieve his goals. The noted Soviet expert Archie Brown, for example, has argued that Gorbachev was by far the most reformist member of the Politburo that voted him into power, and that Gorbachev waited to introduce key reforms until he could replace conservative Politburo members with his own reformist allies, including Shevardnadze and Yakovlev.[54] There are some indications from Politburo decisions, Soviet statements to Eastern European governments, and memoirs that Gorbachev had ruled out the use of force in Eastern Europe as early as 1986 or even 1985.[55] In this same period, however, Gorbachev's public statements kept the conservatives on board by denouncing U.S. imperialism and calling for the reinvigoration of the Soviet economy so that the Soviet Union could remain a great power.

Leaders of the MIP coalition were also reluctant to challenge Gorbachev's policies because they realized the dire straits of the Soviet economy. As Dmitry Yazov, Soviet minister of defense in the late 1980s, stated in a 1999 interview: "Thanks to [nuclear] parity, we could live in peace. But it seemed to me that we had to gradually come to agreement and to reduce, reduce, reduce, especially expensive weapons."[56] This fits the realist explanation, of course, but with the added proviso that this explanation had to work through the minds

---

54. Brown, *Gorbachev Factor.*
55. Ibid., 244; 248, 249; Shevardnadze, *The Future Belongs to Freedom,* 121.
56. Transcript of interview by Oleg Skvortsov, director of the Oral History Project at the Institute of General History, with Dmitry Yazov, March 11, 1999, Moscow, p. 24 (on file at the National Security Archive, Washington, D.C., and the Institute of General History, Moscow, 1999). Hereafter cited as "Skvortsov interviews."

and actions of specific Soviet leaders, which was not a foregone conclusion. Yazov, for example, had been promoted by Gorbachev over the heads of dozens of more senior officers, probably because Gorbachev found Yazov's views congenial, although Yazov later joined those who attempted to over-throw him in August 1991.

Even more striking is the fact that MIP leaders appear to have accepted much of the new thinking on the costs of using force, using many of the same historical analogies as Gorbachev and Shevardnadze. The MIP leaders were on the whole not convinced that they could trust the United States, but most believed that nuclear weapons guaranteed Soviet security, many believed that Eastern Europe was a burden on the Soviet economy, and in light of the ongo-ing failures in Afghanistan by 1989 most shared the new thinkers' aversion to using force. In fact, perhaps the most remarkable fact about 1989 is that *thus far no evidence has come to light that any top Soviet leader argued for using force in Europe in 1989, or that the military or security bureaucracies were asked for or vol-unteered operational plans for using force.* Of course, one cannot "prove a nega-tive," especially as the documentary evidence on this issue remains far from complete, but this conclusion is based not only on extant secondary sources, but on the published memoirs and interviews of key officials, declassified Soviet documents, and declassified documents from Eastern Europe.[57] In the Endgame transcripts, for example, Chernyaev states that

when I am asked, and when Gorbachev is asked, "What was your reaction to the fall of the Berlin Wall? Was it panic?" Some people think that there was panic in Moscow. Some people think there were plans to use tanks, that there were plans to let the troops out of the barracks. This did not happen, there was no panic. He saw that that was inevitable. People say, although I don't know whether that is true, that the Soviet troop commanders in Germany several times called Moscow and asked what they were sup-posed to do in this situation, but I know for a fact that Marshal [Dmitry] Yazov, who was defense minister at that time, never even asked Gorbachev that question. He couldn't afford to ask that question, because he knew what the answer would be, that Gorbachev would never allow any kind of use of Soviet troops that were at that time in Germany.[58]

Thus, while individual units may have asked for orders or perhaps even advocated the use of force, there is no evidence that such requests were trans-

57. An excellent and well-footnoted overview of many of these sources is Zubok, "New Evidence." Similar to the present argument, Zubok notes that even "those Gorbachev critics closely involved in security affairs (such as former KGB chief Vladimir Kryuchkov and Marshal Dmitry Yazov), conspicuously avoid blaming Gorbachev for the 'loss' of Central and Eastern Europe" (5).

58. Chapter 2, pp. 53–54.

lated into a comprehensive option for using force or that any such option was presented to the Politburo.

Perhaps most striking is the fact that, even in retrospect, those who joined the coup attempt against Gorbachev in 1991 and who therefore have political motivations for subsequently questioning his policy choices have not criticized the decision to refrain from using force in 1989. The conservative Politburo member Yegor Ligachev, for example, agreed in 1989 and even earlier that Soviet military intervention in Europe was not an option.[59] Similarly, Vladimir Kryuchkov, head of the KGB in the late 1980s, stated in an interview in 1998 that

in the 1950s–1960s, the use of force for resolving conflicts in those [Eastern European] or other countries was, I would say, not expedient, but possible. In the 1980s to use force became impossible, as in both Soviet society and the Eastern European countries there had taken place a deep change, which played out through the 1980s, producing a negative attitude toward such means of resolving conflicts. . . . the troops we had then in the GDR were fully prepared for the eventuality of resolving the problem by military means, but the qualitative change in the consciousness of people that I mentioned would not allow it.[60]

Finally, Yazov has also stated categorically that the use of force in 1989 was not possible and that because of "the political situation in Europe, even if Gorbachev had wanted to use force, it is not likely that it would have been expedient."[61]

These three leaders, and many others as well, were far more critical of Gorbachev for conceding too much in the negotiations on German unification and failing to obtain sufficient written guarantees of Soviet security and of formal limits on NATO's eastward expansion.[62] As the Endgame transcripts indicate, even Shevardnadze, ordinarily more liberal in his views than Gorbachev, was uneasy at the pace and conditions under which Gorbachev

---

59. Raymond L. Garthoff, *The Great Transition: American-Soviet Relations and the End of the Cold War* (Washington, D.C.: The Brookings Institution, 1994), 605 n. 161.

60. Skvortsov interview with Vladimir Kryuchkov, December 7, 1998, p. 3. In a separate interview, Kryuchkov praised János Kádár's "stabilization" of Hungary in 1956, but noted that in 1989 Hungary was beset by so many strong internal contradictions that it was impossible to manage them. Skvortsov interview with Kryuchkov, October 13, 1998, pp. 2–3. In other respects, Kryuchkov was harshly critical in these interviews of Gorbachev and Yakovlev for allowing the crisis in 1989 to emerge in the first place and for conceding to German unification without exacting sufficient benefits and security guarantees in return. He also stated that if there had been a leader like Andropov, the "tragic events in our government" would not have happened (October 13 interview, p. 26).

61. Skvortsov interview with Yazov, December 16, 1998, p. 21.

62. Skvortsov interviews with Kryuchkov, Boldin, Yazov, and Ligachev.

allowed unification to succeed. Gorbachev had sufficient power as general secretary to push this policy through in early 1990. By the end of 1990, however, a debate erupted over the "loss" of Eastern Europe, and Shevardnadze felt compelled to resign under pressure from hard-line factions. In this same time period, Gorbachev began making policy compromises with his conservative opponents as the Soviet Union itself faced secessionist pressures from the Baltic republics. German unification thus owes much to Gorbachev's personal views, his trust in the West, and his power as general secretary, while the non-use of force in 1989 was widely agreed upon by Soviet leaders who shared a reluctance to use force.

In short, standard domestic politics models based on material coalitions add surprisingly little independent force to explaining the puzzles of 1989–90. Organized opposition to Gorbachev's new thinking emerged only in late 1990 despite the shift in resources and power away from the MIP coalition that had begun much earlier. Gorbachev's power as general secretary helps explain this outcome, but equally important was the fact that the MIP coalition shared his awareness of relative Soviet decline and agreed to a large extent with his unwillingness to use force in Eastern Europe in the way that previous leaders had done in 1956 and 1968.

Conclusions

Few would dispute that international, relational, cognitive, and domestic factors all contributed to the remarkable events of 1989–90 and the emergence of Soviet trust. Anatoly Chernyaev's insightful opening statement at the Endgame conference captures this mix very well: "No one was going to attack us" (realism); "We relied less on the art of diplomacy and more on human relationships" (argumentative rationality); Gorbachev's "moral principles evolved over his entire life, and basically they boiled down to the rejection of violence" (cognitive learning); and "It is often said—with some truth—that Gorbachev's foreign policy . . . was based mostly on Gorbachev's domestic concerns" (domestic politics). Where scholars disagree is on the particular weight to be accorded to each factor and the mechanisms through which the various factors interacted. William Wohlforth has identified the broad outlines of an emerging consensus that synthesizes various accounts of the Cold War's end into four phases: material and social pressures, both domestic and international, provided an impetus for change; Gorbachev came to power with some initial ideas for reform but did not pursue ambitious reforms right away; as he gained in power and learned more radical ideas from his experiences on the job, his advisers, and his encounters with Western leaders, he instituted more dramatic policy changes; and his policy changes unleashed unintended consequences—the overthrow of socialist regimes in Europe, the rapid unification of Germany within NATO, and ultimately the dissolution of the Soviet Union itself—to which Gorbachev reacted with a mixture of new thinking and political expediency.[63]

The present analysis falls within these broad parameters, but makes more specific arguments about the mix of different variables and the counterfactual assertions they justify. It argues that stable nuclear deterrence and relative Soviet economic decline lessened the value of Eastern Europe to Soviet security and provided incentives for Soviet concessions, but that other options were open to Soviet leaders. This leads to the counterfactual assertion that without changing the material context, dramatic changes in Soviet foreign policy could have taken place any time from about 1973 (the rough date by which the Soviet Union attained nuclear parity and the time at which the spike in oil prices raised the opportunity cost of Soviet energy transfers to Eastern Europe) until about the mid-1990s (when cumulative decline would have forced changes). Second, argumentative rationality mattered less than either material decline or cognitive change but as Vladislav Zubok's chapter in this volume argues it mattered more to Gorbachev than to other Soviet leaders and his views carried great weight. This contributes to a second counterfactual claim: without Gorbachev, German unification on the terms achieved in 1990 was unlikely.

Third, cognitive change, including an aversion to force even in the Soviet military, is key to understanding the non-use of force in 1989. The corresponding counterfactual is that the change in thinking across the Soviet spectrum, though uneven, would have made the use of force unlikely in 1989 even if the Soviet economy had grown substantially in the late 1980s. Conversely, if the threat of Soviet force and the internal crackdown in Poland in 1980–81 and the Soviet intervention in Afghanistan in 1979 had been successful, it is likely that key Soviet officials and organizations would have favored the threat or use of force in 1989. Fourth, given the MIP coalition's awareness

63. Wohlforth, "Reality Check," 660.

of Soviet decline and its partial new thinking, the use of force in 1989 was
unlikely even if this coalition had come to power at that time. In other words,
even if several leaders other than Gorbachev had been in power, it is unlikely
that the Soviet Union would have used massive force to contain reformist and
independence movements in Eastern Europe (though some leaders, notably
Andropov, probably would have used force). At the same time, the MIP coalition differed greatly from Gorbachev in its views on the unification of
Germany, so that German unification on such pro-Western terms would have
been unlikely if Gorbachev had not been in power.

In short, the non-use of force in 1989 is attributable in a deep sense to
material conditions (the diminished strategic value of Eastern Europe in the
nuclear age) and in a proximate sense to shared ideas (inhibitions on the use of
force). The unification of Germany on Western terms, in contrast, is proxi-
mally attributable to Gorbachev's individual ideas and his power as general
secretary, as well as to economic constraints, and it took place despite the fact
that few in the bureaucracy fully shared Gorbachev's ideas on German unification. If scholars can move as new information becomes available toward a consensus that these are the relevant counterfactual questions, and perhaps even
narrow the range of disagreement on their answers, then we can gain confidence that we have explained the Cold War's end.

PART III
Debates

7 Gorbachev and the End of the Cold War: Different Perspectives on the Historical Personality

Vladislav M. Zubok

IT IS A PERENNIAL human illusion to attribute great events to great causes. Particularly during the past century scholars have tended to attribute transitions from one historical period to another to grand, impersonal forces—shifts in balance of power, inter-imperialist contradictions, revolutions, the rise of new ideologies and social movements, and so on. In the current scholarly climate the other extreme has become fashionable: to highlight the microlevels of history—the role and beliefs of "common people," incremental changes in social life, and power as a phenomenon of everyday life. As a result of these two trends, the view that history is shaped by "great men" is utterly discredited. Today, many historians would rather die than admit that the character of a personality in a position of power at a critical juncture can make a major difference in the course of history.

Among recent exceptions is the figure of Mikhail Sergeyevich Gorbachev. This energetic, handsome man with sparkling eyes and charming smile "did more than anyone else to end the Cold War between East and West," asserts British political scientist Archie Brown in his seminal study, *The Gorbachev Factor*. Yet his book deals more with the domestic field of Gorbachev's activities than with his foreign policy. And surprisingly, in discussing the reasons for Gorbachev's policies, Brown gives only slight attention to the character and personal traits of the last Soviet leader: Gorbachev is a "factor" in his study, not a human being in flesh and spirit.[1]

Perhaps this reluctance to address Gorbachev the person can be excused. It is indeed very hard to write about a living historical personality. Proximity warps our vision. But is it possible to evaluate recent history without evaluating a person who so dramatically influenced its course? It is worth quoting Anatoly Chernyaev, the most loyal and supportive of Gorbachev's assistants.

---

1. Archie Brown, *The Gorbachev Factor* (London: Oxford University Press, 1996), 317. An exception to the rule of downplaying the personality factor—focused on an earlier phase of the end of the Cold War—is Fred I. Greenstein, "Reagan and Gorbachev: What Difference Did They Make?" in William Wohlforth, ed., *Witnesses to the End of the Cold War* (Baltimore: Johns Hopkins University Press, 1996).

Gorbachev, he claims, "was not 'a great man' as far as a set of personal qualities was concerned." But he "fulfilled a great mission," and that is "more
important for history."[2] A more critical Dmitry Volkogonov provides another,
yet also remarkable estimate: Gorbachev "is a person of great mind, but with a
weak character. Without this paradox of personality it is hard to understand
him as a historical actor." Volkogonov writes that the "intellect, feelings, and
will of Gorbachev" left a unique imprint on the Soviet transition.[3]

The purpose of this chapter is to demonstrate in what ways Gorbachev's
less-than-great personality shaped the end of the Cold War. I proceed in three
sections. In the first, I discuss the standard explanations of the Cold War's end
that highlight structural changes in the international system, a structural
domestic crisis within the Soviet Union, and a radical shift of ideas in the
Soviet leadership, showing the important anomalies they all leave unexplained.
I then analyze Gorbachev's personality and character in general, revealing
what it was that set him apart from other leaders. In the third section, I assess
in detail how these personality and character traits influenced the ending of
the Cold War. The bottom line is that many of the most extraordinary aspects
of this remarkable series of events can *only* be understood by according primary importance to the Gorbachev *personality* factor.

The Standard Explanations—and Their Shortcomings

Realists argue that by the mid-1980s the distribution of capabilities shifted
drastically in favor of the United States and the West. Relative decline offered
the Soviets no practical alternative to a policy of imperial retrenchment and
engagement with the powerful West.[4] When the Kremlin leadership perceived this power shift, it brought its behavior in accordance with reality.

It is obvious, however, that that reality, as harsh as it was, did not automatically dictate one set of perceptions (or a single "narrative" as a modern
theorist would say). In the Kremlin, as everywhere else, the distance between
reality and perception was great and conditioned by many intersecting
motives, interests, and above all, diverging perspectives stemming from social
and historical experience. And most important, people in the Kremlin perceived more than one option by the mid-1980s.

2. Anatoliy Chernyayev, "Fenomen Gorbacheva v kontekste liderstva," *Mezhdunarodnaya Zhizn'*, no. 7
(1993). Also see his *Shest' let s Gorbachevym: po dnevnikovym zapisyam* (Moscow: Progress-Kul'tura, 1993), and
his *1991 god: Dnevnik pomoshnika prezidenta SSSR* (Moscow: Terra, Respublika, 1997).

3. Dmitriy Volkogonov, *Sem' Vozhdey: Galereya liderov SSSR* (Moscow: Novosti, 1995), 2:322–23.

4. See Chapter 9, and sources cited therein.

One option—the most dangerous for the world and the Soviet Union itself—was discussed in 1981–84 by the aged Soviet leaders, who felt threatened by the military buildup and "aggressive" behavior of the Reagan administration. Leaning on their experience of the Stalin era and the Second World War, Yury Andropov and Marshal Dmitry Ustinov contemplated emergency measures to mobilize Soviet society and state for the task of preserving "strategic parity" with the United States in the all-out arms race.[5] Veteran Russian diplomat Oleg Grinevsky even cites plans to repeat "the Cuban scenario" of 1962 by responding to U.S. deployment of the Pershing II missiles in West Germany with equally provocative deployments of Soviet arms in the immediate vicinity of the United States.[6] The core of this response was mistrust, fear, and reliance on deterrence by force—very similar to Soviet behavior in the last years of Stalin's life. Even Gorbachev, when he first came to power, was under the influence of Andropov's opinion that no compromise could be reached while Reagan was in power.[7]

Another option was an "amicable agreement" with the West on the basis of mutual reductions of arms and withdrawal from the Third World. This option was offered at the end of the Second World War by, among others, Maksim Litvinov, and came into focus after Stalin. Nikita Khrushchev and Leonid Brezhnev called it "peaceful coexistence" and adhered to it despite all failures and frustrations in Soviet-American relations. At the core of this option was a "realpolitik" not dissimilar to the Nixon-Kissinger strategy of the early 1970s. It aimed to preserve essential elements of Soviet imperial influence in the world, including strategic "parity" with the United States; Soviet allies abroad; and ideological support of international communist and "progressive" movements. According to Chernyaev, Gorbachev in his first years in office also believed that "peaceful coexistence" was the option of "common sense" and that socialism and capitalism "could coexist without interfering with each other."[8]

5. On the reasons for Soviet fears, see Ben B. Fischer, *A Cold War Conundrum: The 1983 Soviet War Scare*, An Intelligence Monograph (Center for the Study of Intelligence, September 1997); on the Andropov-Ustinov response, see Robert D. English, "Sources, Methods, and Competing Perspectives on the End of the Cold War," *Diplomatic History* 23, no. 2 (spring 1997): 286. Also see Anatoly F. Dobrynin, *In Confidence: Moscow's Ambassador to America's Six Cold War Presidents (1962–1986)* (New York: Random House, 1995), 482.

6. Oleg Grinevsky, senior Soviet arms negotiator, in "Understanding the End of the Cold War, 1980–1987," An Oral History Conference, Brown University, May 7–10, 1998, translated and transcribed by Jeffrey W. Dillon, edited by Nina Tannenwald (provisional transcript, the author's copy), 257–58.

7. Anatoly Chernyaev, personal foreign policy assistant to Gorbachev, in "Understanding the End of the Cold War," 77–78.

8. Ibid., 78.

There was also a third option of unilateral, calibrated reductions of
Soviet armed forces, similar to what the Kremlin carried out in the first years
after Stalin's death. It did not mean bailing out of the arms race with the
United States, but rather procuring "a breathing spell" in order to lift the burden of the military-industrial expenditures on the Soviet economy. This
option, by contrast to the first one, corresponded to the needs of a gradual
reform of the Soviet centralized system, but implied gradualism and firm control over the society and economic life. A majority of analysts in Washington
suspected and feared until 1989 that this was exactly what Gorbachev intended
to do.[9] Indeed, some elements of this option were present in Gorbachev's
arguments before the Politburo during 1986–87 and became public after 1988
in the doctrine of "strategic sufficiency."

The key—and frequently unrecognized—point is that *Gorbachev never
pursued any of these options systematically*. While some domestic critics and
Western policymakers might have *thought* he was following "peaceful coexistence" or "breathing spell" strategies, in fact, he was doing something quite
different and arguably far less coherent and calculated. This is recognized,
after the fact, by Gorbachev's loyalists and particularly by his critics, who continue to speak about it as a missed opportunity to take "a Chinese road."[10]

Soviet domestic politics is the second standard explanation for the end
of the Cold War. Deterioration of Soviet economy, ecology, and quality of
everyday life—the so-called stagnation—as well as deep and growing problems of the multinational state contrasted dramatically with the spectacular
upsurge of the United States and Western Europe in the 1980s. Even before
Gorbachev, under Konstantin Chernenko, the old leadership of the Soviet
Union agreed that a policy of détente and taming the arms race was imperative for the country. Gorbachev's foreign policy during 1985–86 can be largely
explained by this search for détente for the sake of perestroika of the USSR.
Gorbachev's primary foreign policy goal was to prevent a new round of the
arms race (associated with Reagan's Strategic Defense Initiative). He is on
record saying to the Politburo that this race will be "beyond our capabilities,
and we will lose it, because we are at the limit of our capabilities. Moreover,

9. See Robert M. Gates, *In from the Shadows: The Ultimate Insider's Story of Five Presidents and How They
Won the Cold War* (New York: Simon & Schuster, 1996), 330–34, 335–40.

10. Obviously, "the Chinese road" was not the term the Soviets used in the 1980s. At that time China
was barely out of the travails of the cultural revolution, and the scope and direction of reforms of Deng
Xiaoping were still not clear.

we can expect that Japan and the FRG could very soon join the American potential. . . . If the new round begins, the pressure on our economy will be unbelievable."[11]

This crisis of the communist political and economic system inherited from Stalin and preserved essentially intact, was, of course, inevitable. By 1985 the USSR—plagued by its long-term systemic crisis—was a superpower only in the military sense. Under Gorbachev's leadership, the domestic political and economic systems deteriorated further and faster. Some on the U.S. side, among them Secretary of State George Shultz and top CIA watcher Robert Gates, realized it was very advantageous for U.S. interests that the deepening crisis pushed the Soviet leadership to move unilaterally to meet U.S. demands and conditions for the end of the confrontation. In fact, if it were not for Presidents Reagan and Bush, who took significant steps to meet Soviet concerns, the end of the Cold War might have looked like a Soviet surrender.[12]

The "domestic structural" explanation seems persuasive, but a closer look reveals that it, too, is less "structural" than man-made—not to say one-man-made. The key is that the grave economic, financial, and state crisis began only between 1986 and 1988, and its *immediate cause* was Gorbachev's choices and policies. Most consequential were two. First, instead of relying on the most pragmatic elements of the old nomenklatura in the restructuring of the country, Gorbachev tried to build up new political forces and movements while gradually diminishing the power of the party and centralized state structures. Second, instead of moving to economic reforms within the framework of the existing political system, he encouraged a very rapid dismantling of this system and the communist ideology that gave it legitimacy. These choices led after 1988 to political chaos and economic catastrophe. "Doctor" Gorbachev's "remedies" were killing the patient.[13]

11. Politburo Sessions, October 4 and 8, 1986, notes of Anatoly Chernyaev, the Archive of Gorbachev Foundation, *fond* 2, *opis'* 1.

12. Gates, *In from the Shadows*, 385–88, 439; George P. Shultz, *Turmoil and Triumph: My Years as Secretary of State* (New York: Charles Scribner's Sons, 1993), esp. 765; George Bush and Brent Scowcroft, *A World Transformed* (New York: Alfred A. Knopf, 1998); also the analysis of Raymond L. Garthoff, *The Great Transition: American-Soviet Relations and the End of the Cold War* (Washington, D.C.: The Brookings Institution, 1994).

13. On this, see Michael Ellman and Vladimir Kontorovich, eds., *The Destruction of the Soviet Economic System: An Insiders' History* (Armonk, N.Y.: M. E. Sharpe, 1998), 22–23, 165–69. The authors convincingly conclude that "the USSR was killed, against the wishes of its ruler, by politics, not economics. The immediate cause of death, the dissolution of the Union, was the result of the chain of events set in motion by Gorbachev starting in 1985. . . . Unlike much of the Soviet elite, he was ambitious and optimistic about the system's capabilities" (26). Also see, by the same authors, "The Collapse of the Soviet System and the Memoir

And even with the economy and finances in steep decline, the Soviet Union still could, until 1988, maintain a respectable Potemkin facade on its weakness and negotiate with the United States from a position of relative parity. During 1988 this situation drastically changed: Gorbachev's decision to launch radical political and state reforms, coupled with the removal of the party nomenklatura from economic life, created a most severe crisis of the state and unleashed centrifugal political forces that grew like mushrooms. All this was tantamount to revolution, was visible to the world, and engulfed the Soviet leadership. These policies essentially destroyed the Soviet capacity to act like a superpower in the international arena. The Soviet Union was in no position to bail out its allies or to present itself as an equal partner to the United States in negotiations. A close assistant to Foreign Minister Shevardnadze asserts that after mid-1988, "when we encountered domestic difficulties, we began to realize that we would be able to stay afloat for a while and even to preserve the status of great power only if we leaned on the United States. We felt that if we had stepped away from the United States, we would have been pushed aside. We had to be as close as possible to the United States."[14]

There are other aspects that also contradict the "domestic structural crisis" as a determining factor in the Soviet desire to end the Cold War as soon as possible and on the best available terms. First, Soviet negotiating behavior began to change drastically as early as 1987, long before the crisis became grave and visible. On the other hand, the Gorbachev administration continued, even with empty coffers, to throw billions of dollars at and supply military equipment for its clients in Cuba, Ethiopia, and Afghanistan. Gorbachev, Shevardnadze, and others did this during 1989, 1990, and even part of 1991.[15] The U.S. side tried to reason Gorbachev into cutting pipelines to Castro, and radical Soviet reformers even proposed to get into an alliance with Cuban anti-Castro émigrés in Miami. But Gorbachev never took these steps, although they would have earned the gratitude of many in the U.S. political establishment.

Literature," *Europe-Asia Studies* 49, no. 2 (March 1997). A similar argument can be found in David Kotz, with Fred Weir, *Revolution from Above: The Demise of the Soviet System* (London: Routledge, 1997).

14. Transcript of interview by Oleg Skvortsov, director of the Oral History Project at the Institute of General History, with Sergei Tarasenko, March 19, 1999, Moscow (on file at the National Security Archive, Washington, D.C., and the Institute of General History, Moscow, 1999). Hereafter cited as "Skvortsov interviews."

15. Documents on Soviet assistance from *fond* 89 and other archival collections from Moscow are available on file at the National Security Archive, Washington, D.C.

Although many scholars and politicians contend that there was no way to reform the USSR without dismantling the old Soviet system, it is possible to imagine another option: a gradual transformation of the post-Stalinist communist model into a postcommunist authoritarian model. A leader supported by the pragmatic elements of the nomenklatura might have gradually privatized state property. The remarkable transformation of party secretaries and communist ministers into bankers and rich oligarchs under Yeltsin prompted one observer to suggest that even under Gorbachev "the higher echelons of the party" would have been ready "to send to Hell at any moment the whole of Marxism-Leninism, if such an act would only help them preserve their hierarchical positions and continue their careers."[16] Instead of co-opting the old elite, Gorbachev chose to lead Soviet society to "democracy" over the heads of the nomenklatura; and this "populism" soon brought to the fore elements of liberal and nationalist intelligentsia that turned vehemently against him. This, and the growing sabotage of the nomenklatura in all spheres of state policies and in economic life, left Gorbachev hovering without real political support. Denied political recognition and support at home, he increasingly looked for it abroad, from the Western public and foreign leaders.

In sum, at each stage of the Cold War endgame, Gorbachev made choices that destabilized the USSR and sapped its ability to act coherently as a superpower. And as I show below, those choices can be explained only by reference to Gorbachev's peculiar preferences and personality traits.

A third standard explanation for the end of the Cold War is the shift of ideas of the Soviet leadership, both as a product of the longer-term erosion of communist ideology and as a short-term by-product of the glasnost of 1987–89. Some focus on Gorbachev's "new thinking" as a set of ideas that replaced the old Soviet "mentality," in particular the core ideological thesis about class struggle and the inevitability of the world's division into two camps. As Robert English demonstrates in Chapter 8, the roots of new ideas about the world can be traced inside Soviet political establishment and intelligentsia as far back as the 1940s and 1950s. Some scholars point out that Gorbachev absorbed "new thinking" from various international sources and from his liberal-minded advisers. Archie Brown stresses Gorbachev's "capacity for learning."[17]

---

16. Dmitriy Furman, "Fenomen Gorbacheva," *Svobodnaya mysl'* (Moscow), no. 11 (1995): 70–71.
17. Brown, *Gorbachev Factor,* 59.

He clearly regards "new thinking" as an antithesis to "structural" explanations for the end of the Cold War.[18]

Indeed, the role of ideas in changing Soviet international behavior was great. But even at the time there was something bizarre about this role. To put it simply, Gorbachev took ideas *too seriously*. They played an *excessive* role in Soviet behavior. They took precedence, not only to the immediate interests of the negotiating process, but also to the formulation of state interests. The real action is thus not in the ideas themselves, but in the historical personality that espoused them and made them his own.

Again, the key evidence against the "ideas" theory is that there were other scenarios under which the rejection of communist ideology would have proceeded differently. First, the ideological revision could have been carried out more slowly, under more control from above. Gorbachev and his assistants let the process of glasnost go until it became a whirlwind of revelations that discredited the entire foundations of Soviet foreign policy. The emerging attitude among the "progressive intelligentsia" (later shared by Gorbachev himself) was radical antistatist revisionism. The Soviet Union was held to be solely and exclusively responsible for the Cold War. The policies of the West were considered to be purely reactive and dictated by the need to fight Stalin's communist aggression and totalitarian threat. Another, more conservative approach (as, for instance, is practiced in China today) would have held "historic revisionism" in check and diminished its radicalizing pressure on foreign policy.

Second, the rejection of the old ideology could have led to a pragmatic and flexible attitude, a version of realpolitik based less on lofty principles and ideas than on a modest and clear formulation of state interests. When Margaret Thatcher said in 1984 that one could do business with Gorbachev, she was particularly impressed with his citation from Lord Palmerston about the value of permanent interests.[19] Yet the thrust of Soviet foreign policy since 1988 was far from Palmerston's dictum. It was highly idealistic and imbued with messianic spirit. In mid-1987 Gorbachev wrote a book called *Perestroika for Our Country and the Entire World*. It contained a universalist image of international relations based on a new just and democratic world order, where the USSR

18. Ibid., 220–30.
19. Oral communication of Geoffrey Howe, in Deborah Hart Strober and Gerald S. Strober, *Reagan: The Man and His Presidency: An Oral History* (Boston: Houghton Mifflin, 1998), 327.

would play a key role and the United Nations would reign supreme. In a word, Gorbachev replaced one messianic "revolutionary-imperial" idea of communism with another messianic idea "that perestroika in the USSR was only a part of some kind of global perestroika, the birth of a new world order."[20]

Third, the new ideological motives of foreign policy did not necessarily dictate a total rejection of use of force and projection of power in one form or another. For Gorbachev's predecessors, from Stalin to Andropov, and for most of his colleagues in the Politburo in 1985–88, "realism" based on strength, coercion, and balance of power was even more important than communist ideology. They cared about power and empire as much, if not more, than they did about "socialism" and "proletarian internationalism." In his shift of paradigm Gorbachev rejected, not only the communist tenets of class struggle, but also post-Stalin imperialist realpolitik.

While the collapse of the Soviet Eastern European empire was inevitable, there could have been some combination of policies consistent with the new thinking to try to direct political processes in Eastern Europe, to apply the brakes, to mitigate their impact on Soviet international position and negotiating interests. Another option was a preemptive diplomacy of reaching agreements with the United States or key Western European countries that would have protected Soviet security interests in Eastern Europe (for example, the ban on NATO eastward expansion), exploiting American inability to see the full extent of Soviet decline. Instead of trying such options, Gorbachev simply presided as a benign observer to the rapid dissolution of Soviet "empire." He gave up diplomatic and military positions the USSR had retained and expanded since World War II, *in the name of the idea of perestroika, to promote his "new thinking."*

There is nothing intrinsic to the ideas of the new thinking themselves that necessitated Gorbachev's radically conciliatory course. One could subscribe to the whole package of ideas and yet completely part ways with Gorbachev on the question of whether or when to draw a line in the sand and call a halt to Soviet imperial decline. For most statesmen ideas are tools—and to understand their impact on history, one must examine how they are molded and manipulated by the human agents who espouse them. In Gorbachev's case, he clearly overreached himself when he tried to mold Soviet realities according to the ideas of new thinking.

20. Furman, "Fenomen Gorbacheva," 71.

There are few, if any, precedents in history when the leader in charge of
a huge ailing state would willingly risk the geopolitical positions of a great
power and the very foundations of his political position for the sake of a global
moral project. Even Lenin, Gorbachev's hero, compromised away the project
of world revolution in 1918 for the sake of staying in power. Gorbachev, however, did exactly the opposite. By the spring of 1989 it became obvious even to
his closest assistants that he was irreversibly losing control over foreign and
domestic events. Anatoly Chernyaev in May 1989 wrote in his diary with
anguish and amazement: "Inside me depression and alarm are growing, the
sense of crisis of the Gorbachevian Idea. He is prepared to go far. But what
does it mean? His favorite catchword is 'unpredictability.' But most likely we
will come to a collapse of the state and something like chaos."[21] Indeed,
Gorbachev ended as a pathetic figure, hated and despised by a vast majority of
his fellow countrymen and former Soviet allies around the world. Even his
partners, the Western statesmen who took advantage of the direction of his
policy, did not fully repay him, refusing to grant him the $20 billion aid pack-
age he requested in 1990.[22]

The Gorbachev Enigma: Outline of a Historically Fateful Personality

The standard explanations for the end of the Cold War are important and necessary—to describe the critical material, political, and intellectual setting in
which Gorbachev's peculiar personality and leadership style wrought their
powerful effect. Both critics and admirers of Gorbachev inevitably come to a
point at which they just scratch their heads in astonishment and begin to talk
about his personal "enigma." One admirer, a perceptive scholar, concludes
that "those six years of systematic dismantling [of the Cold War and commu-
nism] were not an organic Soviet and Russian development. Rather, it was a
contribution to history linked to Gorbachev's individuality."[23] Yegor Ligachev
writes that politics "cannot explain the zigzags of the political course associated so closely with Gorbachev's name. There was an entire complex of interrelated causes, including Gorbachev's personal qualities."[24]

---

21. Chernyayev, *1991 god*, 15–16.

22. See the discussion between Chernyaev and Baker in Chapter 4.

23. Furman, "Fenomen Gorbacheva," 62.

24. Yegor Ligachev, *Inside Gorbachev's Kremlin: The Memoirs of Yegor Ligachev*, trans. Catherine H.
Fitzpatrick, Michele A. Berdy, and Dobrochna Dyrcz-Freeman (New York: Pantheon, 1993), 126, 128. Note
that this book was titled "The Gorbachev Enigma" in the Russian version.

Sources: Frustrating but Fruitful

The sources for information about Gorbachev's personal qualities are nearly all problematic. It is not easy to glean evidence from Gorbachev's memoirs; they are so craftily opaque and carefully edited that only the most expert reader can tease real data from them. The same reservations apply to the retrospective observations of many of his critics. Some of them seem to seep with poison and viciousness, for example, the books of Valery Boldin (the person who was closest to the Gorbachevs) and former prime minister Nikolai Ryzhkov. Still, such books—as well as the more measured writings of and interviews with KGB Chief Vladimir Kryuchkov, Deputy General Secretary Yegor Ligachev, Vice-President Gennady Yanaev, Deputy Foreign Minister Georgy Kornienko, Gorbachev's personal bodyguard Vladimir Medvedev, and many others—*do* reward careful reading.[25]

The observations of Gorbachev's friends present another kind of problem. Chernyaev, Georgy Shakhnazarov, Vadim Medvedev, Andrei Grachev, and other Gorbachev aides and admirers spare their former boss and elide over his mistakes and weaknesses.[26] A very important source on Gorbachev's

25. Valeriy Boldin, *Krusheniye pedestala: Shtrikhi k portretu M. S. Gorbacheva* (Moscow: Respublika, 1995); Yegor Ligachev, *Zagadka Gorbacheva* (Novosibirsk: Interbuk, 1992); Vitaliy Vorotnikov, *A bylo eto tak . . . Iz dnevnika chlena Politbyuro TsK KPSS* (Moscow: Sovet veteranov knigoizdaniya SI-MAR, 1995); Nikolay Ryzhkov, *Desyat' let velikikh potraysenii* (Moscow: Kniga, Prosveshcheniye, Miloserdiye, 1996); idem, *Perestroyka: istoriya predatel'stv* (Moscow: Novosti, 1992); Vladimir Kryuchkov, *Lichnoye delo*, 2 vols. (Moscow: Olimp, 1996); Nikolay S. Leonov, *Likholet'e* (Moscow: Mezhdunarodniye otnosheniya, 1994); Vladimir Medvedev, *Chelovek za spinoi* (Moscow: Russlit, 1994); Oleg Shenin, *Rodinu ne prodaval* (Moscow: Paleya, 1994); Sergey Akhromeyev and G. M. Korniyenko, *Glazami marshala i diplomata: Kriticheskiy vzglyad na vneshnyuyu politiku SSSR do i posle 1985-go goda* (Moscow: Mezhdunarodniye otnosheniya, 1992); Georgiy Korniyenko, *Kholodnaya voyna: Svidetel'stvo yeye uchastnika* (Moscow: Politizdat, 1994); Valentin Falin, *Politische Erinnerungen*, trans. Heddy Pross-Werth (Munich: Droemer Knaur, 1993); Vadim Pechenev, *Gorbachev: K vershinam vlasti: Iz teoretiko-memuarnykh razmyshlenii* [Gorbachev: To the pinnacle of power: memoir and theoretical reflections] (Moscow: Gospodin narod, 1991); idem, *Vzlet i padeniye Gorbacheva: Glazami ochevidtsa* (Moscow: Respublika, 1996); Anatoliy Gromyko, *Andrey Gromyko v labirintakh Kremlya. Vospominaniya i razmishleniya syna* (Moscow: IPO Avtor, 1997); Boris Yeltsin, *Ispoved na zadannuyu temu* (Moscow: PIK, 1990); Dobrynin, *In Confidence*, and the Russian edition, *Sugubo doveritel'no: posol v Vashingtone pri shesti prezidentakh SShA (1962–1986 gg.)* (Moscow: Avtor, 1997). Also, I used transcripts of the interviews with Soviet officials produced by the Oral History Project on the End of the Cold War under the leadership of Dr. Oleg Skvortsov under auspices of the Institute of General History, Academy of Science, and with the sponsorship of the National Security Archive, George Washington University.

26. Chernyayev, "Fenomen Gorbacheva"; also see his *Shest' let s Gorbachevym* and his *1991 god*; Georgiy Shakhnazarov, *Tsena svobody: Reformatsiya Gorbacheva glazami yego pomoshchnika* (Moscow: Rossika-Zevs, 1993); Vadim Medvedev, *V komande Gorbacheva: Vzglyad iznutri* (Moscow: Bylina, 1994); idem, *Raspad: kak on nazreval v "mirovoi sisteme sotsializma"* (Moscow: Mezhdunarodniye otsnosheniya, 1994); Aleksandr Yakovlev, *Predisloviye, obval, poslesloviye* (Moscow: Novosti, 1992); Eduard Shevardnadze, *Moy vybor v zashchitu demokratii i svobody* (Moscow: Novosti, 1991); Andrey Grachev, *Dal'she bez menya. Ukhod Prezidenta* (Moscow: Progress-Kul'tura, 1994); idem, *Kremlevskaya khronika* (Moscow: EKSMO, 1994); Pavel Palazchenko, *My Years with Gorbachev and Shevardnadze: The Memoir of a Soviet Interpreter* (University Park: Pennsylvania State University Press, 1997). In addition to these sources, I was able to use the materials of "oral history conferences" on the end of the Cold War, with participation of some of the same figures. See Nina Tannenwald,

personality are the minutes taken by his assistants at the Politburo sessions and the records of Gorbachev's conversations with foreign leaders and public figures, in part published, in part available in the archive of the Gorbachev Foundation in Moscow. Finally, perhaps the most important source on Gorbachev's personality continues to be Gorbachev himself. Though they are carefully crafted political documents, his memoirs and other recollections on his years in power do bear the strong imprint of his personality. After all the years since he abandoned the post of general secretary of the CPSU and the presidency of the USSR, it is unmistakably the same personality, with the unique behavior and discourse that even today set him far apart from the rest of Russian politicians of all brands.[27] Sometimes wittingly and more often not, Gorbachev reveals himself in his voluminous retirement writings.

All the arguments regarding Gorbachev's personality mentioned by his friends, critics, and foes deserve a careful and balanced scholarly analysis. Negative comments should be treated with an immense grain of salt. However, it would be a mistake to disregard them entirely. To admit that Gorbachev was not a great statesman is not to denigrate or deny his historic contribution to the process of the peaceful ending of the Cold War. Besides, Gorbachev is so unpopular at home that a serious and unvarnished study of his personality and statesmanship can only contribute to dispelling the cloud of slander that currently hangs over him in Russia.

In short, the sources on Gorbachev's personality are vast; yet they must be treated with extreme circumspection. Only by "triangulating" among a variety of sources—the writings of supporters, opponents, and the man himself—as well as the concrete record of Gorbachev's real behavior in office, can we construct even a rough portrait.

The Twin Pillars of Gorbachev's Character

Western scholars often compare Gorbachev to Nikita Khrushchev. Despite a huge difference in generational experience, education, and style, both of them,

ed., *Understanding the End of the Cold War, 1980–87*, An Oral History Conference, Brown University, May 7–10, 1998, translated and transcribed by Jeffrey W. Dillon, May 1999, and *The End of the Cold War in Europe, 1989: "New Thinking" and New Evidence*, Transcript of the Proceedings of the Musgrove Conference on the Openness in Russia and Eastern Europe Project, Musgrove Plantation, St. Simon's Island, Ga., May 1–3, 1998, prepared by Svetlana Savranskaya under the auspices of the National Security Archive, George Washington University.

27. Mikhail Gorbachev, *Zhizn' i reformy*, 2 vols. (Moscow: Novosti, 1995); idem, *Avgustovskiy putch: Prichiny i Sledstviya* (Moscow: Novosti, 1991); idem, *Dekabr-91: Moya pozitsiya* (Moscow: Novosti, 1992). See

indeed, had something in common as personalities: a peasant social background, a sincere and feverish reformist urge, unflagging optimism and ebullient self-confidence, moral revulsion against the Soviet past, and a simple-minded belief in the common sense of the Soviet people and their innate potential to make for themselves better lives if only they were permitted to. Gorbachev makes this comparison in his memoirs, putting himself in the same boat with Khrushchev and making a point that in Russia "no reformers" had "a happy life."

This comparison can go deeper and exploit methodological instruments and approaches of modern social history, historical sociology, and social psychology. For instance, Russian scholar Natalya Kozlova has recently studied diaries, letters, and other written evidence on the peculiarities of socialization of the Russian peasantry in the USSR. She found how the rapid collapse of "peasant civilization" led to breathtaking social and physical mobility of young peasants to big cities. New recruits to urban civilization were burning with desire to leap from the "idiocy of village life" to the "culture" and the highest social status they could obtain. The first cohort of such people was shaped by the 1930s and the Second World War. The second cohort came in the 1950s, during the final stages of Soviet urbanization. An immense vitality and naïve belief in the "ideas" and "words" of "cultured" discourse distinguished them from the sophisticated, cynical, double-thinking urbanites.[28] The roots of both Khrushchev and Gorbachev should be sought there.

Arguably the central and most consequential feature of Gorbachev's personality was his remarkable *self-confidence and optimism.* His ability to "recoup," to "bounce back," was extraordinary. There is a psychological foundation to this, and political psychologists one day may explain it. Undoubtedly, as an individual, Gorbachev possessed a very healthy ego and stable values. The political and social environment he lived in—the Moscow State University, the region of Kuban Cossacks in the south of Russia, the Politburo where he was the only young member—fostered his healthy self-esteem. In any case, he had unflagging faith in his own capacities to succeed.

---

also his conversation with Russian intellectuals in *Perestroyka desyat' let spustya (aprel' 1985–aprel' 1995)* (Moscow: Aprel'-85 Publishing House, 1995).

28. N. N. Kozlova, *Gorizonti povsednevnosti Sovetskoy epokhi. Golosa iz khora* [Horizons of Everyday Life of Soviet Era: Voices from the Chorus] (Moscow: Institute of Philosophy, 1996).

Flowing from this essential optimism, admirers say, was Gorbachev's natural liberalism and democratic instincts, based on the assumption that the Soviet people and Soviet society were essentially as good, healthy, and well-intentioned as he was himself. In Chernyaev's estimation, Gorbachev's "natural [*prirodnye*] democratic instincts had not been completely spoiled by his long career in the party apparat, although he acquired some 'pockmarks.'"[29] These instincts lived side by side with a discovery of how terrible and corrupt was the system under which the Soviet people lived. In Chernyaev's words, "Gorbachev was a very healthy personality, physically and morally. [And] he suffered a genuine shock from observing the society, the norms, and mores which everybody had to live with, but which unveiled themselves before him in all their ghastly light when he moved to Moscow and joined the ruling party and state strata." This moral revulsion against the existing regime, continues Chernyaev, remained a "backbone" supporting Gorbachev in his actions, despite many transgressions and dirty compromises of politics.[30]

A second key attitude, in the opinion of supporters, was his *naïveté*. One of his assistants, Georgy Shakhnazarov, points to this in his book, stressing Gorbachev's "naïve belief in his colleagues' common sense."[31] But, he argues, Gorbachev's perestroika was a "reformation," and he needed those features of an evangelist seeking to convert the pagans of communism to a fairer and better creed, to free them from the captivity of Stalinism, militarism, and pauperism and lead them to the kingdom of "common sense." Even today, observes a reviewer of Gorbachev's memoirs, "it seems to him that this or that idea whose truth he discovered, is so obvious, that people will absolutely grasp it. In the same way, Luther probably thought that his truths were so obvious, that he could easily convince the Pope with them."[32] Indeed, in his most recent publications—over a decade out of power and almost completely ignored at home and increasingly even abroad—Gorbachev continues to preach the virtues of new thinking for the entire world, as if the truth and usefulness of this political philosophy were self-evident.[33]

29. Chernyayev, "Fenomen Gorbacheva," 52.
30. Ibid.
31. Shakhnazarov, *Tsena svobody*, 47.
32. Furman, "Fenomen Gorbacheva," 66; also, Vladimir Shemyatenkov, deputy head of the Cadre Department of the CC CPSU in 1985–88, implies that Gorbachev was too good for the Soviet society. Skvortsov interview with Shemyatenkov, Moscow, November 18, 1998.
33. Mikhail Sergeevich Gorbachev, *Gorbachev—On My Country and the World*, trans. George Shriver (New York: Columbia University Press, 2000).

It was not Luther, but Lenin who remained Gorbachev's role model as late as 1989. Sympathizers notice this special affection for Lenin and attribute it to the profound impact of the Soviet political culture on Gorbachev. But Gorbachev must also have felt attached to the personality of Lenin in whom (rather, in his idealized, censored image) he saw a reflection of his own traits, particular feverish intellectualism, "historic" optimism, and unflagging determination to muddle through social and political chaos. Gorbachev confessed to Chernyaev that he mentally "asked for Lenin's advice" until early 1989.[34]

The critics see Gorbachev's self-confidence, optimistic nature, and "democratism" in a completely different light. Ligachev argues that Gorbachev "did not have in his character a room for understanding how difficult [the reforms]" would be.[35] Gorbachev's chief of chancellery Valery Boldin, head of his personal security Vladimir Medvedev, and Boris Yeltsin stress, almost in unison, the fact that the Gorbachevs, as a couple, displayed an exceptional talent to enjoy the luxurious, comfortable life of the party nomenklatura. In Medvedev's view, Gorbachev was no more "democratic" than other bonzes of the party elite. There was, Medvedev observes, a profound psychological gap between him and the vast majority of the Soviet people. Medvedev writes that Gorbachev, unlike patriarchal Brezhnev, felt uncomfortable with the Soviet masses and at ease when talking to Westerners.[36]

Gorbachev's friends recognize how much Gorbachev's personality was (and still is) at loggerheads with the mainstream of Russian-Soviet mentality. But they side with him, not with the people. Chernyaev, for instance, defines Soviet society as "a totalitarian boulder," "a lumpenized population with a give-me psychology." In the opinion of his friends, Gorbachev accomplished a Herculean feat of waking the society from the terrible stupor and slavery of Soviet totalitarianism. He pushed the "boulder" off of its resting place. The rest, Chernyaev contends, was inevitable: society turned out to be unworthy of the leader; the new thinking was ahead of its time. Given all this, Gorbachev could not really apply the brakes when the boulder of Soviet society began to roll downhill, crushing everything in its way.[37] Another author argues that Gorbachev had a "simple-minded" and "unfailing" faith that "the people

34. Chernyayev, *Shest' let s Gorbachevym*, 278, 280.
35. Skvortsov interview with Yegor Ligachev, December 17, 1998, Moscow.
36. Medvedev, "Chelovek za spinoi," 214–15, 225; Skvortsov interview with Valery Boldin, Moscow, February 24, 1999; Yeltsin, *Ispoved na zadannuyu temu,* 125.
37. Chernyayev, "Fenomen Gorbacheva," 59.

simply need to be awakened" and that the "living creative work of the masses" would by itself lead to everything good."[38]

Foes and friends alike debate Gorbachev's personal abilities for states-manship and state management. They nearly all highlight a key consequence of Gorbachev's essential optimism and naïveté: his *"ad hocism,"* his *congenital lack of a long-range strategic plan,* and his *aversion to the practical details of governance.* They all recognize that "perestroika" had no plan and "new thinking" was vague and could not be a practical guide for reforms. Gorbachev's favorite phrases, besides "unpredictability," were "let processes develop" and "processes are on the go" (*protsessi poshli*).[39] In the judgment of one of his sympathizers, it was an extension of his excessively optimistic view of people, particularly of Soviet people. "It always seemed to him that people could not help but be glad to organize their own lives for themselves."[40] He had little doubt that it would be best just to wait and watch while "processes" ran their course to the most sensible outcome.

Even sympathizers admit that this psychological feature contributed to Gorbachev's chronic inability to chart a practical course for the state apparat, to carry out a sustained and thought-through program of actions, to prevent psychological disarray and ideological breakdown in the society. Chernyaev's political memoirs are replete with his frustration and nagging doubts about this shortcoming.[41] Gorbachev, he writes, failed to begin meaningful economic reforms when he still could undertake something; he let the Brezhnev-Andropov-Gromyko war in Afghanistan become "Gorbachev's war"; he let Yeltsin seize the political initiative by breaking with the old discredited political order.[42] Still, the sympathizers stress that all this was not a crucial flaw. They argue that since nobody knew how to transform the totalitarian country, it could be done only by trial and error. Also, in the words of one sympathizer, "the work that Gorbachev did could only have been done without accurately perceiving all its complexity and danger. If he had started to compute everything, to think through various alternatives in his head, he simply could never have undertaken it."[43] Quite obviously, this assessment of Gorbachev's abilities

38. Furman, "Fenomen Gorbacheva."
39. See, e.g., Chernyaev's comments in Chapter 2.
40. Furman, "Fenomen Gorbacheva."
41. See, for example, *Shest' let s Gorbachevym,* 343.
42. Chernyayev, "Fenomen Gorbacheva," 56; idem, *Shest' let s Gorbachevym,*" 241.
43. Furman, "Fenomen Gorbacheva," 67.

is based on an assumption that nobody could have reformed the old system; it only could be destroyed in one way or another.

Ten years after he lost power, Gorbachev himself, in a candid discussion, agreed that there was "a lot of naïveté and utopianism" in his actions. But he adamantly stuck to his ideals of new thinking. He admitted that he deliberately ran a risk of political destabilization since 1988, but insisted that it was necessary. Radical political reforms were "deliberately designed" to "wake up [the Soviet] people." Otherwise, he said, "we would have shared the fate of Khrushchev. Even after we introduced new fresh forces into the already liberated structures—the party nomenklatura set a goal . . . to remove the General Secretary because he intended to bury its privileges."[44]

The critics deny there was ever a serious challenge to Gorbachev's authority on the part of the party nomenklatura.[45] They believe that Gorbachev's zigzags, procrastination and tolerance of chaos was the key flaw in his character, accounting for his lack of ability as a statesman. Ligachev writes that "being too late, reacting too slowly to events, was one of the most characteristic traits of Gorbachev's policies."[46] In a recent interview he added: "When some controversial things happened, Gorbachev often reacted with delay. My explanation is that he wanted others to analyze what affected the society, was painful to the society. He wanted a ripe fruit to fall onto his lap, the one he could pick up. But often it was necessary to row against the tide. There were many instances in history when the leader remained in the minority, but turned out to be right. Gorbachev, unfortunately, lacked this quality."[47] Kryuchkov talks and writes about Gorbachev's "impulsiveness that is linked to his personality, to the traits of his abnormal character."[48]

The critics are convinced that another type of leader, with a stronger and steadier hand, would have made a huge difference. This hypothetical "other" could have brought about "détente" with the West and gradually transformed

44. *Perestroyka desyat' let spustya (aprel' 1985–aprel' 1995)* (Moscow: Aprel'-85 Publishing House, 1995), 102–3; Gorbachev's last words give credibility to Ligachev and Boldin's assertion that the post-1986 political confrontation between Gorbachev and the party cadres *was the first result* of political liberalization and "democratization" of the Soviet regime.

45. This important debate cannot be resolved on the basis of today's scholarship. It is true that when Gorbachev introduced "elements of democracy" into the party, he made it possible for the CC Plenums to oust him from power. But Gorbachev then and much later (even in 1990) was able to prevail quite decisively in party "politics."

46. Ligachev, *Inside Gorbachev's Kremlin,* 128.

47. From the Skvortsov interview with Ligachev, Moscow, December 17, 1998.

48. From the Skvortsov interview with Kryuchkov, Moscow, October 13 and December 7, 1998.

the Communist Party and the Soviet Union, but, unlike Gorbachev, without
destroying the foundations of state power and without creating overall political and social chaos.

Gorbachev's Personality and the End of the Cold War

Gorbachev's self-image as a leader is extremely important for understanding the
end of the Cold War. It was linked to his goals and ideals, but at the same time it
reflected the personal, intimate psychological core that allowed him to stick to
these ideals and goals. In late October 1988 Gorbachev began preparations to
announce this core to the world from the most salient podium, the General
Assembly of the United Nations. He told his brain trust of Shevardnadze,
Yakovlev, Dobrynin, Falin, and Chernyaev to prepare a speech that would be an
answer to Churchill's famous speech at Fulton, Missouri, in March 1946. It
"should be an anti-Fulton—Fulton in reverse," he said. "We should present our
worldview and philosophy based on the results of the last three years. We should
stress the demilitarization and humanization of our thinking."[49]

This episode reveals how a comparison with Stalin can help clarify the
impact of Gorbachev's personality. Consciously or not, Gorbachev posed and
acted as an "anti-Stalin," both in the sense of direction he gave to the Soviet
Union, but also on the world arena. The creator of the Soviet state and
empire, Stalin barely distinguished his personality from his creations. He
took the slightest challenge to them as a personal assault and, vice versa,
regarded any slight to his prestige and authority (particularly from foreigners) as an intolerable insult to the prestige of the USSR as a great power.[50]
Gorbachev's creation was perestroika, and as Dmitry Furman observes with
sympathy, for him "perestroika of the USSR was only a part of some kind of
global perestroika, the birth of a new world order."[51] At the same time
Gorbachev did not identify with the Soviet state and empire in the form and
shape he had inherited them from his predecessors. Later he claimed that he
did everything "to preserve the Union," but as an individual, he sought to

49. Chernyaev's notes, October 31, 1988, in the Archive of the Gorbachev Foundation; also see Pavel
Palazchenko, *My Years with Gorbachev and Shevardnadze: The Memoir of a Soviet Interpreter* (University Park:
Pennsylvania State University Press, 1997), 103–4.
    50. For ample illustrations of this attitude, see Vladimir O. Pechatnov, "'The Allies Are Pressing You on
to Break Your Will . . .' Foreign Policy Correspondence Between Stalin and Molotov and Other Politburo
Members, September 1945–December 1946," trans. Vladislav Zubok, Cold War International History
Project Working Paper no. 26 (Washington, D.C., September 1999).
    51. Furman, "Fenomen Gorbacheva."

become a creator of a new state based on the principles and ideas that he had internalized.

Stalin, particularly when the Soviet Union became a world empire, played two roles, that of the leader of the internationalist revolutionary movement and that of a Russian tsar. The second role was, credibly, a central part of his self-image. Gorbachev, wittingly or unwittingly, stepped into the shoes of Russian tsars and, by all his personal inclinations, meant to be a kind, good tsar. But, after all, it is hard to fit Gorbachev into this category.[52] For he had other priorities than the power, prestige, and stability of the state. His first priority, as mentioned earlier, was the construction of a global world order on the basis of new thinking. This puts Gorbachev, at least in his own self-image, in the ranks of such international figures of the twentieth century as Woodrow Wilson, Mahatma Gandhi, and other prophets of universalism. But those people did not excel as state-builders and statesmen.

Thus, both Stalin and Gorbachev had enormous influence on the fate of the Soviet Union, though, of course, the contrast between the "statesmanship" of the two could not be greater. Stalin permeated the entire Soviet state and society with extreme xenophobia; he regarded Western cultural influences as a mortal threat to his regime. Khrushchev and Brezhnev were heirs to this malignant legacy. By contrast Gorbachev had not a trace of xenophobia and cultural hostility toward the West. Stalin was intolerant of different opinions, once he made up his own mind on any issue. He counted the slightest deviation from his "line" as an intolerable sign of dissent, a threat of chaos, a symptom of loss of governability. He displayed an uncanny ability for imagining "worst-case scenarios" and suspected all Western statesmen and politicians, even those who sought to appease the USSR, of the worst anti-Soviet schemes. Personally, he had little or no respect for Western public opinion and called Western leaders every obscene word in the Russian dictionary.[53] Gorbachev, by contrast, liked the West and Westerners, and respected Western statesmen of all creeds, and came to regard some of them as personal friends. He had a striking capacity for "best-case" thinking and began to act on assumption of good faith, honesty, integrity, and fealty to agreements in international affairs.

---

52. I am thankful to Jack Matlock for this observation.
53. On Stalin's features as a statesman, see Vladislav Zubok and Constantin Pleshakov, *Inside the Kremlin's Cold War: From Stalin to Khrushchev* (Cambridge: Harvard University Press, 1996), chap. 1, and Pechatnov, "The Allies Are Pressing," 10–11.

Stalin was, in his crude and bloody way, an architect of realpolitik for the Soviet Union; his policies turned the country into a superpower. His favorite modus operandi was carving up "spheres of influence," making these spheres totally impervious to the influence of and penetration by other great powers, and imposing complete control over them through threats and devious political manipulation. As for Gorbachev, he resolutely refused to treat even the countries where Soviet troops were stationed as part of some Soviet "sphere of influence." In fact, he meticulously avoided interfering in the internal affairs of Eastern European countries. When in January 1989 Henry Kissinger attempted to discuss in Moscow the idea of a U.S.-Soviet condominium over Europe—an idea Stalin would have grasped immediately—Gorbachev, as the evangelist of "new thinking," dismissed the proposal out of hand.[54]

The only common feature between Stalin and Gorbachev was a remarkable "chutzpah." Stalin pushed for recognition of "legitimate" territorial annexation even when the Nazis stood at the door of Moscow. Gorbachev attempted to talk as a world leader and peacemaker (he even tried to negotiate a U.S.-Cuban rapprochement) when the Soviet empire in Europe was already in political ruins and his own domestic base was falling to pieces. Clearly, the manifestations and consequences of this overconfidence were dramatically different in the case of the two leaders. In particular, while Stalin was the archetypal xenophobe and anti-Westerner, Gorbachev was by nature open and inclined toward the West. And while Stalin prided himself on his cold-blooded ruthlessness and willingness to spill others' blood, Gorbachev retained a deep inner aversion to the use of force.

Gorbachev's Westernism

In the opinion of his foreign admirers, Gorbachev was the first Soviet statesman who acted almost like a Western politician, a phenomenon that, given his background, they fail to comprehend. Indeed, by contrast to his predecessors, Gorbachev had not a slightest tinge of xenophobia and psychological hostility toward the West. To be sure, in his first years in power he retained many stan-

54. He told the Politburo on January 21, 1989, that Kissinger "hinted at the idea of a USSR-USA condominium over Europe." He was hinting that Japan, Germany, Spain, and South Korea were on the rise, and so, let us make an agreement so that the "Europeans do not misbehave." "We should work on this range of issues also," Gorbachev concluded, "but in such a way that it would not leak," so that Europeans would not see it as "an effort at conspiracy between the USSR and the USA over Europe." Chernyaev's notes, Archive of the Gorbachev Foundation; according to Anatoly Chernyaev, Gorbachev in effect was not interested in Kissinger's proposal. *The End of the Cold War in Europe, 1989,* 158–59.

dard Soviet political and ideological stereotypes of Western countries, particularly of the United States. But even when he treated Reagan, Kohl, and their colleagues as "adversaries," he began to dismantle the Iron Curtain, first allowing free contacts with foreigners for the select group of establishment intellectuals and officials,[55] then opening the outside world for the rest of the society.

As Gorbachev's sympathizers argue, this was not just a calculated policy of "showing Europe to Ivan" and breaking a lock of obscurantism and isolationism on the mentality of Soviet people. Dmitry Furman remarks that Gorbachev's Westernism was a complex of cultural and psychological dependency shared by his own milieu of educated Russians. "For all Soviet people, including the higher echelons of the party," he writes, "the West has always been an object of longing. Trips to the West were a most important status symbol. There is nothing you can do about this; it is 'in the blood,' in the culture. It is obvious that such was to some extent the case of the Gorbachevs." Furman establishes that Gorbachev, unlike his predecessors, had no aggressive complex of inferiority/superiority toward the West.[56] Gorbachev, Furman continues, liked his huge personal success in the West, including the United States. But "Gorbymania" was not so much the result of a contrived effort, but rather the product of natural mutual affinity between Gorbachev and Western public opinion.[57]

Chernyaev also believes that Gorbachev was successful in his personal diplomacy and attributes this success, not only to Gorbachev's new thinking, but also to his personality: his charm, sincerity, and ability to be on the same wavelength with the West. He waxed enthusiastic in his diary about Gorbachev's talent in establishing a friendly relationship with West German chancellor Helmut Kohl. After all, he observes, the entire new thinking in foreign policy was neither original nor terribly new. What was new was that the leader of the Soviet system, though conditioned by Soviet society, could so quickly and decisively break out of Soviet mentality. "When I saw this striving [of Gorbachev and Kohl] to speak as one human being to another human being (mutually), I felt physically that we are entering a new world where class struggle, ideology, and in general polarity and enmity are no longer determinate. And something all-human is taking the upper hand."[58]

55. Roald Z. Sagdeev, *The Making of a Soviet Scientist: My Adventures in Nuclear Fusion and Space from Stalin to Star Wars*, ed. Susan Eisenhower (New York: Wiley, 1994), 268–69.

56. Furman, "Fenomen Gorbacheva," 70–71.

57. Ibid., 68.

58. Chernyayev, *1991 god*, 11–12.

The critics take an ominous view of Gorbachev's affinity with the West. They claim that Gorbachev's stunning personal success among West European and American audiences made his head swell. He began to put his friendly relations with foreign leaders ahead of "state interests." Psychologically, they argue, Gorbachev turned to the West for recognition all the more as his popularity at home began to sink rapidly as a result of the growing social and political chaos. As Valery Boldin sees it, "Democratization began, but it suddenly took a wrong turn and not Gorbachev, but his arch-enemy Yeltsin became its leader. Then Gorbachev placed all his hopes on the West."[59] Also, the critics point out that Western advice played an ever increasing and sinister role in "diverting" Gorbachev from the foreign and domestic policy course of 1985–87 toward a new course of radical political reforms. They suspect Gorbachev's "euphoria" from his Western trips and high-level contacts as the main reason for his "hurry" in all policy areas, including the diplomacy of ending the Cold War.[60]

Soviet diplomats Anatoly Dobrynin and Georgy Kornienko are particularly blunt in stating that Gorbachev "frittered away the negotiating potential of the Soviet state" in exchange for ephemeral popularity and good relationships with Western statesmen. They sketch a gloomy picture of how Gorbachev's desire to reach an understanding with the West degenerated into a psychological and later political dependence on the West. In Dobrynin's opinion, Western statesmen exploited Gorbachev's weaknesses. After 1988 Gorbachev was in a hurry to end the Cold War because he had a personal need to compensate for his declining prospects at home with breakthroughs in foreign policy. As a result, "Gorbachev's diplomacy often failed to win a better deal with the United States and its allies."[61] Kornienko also believes that Gorbachev's excessive sensitivity to Western opinion and advice explained his hasty move to set up a new political system. Gorbachev the statesman was eager to replace the dubious legitimacy of the chief of the Communist Party with a broadly recognized international title of the President of the Republic. Western advice also can be traced in Gorbachev's political reforms that amounted to a political "shock therapy" for the Communist Party and the people.[62]

59. Skvortsov interview with Valery Boldin, Moscow, February 24, 1999, pp. 126, 127.
60. Dobrynin, *In Confidence*, 624–27.
61. Ibid., 627.
62. Kornienko's personal communication to the author, Moscow, October 1996.

Analysis of the records of Gorbachev's conversations with foreign leaders stored in the Archive at the Gorbachev Foundation reveals beyond any doubt that after 1988, if not earlier, Westerners—from social democrats to anticommunist conservatives—became perhaps the most crucial reference group for Gorbachev. There he found the understanding, willingness to listen, and most important, the ability to appreciate the grandiose universalist scope of his perestroika that he missed among his colleagues in the Politburo and even among his intellectual advisers.

It is significant that this dependence on the West is acknowledged, although in a less negative way, by Gorbachev's sympathizers. According to Furman, "Gorbachev's attention was diverted in the extreme to the West. He clearly relaxed his soul during his frequent trips, while in the country opposition and chaos grew." The same author rejects the notion that the West took advantage of Gorbachev and hastened the collapse of the USSR. But he deplores the fact that Gorbachev took so much of Western advice literally. In his opinion, it would have been better for the country, and for the "correctly understood" interests of the West itself, "if Gorbachev had showed more indifference" to the recommendations of American, German, and other politicians.[63]

Aversion to the Use of Force

An additional feature of Gorbachev's personality that perplexed contemporaries and witnesses was his deep aversion to the use of force. To be sure, as Andrew Bennett argues, Gorbachev's skepticism about the efficacy of force was widely shared among new thinkers.[64] Former Soviet foreign minister Andrei Gromyko, for example, privately called Gorbachev and his advisers "the Martians" for their ignorance of the laws of realpolitik. "I wonder how puzzled must be the U.S. and other NATO countries," he confessed to his son. "It is a mystery for them why Gorbachev and his friends in the Politburo cannot comprehend how to use force and pressure for defending their state interests."[65] As

---

63. Furman believes that "the West" was one of the two crucial reference groups for Gorbachev (the other was the "intelligentsia"). In his opinion, they diverted Gorbachev from his "reformist course." "Fenomen Gorbacheva," 71–72.

64. Andrew Bennett, *Condemned to Repetition? The Rise, Fall, and Reprise of Soviet Russian Military Interventionism, 1973–1996* (Cambridge: MIT Press, 1999). For another study that also gives the reluctance to use force the credit it is due, see Jacques Lévesque, *The Enigma of 1989: The USSR and the Liberation of Eastern Europe*, trans. Keith Martin (Berkeley and Los Angeles: University of California Press, 1997), esp. 252.

65. Anatoliy Gromyko, *Andrey Gromyko v labirintakh Kremlya. Vospominaniya i razmishleniya syna* (Moscow: IPO Avtor, 1997), 182, 184.

a keen observer of Russia Anatol Lieven commented ten years later, there was the growing social trend toward nonmilitarist, nonviolent attitudes since Stalin's death, when Soviet state and its controlling ideology began to weaken. Those attitudes, Lieven writes, "grew slowly through the last four decades of Soviet life."[66]

Yet it is clear that Gorbachev himself personified the reluctance to use force. Indeed, for him it was less a reasoned lesson from experience than a fundamental part of his character. The principle of nonviolence was not only Gorbachev's sincere belief, and the foundation of his domestic and foreign policies, but it also matched his personal "codes." Gorbachev's collaborators and assistants emphasize that "the avoidance of bloodshed was a constant concern of Gorbachev," that "for Gorbachev an unwillingness to shed blood was not only a criterion but the condition of his involvement in politics." Gorbachev, they observe, was a man of indubitable personal courage. Yet "by character he was a man incapable not only of using dictatorial measures, but even of resorting to hard-line administrative means"; that "harsh and dictatorial methods are not in the character of Gorbachev." The critics claim that Gorbachev "had no guts for blood," even when it was dictated by reasons of state.[67]

And it is important to note that Gorbachev's renunciation of force was not an inevitable consequence of new thinking or democratic values. Liberals will use force for liberal ends. A substantial number of liberals and former dissidents believe that Gorbachev's absolutist rejection of force was erroneous and perhaps even not moral. For instance, liberal philosopher Grigory Pomerantz praised Gorbachev's decision "to let go" of Eastern Europe. But simultaneously, he said, Gorbachev "let go the forces of destruction"—forces of barbarism, ethnic genocide, and chaos—in the South Caucasus, Central Asia, and other areas of the Soviet Union. "The first duty of the state was to contain chaos." Gorbachev's inactivity, however, opened the Pandora's Box. Another critic, Vladimir Lukin, noted: "Firmness [zhestkost'] was necessary in such a country as Russia, not to mention the Soviet Union."[68]

66. Anatol Lieven, *Chechnya: Tombstone of Russian Power* (New Haven: Yale University Press, 1998), 204.

67. Interviews with Aleksandr Yakovlev and Andrei Grachev, cited in Brown, *Gorbachev Factor*, 383–84; Vladimir Yegorov, *Out of a Dead End into the Unknown: Notes on Gorbachev's Perestroika*, trans. David Floyd (Chicago: Edition, 1993); Georgiy Shakhnazarov, *Tsena svobody: Reformatsiya Gorbacheva glazami yego pomoshchnika* (Moscow: Rossika-Zevs, 1993), 147.

68. *Perestroyka desyat' let spustya*, 29–30, 60.

As the Cold War was ending in Europe, the first fissures appeared in the Soviet state. And it was not a mere coincidence. Rather, in both cases, Gorbachev's approach—linked to his personality—played a major and indispensable role. On the ideological level, the Soviet leader had a firm linkage between the two goals, the end of the Cold War and the successful transformation of the Soviet Union. One of the staples of this was the idea of nonviolence that was a continuation of Gorbachev's personal aversion to using force. After the tragedy in Tbilisi in April 1989 (when Russian troops protected the Georgian communist leadership against the nationalist demonstration and killed Georgian civilians), Gorbachev forbade the use of force, even though nationalist forces began to break the country apart. He said to the Politburo: "We have accepted that even in foreign policy force is to no avail [*nichego ne dayet*]. So especially internally—we cannot resort and will not resort to force."[69] Despite various setbacks, Gorbachev adhered to this with remarkable tenacity until his last day in power.

Western politicians, particularly Bush and Baker, understood very well that feature of Gorbachev's statesmanship and successfully appealed to it. At Malta, for instance, Bush suggested to Gorbachev a gentleman's agreement on the Baltics where popular movements had begun to demand complete independence from the USSR. This was in violation of a long-standing taboo in U.S.-Soviet relations, interference in the internal affairs of a superpower. Bush, however, found the correct approach. "I would like to have a fullest understanding of your approach to the Baltics," he said. "There should be no setbacks here. Perhaps it would be better to discuss this issue in a confidential way, since I would very much like to perceive the core of your thinking on this extremely complicated issue." Since the internal issue of the Baltics was presented in the context of concern for Gorbachev's new thinking, to prevent setbacks for U.S.-Soviet partnership for the sake of a new global order, Gorbachev readily agreed. As a result, there was an understanding that the Americans would refrain from any attempts to help the Baltic nationalists, while in return Gorbachev would refrain from using force in dealing with the Baltic problem.[70]

69. Chernyaev's and Medvedev's notes at the Politburo, May 11, 1989; discussion of the Memorandum of six Politburo members on the situation in the Baltic Republics, the Archive of Gorbachev Foundation, *fond* 4, *opis'* 1, and *fond* 2, *opis'* 3; published in *The Union Could Be Preserved: The White Book: Documents and Facts about the Policy of M. S. Gorbachev to Reform and Preserve the Multi-National State* (Moscow: April Publishers, 1995), 52, 55.

70. See "At Historic Crossroads: Documents on the December 1989 Malta Summit," *Cold War International History Bulletin*, no. 12/13 (fall/winter 2001): 229–41, and Philip Zelikow and Condoleezza Rice, *Germany Unified and Europe Transformed: A Study in Statecraft* (Cambridge: Harvard University Press, 1995), 129.

Gorbachev himself, years after he lost power, continues to be an adamant opponent of the use of force to achieve political goals. He regrets the cases when he used force against nationalists inside the USSR. Referring to other crisis situations (the pogrom against Armenians by an Azeri mob in Sumgait in February 1988, bloodshed in Tbilisi in April 1989, a riot in Baku in January 1990, crackdowns in Vilnius and Riga in January 1991), Gorbachev said: "How many were [the] attempts to baptize me by blood. But they failed."[71] Essentially, Gorbachev agrees with what Ligachev said about him: "As far as the measures involving the use of violence that were required to save people, were concerned, Gorbachev resorted to them only when the last citizen in the country became convinced there was no other choice. It was a trait of Gorbachev's character."[72] Every time limited military force was used against nationalist crowds, on ambiguous (probably oral) order from Moscow, Gorbachev immediately stepped aside and left the military in the lurch, exposed to the fury of the nationalist and liberal media. This pattern had a double effect of paralyzing the Soviet army and magnifying the forces of those who wanted to destroy the Soviet Union.[73]

Gorbachev's decision to renounce the use of force in foreign and domestic policies as a matter of high principle was remarkable, unique, and encouraging for world history. Canadian scholar Jacques Lévesque writes that "the way the USSR separated itself from its empire and its own peaceful end" are interlinked and "may seem to be its most beneficial contributions to history. These episodes are, in any case, masterpieces of history."[74] But Gorbachev's principled nonviolence, so much appreciated in the West, is not likely to evoke admiration inside Russia. For all of his other roles, for his fellow countrymen Gorbachev was, first and foremost, a tsar, guarantor of their stability and livelihood, of the very existence of the state. The clear inability and even refusal of Gorbachev to perform this role contributed to the collapse of the Soviet Union and dislocation and misery for tens of millions of people and earned him the long-standing scorn among the vast majority of the Russians. Younger Russians today, if they remember Gorbachev at all, are likely to perceive him as a "holy fool" on the throne of the communist tsars.

71. *Perestroyka desyat' let spustya*, 19.
72. Skvortsov interview with Ligachev, December 17, 1998, Moscow.
73. See William Odom, *The Collapse of the Soviet Military* (New Haven: Yale University Press, 1998).
74. Lévesque, *Enigma of 1989*, 2.

The Case of German Unification

The effect of this complex mix of character traits—optimism, naïveté, ad hocism, Westernism, and aversion to force—is well illustrated by the diplomacy of German unification. On this as on other issues, Gorbachev himself made Soviet foreign policy with remarkably few bureaucratic constraints. Critics and supporters point out that Gorbachev's foreign policy after 1987 was rarely discussed formally at the Politburo, but rather informally within a narrow circle of advisers. In conducting negotiations, Gorbachev relied on Eduard Shevardnadze, but increasingly discussed issues "between four eyes," that is, directly with foreign leaders. The multi-institutional, bureaucratic decision-making structures (the Defense Council, "the panel of Five" that worked out proposals on arms reductions, the informal "alliance" of the KGB and the Ministry of Defense) were often not in the loop. On Germany, as one participant affirms, Gorbachev handled "all the negotiations . . . virtually by himself or in tandem with Shevardnadze, sweeping aside our professional diplomats and scarcely informing the Politburo."[75]

Thus, Gorbachev's personal traits and his peculiarities as a statesman determined Soviet policy with remarkably few constraints. In particular, Gorbachev's "anti-Stalin" personality had a lot to do with the peaceful death of communism in Eastern Europe (with the exception of Romania). It is stunning, in retrospect, to observe how easily Gorbachev let the Soviet geopolitical props in Eastern Europe go. On March 3, 1989, Chairman of the Council of Ministers of Hungary Miklós Németh informed Gorbachev about the decision "to completely remove the electronic and technological protection from the Western and Southern borders of Hungary. It has outlived the need for it, and now it serves only for catching citizens of Romania and the GDR who try to illegally escape to the West through Hungary." He added cautiously: "Of course we will have to talk to comrades from the GDR." The only words for the record from Gorbachev were: "We have a strict regime on our borders, but we are also becoming more open."[76]

75. Interview with Ligachev, Moscow, December 17, 1998; on the evidence on the process of cutting off "conservative" elements, party structures, and other bureaucratic players from the foreign policy field, see Carolyn McGiffert Ekedahl and Melvin A. Goodman, *The Wars of Eduard Shevardnadze* (University Park: Pennsylvania State University Press, 1997), 71–98.

76. Record of conversation between M. S. Gorbachev and the member of the central committee of the Hungarian Socialist Workers' Party and chairman of the Council of Ministers of the People's Republic of Hungary Miklós Németh, March 23, 1989, Chernyaev's notes, the Archive of the Gorbachev Foundation.

On October 5, Chernyaev wrote down in his diary: "Gorbachev is flying to the GDR to celebrate its fortieth anniversary. He is very reluctant. Called me two times. Today called and said: I will not say a word in support of [the GDR leader Erich] Honecker. But I will support the Republic and the revolution." The KGB reported to the leadership the lineup in the GDR leadership and indicated (without giving political recommendation) that the situation urgently dictated Honecker's removal.[77] But Gorbachev took no preemptive actions to avoid "the loss of the GDR." Chernyaev, a veteran of the Second World War and an expert of the Central Committee's International Department, believed that the Soviet leader had outgrown old fears and state geopolitical concerns. He jotted in his diary: "A total dismantling of socialism as a world phenomenon has been taking place. This may be inevitable and good. For this is a reunification of mankind on the basis of common sense. And a common fellow from Stavropol [i.e., Gorbachev] set this process in motion."[78]

At work here were two conflicting impulses within Gorbachev. On one hand, he could not recognize that his vision of reform communism was doomed in Eastern Europe and East Germany. Gorbachev continued to believe that "the socialist basis" would be preserved, and these illusions helped him to ignore a torrent of alarmist voices and watch with sympathy the spectacular process of the dissolution of communist regimes, first in Poland and Hungary and then in the GDR and the rest of Eastern Europe. Gorbachev's friends stress his moral principles and different generational experience that contrasted with his predecessors' fears of losing Central Europe.[79] But also at work here were all the above-mentioned traits of Gorbachev's character: his remarkable optimism, his ad hoc impulse to "let processes develop," his aversion to detailed strategic plans and affinity for larger principles, and his ultimate belief in his "lodestar" and the magic of persuasion as a substitute for actions.

On the other hand, he rejected as immoral any agreement with the West to preserve Soviet "interests" in the region. As Dobrynin puts it: "In exchange for the generous Soviet concessions Gorbachev and his devoted lieutenant

77. Ivan N. Kuzmin, *Krusheniye GDR: Istoriya. Posledstviya* (Moscow: Nauchnaya kniga, 1996), 112–13.

78. The Archive of Gorbachev Foundation, *fond 2, opis' 2*. This entry was omitted from Chernyayev, *1991 god: Dnevnik pomoschnika prezidenta SSSR*.

79. Lévesque, *The Enigma of 1989*, 83, 178–81, 255. I disagree that Gorbachev was misinformed about the seriousness of the brewing crisis in Eastern Europe. On the contrary, Soviet ambassadors and intelligence chiefs in Eastern European capitals, as well as some "roving" Soviet ambassadors (such as, for example, Vadim Zagladin, who traveled to Czechoslovakia in July 1989) warned Moscow repeatedly of the grave situation. At the same time, few could predict what direction and character the revolutions in Eastern Europe would take.

Shevardnadze offered the West [on Germany in particular—V. Z.], they could and should have obtained a more important role for the Soviet Union in European security and a stronger Soviet voice in European affairs. But they did not. Able but inexperienced, impatient to reach agreement, *but excessively self-assured* and flattered by the Western media, Gorbachev and Shevardnadze were often outwitted and outplayed by their Western partners."[80] Gorbachev in particular failed to state squarely and early enough Soviet terms for reunification (Germany's neutrality, demilitarization, compensation for withdrawal of Soviet troops, and so forth). Instead, he temporized, played by ear, yielded one position after another. Dobrynin cites Western publications as a proof of how unprepared, naïve, and reactive Gorbachev was in comparison with Helmut Kohl, whose well-calibrated steps toward swallowing the GDR enjoyed the full support of the United States.[81]

Dobrynin returns to such features of Gorbachev as optimism, self-confidence, and an unbounded belief in "processes" and forces of history as essentially good and healthy. This, he argues, served him badly in international affairs, as he, in an increasingly desperate situation, preserved unwarranted expectations that he would, despite the odds, convince his Western counterparts of the correctness of his initiatives. This "emotional set up of gambler," Dobrynin writes, was visible even at Reykjavik in October 1986. Later, in 1989–91, it mystified Gorbachev's Western partners.[82] Dobrynin continues that Gorbachev "was fascinated by the huge challenge of the [disarmament] tasks and carried away by the cheering international audience. So he moved forward without seriously contemplating the consequences. Here lay his weakness. He was either unable or in too much of a hurry to think about the prospective turn of events."[83]

The key—as both Bennett and Derek Chollet and James M. Goldgeier show—lies in the *interaction* between Gorbachev's personality and his Western interlocutors. Initially, the Bush administration was cautious and defensive as it watched the triumphal march of "Gorbymania" in West Germany. The predominant mood among Bush's lieutenants was one of skepticism toward "new thinking" and Gorbachev himself. Even Soviet withdrawal from Afghanistan,

---

80. Dobrynin, *In Confidence*, 627–28 (emphasis added).
81. Ibid., 630–31; also personal communication with Dobrynin, Moscow, June 18, 1999.
82. Dobrynin, *Sugubo doveritel'no*, 642; also see G. M. Korniyenko, *Kholodnaya voyna: Svidetel'stvo yeye uchastnika* (Moscow: Mezhdunarodniye otnosheniya, 1994), 261–68.
83. Dobrynin, *In Confidence*, 626.

completed by February 1989, did not convince them. Brent Scowcroft interpreted it as "cutting the losses" and retrenchment of Soviet power. "What was
not evident was whether their [Soviet] appetite also had been dampened. . . .
Instead of changing, Soviet priorities seemed only to narrow."[84] U.S. intelligence analyses stressed that Gorbachev had opened "Pandora's Box" of radical
changes and that he was "gambling" with the future of the state. Bush and his
secretary of state James Baker, however, came to an opposite conclusion, that
Gorbachev's personality and statesmanship were crucial. "Look, this guy *is*
perestroika," Bush said to the skeptical experts.[85] He dismissed the analysis of
the CIA's Soviet desk, which indicated that Gorbachev was losing control over
events and implied he could not be a stable long-term partner.[86]

After the fall of the Berlin Wall the Bush administration quickly plucked
the initiative from the weakening hands of Gorbachev and played a very active
and stabilizing role in ending the Cold War in Europe. For Gorbachev, this
was a very important development. He found in Bush what he had missed
since Reagan had left the White House: an understanding and reassuring partner. On December 2–3 at the Malta summit Bush and Gorbachev achieved
what they had wanted to do months before, the creation of a personal relationship of mutual trust and respect.[87]

It is remarkable, in retrospect, how much Bush, like Reagan before him,
came to believe in Gorbachev as a person of "common sense" who would
admit that the West had won the Cold War. In preparations for the summit,
Bush told NATO secretary general Manfred Woerner on October 11 that the
main thing was to persuade the Soviets to allow continued change in Eastern
Europe and the GDR. When Woerner warned that Gorbachev would not
let the GDR leave the Warsaw Pact, Bush wondered if he could persuade
Gorbachev to let the Warsaw Pact go, to decide its military value was no

84. Bush and Scowcroft, *A World Transformed*, 135.

85. Quoted by Michael Beschoss and Strobe Talbott, *At the Highest Levels: The Inside Story of the End of
the Cold War* (Boston: Little, Brown, 1993), 73–100.

86. See, for example, the analytical paper of Fritz Ermarth, chairman of the National Intelligence
Council, CIA, "The Russian Revolution and the Future Russian Threat to the West: Geostrategic
Woolgathering," May 18, 1990, declassified and posted on the Johnston Reading List, June 30, 1999. Also see
Directorate of Intelligence (CIA), "Rising Political Instability Under Gorbachev: Understanding the Problem
and Prospects for Resolution, An Intelligence Assessment" (April 1989), and "Gorbachev's Domestic
Gambles and Instability in the USSR, An Intelligence Assessment" (September 1989); both documents were
declassified by FOIA request and are on file at the National Security Archive, George Washington
University.

87. James A. Baker III, with Thomas M. DeFrank, *The Politics of Diplomacy: Revolution, War, and Peace,
1989–1992* (New York: G. P. Putnam's Sons, 1995), 144–52; Bush and Scowcroft, *A World Transformed*, 173.

longer essential. "That may seem naïve," Bush said, "but who predicted the changes we are seeing today?"[88] One could hardly imagine any U.S. leader trying to persuade Stalin, Khrushchev, Brezhnev, or Andropov "to let go" of the Soviet sphere of influence in Europe. However, there was a rare harmony between Bush and Gorbachev, as they talked one-on-one and almost effortlessly agreed on all the main issues at their first official summit.

At first, Bush startled Gorbachev opening the discussion with, not the question of the future of Europe, but the issue of the "export of revolution" and the Soviet presence in Central America. The Americans were relieved when Gorbachev assured them that the Soviet Union "has no plans regarding spheres of influence in Latin America."[89] So revolutionary and improbable it seemed to them that the Soviet leadership was renouncing its geopolitical ambitions, that even a year after Malta Bush had lingering doubts. When Gorbachev joined the United States in a coalition against its long-time ally and debtor Saddam Hussein, Bush, speaking to his advisers, vowed not to "overlook the Soviet desire for access to warm water ports."[90]

But despite this skepticism, Bush found it easy to deal with Gorbachev. When the two leaders began to discuss the German Question, there was an excellent opportunity for Gorbachev to set the terms for the reunification of Germany and demand from Bush, in exchange for support for reunification, a firm commitment to the construction of "a new European home" with simultaneous dissolution of two military-political blocs in a new security structure. However, he just came down heavily on Kohl's plan of "ten points," a decisive move by the West German chancellor to swallow the GDR. In his words, this move "put in question trust in the government of the FRG. What would happen? A unified Germany would be neutral, not belonging to military-political alliances, or a member of NATO? I think we should let everybody understand that *it would be premature to discuss now one or the other scenario.*" He then continued: "There are two German states, so history ordered. And let history now decide how the process should evolve and where it should lead in the context of new Europe and the new world."[91]

88. The record of the meeting is cited in Zelikow and Rice, *Germany Unified*, 398–99.
89. Soviet record of conversation with President George Bush, December 2, 1989, the Archive of the Gorbachev Foundation, Moscow. On the startled reaction of Gorbachev, personal communication from Pavel Palazchenko, who interpreted for this conversation. Also see Bush and Scowcroft, *A World Transformed*, 165.
90. Bush and Scowcroft, *A World Transformed*, 317.
91. Soviet record of conversation with President George Bush, December 2, 1989, the Archive of the Gorbachev Foundation, Moscow.

This was a vintage Gorbachev preferring to talk about principles on which a new global order and "new European house" should be based, rather than to haggle about practicalities of German settlement. Again, it was a stark contrast with Stalin as a statesman if one compares the record of Malta's summit with the records of Stalin's negotiations of 1939–45. The Soviet dictator acted like a stubborn bulldog and sly fox simultaneously, fighting for every inch whenever Soviet "state interests" (in his understanding) were at stake and making "generous" concessions only when it fit his overall plan of negotiations. Stalin's foreign policy was imperialistic and very costly for his country, yet his negotiating techniques evoked grudging admiration from other imperialist masters, such as Winston Churchill and Anthony Eden. Gorbachev, by contrast, did not even seek to elicit any specific agreements and promises from Bush. At that time he obviously considered the "special relationship" with Bush his paramount interest. He was satisfied with his assurance "not to leap on the Berlin Wall" or to "jumpstart" the process of German unification.

Various officials in Moscow, including the ambassador to the FRG Yuly Kvitsinsky and Eduard Shevardnadze, had admitted since November that the GDR was about to disappear and suggested a preemptive strategy: to impose on Kohl the idea of a confederation of the two states. Alternatively, Anatoly Chernyaev proposed something that can in retrospect be viewed as "a new Rapallo"[92] by reaching an early agreement with Kohl about German reunification by linking it to Germany's commitment to a new pan-European security structure.

But Gorbachev revealed no inclination for preemptive actions and *realpolitisch* deals, no matter how serious were their chances for success. For two crucial months Soviet foreign policy on the German reunification was adrift. Only at the end of January 1990, in preparation for the Canadian meeting of foreign ministers, did Gorbachev hold a policymaking conference that accepted the "four-plus-two" formula for negotiations on German reunification. While Gorbachev finally admitted that the "processes" would lead to reunification, he still hoped against hope that the GDR could survive thanks to its own "perestroika." (Gorbachev was prompted in his illusion by false advice of some German experts who reflected antireunification opinions of the West German social democratic establishment. At the same time, in fairness,

92. This term was born in 1922 when Germany and the Soviet Union struck a bilateral agreement behind the backs of the rest of the world.

other experts warned him very early that the GDR would not sustain itself for long.) Also the Soviet leader preferred to let "two German states" take a lead in the settlement talks and later accepted with easy heart the replacement of the "four plus two" formula with the final "two plus four" version.[93] Finally, in July 1990, he took Chernyaev's advice and reached a unilateral settlement with Kohl at Arkhyz. By that time, of course, Gorbachev's negotiating hand was extremely weak; but even then he never attempted to use the last waning "asset," namely, the presence of Soviet troops on German soil. No "new Rapallo" took place, and Gorbachev did not seek it, very much to the relief of the United States and other Western countries.

On the contrary, it was a determined policy of both Kohl and the Bush administration to nudge "history" in the right direction at a rapid, but coordinated pace. Their joint actions, called by two younger "realistic" members of the Bush administration "a study in statecraft"[94] helped produce the desirable result: Germany became part of NATO, while the USSR did not get any firm commitments about future structure of European security and Moscow's role in it.

Conclusion

Mikhail Gorbachev's character was a serious factor in the history of the end of the Cold War. It conditioned his preferences and choices. In retrospect, Gorbachev, in his determination to end the Cold War, had to wage two political campaigns: one aimed at the West and another at his own people. The main characteristics of his personality—tolerance for different opinions, idealistic and moralistic optimism, staunch belief in common sense, and universalist interpretation of "all human values"—made him the darling of the West, but a pariah at home. For this reason, the relationship between his foreign and domestic priorities gradually became reversed. Initially, foreign policy was meant to overcome the international isolation of the USSR, to improve economic and trade relations with the West, to wind down the arms race. But around 1987–88, Gorbachev, increasingly sabotaged by the party nomenklatura and without real domestic support, assigned priority to integration of the USSR in the world community as the way to its restructuring, that is to

93. Julij A. Kwizinskij, *Vor dem Sturm: Errinerungen eines Diplomaten*, trans. Hilde Ettinger and Helmut Ettinger (Berlin: Siedler, 1993), 16–17; Zelikow and Rice, *Germany Unified*, 124–25; record of the meeting on Germany at the CC CPSU, January 28, 1990, from Anatoly Chernyaev's journal.

94. Zelikow and Rice, *Germany Unified*.

say, foreign policy came to determine domestic policy. His "new thinking" became a goal in itself, a substitute for a "normal" strategy of statesmanship. Gorbachev, in his idealism, believed it was "a ticket" for him and the USSR to join the community of "civilized nations." While his domestic choices undermined the Soviet economy and the Soviet state, his international vision precluded any chance for the USSR to get "better terms" from the West for ending the confrontation.

No doubt the debates about Gorbachev's personality and his personal choices will continue as long as Russia struggles between its need for a solid state, stability, and prosperous economy, on one hand, and the need to develop a dynamic, self-reliant civil society on the other. Perhaps a consensus on this question is impossible; in the similar revolutionary circumstances in the past the vision of liberal internationalists in Russia differed sharply from the concerns of conservative statists, even the most enlightened ones. For instance, here is an opinion of enlightened conservative, Russian count Sergei Trubetskoi, about Georgy L'vov, the first head of the 1917 Provisional Government. To a remarkable extent, it echoes the modern criticisms of Gorbachev. Trubetskoi wrote in emigration in Paris in 1940:

The populism [*narodnichestvo*] of L'vov was of a rather fatalistic nature. I am groping for proper words to characterize his belief in Russian people in general, in the common people in particular. He imagined them in false tones, as if through rosy glasses. . . . "Do not worry," L'vov said to me on the eve of the first assault of the Bolsheviks in Petersburg in the summer of 1917. "We need not use force. Russian people do not like violence. . . . All will settle down *by itself*. All will turn out to be well. . . . People *themselves* will create from their wise instincts just and light forms of life." I was shocked by these words of the head of the government in those difficult minutes when he ought to take energetic actions. A true fighter in the matters of economy, in the affairs of the state he was some kind of "*neprotivlenets*" [a believer in nonviolence under any circumstances].[95]

Recently, another Russian émigré, Mikhail Geller, wrote about Gorbachev in a book on the history of Soviet society (edited by a former radical democrat Yury Afanasyev): "Gorbachev continued to live in the world of illusions. He assuaged himself with chimerical schemes, in the belief that political zigzags would allow him to retain power, in fact, to aggrandize it." As to the decision to agree to the reunification of Germany on Western terms, "the decision of Gorbachev was not the act of a statesman who carefully thought through the

95. Sergey E. Trubetskoy, *Minuvsheye* (Moscow: DEM, 1991), 109, 110.

consequences of his step. Rather, it was an act of a gambler who believed that, if he sacrificed the GDR, he would get in return some aces that he would use at home. Gorbachev seemed to behave like a balloonist who, having discovered that his balloon was falling, would toss overboard everything that one could find in the basket."[96]

But other émigrés and even some Russians at home raise, from time to time, glasses to Gorbachev's health. And they have a point. Without Gorbachev, the dismantling of the Cold War would not have happened so quickly. A different person could have taken a very different course of action and, who knows, perhaps as a result the Soviet Union would exist even today. But so would the Cold War. For millions of people, the end of the superpowers' confrontation and the Iron Curtain created new opportunities, opened new choices for their life and work.

Opposed perspectives on Gorbachev take root not in his personality but in the gigantic consequences of his actions and inactivity. Every group, faction, or school sees him as a function of these consequences. Gorbachev cannot be all these functions at one time. But certain qualities of Gorbachev's character help explain the quick end to the Cold War and the quick dissolution of the Soviet Union. The former fact secures Gorbachev's place in international history. The latter one makes him one of the most controversial figures in the history of Russia—the country that, some argue, sank into ultimate lawlessness, cynicism, corruption, and misery as a result of the "unpredictability" that Gorbachev set into motion.

96. Yuriy Afanasyev, ed., *Sovetskoye obshchestvo: vozniknoveniye, razvitiye, istoricheskiy final*, vol. 2 (Moscow: Rossiyskiy gosudarstvenniy gumanitarniy universitet, 1997), 560, 562.

8 The Road(s) Not Taken: Causality and Contingency in Analysis of the Cold War's End

Robert D. English

> Two roads diverged in a wood, and I—
> I took the one less traveled by,
> And that has made all the difference.
>
> —*Robert Frost*

APPRECIATION OF THE element of historical contingency in the Cold War's end—an understanding of how and when critical turning points appeared, of what plausible alternatives existed and where different choices might have led—is generally poor. In much of the literature there prevails instead a sense of inevitability, a more or less explicit assumption that by the mid-1980s the USSR had little choice but to undertake major domestic reforms and a broad retreat from empire. It was the unforgiving calculus of power that so dictated, as deepening economic crisis made it impossible to keep up the military rivalry with a newly assertive West; the so-called new thinking—if not merely rationalizing the unavoidable—reflected ideas driven mainly by instrumental and not idealistic concerns.[1] The greatest drama, the "moment of truth" in this telling, came only at the end of the 1980s when Mikhail Gorbachev faced the inescapable consequences of his attempted reforms: the collapse of East European socialism in 1989, and the march of German reunification in 1990. These were the crises that, successfully surmounted by skillful diplomacy, represented a point of no return whose passage marked the real end of the Cold War.

The importance of this narrative's accuracy is enormous: in its own right, as a matter of historical record; as a series of events suggesting vital lessons for U.S. foreign policy; and as a case of momentous change with crucial implications for theories of international relations. And yet, owing largely to its misunderstanding of the element of contingency, it gets the story—and the attendant lessons—wrong in all three areas. Put briefly, the decisive turn

---

1. The most persuasive "materialist" interpretations are Wohlforth and Brooks's chapter herein; Stephen G. Brooks and William C. Wohlforth, "Power, Globalization and the End of the Cold War: Reevaluating a Landmark Case for Ideas," *International Security* 25, no. 3 (2000/2001): 5–53; and Randall Schweller and William Wohlforth, "Power Test: Updating Realism in Response to the End of the Cold War," *Security Studies* 9, no. 2 (winter 2000). A prominent ideational account that emphasizes instrumental aspects of the rise of "new thinking" is Jeffrey T. Checkel, *Ideas and International Political Change: Soviet/Russian Behavior and the End of the Cold War* (New Haven: Yale University Press, 1997).

actually came in the mid-1980s and was propelled as much by the force of *ideas* as the imperatives of power. There was a viable and politically powerful alternative to Gorbachev and broad liberalization in 1985, and it lost out less because, and more *in spite*, of the renewed U.S. hard line in foreign policy. But, once chosen, Gorbachev's path led swiftly to a decisive break with the deep-rooted posture of East-West rivalry and confrontation, and thence to a conclusion that, for all its drama and danger, was now arguably more "inevitable" than its inception.

Again, this had as much to do with the power of ideas as a crisis of power, abetted as it was by an influential group of reformist, "Westernizing" intellectuals who had done much to propel the launch of perestroika and new thinking in the first place. Many of them had been promoting such reforms for over a decade, long before it was popular or profitable to do so. By late 1986 or early 1987—that is, prior to the sharp economic downturn that followed—Gorbachev and his allies had crossed a key ideological divide and definitively embraced a liberal-humanist-integrationist conception of their country and its place in the international community. With this critical turn, the Cold War's end was now largely a matter of time; indeed, in an important sense it had already ended with the decisive rejection of perhaps its most vital sustaining force.

It would still require much skillful diplomacy to negotiate specific terms, and of course could easily have been halted by a political reversal in Moscow. But, as the hard-liners' putsch of August 1991 served to demonstrate, this would have required the removal of Gorbachev.[2] So long as he was in charge, one of the Soviet conferees reminds his American colleagues, the hard-liners did not even dare to suggest use of military force to halt the collapse of socialism in Eastern Europe.[3] It is a point—like others from the Soviet side, on the *intellectual* impetus behind new thinking—that is not so much disputed as ignored. This is understandable; for all their expertise, the internal story of perestroika's inception and implementation is still very difficult for many Western policymakers to comprehend. There is also the tendency of statesmen to view their opposite numbers as operating in a familiar context (if not

---

2. Since the coup failed so quickly, rarely are the implications that its success would have had for Soviet foreign relations pondered. But given the number of troops then still abroad, not to mention spiraling national-separatist sentiments on the USSR's periphery, those implications were certainly difficult. Even more problematic would have been a decision to remove or block Gorbachev in 1987 or 1988—that is, *before* the acceleration of glasnost (including openness on foreign affairs), *before* his democratization of the political system (probably his most fateful step), and *before* implementation of his major foreign policy concessions.

3. Anatoly Chernyaev, in Chapter 2, p. 54.

always cast in a favorable light), as well as to magnify the importance of events in which one took part and to credit one's own actions as decisive in shaping a positive outcome.[4]

But understandable or not, these tendencies can lead to misperception of the inevitable and contingent, to confusion between distant and proximate or actual and illusory sources of causation, and so to the drawing of one-sided historical conclusions and misleading policy lessons. My argument about contingency and causality in the Cold War's end is clearly an unconventional one. In the space of this chapter it can only be outlined and illustrated in brief, something best accomplished by examining several key phases in the accession of Gorbachev and the evolution of his foreign policy.[5]

Crisis and Leadership in Transition

Was the launching of far-reaching domestic changes unavoidable or "objectively necessary" for the Soviet Union in the mid-1980s? And was economic crisis so deep that it also required a broad retreat from empire and "suing for peace" in the global contest with the West on highly concessionary terms? The simple answer to these questions is no. For all its now well-documented weaknesses—negligible or nonexistent growth, technological backwardness, chronic shortages—the Soviet economy was nevertheless strong enough to sustain the country on a largely status quo course well into the next century.[6]

Arguments from hindsight—reading a near-desperate "necessity" back into 1985 from the disintegration that came in 1991—are both empirically and analytically flawed. It is manifestly *not* the case that collapse occurred because of the same problems that supposedly necessitated radical reforms; collapse was a direct (albeit unintended) result of those reforms themselves, in whose absence the Soviet system would almost surely still be intact today.[7] A similar confusion of cause and effect attends projecting back into the minds of decision makers in 1985 a situation that did not obtain until perhaps five years later.

4. The classic work on such issues remains Robert Jervis, *Perception and Misperception in International Politics* (Princeton: Princeton University Press, 1976).

5. For more detail, see Robert D. English, *Russia and the Idea of the West: Gorbachev, Intellectuals, and the End of the Cold War* (New York: Columbia University Press, 2000).

6. Perhaps the best single source for this assertion—containing both economic analysis and participant recollections—is Michael Ellman and Vladimir Kontorovich, eds., *The Destruction of the Soviet Economic System: An Insiders' History* (Armonk, N.Y.: M. E. Sharpe, 1998).

7. Ibid. A defense of realism that conflates Soviet stagnation of 1985 with the accelerating crisis of 1988–89 is Stephen M. Walt, "The Gorbachev Interlude and International Relations Theory," *Diplomatic History* 21, no. 3 (summer 1997).

Some, principally Gorbachev, were indeed convinced that only major changes could stave off a looming crisis. But most others did not share his degree of concern, viewing Soviet problems in less dire terms and so favoring quite different measures to address them. These alternative prescriptions concerned both domestic and foreign policy, ranging from the status quo abroad and only modest changes at home, to a harder foreign policy line and sharp tightening of the screws in domestic life.[8] Only by close examination of how a particular course (and leader) was chosen can we begin to understand why one prevailed and others did not, as well as how likely these alternatives were and what difference they might have made to the course of the Cold War.

Brezhnev, under whose rule the Soviet Union had achieved superpower status, global reach, and nuclear parity with the United States but whose later "gerontocratic" regime saw the country slip into stagnation, died in November 1982. Concerned about declining growth and rising socioeconomic problems (such as absenteeism, alcoholism, and mortality), his successor Yury Andropov briefly shook up the country's leadership before succumbing to kidney disease and premature death in April 1984. During his approximately nine months of active leadership, Andropov decried corruption, waste, and inefficiency while launching a series of "experiments" in economic decentralization. He also stumbled into a series of foreign policy crises—the downing of a Korean Airlines passenger jet, the breakdown of arms talks over the issue of NATO missiles in Europe, and a growing confrontation over space-based weapons—that were only partly of his own making.[9]

Perhaps his most important step was the promotion of a group of officials in the senior leadership—Gorbachev, Yegor Ligachev, Nikolai Ryzhkov, and several others—whose relative youth, energy, and freedom from the taint of corruption distinguished them from the majority of Brezhnev-era functionaries. But Andropov's untimely death interrupted any long-range plans he may have had, and under his successor, the emphysematic Brezhnev crony Konstantin Chernenko, the country fell back into the rut of his longtime patron. Meanwhile, hard-liners took advantage of this leadership vacuum to advance their agenda—from plans for a sharp increase in military spending, to a purge of too-outspoken reformist academics and policy advisers.[10]

8. English, *Russia and the Idea of the West*, chaps. 5–6.
9. The classic work on superpower diplomacy of this period is Raymond L. Garthoff, *The Great Transition: American-Soviet Relations and the End of the Cold War* (Washington, D.C.: The Brookings Institution, 1994).
10. English, *Russia and the Idea of the West*, chap. 5.

Still, Andropov's personnel legacy continued in the preparation of his protégés for yet another near-term leadership transition. Ligachev oversaw turnover in the Central Committee, while Ryzhkov helped manage the analysis of proposals for economic change. Gorbachev became the Politburo's "second secretary" and unofficial heir-apparent, though his rise was strongly resisted by some hard-liners, particularly Prime Minister Nikolai Tikhonov and Military Industry Secretary Grigory Romanov. Negative too, though less actively so, was the attitude of such Brezhnevite Politburo members as the republican party bosses Vladimir Shcherbitsky and Dinmukhamad Kunayev; as one longtime apparat staffer observed, Gorbachev was generally "feared and distrusted by the old guard," who regarded him as "a mysterious, alien, even hostile figure."[11]

The stance toward Gorbachev of Foreign Minister Andrei Gromyko and Defense Minister Dmitry Ustinov was rather more ambiguous. The former—no new thinker, but distressed at rampant corruption—had been instrumental in Gorbachev's "temporary" appointment as second secretary upon Chernenko's accession.[12] This greatly strengthened his hand when Chernenko died just a year later, at which time Gromyko also formally nominated Gorbachev for the position of general secretary.[13] Ustinov's attitude was perhaps more skeptical but ultimately less important. He died in December 1984 (three months before Chernenko) and thus played no part in the last-minute maneuvering that finally settled on Gorbachev.[14]

The Politburo indeed "unanimously" recommended Gorbachev to the Central Committee, which elected him general secretary in March 1985. But as even the brief summary just given is sufficient to show, this was unanimity only in the most formal, procedural sense (for decades, *every* decision taken by the Politburo had been officially unanimous). As various insider accounts reveal, Gorbachev's triumph was more of a touch-and-go affair with a slight Politburo majority (thanks also to the timely absence of Shcherbitsky and Kunayev) only grudgingly deciding to take a chance on the young leader for lack of a better alternative.[15] Why this ambivalence? Why the hesitation to

11. Valery Boldin, *Ten Years That Shook the World: The Gorbachev Era as Witnessed by his Chief of Staff*, trans. Evelyn Rossiter (New York: Basic Books, 1994), 53.

12. On Gromyko's motives, see A. S. Chernyayev, *Shest' let s Gorbachevym: po dnevnikovym zapisyam* (Moscow: Progress-Kul'tura, 1993), 30–31.

13. Vadim Pechenev, *Gorbachev: K vershinam vlasti: Iz teoretiko-memuarnykh razmyshlenii* (Moscow: Gospodin narod, 1991), 109–10.

14. Archie Brown, *The Gorbachev Factor* (New York: Oxford University Press, 1996), 69–71.

15. Other sources here include Nikolay Ryzhkov, *Perestroyka: istoriya predatel'stv* (Moscow: Novosti, 1992), and Yegor Ligachev, *Inside Gorbachev's Kremlin: The Memoirs of Yegor Ligachev*, trans. Catherine H. Fitzpatrick, Michele A. Berdy, and Dobrochna Dyrcz-Freeman (New York: Pantheon, 1993).

elect the candidate who was far and away the most intelligent and energetic among them, and who in any case had been "anointed" by Andropov for the post more than a year earlier?

Several factors complicated Gorbachev's rise, including an international atmosphere of heightened confrontation that strengthened the hard-liners and made Politburo members loathe to gamble on their youngest and least experienced colleague. There was also the fear—raised by various of his statements and personal associations—that Gorbachev might move too far, too fast.[16] Such concerns were of course well founded (exactly why will be examined presently), and many would later bitterly complain of a "betrayal." In the words of one of the Politburo's centrist, "swing" voters in 1985, "Nobody thought that he'd be a reformer. . . . He didn't turn out to be the man that we'd voted for."[17] So who was the man they'd voted for, or rather, what sort of policies had they anticipated?

Continuation of the Brezhnev-Chernenko status quo was one option, though the steady decline to which it was increasingly obviously leading left it the preferred choice of a dwindling number of the old guard.[18] Another group, as noted, advocated a hard-line turn. Comprised of various members of the military-industrial complex and neo-Stalinist party officials, they sought greatly increased defense spending (with emphasis on high-technology weapons), a crackdown on dissent (to include not only open critics but even the reform-minded "loyal opposition"), and a return to pre-détente ideological orthodoxy and societal discipline. Their strength was seen in Stalin-style pronouncements about apocalyptic confrontation with the West and even a partial rehabilitation of Stalin himself (in books and movies, and symbolically as well in the readmission to the party of Stalin's longtime henchman and foreign minister, Vyacheslav Molotov). Less visible at the time, but perhaps even more portentous, was their assault on liberal academics, their advocacy of a Soviet "Star Wars" system, and their efforts to humiliate and undermine Gorbachev.[19] Had these reactionaries succeeded, the likelihood

---

16. Boldin, *Ten Years*, 50–51. See also then-director of the KGB Vladimir Kryuchkov, in *Sovetskaya Rossiya*, February 13, 1993.

17. See the interview with Gaidar Aliyev in Andrey Karaulov, *Vokrug kremlya: Kniga politicheskikh dialogov*, 2 vols. (Moscow: Novosti, 1990, 1992), 1:268.

18. The Brezhnevites' preferred candidate could have been Prime Minister Nikolai Tikhonov or Moscow party boss Victor Grishin (both over seventy years old at the time) but not far behind might have been military industry secretary Grigory Romanov (still in his sixties, and an outspoken hard-liner).

19. For detail on all these positions and initiatives, see English, *Russia and the Idea of the West*, chap. 5.

of a very different, far more perilous, ending to the Cold War would have been great.

Others favored a path lying between the neo-Stalinists and neo-Brezhnevites, essentially a return to the changes Andropov had begun. Where might these have led? Domestically, various streamlining and anticorruption measures could have prolonged the life of the old system well into the next century; with heightened discipline and renewed "vigilance," popular dissatisfaction would not have been a near-term concern. Internationally, the USSR might have quit Afghanistan and ceded other Third World contests—but surely not as easily as it actually did—while a precarious nuclear confrontation would likely continue.[20] Thence one can imagine multiple scenarios. In one, an "Ottoman" variant, a steadily declining USSR might find itself drawn into a cycle of dissent, repression, and eventual rebellion in Eastern Europe that could also spread to parts of Ukraine, the Baltics, and the Caucasus (all fraught with dangerous international implications). In another, "Romanian" scenario, a more defiant USSR might more determinedly keep its subjects in order, delaying the regime's eventual denouement but thereby ensuring that it would be more violent and destabilizing (especially if hard-liners clung to power by mobilizing against such "threats" as Afghanistan/Pakistan, Turkey, or China). And Ceauşescu, of course, possessed neither a foreign empire nor nuclear weapons.[21]

Perhaps yet another option—though it seems to have risen mainly in hindsight, with scant evidence that it was broadly considered at the time—was to undertake more radical, Chinese-style economic reforms. Notwithstanding the great political and socioeconomic differences in the Soviet situation that made this scenario highly problematic, its foreign policy implications might have been even more troubling. As a global (not regional) power with a vast strategic arsenal and extensive international commitments and entanglements, the domestic upheaval ensuing from such a course would have had dangerous reverberations abroad. This is particularly so if, as some post hoc advocates of Soviet Chinese-style reforms themselves allow, maintaining order might have required a broad domestic crackdown or even imposition

20. On Gromyko's subsequent astonishment at Gorbachev's unwillingness "to use force and pressure to defend state interests"—a revealing observation when considering where alternatives to Gorbachev's leadership might have led—see Anatoli Gromyko, *Andrey Gromyko v labirintakh Kremlya. Vospominaniya i razmyshleniya syna* (Moscow: IPO Avtor, 1997), 184 and passim.

21. For a slightly different view of Soviet options in 1985, see Vladislav Zubok's analysis in Chapter 7.

of martial law.[22] And this is assuming that such reforms would have eventually succeeded; had they not, the international repercussions could have been truly explosive.

While it is impossible to state so definitively, the alternatives under consideration seem to have ranged from minimal to modest reforms at home, and from essentially the status quo to a harder line abroad.[23] In the end, it appears that resumption of an Andropov-style course won out. That is what the Politburo elected Gorbachev to enact, and that is what he gave them good reason to expect.[24] But his private ambitions already went considerably further, and the radical changes that ensued—nowhere among the options considered by the Politburo in early 1985, yet to begin very soon after Gorbachev's assumption of power—had as much to do with the catalyst of ideas as a crisis of power.

Gorbachev and the Intellectual Origins of New Thinking

For over two decades—in fact, since soon after the death of Stalin in 1953—there had been developing a strong intellectual current of liberal, humanist, global orientation. Beginning among writers, historians, and philosophers, by the early-to-mid-1960s a distinct "Westernizing" intellectual elite had grown to include scientists, economists, and foreign affairs specialists as well. They were the "children of the Twentieth Congress," that landmark event of de-Stalinization, who had studied and matured during the cultural awakening, domestic liberalization, and international opening of Khrushchev's reform epoch. Instead of Stalin's "hostile capitalist encirclement" and terror, they were shaped by "peaceful coexistence" and thaw. Beyond general inspiration, such changes also brought the specific prerequisites of new thinking: access to Western humanities, social science, and media; travel for research and confer-

22. Jerry F. Hough, *Democratization and Revolution in the USSR, 1985–1991* (Washington, D.C.: The Brookings Institution, 1997), 96–97, 106, 118.

23. Brooks and Wohlforth disagree, claiming that the Soviet leadership shared a broad sense of impending crisis and broad agreement on the need for international retrenchment and arms reductions. This they argue in part by adding to the familiar litany of Soviet economic woes an ostensibly new factor: the globalization of production (see their chapter in this volume as well as their "Power, Globalization, and the End of the Cold War"). But as important a *qualitative* shift as this appears in hindsight, the evidence on how it was viewed by the leadership at the time suggests it was in less alarmist, more *quantitative* terms, that is, as just another in a sizable list of economic woes (shortages and bottlenecks, flagging growth, scientific-technological backwardness, etc.). In general, I argue that Brooks and Wohlforth overstate the conservatives' agreement with a policy of retrenchment and understate the opposition to its implementation. For a more detailed reply to Brooks and Wohlforth, see Robert D. English, "Power, Ideas, and New Evidence on the Cold War's End," *International Security* 26, no. 3 (2001/2002): 1–22.

24. Ryzhkov, *Perestroyka*, 79; Pechenev, *Gorbachev: K vershinam vlasti*, 90, 92.

ences abroad; and increasing freedom to criticize and debate at home (particularly among specialists, in many new or rejuvenated academic institutes). While their professional concerns varied widely, they were intellectually—and often personally—united in rejecting the two-camp, confrontational outlook of Leninist-Stalinist dogmas, and in embracing an increasingly liberal, integrationist, social democratic worldview.

By the early 1970s, many of them—still a minority among Soviet intellectuals, and an even smaller one in the party apparat—also grew increasingly active in promoting liberal ideas and proposing policy reforms. At odds with the party line, most such efforts could not be publicized openly and so were (and remain) largely unknown to outside observers. They were mainly seen in specialized literature and classified analytical reports; they ranged from blunt criticism of Soviet economic isolation and bold calls for its marketization and integration with the world economy, to analyses that faulted Soviet foreign policy for its too-aggressive posture in theaters from Europe and Asia to the Third World.[25] It is important that this "mobilization" began well *before* the economic slump that followed. It also began before a "second thaw" came in the bright but brief flowering of détente.

But while it did not launch Soviet new thinking, the détente epoch of the mid-1970s gave it a vital boost. This it did through rapid expansion of cultural and educational ties, and especially via the institutionalization of contacts between Soviet and Western economists, scientists, security specialists, and other professions. These links served to strengthen the "Westernizing" intellectual current and, in particular, to advance various cooperative approaches to arms control and international security.[26] By the end of the 1970s and beginning of the 1980s, even as Soviet-Western relations collapsed and they came under conservative attack, many members of this new-thinking elite redoubled their efforts to salvage détente and encourage liberalizing reforms. Oblique questioning of the invasion of Afghanistan and "Aesopian" criticism of Soviet Third World activism even appeared publicly, while blunter critiques

25. These usually classified or limited-circulation sources—far too numerous to be specified in a chapter-length summary—confirm the new thinking's early and extensive development among a policy-academic elite. They also illustrate how many of that elite were willing to swim against the official tide, risking rebuke or worse with advocacy that butted up against a tightly closed "policy window." A few of these writings are summarized in Robert English, "Sources, Methods, and Competing Perspectives on the End of the Cold War," *Diplomatic History* 21, no. 2 (spring 1997).

26. See Matthew Evangelista, *Unarmed Forces: The Transnational Movement to End the Cold War* (Ithaca: Cornell University Press, 1999).

of these policies, together with those toward Europe and Asia, were found in the closed-specialized literature.[27] Still, as the Cold War grew more heated and Soviet hard-liners circled the wagons, such ideas appeared increasingly heretical and their advocacy became increasingly perilous.

The most outspoken individuals were punished, with sanctions including reprimand by (or expulsion from) the party, public denunciation, and loss of employment. Another popular measure was slightly subtler, with the offender officially retaining his or her job but being barred from publishing, banned from foreign travel, and otherwise blocked from pursuit of serious analytical work. At the behest of party reactionaries, and with the cover of various "investigatory commissions," similar attacks were launched against entire research centers. Those best known for a reformist-Western orientation—including Georgy Arbatov's Institute of the USA and Canada, Nikolai Inozemtsev's Institute of World Economy and International Relations, and Abel Aganbegyan's Novosibirsk Institute of Economic and Industrial Organization—were punished for "misleading the country's leadership," for "harboring zionist elements," and for alleged security breaches.[28]

The new thinkers' influence, never great, had virtually vanished, and their prospects looked even bleaker. They would have been too, were it not for the rise of a small group of change-minded officials within the party, a group whose emergent leader was Gorbachev. He had met many of the reformers in the late 1970s, and over the next few years he forged close ties with some of the most prominent: economists Aganbegyan and Vladimir Tikhonov, sociologist Tatyana Zaslavskaya, physicist Yevgeny Velikhov, and foreign affairs analysts Inozemtsev and Arbatov. Influential in their own right, in another sense these individuals were also the "ambassadors" to Gorbachev of a considerably larger liberal policy-academic elite. By the early 1980s he was also consulting, directly or indirectly, with such experts as foreign policy specialist Yevgeny Primakov, scientist–arms control advocate Roald Sagdeyev, and—most influential of all—the apparatchik scholar-cum-diplomat Aleksandr Yakovlev.[29]

27. In addition to those sources already cited, useful overviews of the activities of "within-system reformers" during the Brezhnev years are Georgy Arbatov, *The System: An Insider's Life in Soviet Politics* (New York: Times Books, 1992); Andrey Grachev, *Kremlevskaya khronika* (Moscow: EKSMO, 1994); and Evgenij Primakov, *Gody v bol'shoi politike* (Moscow: Sovershenno Sekretno, 1999).

28. Arbatov, *The System*; Primakov, *Gody v bol'shoi politike*. See also English, *Russia and the Idea of the West*, chap. 5, for additional argumentation and evidence against the view that new-thinking "policy entrepreneurship" was in one's professional or institutional interests, at least not until 1986 or 1987.

29. Examples of these ties abound in the noted works of Arbatov, Chernyaev, Primakov, and others. Additional sources of insight range from Roald Z. Sagdeev, *The Making of a Soviet Scientist: My Adventures in Nuclear Fusion and Space from Stalin to Star Wars*, ed. Susan Eisenhower (New York: Wiley, 1994), and

In a number of semiformal "seminars," in many more informal meetings, and through numerous memoranda and reports, Gorbachev studied their advice. Such a practice—particularly as it involved ties to some who had recently come (or remained) under the ideologues' fire for their "heresies"— was absolutely unprecedented for a member of the top leadership. As noted, it would later complicate his chances for the office of general secretary. Why did he do it?

Even a cynical or largely instrumental interpretation—that looming crisis forced leaders to consider new alternatives, thus creating opportunities for ambitious "policy entrepreneurs"[30]—necessarily draws attention to the specific origins of reformist ideas. For without much prior development, they simply would not have been available when the need arose. Nor, it appears, did any others in the Politburo besides Gorbachev perceive much use in consulting these entrepreneurs. Close examination of how this entrepreneurship actually occurred highlights the *normative*, not just instrumental, role of ideas. And, above all, analysis of reformist ideas' remarkable and ultimately successful swim against a tide of early 1980s reaction (which hardly made their advocacy a "rational," self-interested choice at the time) directs attention back to the beliefs and values of the one who would become their chief sponsor.[31]

Gorbachev, notwithstanding the unfortunately still-prevalent image of him as a fairly typical (if particularly cunning and ambitious) party functionary, was anything but.[32] There is no denying that his intelligence and ambition were unusual, but from the outset of his career he also showed a strong innovative and idealistic bent. He also stood apart from other high party officials by virtue of his broad exposure—through a relatively diverse legal-humanitarian education, through considerable Western travel, and through extensive private study—to unorthodox, social democratic ideas about international relations.[33]

Aleksandr Yakovlev, *Gor'kaya chasha. Bol'shevizm i reformatsiya Rossii* (Yaroslavl: Verkhne-Volzhskoe Knizhnoe Izdatel'stvo, 1994), to Yegor Gaidar, *Dni porazhenii i pobed* (Moscow: Vagrius, 1996). There is a large memoir literature, to which numerous shorter articles and interviews must be added as well. Some important examples of the latter are found in sources as varied as Andrey Karaulov, *Vokrug Kremlya: Kniga politicheskikh dialogov*, 2 vols. (Moscow: Novosti, 1990, 1992), and William C. Wohlforth, ed., *Witnesses to the End of the Cold War* (Baltimore: Johns Hopkins University Press, 1996).

30. Checkel, *Ideas and International Political Change*.

31. Most of this "intellectual preparation" on Gorbachev's part, as well as evidence of intense discussion among the reformers over the principles of foreign policy almost from the moment Gorbachev took office, is simply and strikingly absent from materialist accounts of the Cold War's end.

32. Brown, *Gorbachev Factor*.

33. English, *Russia and the Idea of the West*, 180–86 and passim.

It is difficult to characterize simply Gorbachev's worldview of the early 1980s, particularly as it was undergoing rapid change. From the accounts of close observers, several aspects of his international outlook appear most notable: a strong desire to end the arms race and East-West confrontation; belief in the possibility of socialism's liberal-humanistic revival, and its prospects for broad cooperation with capitalism (particularly social democratic Europe); and scorn for the West's exploitation of the Third World (together with the same for Soviet behavior in Eastern Europe). There is no doubt that an urgent priority was to halt the sapping U.S.-Soviet military rivalry. But it is also evident that his concern about global, humanitarian problems was genuine and deep. And notwithstanding various contradictions and certain persistent dogmas, it is quite clear that by early 1985 his ambitions for foreign policy change went far beyond the various hints and suggestions—principally, that of "a common European home"—that he had so far publicly voiced.[34]

These were revealed in some of his very first steps after taking power in March 1985. At the receptions for foreign dignitaries that accompanied Chernenko's funeral—in other words, only days after taking office—Gorbachev warmly greeted some social democratic leaders (and also the head of the Italian communist party, a "renegade" organization for its long criticism of Soviet foreign policy and its pioneering of the Eurocommunist heresy) while demonstrably snubbing most East European party bosses. When he met the latter privately, he warned them in no uncertain terms that the days of the "Brezhnev Doctrine" were over, that they must undertake long-overdue reforms and henceforth would sink or swim on their own.[35] Shortly thereafter he ordered the beginning of preparations for a withdrawal from Afghanistan.[36] And less than a month later, at the now-famous "April plenum" of the Central Committee, Gorbachev decried the inefficiency, waste, and corruption in domestic socioeconomic life in terms considerably bolder than any heard under Andropov.

That summer he met privately with his top military brass and warned them of coming cuts in their once-sacred budgets; he also reiterated his call,

34. A prescient early analysis of how Gorbachev's worldview evolved is Janice Gross Stein, "Political Learning by Doing: Gorbachev as Uncommitted Thinker and Motivated Learner," *International Organization* 48, no. 2 (spring 1994).

35. A witness recalls Gorbachev saying "We're all equals now. The Brezhnev doctrine is dead." Anatoly Chernyaev (Princeton University seminar, February 24, 1993).

36. Chernyayev, *Shest' let s Gorbachevym*, 41.

first voiced at the April plenum, for a new defense doctrine based on the criteria of "sufficiency."[37] And publicly, on the anniversary of the U.S. atomic
bombing of Japan in the Second World War, he announced a unilateral moratorium on the testing of nuclear weapons. Since these bold initiatives had
bypassed traditional Ministry and Central Committee channels, distressed
conservatives wondered: "Just how is he deciding defense issues?"[38]

The answer is that Gorbachev was relying on the same informal advisers, the same "brain trust," that he had gathered in the early 1980s.[39] These
reformers were further strengthened with Yakovlev's promotion to a Central
Committee secretaryship, that for ideology and propaganda, from which he
exercised a decisive influence on the emergence of glasnost in all areas, including foreign policy. Also crucial was the mid-year appointment of Eduard
Shevardnadze to replace Gromyko as foreign minister. Had Gorbachev merely
sought to "put his personal stamp" on foreign policy, as many believed at the
time, then any of several deputies could have been promoted. Instead, by
selecting the Georgian party boss (and probably the most innovative of republican leaders), Gorbachev not only chose a longtime confidant of proven
reformist credentials, he also chose a man whose apparent weakness—a lack of
international experience—was actually a strength for a leader seeking to encourage new ideas and break the grip of a hidebound, "Gromykoite" foreign policy
apparat.[40]

Gorbachev's next major step was his November 1985 meeting with
President Reagan in Geneva, the first such summit in six years and a move
strongly opposed by Soviet hard-liners. When the meeting failed to produce

37. Dale R. Herspring, "The Military Factor in East German Soviet Policy," *Slavic Review* 47, no. 1
(1988); Garthoff, *Great Transition*, 214.

38. Sergey F. Akhromeyev and G. M. Korniyenko, *Glazami marshala i diplomata: Kriticheskiy vzglyad na
vneshnyuyu politiku SSSR do i posle 1985-go goda* (Moscow: Mezhdunarodniye otnosheniya, 1992), 65–66, 91. It
should be noted that defense spending under Gorbachev initially showed a slight increase, though this apparently reflected the continuation of previously established plans as well as an effort to stimulate the economy
by raising investment in its most productive industrial sectors. But, notably lacking major new weapons pro-
curement, it did *not* represent a decision by Gorbachev to continue the arms race.

39. For more on "Gorbachev's team," see Sagdeev, *The Making of a Soviet Scientist*, 267–69.

40. The two had established close, cooperative ties during Gorbachev's tenure as party boss of the
Stavropol *krai* (region) bordering Shevardnadze's home republic of Georgia. This cooperation ranged from
various local economic innovations to discussion of the folly of Afghanistan. The latter weighed rather more
heavily on them than it did on most other republican-regional officials, since their Caucasian districts served
as transit points for equipment and troops to—and dead and wounded from—Afghanistan. See
Shevardnadze's *Moy vybor v zashchitu demokratii i svobody* (Moscow: Novosti, 1991); also Carolyn McGiffert
Ekedahl and Melvin A. Goodman, *The Wars of Eduard Shevardnadze* (University Park: Pennsylvania State
University Press, 1997).

any real progress, Gorbachev unveiled a sweeping arms-reduction proposal in January 1986. Although too ambitious to be immediately, practically nego-tiable, it offered various concessions (deep cuts in strategic weapons, including the heretofore untouchable Soviet heavy missile force, as well as reductions in shorter-range weapons) that pointed the way toward precisely the agreements later reached.[41]

There is no doubt that Gorbachev's primary concern during his first year in office was reinvigorating the Soviet economy. As Shevardnadze later described, they were acutely aware that reform at home required tranquillity abroad, partic-ularly a halt to the arms race that was such an economic burden.[42] But if that had been the only, or even the primary, factor in the evolution of Gorbachev's foreign policy, then a breakthrough toward new thinking would have been highly unlikely. Hard-liners on both sides now dug in their heels, and even though his steps to date had produced no major policy changes, some senior Soviet officials went so far as to question publicly Gorbachev's efforts.[43] Yet a major breakthrough was in the making, which close examination reveals was propelled less by an economic "push" than an intellectual "pull."

Crossing the Rubicon in International Relations

Nineteen eighty-six was the most critical year in the evolution of Gorbachev's foreign policy. It was the year that, despite still-modest policy change, saw the most critical cognitive-conceptual change among Gorbachev and his closest allies that then made possible the progress that came so quickly thereafter. This intellectual turn—in the making, as seen, since the early 1980s—acceler-ated with preparations for the Twenty-seventh Party Congress, scheduled for February–March 1986. Such congresses, usually held every five years, were the gatherings at which major policy changes were endorsed by the party's most authoritative conclave (such as Khrushchev's campaign of de-Stalinization, begun at the Twentieth Party Congress in 1956), and so this one represented an important early milestone and critical opportunity in the launch of pere-stroika. This was particularly so as the Twenty-seventh Congress would approve a new party program, to replace the outdated, utopian one inherited from the early 1960s. But equal importance attached to the general secretary's report, a

41. For fascinating participants' accounts—including the military's attempts to co-opt the initiative—see "Peregovorshchik—razoruzhenets," *Nezavisimaya Gazeta*, February 19, 1997.

42. "Eduard Shevardnadze's Choice," interview in *International Affairs* (Moscow), no. 11, 1991, p. 7.

43. *Izvestiya*, November 28, 1985.

document that at Brezhnev-era congresses had been prepared by the apparat and mainly served to ratify the status quo.

This time the usual apparat-managed committees and conservative-dominated drafting groups were enlivened by an infusion of new blood and fresh ideas. But even more important were the private gatherings of Gorbachev and his inner circle—principally Shevardnadze, Yakovlev, Primakov, and Raisa Gorbacheva, as well as occasional others, such as Anatoly Chernyaev, Gorbachev's newly appointed aide for international affairs—that grappled with the fundamental "philosophy of foreign policy."[44] Shevardnadze recalled the "incredible difficulty" with which they embraced the view of an integral world instead of one divided by social systems; in near daily sessions he "observed Gorbachev's ideas heading into dangerous, uncharted waters."[45] Though alien to Leninist thinking, these waters had in fact been well mapped; as Yakovlev noted, they were guided by "the leading minds of the century—Einstein, Kapitsa, Russell, and Sakharov"—in "discarding the besieged-fortress [Stalinist] psychology."[46] Gorbachev too recalled the days that he, Yakovlev, and Shevardnadze spent arguing over rejection of Lenin's basic precept of a class-divided world: "We were at Zavidovo [a government dacha] working on the report, and we really quarreled, for a day and a half we even stopped speaking to each other. What was the argument about? About . . . the fact that we live in an interdependent, contradictory, but ultimately integral world. No, the new thinking wasn't just some policy shift, it required a major conceptual breakthrough."[47]

This breakthrough was largely (but not completely) reflected in the Congress's documents. The worst contradictions of the Khrushchev-era program—that peaceful coexistence is another form of class struggle, and that nuclear war, while not inevitable, would nevertheless see socialism triumph should it occur—were absent from the new one. It is not surprising that Gorbachev's report was the far bolder document. Here was the greatest emphasis on global problems, interdependence, and an integral world, on political means of ensuring security and "reasonable sufficiency" in defense.[48] Still, the changes did not come easily. Gorbachev's report generated fierce

44. Shevardnadze, *Moy vybor*, 96,
45. Ibid., 94, 96.
46. Aleksandr Yakovlev, *Muki prochteniya bytiya. Perestroyka: nadezhdy i real'nosti* (Moscow: Novosti, 1991), 181, 188.
47. "Razgovor s Prezidentom SSSR za chashkoi chaya," *Izvestiya*, September 20, 1991.
48. Mikhail Gorbachev, *Political Report of the CPSU Central Committee to the 27th Party Congress* (Moscow: Novosti, 1986).

opposition, and the final version retained criticism of "American aggression" and "imperialism."[49] Elsewhere, a reference to Afghanistan as "a bleeding wound" was deleted by the conservatives in draft and only restored at the last moment upon the insistence of Gorbachev and Shevardnadze.[50]

The Congress preparations had set in motion a process of searching reflection that would continue in its aftermath. Beyond the familiar channels of policy input—now much invigorated, with younger, new-thinking analysts such as Andrei Grachev and Andrei Kozyrev promoted in the Central Committee and Foreign Ministry—Gorbachev and his closest allies tapped many other sources of ideas. These included studies performed by the most reform-minded and Western-oriented academic institutes,[51] as well as the works of such original thinkers as the philosopher Aleksandr Tsipko, the economist Stanislav Shatalin, and the foreign affairs analyst Vyacheslav Dashichev.[52] Gorbachev's "insatiable search" also led to private study that ranged from Western political science to the memoirs of Western leaders such as Churchill, works long available to the Soviet elite in classified Russian translations.[53] On broader philosophical issues, Raisa introduced him to the integrationist, social democratic–leaning ideas of "semi-dissident" Moscow scholars. And on specific foreign policy matters, Arbatov offered the works of the Palme Commission on disarmament and other European writings on new approaches to global security.[54]

In tandem with Gorbachev's study came an intensive series of meetings with foreign statesmen, activists, and intellectuals, a process that Chernyaev recalled as "the way he came to know the other world."[55] His interlocutors

49. See Chernyayev, *Shest' let s Gorbachevym*, 60.

50. Shevardnadze, *Moy vybor*, 93–94. See also A. G. Kovalev, "Politik poroi obyazan skhodit' s tribuny pod skrip svoikh botinok," *Novaya Gazeta*, April 22, 1996.

51. In addition to numerous liberal sources, the influence on Gorbachev of institutes such as IMEMO (via Yakovlev) as well as that of various social democratic leaning intellectuals (via Gorbachev's wife, Raisa) is confirmed by many of Gorbachev's conservative critics as well; see Boldin, *Ten Years*, 73, 115.

52. Ibid., 73; see also Aleksandr Tsipko, "Gorbachev postavil na 'sotsialisticheskiy vybor' i proigral," *Nezavisimaya Gazeta*, October 17, 1996.

53. See Mikhail Gorbachev and Zdenek Mlynar, "Dialog o perestroike, 'Prazhske vesne' i o sotsializme" (MS), 159–64. Elsewhere such insiders as Chernyaev, Anatoly Dobrynin, and Aleksandr Bessmertnykh have commented on Gorbachev's "insatiable appetite" for reading, emphasizing topics that ranged from the New Economic Policy of the 1920s to European social democratic ideas for arms control of the early-mid-1980s (author's interviews, Princeton and Moscow, 1993–94).

54. Arbatov, *The System*, 324. See also Mikhail Gorbachev, *Zhizn' i reformy* (Moscow: Novosti, 1995), 1:190; Grachev, *Kremlevskaya khronika*, 137; and Pechenev, *Gorbachev: K vershinam vlasti*, 27.

55. Chernyayev, *Shest' let s Gorbachevym*, 75; see also Gorbachev, *Perestroika: New Thinking for Our Country and the World* (New York: Harper & Row, 1987), 139, 144.

included French president François Mitterrand and former U.S. president Richard Nixon, both of whom encouraged his early new thinking and argued that further steps would meet a positive Western response. They also included writers and cultural figures, who fanned his interest in global, humanistic concerns. And they included representatives of Western arms control organizations, such as the Federation of American Scientists, International Physicians for the Prevention of Nuclear War, and the National Resources Defense Council. These groups applauded Gorbachev's early steps but also encouraged bolder ones, such as dropping his demand that the United States halt the Strategic Defense Initiative (SDI, or "Star Wars") before moving ahead on other nuclear issues, or easing the USSR's traditional resistance to on-site verification of arms agreements. They also pressed him to end the exile of Andrei Sakharov, the renowned physicist-dissident who embodied two liberalizing currents simultaneously—that of conciliation and cooperation abroad, and of human rights and democratization at home.[56]

From a completely different corner came similar advice, from Spanish prime minister Felipe Gonzalez. He was perhaps the single most influential of Gorbachev's foreign interlocutors, and they immediately established a bond of intimacy and trust. As his "comrade in the socialist movement"—and, more important, as the leader of a country that was completing a successful transition away from decades of dictatorship—Gorbachev paid close heed to Gonzalez's arguments.[57] They ranged from the importance of genuine democracy, to the necessity of a free market (and foreign investment) in order to achieve socialist goals. Gonzalez also criticized Lenin harshly, for sins that included a lack of humanism, suppression of legality, and his responsibility for the world's division into antagonistic camps.[58]

Viewing all this activity over the post-Congress months, conservatives were aghast. It was the beginning of what they would later describe as the hijacking of perestroika from its intended Andropovian course. In their view, Gorbachev had entered into a "conspiracy of academicians," falling under the

---

56. Sakharov's 1968 samizdat memorandum, *Progress, Coexistence, and Intellectual Freedom* (London: Penguin Books, 1968), a work rather widely known in reformist-specialist circles, was in many ways the pioneer manifesto of Soviet "new thinking."

57. Zubok places even more weight on this factor, finding that at the heart of Gorbachev's embrace of new thinking was his adoption of West European social democracy (and social democrats) as his key "reference group," a transformation that he dates to late 1987 or 1988. Zubok, Chapter 7.

58. M. S. Gorbachev, "Doveritel'nyi razgovor," in *Gody trudnykh resheniy: Izbrannoye 1985–1992* (Moscow: Tortuga, 1993), 235–47.

incompetent and malevolent advice of several "highly politicized research organizations of a pro-Western character."[59] There is more than a little truth to the conservatives' characterization, and their alarm would grow even more after the spring of 1986. That is the time, according to Chernyaev, when Gorbachev resolutely "set himself the task" of achieving a decisive breakthrough in foreign policy.[60] This new urgency flowed directly from another conceptual breakthrough, one triggered by what was probably the most traumatic single event of perestroika.

That event was the Chernobyl tragedy, the deadly reactor explosion and fire that cost thousands of lives and billions of rubles. Many view its impact in mainly the latter terms, as yet another economic drain; but even a brief examination reveals that its cognitive impact was still greater. Chernobyl absolutely consumed the Politburo for three months. A crisis committee, constant meetings and reports, and a summoning of all available civilian and military resources put the government on a virtual wartime footing. Witnesses recall mobilization of a frantic pace and grave intensity "seen only in the years of the Great Patriotic War."[61] The disaster boosted calls for domestic reforms by dramatically exposing the corruption of the Stalinist system, the failures of central planning with its sloppiness and disregard of the human element. But it also boosted the new thinking: "It was a tremendous shock . . . that raised our view of security to an entirely new plane of understanding."[62] Even Sergei Akhromeev, chief of the general staff, recalled the tragedy touching "minds and souls . . . the nuclear danger was no longer abstract, but something palpable and concrete."

Many have compared its impact to that of World War II. But unlike 1941, whose enduring lesson was to build up forces and heighten vigilance, Chernobyl's was the opposite. Traditional military concepts such as surprise or superiority lost meaning when even a small nuclear accident could wreak such havoc. On a more basic level, understanding of Europe's "oneness" was reinforced by the cloud of radiation blowing freely across the Iron Curtain. The concept of an integral world, no longer divided by class, something already

---

59. Valeriy Legostayev, "God 1987-yy—peremena logiki," *Den'*, no. 14, 1991, p. 2.
60. Cited in Fred Greenstein and William Wohlforth, eds., *Retrospective on the End of the Cold War* (Princeton: Center of International Studies, 1994), 40.
61. Akhromeyev and Korniyenko, *Glazami marshala i diplomata*, 99, 105. For further detail see Ryzhkov, *Perestroyka*, 133–52.
62. Anatoly Chernyaev (author's interview: Moscow, December 16, 1993).

accepted in theory, took on concrete meaning in the outpouring of Western aid and sympathy that also briefly reached a level unseen since the Second World War. This support—an "unprecedented campaign of solidarity" despite the ill will caused by initial Soviet secrecy (and consequently some anti-Soviet demonstrations in the West)—was a vote of confidence in Gorbachev's reforms, reinforcing the primacy of global concerns and the cause of openness and East-West cooperation.[63] As Shevardnadze recalled, "It tore the blindfold from our eyes" and "convinced us that morality and politics could not diverge."[64]

For Shevardnadze, Gorbachev, and others fighting to improve ties abroad, the shame of having initially misinformed their foreign colleagues about the disaster (as they themselves were misinformed by their own military-industrial complex) and so aiding a cover-up was a watershed experience. It was "outright sabotage of the new thinking [and of] the trust we had worked so hard to build."[65] They had been betrayed, only not by the West but by their own hard-liners. But the end result was the opposite of what the hard-liners had hoped for.

Velikhov observed that Chernobyl pushed Gorbachev toward "a great, instinctive leap"[66] to break the deadlock in Soviet-Western relations, something clearly seen in his bold address to a Foreign Ministry conference in May (which only appeared in print a year later, and then only in summary form). Though not uncritical of the United States, his main emphasis was on Soviet shortcomings. These included the lack of progress on a withdrawal from Afghanistan as well as ideological opposition to the settlement of other Third World conflicts, "panicked" reporting on the progress of SDI and other threat inflation that supported unnecessary military expenditures, a paternal attitude toward Eastern Europe as if the USSR were "running a kindergarten for little children," and an approach to China that still viewed relations "through the prism of the 1960s."[67]

But the centerpiece of Gorbachev's broadside was his insistence on a "radical restructuring" of the underlying approach to foreign policy. The new priorities included facilitating economic integration, expanding cultural ties,

63. Gorbachev, *Zhizn' i reformy*, 1:302.
64. Shevardnadze, *Moy vybor*, 294.
65. Ibid., 291. See also Sagdeev, *The Making of a Soviet Scientist*, 286–92; Gorbachev, *Perestroika*, 221; and "Chtoby pokoleniya ne zabyli ob etom fakte," *Vestnik*, no. 5 (1996): 87–103.
66. Yevgeny Velikov (author's interview: Moscow, December 30, 1993).
67. "U perelomnoy cherty," in Gorbachev, *Gody trudnykh resheniy*, 46–55.

cooperating in the fight against terrorism, and above all, raising the profile of "humanitarian issues."

The very words "human rights" are put in quotation marks and we speak of so-called human rights, as if our own revolution had nothing to do with human rights. . . . But would there even have been a revolution if such rights had been observed in the old society? We need to reject decisively this outdated approach to the problem . . . and view it more broadly, particularly with regard to such specific issues as reunification of families, exit and entry visas . . . all this is part of the process of building trust.[68]

That same month, Soviet delegates to the Stockholm conventional force talks received new instructions—to accept unprecedented on-site verification measures—and by July a treaty was completed. Shortly thereafter Gorbachev decided to seek an "interim" summit, before the next scheduled U.S.-Soviet gathering (which would become the Reykjavik conclave of October 1986). And as he prepared for that summit, his frustration at the still-timid proposals generated by the apparat boiled over. He turned to Chernyaev for advice, and the latter assessed the latest such proposal harshly:

It proceeds from the old view: "If there is war, the two sides must have equal abilities to destroy each other." What's in here is the arithmetic, not the algebra, of contemporary world politics. . . . Instead, it must begin with the need to liquidate all nuclear weapons. [On strategic forces] it should stress our idea of a 50 percent cut as a first step. In contrast to our earlier positions, such reductions needn't hinge on an agreement over SDI. Otherwise it will be another dead end. [On intermediate forces] we must not begin with an interim but optimal variant: liquidate all medium-range missiles in Europe. The [ministry] proposal again raises a scare over French and English forces. But it's impossible to imagine any circumstances . . . under which they would push the button against us. Here we are only frightening ourselves and raise anew the obstacle that has blocked European disarmament for a decade.[69]

With the exception of dropping opposition to SDI—though he eased the proposed restrictions on it considerably—Gorbachev accepted Chernyaev's recommendations across the board. But others did not, and the Reykjavik proposals generated enormous high-level opposition in the fall of 1986.[70] Akhromeev nearly resigned over the issue, while others in the military-industrial complex pushed even harder for a Soviet "Star Wars" program. Also at this time, the promulgation of a new defense doctrine of "reasonable sufficiency," which

68. Ibid., 53.
69. Chernyayev, *Shest' let s Gorbachevym*, 110.
70. Akhromeyev and Korniyenko, *Glazami marshala i diplomata*, 109, 126; Sagdeev, *The Making of a Soviet Scientist*, 272–73.

Gorbachev had said was coming over a year before, provoked a rebellious outcry among some senior officers.[71] Meanwhile, having earlier warned about the
dangers of incipient glasnost, the KGB now shrilly argued that openness was
facilitating the subversive designs of Western spy agencies.[72]

Conservatives (and many moderates too) grew alarmed, and some felt
that they had been duped. For they were now faced with radical policy changes
that they themselves had earlier endorsed in principle, but with the expectation that they would only serve propaganda purposes and never really be put
into practice.[73] But Gorbachev had different ideas, and the Politburo became
an open battleground. The hard-liners fought fiercely, but Gorbachev stood
his ground: "He fended off all the arguments against [his new proposals] with
a critical, rhetorical question: 'What are you doing, still preparing to fight a
nuclear war? Well, I'm not, and everything else follows from that. . . . If we
still want to conquer the world, then let's decide how to arm ourselves further
and outdo the Americans. But then that'll be it, and everything we've been
saying about a new policy has to go on the trash heap.'"[74]

The hard-liners' last stab at derailing Reykjavik was the "Daniloff affair,"
the arrest on trumped-up charges of an American journalist in, at best, a massive overreaction to the U.S. arrest of a low-level Soviet agent. But the gambit
failed—intense, eleventh-hour negotiations resolved the crisis and permitted
the summit to go forward—and ultimately even backfired. For rather than
derailing the drive toward new thinking, this attempted "sabotage" infuriated
Gorbachev and Shevardnadze; they looked again at the hard-liners, wondering if it was they and not the Americans who were their real adversaries.[75] A
similar irony attended the Reykjavik summit itself. Though it ultimately

71. When it was presented to the General Staff Academy in late 1986, the new doctrine met with
"incomprehension, confusion, fear . . . and accusations that it was flawed, unacceptable, and bordered on
treasonous." Akhromeyev and Korniyenko, *Glazami marshala i diplomata*, 126.

72. Chernyayev, *Shest' let s Gorbachevym*, 96–97; Sagdeev, *The Making of a Soviet Scientist*, 290.

73. Aleksandr G. Savel'yev and Nikolai N. Detinov, *The Big Five: Arms Control Decision-Making in the
Soviet Union*, trans. Dmitry Trenin (Westport, Conn.: Praeger, 1995), 93; Georgiy Shakhnazarov, *Tsena svobody: Reformatsiya Gorbacheva glazami yego pomoshchnika* (Moscow: Rossika-Zevs, 1993), 89–91.

74. Chernyayev, *Shest' let s Gorbachevym*, 112.

75. Brooks and Wohlforth (Chapter 9) downplay the evidence of conservative resistance to Gorbachev's
foreign policy, finding the examples cited herein (ranging from public criticism, to foot-dragging on implementation, to outright "sabotage") relatively feeble or half-hearted. They interpret the absence of more vigorous conservative opposition, and of more clearly articulated policy alternatives, as evidence instead of the
conservatives' essential agreement with a need to retrench. Space does not permit a detailed rebuttal here
(see English, "Power, Ideas, and New Evidence"), but I do wish to emphasize two brief points in reply. One is
that their interpretation seems to project today's more pluralistic Russian politics into the past, forgetting that
the hierarchy and discipline of even late Soviet-era Communist Party politics made open opposition to the

failed—with agreement on broad nuclear disarmament only foundering over the U.S. refusal to brook restrictions on SDI—Gorbachev's disappointment was tempered by hope and exhilaration over just how close they had come.

With this optimism, the final months of 1986 saw Gorbachev take important further steps that reflected his near-complete conversion to new thinking. Ideologically, he now embraced a position that went far beyond what had seemed so bold at the party congress just eight months earlier; in a November speech, he argued that "universal human values take precedence over the interests of any particular class."[76] And politically, in a move of enormous symbolic and practical significance, he "rehabilitated" one of the new thinking's greatest pioneers; in December, again overruling a skeptical Politburo, he ordered that the exile of Andrei Sakharov be ended.

The Cold War's Endgame

Sakharov immediately resumed public advocacy on the two issues of his greatest concern: human rights and arms control. He called on Gorbachev to free other prisoners of conscience, and to free U.S.-Soviet negotiations from the linkage that tied arms cuts to restrictions on SDI. In February 1987, Gorbachev did just that, and the Intermediate-Range Nuclear Forces (INF) treaty followed soon thereafter, the first agreement that did not just limit weapons but eliminated an entire class of them. Meanwhile, Shevardnadze informed his U.S. counterpart of Soviet intentions to achieve a near-term settlement in Afghanistan—with or without U.S. help.[77] Publicly, Gorbachev and Shevardnadze still faulted the United States for the stalemated talks; privately, they blamed hard-liners in Moscow and Kabul for blocking progress. The stubborn Karmal was replaced with the more flexible Najibullah as Shevardnadze railed against regimes that "did not stand for anything" and lacked "any real support among the people."[78] This anger was directed at the East European party bosses as well. Having privately reminded them in late

---

"general line" extremely difficult, and so underrating what resistance did occur. And the second is that the retrospective claims of Soviet conservatives—that they did not resist broad arms cuts and other aspects of retrenchment—must be taken with a much larger grain of salt. Apart from a serious issue of credibility, there is the problem of strong incentives to retouch their actual role in the mid-late 1980s, not the least of which is a perceived need to justify their apparent complicity in the loss of Soviet power, their failure to speak out louder, or break ranks earlier.

76. *Literaturnaya Gazeta*, November 5, 1986.

77. Don Oberdorfer, *The Turn: From the Cold War to a New Era: The United States and the Soviet Union, 1983–1990* (New York: Poseidon Press, 1991), 235–40.

78. Pavel Palazchenko, "Interpreting the Whirlwind" (MS), 144.

1986 that Moscow would no longer bail them out (and also having ordered the Soviet military to begin planning for an eventual withdrawal from the region), Gorbachev stepped up the public pressure by such steps as his sensational visit to Czechoslovakia in 1987.

Over 1987–88, the pace of the new thinking's implementation accelerated on all fronts. Progress toward an Afghan settlement quickened, as did cooperation on the resolution of other regional conflicts, from Cambodia to Namibia and Nicaragua. Negotiations over strategic and conventional arms advanced rapidly, as a series of key Soviet concessions—as well as Gorbachev's landmark unilateral initiative announced in his December 1988 United Nations speech—broke long-standing deadlocks. And glasnost spread on issues of foreign as well as domestic politics. Conservatives fought back, but they could not halt the lightning spread of new-thinking ideas from private councils to numerous public forums. Nor could they block such steps as the unjamming of foreign radio broadcasts and the release of the remaining political prisoners.

It was also in 1987 that Gorbachev secured agreement to summon an extraordinary party conference—held in July 1988—where he won approval for a radical restructuring of the Soviet political system via multicandidate elections for a new Congress of People's Deputies. Again, this initiative is rarely considered in connection with foreign policy and instead interpreted as a move exclusively driven by economic necessity, the need to shake up the party in order to advance economic reforms.[79] Once again, this view is only half right, for it misses altogether the vital link the new thinkers now understood between democratization at home and trust abroad. This link is vividly seen in Gorbachev's account of his post-Reykjavik discussions with British prime minister Margaret Thatcher. Contributing to a "sharp turn" (*sil'nyi povorot*) in Gorbachev's thinking about the domestic nexus of foreign policy, he recalled Thatcher's critique of the Soviet system:

You have no democracy, so there's no control over the government. It does what it wants. You stress the will of your people, that they don't want war, but they're denied the means to express this will. Let's say we trust you personally, but if you're gone

79. At the risk of belaboring my earlier point on understating conservatives' resistance to the new thinking over 1985–90, the seemingly unconnected issue of Gorbachev's 1987–88 efforts to democratize the Soviet political system offers an important parallel. Those arguing that conservatives must not have opposed new thinking because they didn't resist more vigorously and openly would, by this logic, also argue that conservatives did not oppose free elections and the end of the Communist Party's monopoly on political power. Of course they did, but—as with various foreign policy initiatives—they went along not only out of party discipline but because they never expected such radical proposals to be effectively implemented.

tomorrow, then what?" . . . We had to think long and hard to grasp that human rights are an extraterritorial, universal, all-human value, and to understand that [without democracy] we'd never achieve real trust in foreign relations.[80]

Regarding Eastern Europe, Gorbachev reported on his discussions with Thatcher to the Politburo as follows:

She focused on trust. She said, "The USSR has squandered the West's faith and we don't trust you. You take grave actions lightly: Hungary, Czechoslovakia, Afghanistan. We couldn't imagine that you'd invade Czechoslovakia, but you did. The same with Afghanistan. We're afraid of you. If you remove your INF, and the Americans do too, then we'll be completely defenseless before [your huge armies]." That's how she sees it. She thinks we haven't rejected the "Brezhnev Doctrine." Comrades, we have to think this over. We can't ignore these arguments.[81]

Gorbachev's reflections thus revealed a key advance in his embrace of the liberal weltanschauung, a near-Kantian understanding of the link between genuine democracy and the foundations of international trust.

Skeptics rightly argue that neither in 1987, nor as late as early 1989, did Gorbachev and his allies foresee that real democratization would lead to the rapid collapse of East European socialism (and later, of party rule in the USSR). And had they so foreseen, it is indeed likely that their subsequent liberalizing steps would have been at least somewhat more cautious. Nonetheless, such views, as well as those that interpret Moscow's restraint in Eastern Europe as mainly driven by fear of endangering hoped-for Western aid, underestimate the extent of the new thinkers' intellectual conversion by early 1987. Far beyond just limits on the arms race or a deeper détente, they now sought for their country to "become a normal member of the world community" and to merge with "the common stream of world civilization."[82]

How differently might events have unfolded if U.S. policymakers had understood the gravity of this conversion instead of greeting his landmark U.N. speech and unilateral arms cuts—which came in December 1988, some *two years later*—as a potential ruse, unsure whether or not Gorbachev was "for real" and so "going slow" at such a critical junction in perestroika?[83] No doubt they were concerned by such old-thinking pronouncements as Ligachev's

80. Mikhail Gorbachev, "Doveriye—vektor sovremennoy zhizni," *Svobodnaya mysl'*, no. 3 (1995): 6.
81. Chernyayev, *Shest' let s Gorbachevym*, 139.
82. Mikhail Gorbachev, "The Crimea Article," in *The August Coup: The Truth and the Lessons* (New York: HarperCollins, 1991), 119.
83. Scowcroft, in Chapter 1, p. 26.

much-publicized insistence on the enduring class character of international relations. But such outbursts, rather than the boldness of an incipient hard-line turn, reflected instead conservatives' frustration that Gorbachev was going ever further in the opposite direction. Again, how different might foreign analysts' interpretations have been if they had understood that already in 1986 Gorbachev had ordered the preparation of plans for an eventual Soviet withdrawal from Eastern Europe; overriding a skeptical Defense Minister Yazov, Gorbachev had barked: "What are you waiting for? For them to ask you to leave?"[84]

Even though Gorbachev and his allies did not anticipate (nor did observers in the West, or in Eastern Europe itself for that matter) how rapidly party rule there would collapse, they had already understood and accepted that the region would inevitably evolve toward the political-economic orbit of the West.[85] And even though they foresaw it taking decades rather than months, they understood the inevitability of German reunification as well.[86] The most critical decisions of 1987–89 were arguably those of Western leaders to withhold large-scale aid to perestroika, and those of hard-line East European leaders not to launch perestroikas of their own. As for Gorbachev, his decision had already been made; come what may, there would be no use of force to preserve the socialist bloc or a divided Germany. The top brass did not even dare to raise the question in Gorbachev's presence at the Politburo "because they knew what the answer would be."[87]

Lessons, Imagined and Real

What, then, can we conclude from this admittedly unconventional narrative of the Cold War's end? First, regarding lessons for U.S. foreign policy, the argument that is expressed figuratively (and often literally) as "Star Wars brought the Soviets to their knees" is greatly oversimplified at best. The heightened confrontation of the early and mid-1980s strengthened Soviet hard-liners

84. Anatoly Chernyaev (Princeton University seminar, February 24, 1993).
85. This at least is the claim made privately by such Gorbachev advisers as Georgy Shakhnazarov and Anatoly Chernyaev.
86. Shevardnadze, *Moy vybor*, 223; see also Vyacheslav Dashichev, "On the Road to German Reunification: The View from Moscow," in Gabriel Gorodetsky, ed., *Soviet Foreign Policy, 1917–1991: A Retrospective* (London: Frank Cass, 1994), 170–79.
87. Chernyaev, in Chapter 2, p. 54. See also the declassified documents pertaining to Soviet–East European relations during 1989 posted on the web sites of the Cold War International History Project and National Security Archive (cwihp.si.edu, gwu.edu~nsarchiv).

and greatly complicated the accession of reform. The policy of exploiting Soviet weakness "by every available means" *did not* force the Politburo to "choose . . . a man committed to perestroika and disarmament."[88] Gorbachev was chosen because the Politburo sought a far more conservative, Andropov-style course—and because he *concealed* the extent of his ambitions for perestroika and disarmament. And these ambitions, which grew still further after he took office, sprang as much from ideas nurtured during the thaw and openness of the 1960s and 1970s as they did from the military-economic pressures of renewed Cold War in the 1980s.

Similarly, regarding lessons for theories of international relations, the dominant neorealist-materialist view that a crisis of power was essentially responsible for Soviet "imperial retrenchment" is only half right. The old system clearly possessed sufficient reserves to make a go of the Andropov course—modestly reformist at home and mostly status quo abroad—while a powerful constituency favored a harder line. That a different course was chosen had more to do with the power of ideas than a crisis of power. Put differently, material pressures clearly served as a catalyst of change. But that change could easily have gone in a very different direction; that it did not was largely thanks to an earlier intellectual transformation, one whose origins lie largely beyond the reach of materialist, international-system-level approaches.

Nor have most attempts to integrate the critical domestic context of Gorbachev's foreign policy—mainly of the neoliberal-institutionalist school—been much more successful in explaining the Cold War's end. While ideas are no longer seen as purely epiphenomenal to considerations of power, understanding of their origins and impact are still hampered by assumptions of their largely instrumental role. Crisis created "windows" of opportunity through which "entrepreneurs" then leaped, specialists motivated by personal and institutional interests to advance a new policy agenda.[89] While capturing part of the dynamic of new thinking's rapid implementation in some particulars—once its general course had been charted from above—such approaches tell much less about its origins. How was it that Gorbachev chose such a course,

---

88. Richard Pipes, "Misinterpreting the Cold War: The Hardliners Had It Right," *Foreign Affairs* 74, no. 1 (1995): 157–58.

89. This is the basic model of Checkel, *Ideas and International Political Change*. The learning-based account of Bennett—while sweeping and rigorously argued—is also ultimately only partly satisfactory as an interpretation of the Cold War's end, in large part because of its narrow focus on the question of "military interventionism." See Andrew Bennett, *Condemned to Repetition? The Rise, Fall, and Reprise of Soviet Russian Military Interventionism, 1973–1996* (Cambridge: MIT Press, 1999).

THE ROAD(S) NOT TAKEN   269

given the conservative correlation of forces in the top leadership? Where did the "policy entrepreneurs" and their agendas originate? The presumption that new ideas naturally emerged as a result of objective problems, and that their advocacy naturally flowed from pursuit of personal ambition and institutional interests, reflects the pluralistic political systems and attendant rational-actor assumptions upon which such theories have been built. Yet both are belied by much evidence of how the new thinking actually emerged in the Soviet system.

The anti-isolationist, globalist, social democratic–leaning intellectual current that provided the crucial soil for particular reformist policies was fertilized in the optimistic late 1950s and 1960s, not the crisis-ridden late 1970s and early 1980s. Its pioneers championed liberal ideas, criticized old-thinking policies, and advocated proposals for "Westernizing" domestic and foreign policy reforms not only in the heyday of détente, when such advocacy was problematic enough, but also in the post-détente collapse of Soviet-Western relations when such boldness was frequently harshly punished. In other words, it was less in the service of—and more often at risk to—their personal, professional, and institutional interests within a rigid and highly ideologized academic-policy system that the early new thinkers took their most important steps. No more in Moscow than in the West was there any reasonable expectation that a bold reformer would soon be running the Politburo. And far more important than the many who would subsequently join the bandwagon of a new-thinking leader were the few who helped create that new-thinking leader in the first place.

By contrast, it is approaches that privilege the normative over instrumental aspects of ideas that better capture the nature of new thinking as a long-term intellectual phenomenon as well as the contingencies of its near-term influence over leadership. Whether focused in depth on the generation-long rise of new ideas about international security among arms control experts, or emphasizing instead the breadth and diversity of a community of liberal humanists, social and natural scientists, the few such studies to date are distinguished by their empirical as well as analytical insights.[90] And this is no accident, for the analytical and empirical blinders that have hampered understanding of the Cold War's end are closely linked.

90. Evangelista, *Unarmed Forces*; Robert G. Herman, "Identity, Norms, and National Security: The Soviet Foreign Policy Revolution and the End of the Cold War," in Peter J. Katzenstein, ed., *The Culture of National Security: Norms and Identity in World Politics* (New York: Columbia University Press, 1996).

To illustrate this, it is useful to begin by recalling a central claim from one of the most influential pre-perestroika studies of Soviet foreign policy: "In no case was the Politburo confronted with advisers who had the treasonous temerity to . . . challenge the fundamental preconceptions of these old men."[91] As seen, this was flatly wrong: a critical factor in the accession of new thinking was that many advisers *did* early and persistently offer critiques and proposals—up to the highest levels—that challenged the fundamental preconceptions of old thinking. But notwithstanding the problem of asserting a negative, the cited claim was based on sound logic. So firmly was the Leninist-Stalinist confrontational ideology entrenched in the Brezhnevist military-industrial system, and so resolutely was heresy punished, that any challenge to it could only be conceived as a limited, essentially dissident affair. Anything larger, particularly among the ranks of the privileged policy-academic elite, was simply ruled out by the logic of rational self-interest.

And it is fealty to this core assumption of the centrality of materially driven interests that hampers efforts to understand the sources of subsequent changes. If Gorbachev's conciliatory steps confounded the expectations shared by most neorealists as late as 1987–88, then the explanation must be that Moscow's military-economic crisis had been far more severe than was understood. If scores of new-thinking analysts and arguments suddenly emerged, neoliberals reason, it was because that crisis had changed the "incentive structures" for ambitious policy advocates. And guided by their theoretical precepts, both neoliberals and neorealists have sought supporting evidence in particular places. One focuses on the near-term elaboration and implementation of policy innovations, paying little attention to their longer-term origins. And the other privileges evidence of economic over intellectual forces among the factors that influenced Gorbachev.

An example from the latter helps put the problem I am describing in sharper focus. In their public statements and writings, Gorbachev, Shevardnadze, and others make (and made) no secret of the fact that economic woes were one (but only one) of the important factors in the inception of new thinking. And the few available records of Politburo deliberations under Gorbachev can be used to show him acting less out of high-mindedness than necessity.[92] But

---

91. Harry Gelman, *The Brezhnev Politburo and the Decline of Détente* (Ithaca: Cornell University Press, 1984), 26.

92. See, for example, the Politburo resolution of September 4, 1986, "Ne Pozvolim SShA Dostich' Prevoskhodstva," *Istochnik* 2 (1995): 70–72. Additional examples are noted herein by Zubok and Brooks and Wohlforth.

it is infrequently emphasized that those records—still an infinitesimal part of the total—were selected for release less in the interests of historical balance than to embarrass Gorbachev.[93] And almost nowhere is it asked just what Politburo deliberations under Gorbachev really meant. Perhaps a sampling of such long-anticipated, high-level inside sources has made it tempting to overlook something that we learned at the same time from numerous other sources—that little of substance was openly debated at the Politburo, key decisions being taken instead in restricted conclaves, through phone discussions, and in other private venues.

It was so under Brezhnev because the leader was infirm; a rump group decided most issues outside the Politburo, and much of the latter's deliberative and decision-making functions became ritualistic, scripted affairs. And it was so under Gorbachev, at least insofar as foreign policy was concerned. From numerous sources—his allies and critics alike—we know that the conception and elaboration of his main initiatives occurred outside the Politburo, ministries, and even Central Committee apparat.[94] Indeed, it was precisely their loss of influence while that of Gorbachev's academic "brain trust" grew that angered the conservatives. And even when foreign policy was seriously discussed at the Politburo, the intellectual gulf between such as Gorbachev or Yakovlev on one side, and Ligachev, Yazov, or Kryuchkov on the other, has to be borne in mind. How would Gorbachev have best sought approval for settling some conflict or reducing some weapons? By trying to persuade the class-conscious Ligachev about the primacy of universal human values? Or by arguing that, given the state of the economy, they simply had no choice? Of course, by means of the latter—but care must be taken not to confuse Gorbachev's tactics with his strategy.[95]

The need to ponder counterfactuals and rethink familiar assumptions—from the basics of how and where decisions were made, to more fundamental

93. There is also the problem that in the instances where Gorbachev's Politburo proceedings were indeed recorded, the transcripts were subsequently edited—distorted, in the complaints of some staff secretaries—by hard-liner and future putschist Boldin.

94. From the outset, as noted above, conservatives worried that Gorbachev was receiving advice—and formulating options—outside established party-ministry channels. By 1987, key foreign policy decisions were also being taken elsewhere, with the Politburo either consulted only formally or not at all.

95. Brooks and Wohlforth note a pre-Reykjavik Politburo meeting at which Gorbachev fought for acceptance of his radical proposals by emphasizing the USSR's economic difficulties and need to halt the arms race. Brooks and Wohlforth, "Power," 29. But they ignore an immediate post-Reykjavik Politburo meeting at which Gorbachev argued precisely the opposite. See *Zasedaniye Politbyuro TsK KPSS*, "Ob itogakh vstrechi General'nogo sekretariya TsK KPSS M. S. Gorbacheva s Prezidentom SShA R. Reaganom v Reykyavike," October 14, 1986. This switch alone should alert researchers to the possibility that Gorbachev's argumentation at such meetings may have had as much or more tactical, than strategic, significance.

questions on the balance of material and intellectual forces in the genesis of new thinking or the viability of continued old thinking—should by now be clear. It remains only to emphasize one final irony by way of conclusion. And this is that, for all that I have argued in challenging materialist assumptions about the Cold War's end, the realists were absolutely right on one crucial point. Writing in the early and mid-1980s, those who for various political-historical reasons stressed the likelihood of a conflictual future were absolutely correct.[96] The new thinkers were never more than a minority among Soviet intellectuals, and the political "correlation of forces" clearly favored the conservatives. And so the well-trod confrontational path, with its implications for a far more perilous Cold War ending, was indeed the more likely choice in 1985. That a different course was chosen was thanks to the singular influence of ideas and the singular leadership of Gorbachev. He chose the road less traveled, and that is what made all the difference.

96. "There is nothing in the character or tradition of the Russian state to suggest that it could ever accept imperial decline gracefully. Indeed, historically none of the overextended, multinational empires ever retreated to their own ethnic base until they had been defeated in a Great Power war." Paul Kennedy, *The Rise and Fall of the Great Powers: Economic Change and Military Conflict from 1500 to 2000* (New York: Random House, 1987), 514.

9 Economic Constraints and the End of the Cold War

Stephen G. Brooks and William C. Wohlforth

DEBATES ABOUT HOW the various causes of great events interact cannot be resolved conclusively, but neither can they be avoided. All arguments about the implications of the Cold War's end for both policy and international relations theory hinge on rendering some judgment about how changing economic constraints affected this seminal event. Although scholars have spent a great deal of intellectual energy tracing the effects of ideas and leaders, comparatively few studies rigorously analyze how economic shifts independently influenced the final years of the U.S.-Soviet rivalry.[1] The Endgame conference illustrates this problem. James Baker opened the conference with an analysis that highlighted Soviet economic decline and geopolitical exhaustion, yet the subsequent discussions focused on the interaction between leaders, changing ideas, and domestic politics.

Participants, observers, and scholars are convinced that these factors all conspired to end the Cold War. But the analysis of how they interacted is hamstrung by imprecision. The standard approach is to show that because some cause did not wholly determine the outcome, some other cause "matters." The problem is that no one actually claims that any single factor is both necessary and sufficient to explain the end of the Cold War. Unfortunately, scholars routinely succumb to what we have elsewhere termed the "strawman bias": they are led to misrepresent others' work as deterministic in order to showcase the significance of their otherwise unremarkable finding that some cause mattered in explaining a complex outcome.[2] The result is debate in which scholars regularly impute to others clearly untenable claims that some factor wholly determines an outcome, which they then debunk with evidence that another factor actually played a role. Against this confused backdrop, it is no wonder that scholars increasingly question whether qualitative research on important cases like the end of the Cold War can add to our general knowledge of international relations.

---

1. See Stephen G. Brooks and William C. Wohlforth, "Power, Globalization and the End of the Cold War: Reevaluating a Landmark Case for Ideas," *International Security* 25, no. 3 (2000/2001): 5–7.

2. For a discussion of the strawman bias, see Stephen G. Brooks and William C. Wohlforth, "From Old Thinking to New Thinking in Qualitative Research," *International Security* 26, no. 4 (spring 2002).

*but when?
and how?*

We seek to move beyond this standard practice by analyzing the role of economic constraints in a probabilistic manner. Our central finding is that the rapidly escalating economic costs of maintaining the Soviet Union's international position made the Cold War's end on American terms the most likely outcome. Elsewhere, we have demonstrated this finding by carefully sifting through general patterns of evidence concerning this case.[3] Here, our main goal is to evaluate the most influential arguments against the explanatory power of economic constraints in this case. These objections are featured in the chapters by the other scholarly contributors to this volume, and they all entail careful consideration of counterfactual arguments. We find that these rebuttals do not undercut the major implication of the new evidence on economic constraints and superpower decision making. The problem is that these scholars' counterfactual arguments also suffer from the strawman bias: in the end, they only succeed in showing that the actual outcome was not the only possible outcome.[4] Such an argument works only against a deterministic claim concerning a specific event, which, again, no social scientist ever advances. Here, we seek to address these counterfactuals in a more realistic manner; that is, probabilistically.

really?!

We proceed in three main sections. First, we briefly review the nature of the economic constraints facing the Soviet Union during the final phase of the Cold War. Second, we provide a concise portrayal of how our probabilistic conception of the causal effect of economic constraints actually works—that is, how economic incentives pushed events in certain overall directions without determining them. Third, and most important, we analyze the major objections to our analysis and the counterfactual arguments they imply. We conclude that on currently available evidence, economic constraints were more than necessary but less than sufficient to explain the end of the Cold War. Rather, they made Soviet retrenchment the most likely response.

Soviet Decline, Globalization, and the Cold War Endgame

Despite the ambiguity plaguing the literature on the end of the Cold War, there has been marked progress in scholars' knowledge of economic con-

---

3. Brooks and Wohlforth, "Power." We provide further discussion of the probabilistic nature of our findings in Brooks and Wohlforth, "From Old Thinking to New Thinking."

4. This problem concerns not only the use of counterfactuals in analyzing the end of the Cold War, but also more general treatments of the use of counterfactuals in international relations. See, for example, Richard Ned Lebow, "Contingency, Counterfactuals, and International Systems Change," *Political Science Quarterly* 115, no. 4 (winter 2000/2001): 591–619.

Harmony whom ?
This may have been a view, but it wasn't conventional

straints in this case. In the early 1990s, the conventional wisdom was that Soviet material decline was small or nonexistent, and consequently had little causal weight in the end of the Cold War.[5] A second wave of empirical scholarship that emerged in the mid-1990s revised the conventional wisdom. Most now agreed that the Soviet material decline had actually been quite significant beginning in the early to mid-1980s and that it did play a significant causal role.[6] Still, most held that while decline played an important role in prompting a major shift in Soviet foreign policy, the resulting policy change could have just as easily been toward aggression or a new version of muddling through, and so other factors must have played the key role in resolving this uncertainty. This is essentially the position taken in Chapters 7 and 8 herein.

One problem with this view is that we now have much better data about the economic constraints on the Soviet Union, all of which indicate that they were much more pressing than scholars realized in the mid-1990s. In particular, decline began earlier, progressed faster, was far more pronounced, and had far greater effects on policy deliberations than scholars assumed. Moreover, it is now apparent that changes in the world economy—especially the globalization of production—dramatically changed the incentives facing Moscow in the 1980s. In the subsections that follow, we review the basic nature of this evidence.

Decline

The Soviet economy grew at impressive rates in the 1950s and registered respectable performance in the 1960s, but in the second half of the 1970s it entered an acute decline from which it never recovered.[7] By the time Mikhail Gorbachev became general secretary in 1985, the Soviet Union had grown on average at least 1–2 percent slower than the United States over the preceding decade.[8] And U.S. allies such as Germany and Japan were also growing

5. See, for example, Charles Kegley, "The Neoidealist Moment in International Studies? Realist Myths and the New International Realities," *International Studies Quarterly* 37, no. 2 (June 1993).

6. See, for example, Coit D. Blacker, *Hostage to Revolution: Gorbachev and Soviet Security Policy, 1985–1991* (New York: Council on Foreign Relations, 1993), and William Wohlforth, "Realism and the End of the Cold War," *International Security* 19, no. 3 (winter 1994/95).

7. See Brooks and Wohlforth, "Power," 14–20, and sources cited therein.

8. One percent is the CIA's calculation, reported in Joint Economic Committee, U.S. Congress, *Measures of Soviet Gross National Product in 1982 Prices* (Washington, D.C.: U.S. Government Printing Office, 1990). Two percent is the estimate of Russian economist G. I. Khanin, in "Ekonomicheskiy rost: Alternativnaya otsenka" [Economic growth: An alternative estimate], *Kommunist* 17 (November 1988): 83–90. Analysts agree that official data vastly overstated Soviet economic performance. Most now also agree that the CIA's estimates, which were based on a complex reworking of official data, significantly overstated Soviet output. Most

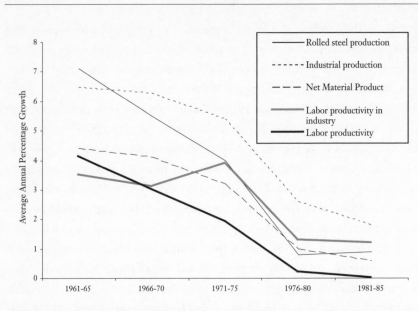

SOURCES: Gertrude E. Schroeder, "The Slowdown in Soviet Industry, 1976-1982," *Soviet Economy*, Vol. 1, No. 1 (January–March 1985), pp. 42–74; Boris Z. Rumer, *Soviet Steel: The Challenge of Modernization in the USSR* (Ithaca, N.Y. Cornell University Press, 1989); and G. I. Khanin, "Ekonomicheskiy rost: Alternativnaia otsenka" [Economic growth: An alternative estimate]. *Kommunist* No. 17 (November 1988), pp. 83–90.

FIGURE 1. *The Soviet Decline*

rapidly, making Moscow's relative decline all the more salient. The entire Soviet economic system was geared toward increasing such industrial-age metrics as steel production. Yet as Figure 1 shows, even those indices declined precipitously after 1976. Meanwhile, the country's long-standing *qualitative* lag increased in exactly this period, with the productivity of research and development (R&D) and technological progress both declining.[9] Compounded over time, an economic growth lag of 1–2 percent below the United States would have devastating effects on the Soviets' ability to keep up with

important, CIA estimates dramatically underreported the severity of the decline that preceded Gorbachev and accelerated during his leadership. See Vladimir Kontorovich, "Economists, Soviet Growth Slowdown and the Collapse," *Europe-Asia Studies* 53, no. 5 (July 2001): 675–95.

9. See Vladimir Kontorovich, "Technological Progress and Research and Development," in Michael Ellman and Vladimir Kontorovich, eds., *The Disintegration of the Soviet Economic System* (New York: Routledge, 1992). A good assessment of the military implications of this technological lag is Central Intelligence Agency, Directorate of Intelligence, "The Soviet Defense Industry: Coping with the Military-Technological Challenge," SOV-87-10035DX (July 1987), declassified and made available on CD-ROM by the CIA's Center for the Study of Intelligence.

their Cold War competitors. Considering U.S. allies as well as the growing technological lag made the equation much worse. And with each passing year, it would become harder for the Soviets to match U.S. capabilities.

The causes of Soviet decline continue to be debated, but there is widespread agreement that an important part of the explanation lies in the large and growing costs of the Soviet Union's international position. As Vladimir Kontorovich sums up, "The achievement of strategic parity with the west and the macroeconomic stagnation, or decline, in the late 1970s to early 1980s, are strongly related."[10] Defense claimed a massive proportion of Soviet resources. Despite daunting measurement problems, different sources converge around an estimate of roughly 40 percent of the budget and 15–20 percent of GDP in the early 1980s, or at least four times the U.S. level.[11] By any comparative standard, this is a punishingly high peacetime commitment to military power. Not only was the defense burden high, but it was generally rising from the mid-1970s on.[12] And these quantitative measures, as dramatic as they are, fail to capture the fact that the Soviet military-industrial complex had a priority claim on scarce qualitative resources, such as high-technology and R&D expertise.[13] Moreover, defense allocations were only part of the story. Moscow's international position imposed other costs that were also increasing in this period. The CIA estimated that the costs of the Soviet Union's "global position" more than doubled between 1970 and 1982.[14] At the beginning of the 1980s, the Central Committee estimated Soviet spending on foreign aid alone at 2 percent of GDP.[15] And, as we shall discuss in more detail, the costs of Moscow's East European dependencies began to escalate in the late 1970s and early 1980s.

Two critical conclusions emerge from this discussion. First, the Soviet Union was in a state of severe relative decline beginning in the second half of

10. Ellman and Kontorovich, *The Disintegration of the Soviet Economic System*, 9.

11. See Noel E. Firth and James H. Noren, *Soviet Defense Spending: A History of CIA Estimates, 1950–1990* (Houston: Texas A&M Press, 1998), for the CIA estimate of around 15 percent in 1980. Using a different methodology (percentage of the workforce in the defense sector), Clifford Gaddy estimates 20 percent; see Gaddy, *The Price of the Past* (Washington, D.C.: The Brookings Institution, 1997), chap. 1.

12. See Brooks and Wohlforth, "Power," 24.

13. As Gorbachev notes, "Of 25 billion rubles in total expenditure on science, 20 billion went to the military for technical research and development." Mikhail Sergeevich Gorbachev, *Memoirs*, trans. from the German edition by Wolf Jobst [which was translated into German from the Russian original by Georges Peronansky and Tatjana Varsavsky] (New York: Doubleday, 1995), 215.

14. Firth and Noren, *Soviet Defense Spending*, 134.

15. Michael Ellman and Vladimir Kontorovich, eds., *The Destruction of the Soviet Economic System: An Insider's Account* (Armonk, N.Y.: M. E. Sharpe, 1998), 293.

the 1970s. Second, declining Soviet economic performance was to a significant degree a reflection of the international environment. The Soviet Union's
position as one pole in a bipolar system, and as a formal challenger to the U.S.-
dominated international status quo, imposed massive and growing burdens on
a Soviet economy that was in desperate need of renewed growth. Moreover,
by the late 1970s, it was becoming increasingly evident to Soviet analysts that
the world's most advanced economies—all of which were arrayed against the
Soviet Union—were undergoing an important transformation involving the
rapid development of high technology. The Soviets dubbed this the "scientific
and technological revolution," and there was little doubt that it was leaving
them behind. And this brings us to a second critical economic shift that influenced the course of the Cold War competition.

The Changing Structure of Global Production

As inefficiencies mounted in the Soviet economy during the 1970s, the global
economy was concomitantly undergoing important transformations that served
greatly to accelerate the opportunity cost of the Soviets' international economic
isolation. Underlying these transformations were two interrelated technological shifts that accelerated in the late 1970s and early 1980s: the massively
increased cost, risk, complexity, and importance of technological development;
and dramatic improvements in transportation and communications technology. The escalating cost and importance of technological development created
strong incentives for crucial shifts in the structure of global production that, in
turn, were facilitated by cheaper and better transport and communications.
Four shifts in the structure of global production were especially relevant to the
superpower rivalry during the Cold War's last years: (1) the upswing in the
number and importance of interfirm alliances; (2) the growing opportunity cost
of being isolated from foreign direct investment (FDI); (3) the increase in international outsourcing; and (4) the enhanced efforts by many global firms to
break up the value-added chain and locate different parts of the production
process in countries that offer the greatest locational advantages.[16]

The Soviet Union and its allies were almost completely isolated from
these global production changes, which achieved their greatest salience among

16. For thorough reviews of these changes in the structure of global production, and the role of technological shifts in producing them, see Stephen G. Brooks, "The Globalization of Production and International
Security" (Ph.D. diss., Yale University, 2001), chap. 4.

the Soviets' international competitors—the United States and its allies. Thus, "globalization" was not global: it took sides in the Cold War. While U.S. and Western multinational corporations (MNCs) could exploit a greatly expanding web of international interfirm alliances during the 1980s to increase their opportunities for technological innovation and reduce the risks and difficulty associated with R&D, the Soviets were completely isolated from this trend.[17] While rapidly increasing FDI inflows allowed the United States to gain access to the latest technologies and production methods from throughout the world, the Soviets were largely dependent on autonomous improvements in technology and production methods.[18] And instead of being able to disperse production throughout the world to reap various efficiencies as firms from the United States and its main allies—Japan, West Germany, France, and Britain—were able to do, Soviet enterprises were forced to generate almost all of their key components and production within the Eastern bloc.[19]

While relative Soviet autarky was a staple feature of the Cold War that had long entailed significant economic handicaps for Moscow, these handicaps greatly increased in relative importance as the cost, complexity, and difficulty of technological development spiraled upward in the late 1970s and 1980s and as the globalization of production concomitantly accelerated.[20] Isolation from the globalization of production increased the difficulty of keeping up with the West in terms of general economic and technological productivity, likely the key concern of many new thinkers. Moreover, Soviet isolation from these global production changes *simultaneously* made it much more difficult to remain

17. The overwhelming majority (more than 90 percent, by many estimates) of interfirm alliances during the 1980s were located within the triad of Western Europe, Japan, and North America. See Stephen Kobrin, "The Architecture of Globalization: State Sovereignty in a Networked Global Economy," in J. Dunning, ed., *Governments, Globalization, and International Business* (Oxford: Oxford University Press, 1997), 150.

18. During the 1980s, the "annual average growth rate for FDI outflows reached 14 per cent." Geoffrey Jones, *The Evolution of International Business* (London: Routledge, 1996), 52. As the absolute level of FDI rose dramatically in the 1980s, the Soviets remained isolated from these flows, while the share of FDI based in Western Europe, the United States, and Canada increased from 62 percent of the world total in 1980 to 70 percent in 1993. Jones, *Evolution*, 48, 54.

19. In combination, these five Western countries accounted for 74 percent of the total world FDI stock in 1980. Ibid., 47. One reflection of the enhanced degree to which the production of U.S. MNCs became strongly integrated internationally during this period is that "the value of United States intra-firm exports increased by nearly two-thirds between 1977 and 1982 and by over 70 per cent between 1982 and 1989." United Nations Conference on Trade and Development (UNCTAD), *World Investment Report 1994: Transnational Corporations, Employment, and the Workplace* (Geneva: United Nations, 1994), 143. Another reflection of this trend is that the value of offshore outsourcing by the United States increased from U.S.$48.8 billion in 1972 to U.S.$356 billion in 1987. See World Bank, *Global Economic Prospects and the Developing Countries* (Washington, D.C.: World Bank, 1997), 45.

20. On the changing nature of technological development, see Kobrin, "Architecture of Globalization," 149–50.

technologically competitive in the arms race—of foremost importance to more traditionally minded old thinkers. Interfirm alliances in the 1980s were concentrated in those sectors with rapidly changing technologies and high entry costs, such as microelectronics, computers, aerospace, telecommunications, transportation, new materials, biotechnology, and chemicals.[21] At the same time, production appears to have been most geographically dispersed in those sectors of manufacturing with high levels of R&D costs and significant economies of scale, such as machinery, computers, electronic components, and transportation.[22] These sectors read like a who's who of dual-use industries. In short, the very sectors that were becoming most internationalized in the 1980s were those that provide much of the foundation for military power in the modern era. For this reason, Soviet isolation from ongoing global production changes became a tremendous handicap relative to the West in the 1980s in the military realm.[23]

Economic Constraints and Policy Shifts

Beginning in the late 1970s, critical conditions that had shaped the Cold War—a Soviet Union that could remain relatively autarkic and yet generate capabilities competitive with and rising relative to those of the United States—thus began to change measurably and consistently. How exactly did these underlying shifts alter the incentives facing policymakers in the Cold War's endgame? And how did these incentives actually affect policy outcomes? We outline answers to these questions in the subsections that follow.

Causal Effects of Rising Economic Constraints

Rising economic constraints had two critical consequences for Soviet foreign policy. First, relative decline and Soviet isolation from ongoing global production changes created strong incentives for the country to retrench internationally; that is, to halt and, eventually, reverse the growth in the costs of Moscow's global position. Given the punishingly high degree to which the Soviets were already pouring scarce economic resources—especially R&D—into the military, the possibility that this burden might increase even further was truly an

---

21. See, for example, Peter Dicken, *Global Shift: Transforming the World Economy* (New York: Guilford, 1998), 229, and Kobrin, "Architecture of Globalization," 150.
22. See World Bank, *Global Economic Prospects*, 42.
23. For a detailed analysis of this point, see Brooks, "Globalization," chap. 5.

ominous prospect for Gorbachev and many other policymakers.[24] By the mid-1980s, even important figures in the Soviet military shared this assessment.[25] Stemming the rising costs of the Soviet Union's international position implied moderating the arms race and scaling back the costs of competition in the Third World. In addition, the general incentive to reduce the rising costs of empire meant limiting Moscow's intervention in the domestic affairs of its Central European allies. The more the Soviet Union and its dependencies declined, the higher the governance costs for Moscow—that is, the higher the marginal cost of maintaining Russian influence over the domestic choices of Central European states—and the greater the incentives to devolve authority.

The second essential casual effect of these shifts is that they affected the bargaining outcome once the Soviet alliance began to unravel. The key here is that both the Soviet Union and its Eastern European allies turned out to be far worse off in economic terms than observers recognized before 1989. By the time the actual terms of the Cold War's settlement were negotiated—in the winter and spring of 1989–90—resource constraints were overpowering the Soviet policy process on all fronts (Table 1). It is often argued that failure to predict the precipitous economic decline of the Soviet Union and its key allies in Eastern Europe somehow impugns an explanation rooted in economic constraints. But the fact that analysts were not aware of how close the Soviet-type economies were to utter collapse is not evidence that the collapse was not of central importance.[26]

The Links Between Economic Constraints and Policy Effects

The connection between economic constraints and policy change is not mechanistic. An economic downturn for one or two years may or may not represent a trend to which decision makers must respond. One only knows whether one is experiencing a "trend" after observations have confirmed it for many years

---

24. The best-researched study that documents this dilemma is Gaddy, *Price of the Past*. For a wide-ranging review, based on Soviet writings and speeches, see Central Intelligence Agency, Directorate of Intelligence, "The USSR Confronts the Information Revolution," SOV 87-10029 (May 1987), declassified and made available on CD-ROM by the CIA's Center for the Study of Intelligence.

25. See William Odom, *The Collapse of the Soviet Military* (New Haven: Yale University Press, 1998), 91, 225.

26. By way of analogy, our ability to detect asteroids is presently imperfect. If, owing to limits on our powers of observation, we fail to foresee an asteroid impact on Earth, this predictive failure would indicate neither that the asteroid did not have an important effect, nor that our theories of astrophysics are flawed. The sole lesson would concern our capacity to measure variables central to the theory concerned. For more, see David Dessler, "Prediction as a Criterion of Theory Appraisal in International Relations: Lessons from the Natural Sciences" (MS, William and Mary College).

TABLE I. *Soviet Economic Performance During the Cold War Endgame*

	1986	1987	1988	1989	1990	1991
GNP growth (percent per year)[a]	4.1	1.3	2.1	1.5	-12	-13
Internal debt as a percentage of GDP[b]	20.0	22	36	43	55	n.a.
Budget deficit as a percentage of GDP	-2.4	-6.2	-8.8	-11	-14	-20
Balance of payments in convertible currencies (in billions of U.S. dollars)[c]	0.637	-2.3	-0.72	-3.7	-11.8[d]	n.a.

SOURCES: David Kotz , with Fred Weir, *Revolution from Above: The Demise of the Soviet System* (London: Routledge, 1997); International Monetary Fund, The World Bank, Organisation for Economic Cooperation and Development, and European Bank for Reconstruction and Development, *A Study of the Soviet Economy* (Paris: OECD, 1991); Sergei Germanovich Sinel'nikov, *Biudzhetnyi krisis v rossii, 1985–1995 gody* (Moscow: Evraziya, 1995); Michael Ellman and Vladimir Kontorovich, eds., *The Destruction of the Soviet Economic System: An Insider's Account* (Armonk, N.Y.: M.E. Sharpe, 1998).

[a] The figures for 1986–90 are CIA estimates; those for 1991 are official Russian data as reported in Sinel'nikov.
[b] The figures for 1986–89 are official data; the figure for 1990 is an estimate reported in Ellman and Kontorovich, *The Destruction of the Soviet Economic System*.
[c] On a settlements basis. Payments deficits in nonconvertible currencies also increased dramatically over the period.
[d] First half of 1990 only.

in a row. In the case of the Soviet Union and the end of the Cold War, observations confirming negative economic trends accumulated in the late 1970s and early 1980s. Growth plunged in 1976. In 1980, the economy entered an outright recession. Then, the economic crisis spread to Moscow's allies in Central Europe.[27] By the early 1980s, the systemic decline of the Soviet Union and its chief allies was undeniable.

Of course, increasing economic constraints did not *force* a response in the way that deterministic causation occurs in nature. For one thing, even after a trend is recognized, it always takes some time to formulate and effect a response, given the standard institutional and organizational lags that characterize any modern polity and the fact that individual leaders are bounded in their ability to process information. Moreover, human beings take action based on expectations. A Soviet leader could have resisted changes for a period

27. Economic growth in Moscow's Eastern European allies declined from an average real GDP growth rate of 3.23 percent in 1971–80 to 0.9 percent in 1981–85, and eventually reached an average growth rate of −1.16 percent in 1989. Calculated from data in Carol Clark, "Relative Backwardness in Eastern Europe: An Application of the Technological Gap Hypothesis," *Economic Systems* 17, no. 3 (September 1993): 170.

of time, the length of which one can argue over counterfactually. An explanation rooted in changing economic incentives simply posits that the agents concerned responded to expectations of economic trends. Here, the most important question is: What were the alternatives to retrenchment? By 1985–87,
there was no evidence that just clinging to the status quo and hoping trends
would miraculously reverse themselves would be a sustainable policy over the
long run. A renewed assault on the West would only increase the economic
burden Moscow already faced. Given the United States's economic and military ascendancy, higher tensions would only reinforce its dominance over its
own alliance and hence its ultimate superiority over Moscow. Preventive war
was out of the question, given overall U.S. material superiority, nuclear deterrence, and the declining economic value of territory.

The evidence concerning perceptions of economic constraints and their
connection to new ideas and policies is strongly consistent with the argument
we have developed thus far. Three general patterns of evidence are indicative
of this overall finding. First, Soviet policymakers at the highest levels began to
agonize over relative decline in the early 1980s, just as the systemic decline of
the Soviet Union became undeniable.[28] Internal assessments of Soviet economic decline either matched or were more pessimistic than the data presented in Figure 1.[29] As we would expect, there was a two-to-three-year lag
between recognition of the systemic trend and the new policy response.
However, even in this period (roughly 1981–85), evidence reveals leadership
efforts to contain foreign policy costs and close the widening gap between
capabilities and commitments. In particular, Brezhnev, Andropov, and
Chernenko all struggled hard to stem the growth in defense spending in the
early 1980s, despite the hard line coming from Washington and heavy pressure from the military.[30]

Second, the data demonstrate how decline and resource constraints
helped propel new policy innovations. Memoirs and other recollections—by

28. See Mark Kramer, "Ideology and the Cold War," *Review of International Studies* 25, no. 4 (October
1999): 539–76.
29. This is the general finding reported in Michael Ellman and Vladimir Kontorovich, "The Collapse of
the Soviet System and the Memoir Literature," *Europe-Asia Studies* 49, no. 2 (March 1997). More specific recollections include Ellman and Kontorovich, *Destruction of the Soviet Economic System*; Gorbachev, *Memoirs*;
Vitaliy Ivanovich Vorotnikov, *A bylo eto tak . . . Iz dnevnika chlena Politbyuro TsK KPSS* (Moscow: Sovet veteranov knigoizdaniya, 1995); Yegor Gaidar, *Days of Defeat and Victory*, trans. Jane Ann Miller (Seattle: University
of Washington Press, 1999); Stanislav Shatalin, "'500 dney' i drugiye dni moyey zhizni," *Nezavisimaya gazeta*,
March 31 and April 2, 1992; Nikolai Ryzhkov, *Perestroyka: istoriya predatl'stv* (Moscow: Novosti, 1992).
30. According to Firth and Noren, *Soviet Defense Spending*, they succeeded in capping budgetary growth,
but because the economy actually declined in 1980–82, defense outlays as a percentage of GDP probably rose.

new and old thinkers alike—consistently document that the mounting evidence of Soviet relative decline and technological inferiority played a role in the evolution of individuals' policy perspectives.[31] The momentum behind new policy directions was intimately related to cascading information on the Soviet Union's material failings compared to the United States and its chief allies. At each wrenching step in the process of discarding old policy approaches and adopting new ones, resource constraints were of central importance.[32]

It is clear, moreover, that both new and old thinkers strongly resisted a complete abandonment of traditional Soviet ideas and policy practices. Gorbachev's initial response did not threaten system fundamentals. He adopted a policy of "acceleration" (*uskoreniye*) of the Soviet economy via discipline, new personnel in key managerial roles, an anti-vodka campaign, and massively increased investment in the machine-tool sector of the economy (roughly 70 percent of which was devoted to military production). In foreign policy, Gorbachev began by reversing the Brezhnev-Andropov-Chernenko policy of capping military spending and programmed into the 1986–90 five-year plan an increase in military outlays; he approved an effort to end the Afghan war by military escalation; and he agreed to increase arms transfers to Third World clients to magnify Moscow's bargaining leverage in talks on regional issues.[33]

The initial policy package failed to turn the economy around (see Table 1) and produced only the beginnings of a potential burden-reducing entente

31. General analyses that demonstrate this point include Aleksandr Shubin, *Istoki perestroyki: 1978–1984 gg.* (Moscow: [n.p.], 1997), and Paul Hollander, *Political Will and Personal Belief: The Decline and Fall of Soviet Communism* (New Haven: Yale University Press, 1999). Particular memoirs that are especially telling on this score are Nikolay Leonov, *Likholet'e* (Moscow: Mezhdunarodniye otnosheniya, 1994); Sergey F. Akhromeyev and G. M. Korniyenko, *Glazami marshala i diplomata: Kriticheskiy vzglyad na vneshnyuyu politiku SSSR do i posle 1985-go goda* (Moscow: Mezhdunarodniye otnosheniya, 1992); Anatoly S. Chernyaev, *My Six Years with Gorbachev*, ed. and trans. Robert D. English and Elizabeth Tucker (University Park: Pennsylvania State University Press, 2000); Vorotnikov, *A bylo eto tak;* and Georgiy Khosroyevich Shakhnazarov, *Tsena svobody: Reformatsiya Gorbacheva glazami ego pomoshchnika* (Moscow: Rossika-Zevs, 1993).

32. Two salient examples of this dynamic are the unilateral conventional force reductions in November–December 1988 (see the accounts in Chernyaev, *My Six Years with Gorbachev;* Akhromeyev and Korniyenko, *Glazami marshala i diplomata;* and Vorotnikov, *A bylo eto tak*) and the twin decisions to demand hard currency for energy exports to the East European allies while reducing interference in their domestic policy choices (see the accounts in Ryzhkov, *Perestroyka,* and Shakhnazarov, *Tsena svobody*).

33. Rhetoric aside, Gorbachev made no effort to increase outlays for consumer welfare in this period. See Sergey Germanovich Sinel'nikov (-Murylev), *Byudzhetnyy krizis v rossii, 1985–1995 gody* (Moscow: Evraziya, 1995), 36. Aleksandr Lyakhovskiy, *Tragediya i Doblest' Afgana* (Moscow: GPI Iskona, 1995), documents the early escalatory policy on Afghanistan. For Gorbachev's own contemporary description of these policy moves in Politburo settings, see, for example, National Security Archive, "Understanding the End of the Cold War: The Reagan/Gorbachev Years" (Providence: Brown University, 1998), esp. docs. 44 and 52. For an analysis of the competitive impulse behind "acceleration," see Vladimir Shlapentokh, *A Normal Totalitarian Country: How the Soviet Union Functioned and How It Collapsed* (Armonk, N.Y.: M. E. Sharpe, 2001).

with the West. The result was dramatically increased resource constraints and a consequent radicalization of the foreign strategy, which by 1988 had moved from graduated initiatives premised on reciprocation to escalating unilateral concessions. By then, resource constraints were escalating even further and there were no obvious quick fixes other than to reduce the external pressure and perhaps exploit the economic benefits of reduced tensions as rapidly as possible.[34] As Shevardnadze's adviser Sergei Tarasenko noted in an interview:

Already after the Nineteenth Party Conference, as we confronted the difficulties inside the country, the realization began to take shape that we would be able to continue on for a little while and perhaps retain the status of a great power only by relying on the United States. We sensed that were we to take two or three steps away from the U.S., we'd be tossed aside. We had to move as close as possible to the United States. . . . [This point of view came to the fore in 1988], when the policy of acceleration turned out so badly. The USA had always wanted to cut us down [*dozhat' nas*]. Had we at that time acted in a confrontational way, the Americans would have easily cut us in two.[35]

This pattern—start with the policies of least resistance and move to riskier measures only under pressure of intensified economic constraints—characterized all key foreign policy areas. For example, one of Gorbachev's initial responses to the technological lag was to foster increased interfirm linkages within the Soviet Union and its economic alliance, the Council on Mutual Economic Assistance (CMEA), and to try to exploit the reputed technological prowess of the military-industrial sector. By 1987, however, it was clear that any attempt to apply the productivity "secret" of the military sector to the overall economy was doomed to failure. As Clifford Gaddy points out, "The 'secret' was that the military sector cannibalized the economy. . . . To ask the military industry to apply its methods to serve civilian industry was not simply politically impossible but also illogical."[36] Moreover, it soon became clear that efforts to duplicate the increasing international production linkages that were occurring in the West by expanding specialization and production

34. For more on this critical reversal, see Chernyaev, *My Six Years with Gorbachev*, 193–95; Akhromeyev and Korniyenko, *Glazami marshala i diplomata*, 55; Ryzhkov, *Perestroyka*, 232–33; Eduard Amvrosiyevich Shevardnadze, *Moy vybor: v zashchitu demokratii i svobody* (Moscow: Novosti, 1991), 110–11; and Vorotnikov, *A bylo eto tak*, 223.

35. Transcript of interview by Oleg Skvortsov, director of the Oral History Project at the Institute of General History with S. P. Tarasenko, March 19, 1999, Moscow (on file at the National Security Archive, Washington, D.C., and the Institute of General History, Moscow, 1999). Hereafter cited as "Skvortsov interviews."

36. Gaddy, *Price of the Past*, 56.

linkages within the CMEA would bear little fruit, in significant part because no country in the Eastern bloc could match Western technology using indigenous sources.[37] The failure of the initial policy of least resistance led Gorbachev to more controversial policies to increase access to MNCs, including allowing majority-owned joint ventures.

Third and finally, the evidence reveals that old thinkers tended to see the same underlying trends, which undercut opposition to Gorbachev's reorientation of Soviet grand strategy. William Odom finds, "In interviews and in their memoirs senior former Soviet military officers uniformly cited the burden of military spending as more than the Soviet economy could bear."[38] Traditionally minded officials such as KGB chief Vladimir Kryuchkov, Gorbachev's chief of staff Valery Boldin, Defense Minister Marshal Dmitry Yazov, Chief of the General Staff and military adviser Marshal Sergei Akhromeev—all of whom participated in or (in Akhromeev's case) sympathized with the August 1991 anti-Gorbachev putsch—agreed that the Soviet economy could not bear the Cold War status quo and that the technological gap was large and widening.[39] Despite deep disagreements with Gorbachev, Akhromeev insisted that "all who knew the real situation in our state and economy in the mid-1980s understood that Soviet foreign policy had to be changed. The Soviet Union could no longer continue a policy of military confrontation with the United States and NATO after 1985. The economic possibilities for such a policy had been exhausted."[40] When asked in a recent interview whether the Soviet Union had to get out of the Cold War, Yazov responded: "Absolutely. . . . We simply lacked the power to oppose the USA, England, Germany, France, Italy—all the flourishing states that were united in the NATO bloc. We had to seek a

37. See Hannes Adomeit, *Imperial Overstretch: Germany in Soviet Policy from Stalin to Gorbachev* (Baden Baden: Nomos Verlagsgesellschaft, 1998), esp. 227, and Charles Maier, *Dissolution: The Crisis of Communism and the Collapse of East Germany* (Princeton: Princeton University Press, 1997).

38. Odom, *Collapse of the Soviet Military*, 225.

39. Based on Skvortsov interviews with Kryuchkov, Boldin, and Yazov. See also Vladimir Kryuchkov, *Lichnoye delo* (Moscow: Olimp, 1996), 1:273, 282; Akhromeyev and Korniyenko, *Glazami marshala i diplomata*; and Aleksandr G. Savel'yev and Nikolai N. Detinov, *The Big Five: Arms Control Decision-Making in the Soviet Union*, trans. Dmitry Trenin (Westport, Conn.: Praeger, 1995). Odom also documents Soviet military concern over the technological gap: "It was becoming clear to Soviet military leaders that they were facing a third wave of new military technologies. The developments in micro-electronics, the semiconductor revolution and its impact on computers, distributed processing, and digital communications were affecting many aspects of military equipment and weaponry. . . . [The] new revolution in military affairs was demanding forces and weapons that the Soviet scientific-technological and industrial bases could not provide." William Odom, "The Soviet Military in Transition," *Problems of Communism* 3a (May-June 1990): 52–53, 63–64. For more, see also Thomas M. Nichols, *The Sacred Cause: Civil-Military Conflict Over Soviet National Security* (Ithaca: Cornell University Press, 1993), 115, 116.

40. Akhromeyev and Korniyenko, *Glazami marshala i diplomata*, 314–15.

dénouement. . . . We had to find an alternative to the arms race. . . . We had to continually negotiate, and reduce, reduce, reduce—especially the most expensive weaponry."[41] And not only did he express these views in hindsight, he used the very same arguments while implementing retrenchment policies as defense minister.[42]

Given their recognition of these underlying trends, old thinkers faced great difficulty in making the case for a plausible alternative to retrenchment. Indeed, despite a sustained and intensive research effort, scholars have yet to uncover contemporary evidence of a strategic alternative.[43] Clearly, many traditionally minded officials were convinced at the time, and remain so in retirement, that they could have implemented a retrenchment strategy better than Gorbachev was able to. But they were not able—in office or in hindsight—to make a coherent case for a general foreign policy alternative.

Counterarguments and Counterfactuals

In March 1985 Mikhail Gorbachev took the helm of an overextended superpower with an inefficient economy that was declining alarmingly in relative terms. Existing policies of maintaining the Cold War status quo demanded increased expenditures, which increased the imperial burden as a share of the economy. A more vigorous prosecution of the Cold War rivalry was unlikely to relieve the economic burdens on the Soviet Union. On the contrary, there was every reason to conclude that a renewed assault on U.S. positions internationally would invite an escalatory response from a stronger rival. As a result, a general strategy of reducing Cold War tensions and scaling back the imperial burdens on the Soviet economy gained numerous adherents in Soviet ruling echelons. In significant part because the Soviet Union's economic fortunes were rapidly declining, Gorbachev's efforts to engage the United States in security negotiations while initiating economic reform were supported or at least tolerated by a critical mass of the Soviet policymaking elite.

While other outcomes were possible, our basic finding is that precipitous Soviet decline made the Cold War's ending on U.S. terms the most likely outcome. Many scholars remain unconvinced by explanations of this type.

41. Skvortsov interview with Yazov, March 11, 1999.
42. See L. G. Ivashov, *Marshal Yazov (Rokovoi Avgust 91-go): Pravda o "putche"* (Moscow: Biblioteka Zhurnala "Muzhestvo," 1992), chap. 2, esp. p. 27.
43. For a discussion of the evidence on this point, see Brooks and Wohlforth, "New versus Old Thinking in Qualitative Research."

Among the counterarguments they offer, the following five are the most prominent.

Counterargument 1: Force in Eastern Europe

Many scholars argue that the Soviet decision to avoid using force in Eastern Europe is the key puzzle that a focus on economic constraints leaves unresolved.[44] We disagree. While economic constraints did not preclude the possibility that force would be used, they clearly stacked the deck against it.

Thus far we have highlighted the growing costs of maintaining the Soviet Union's Cold War foreign policy. Costs, however, are only one half of the balance sheet: benefits obviously matter as well. For the Soviet Union, the key benefit of the dependencies in Eastern Europe in the initial phases of the Cold War was that they provided a security buffer zone.[45] Given the devastation of World War II, the Soviets' preference for such a buffer zone is certainly understandable. But over time this logic lost much of its force. Once the Soviets had an assured "second strike" capability that established mutual nuclear deterrence, the need for a buffer zone faded.[46]

Of course, critics would likely point out nuclear deterrence had diminished the Soviets' security rationale for the East European empires since at least the mid-1960s. Why, they might ask, did the Soviets not abandon the East European empire decades earlier? Two points are particularly relevant here. First, the Soviets had little need to question their Cold War foreign policy commitments as long as there was no reason to think that maintaining these commitments was unbearably costly. Undertaking a decision to abandon the Eastern European dependencies would obviously have been a major policy departure. As any student of institutions knows, major policy departures are not undertaken lightly. So in the absence of palpable costs, the default option was to continue with the existing policy on Eastern Europe.

Second, while the security benefits of maintaining the Soviet empire in Eastern Europe declined following the onset of secure nuclear deterrence in

---

44. See, for example, Jacques Lévesque, *The Enigma of 1989: The USSR and the Liberation of Eastern Europe*, trans. Keith Martin (Berkeley and Los Angeles: University of California Press, 1997).

45. See, for example, Karen Dawisha, *Eastern Europe, Gorbachev and Reform: The Great Challenge* (Cambridge: Cambridge University Press, 1988), 18.

46. As Alex Pravda notes, "Advances in weapons technology had long reduced the military value of the region as a glacis." Pravda, "Soviet Policy Towards Eastern Europe in Transition," in Alex Pravda, ed., *The End of Outer Empire: Soviet–East European Relations in Transition, 1985–1990* (London: Sage, 1992), 5. See also Aleksandr Bovin (in *Pravda*, March 23, 1990, p. 5), and Shakhnazarov, *Tsena svobody*, chap. 6.

the 1960s and remained relatively constant thereafter, the economic opportunity cost of maintaining the Soviet empire only began to escalate rapidly beginning in roughly the mid-1970s. The best-researched account of Soviet–Warsaw Pact economic relations concludes that during the 1980s "Soviet subsidies to the region were becoming an intolerable burden. . . . What had been a serious problem in the early 1970s had grown into a crisis of threatening proportions by the mid-1980s."[47] This imperial crisis stemmed from a variety of factors. Following the rise of Solidarity in Poland and the imposition of martial law in 1981, the Soviets bankrolled a huge outflow of subsidized loans in the early 1980s to Poland, East Germany, and Bulgaria and, at the same time, sought to "ease Eastern Europe's financial situation by accepting increased imports."[48] However, the goods that the allies shipped to the Soviets were falling further and further behind world standards; most were of much lower quality than the Soviets could have obtained on the open world market in exchange for the energy and raw materials they sent to Eastern Europe.[49]

At the same time, the Soviets' marginal cost of extracting the energy and raw materials they supplied to Eastern Europe in exchange for these goods was progressively increasing because most of the easily exploitable sources in the Soviet Union had already been exhausted.[50] By 1983, as noted, Siberian oil production began to decline, and the perennial Soviet problem of "shortage amidst plenty" suddenly worsened.[51] Finally, the East European allies' need for Soviet help increased as time progressed because they suffered a marked slowdown in both technological competitiveness and economic growth—

47. Randall Stone, *Satellites and Commissars: Strategy and Conflict in the Politics of Soviet-Bloc Trade* (Princeton: Princeton University Press, 1996), 134. More evidence for Stone's central conclusion is presented in Adomeit, *Imperial Overstretch*. For an analysis based on earlier data that reaches this same general conclusion, see Valerie Bunce, "The Empire Strikes Back: The Evolution of the Eastern Bloc from Soviet Asset to Liability," *International Organization* 39, no. 1 (winter 1985): 1–46.

48. J. F. Brown, *Eastern Europe and Communist Rule* (Durham: Duke University Press, 1988), 138, 129. As Brown reports, "In the winter of 1980–81, Soviet money almost literally poured into Poland. Some Western observers even put the total of Soviet assistance as high as nearly $5 billion" (54).

49. Smith notes, for example, that Soviet analysts "complained that Soviet imports from Eastern Europe largely consisted of poor quality machinery and equipment that were obsolete on world markets but which were priced at prices equivalent to or even higher than the world market price for higher quality goods." Alan Smith, "Economic Relations," in Alex Pravda, ed., *The End of Outer Empire: Soviet–East European Relations in Transition, 1985–1990* (London: Sage, 1992), 82. See also Mark Kramer, "The Soviet Union and Eastern Europe: Spheres of Influence," in Ngaire Woods, ed., *Explaining International Relations Since 1945* (Oxford: Oxford University Press, 1996), 112, who reports that most of these East European exports to the Soviet Union were of such poor quality that they "would have been unmarketable, or saleable only at highly disadvantageous prices, outside the Soviet bloc."

50. Stone, *Satellites and Commissars*, 37.

51. See Thane Gustafson, *Crisis Amid Plenty: The Politics of Soviet Energy Under Brezhnev and Gorbachev* (Princeton: Princeton University Press, 1989).

declining from an average real GDP growth rate of 3.23 percent in 1971–80, to 0.9 percent in 1981–85, and eventually reaching an average growth rate of –1.16 percent in 1989.[52]

For these and other reasons, by the mid-1980s the Soviets felt "increasingly exploited by the East Europeans," and there was growing Soviet "exasperation at what they considered the self-seeking behavior of their East European liabilities."[53] This led Soviet leaders to take the uncomfortable step of publicly castigating their allies in the CMEA. The most notable public expression of this growing frustration was at the 1984 CMEA summit, where General Secretary Konstantin Chernenko issued a stern warning to the East European countries to start living up to their economic "responsibilities,"[54] and the summit's final document bluntly directed them to start "supplying the USSR with the products it needs."[55] Similarly, at a 1986 summit of CMEA party leaders in Moscow, "the Soviet leadership had repeated complaints about the poor quality of East European manufactured exports to the Soviet Union."[56]

While the economic rationale for cutting back Soviet ties with Eastern Europe was thus becoming stronger and stronger, it would be wrong to say that these changing incentives led mechanistically to a positive Soviet decision to withdraw from Eastern Europe. In fact, available evidence indicates that there was no plan to withdraw from Eastern Europe, whether to reap economic benefits or for any other reason. Some key decision makers—notably, Shevardnadze and Ligachev—retrospectively claimed "that the Politburo renounced the Brezhnev doctrine in 1985."[57] The evidence, however, does not support the argument that such a proactive decision was actually made. On the contrary, Vladislav Zubok's extensive review of recently released archival documents concludes that "All the evidence indicates that Gorbachev and his advisers had no new policy for Eastern Europe."[58] The new evidence

52. Carol Clark, "Relative Backwardness in Eastern Europe: An Application of the Technological Gap Hypothesis," *Economic Systems* 17, no. 3 (September 1993): 167–93, is a good source on declining technological competitiveness. Growth figures are calculated from data on page 170 of the Clark article.

53. Brown, *Eastern Europe and Communist Rule*, 155.

54. Ibid., 154.

55. As Brown points out, "The directness of the above-quoted passage, which was, after all, part of an *agreed* document, gives some idea of what the debates over the issue must have been like and of what the Soviets' *original* suggestions might have been." Ibid., 155 (emphasis in original).

56. Smith, "Economic Relations," 77.

57. Mark Chafetz, *Gorbachev, Reform, and the Brezhnev Doctrine: Soviet Policy Toward Eastern Europe, 1985–1990* (Westport, Conn.: Praeger, 1993), 63.

58. Vladislav Zubok, "New Evidence on the 'Soviet Factor' in the Peaceful Revolutions of 1989," *Cold War International History Bulletin*, no. 12/13 (fall/winter 2001): 7. On security matters, Zubok stresses,

ratifies Pravda's assessment: "It would be unrealistic to argue that the Gorbachev leadership had any well-defined idea of the relationship they wished to achieve. They were clearer about past features they wanted to avoid and the general direction in which the relationship should evolve."[59]

Specifically, it is quite clear what the Soviets wanted: to reduce the burden of subsidies to the allies; to get them to supply better goods; and to lower the strain of maintaining the forward defense posture in Eastern Europe. In short, maintaining the foreign policy status quo in Eastern Europe was becoming very expensive in economic terms, and the Soviets wanted to drastically cut back those costs. As Jacques Lévesque notes, under Gorbachev "Moscow was much more demanding and stingy in its economic relations with its allies than it had been in the past."[60] An obvious way to cut costs was to demand less obedience from the allies. When policymakers such as Shevardnadze and Ligachev recall "renouncing the Brezhnev Doctrine" in 1985, what they probably have in mind is the resolve to reduce Moscow's interference in its allies' domestic choices. This self-restraint is understandable when one considers how very expensive it is to induce obedience from balky allies—as the Soviets discovered in the Polish crisis of 1980–81. Reducing costs and interference is very different, of course, from saying that the Soviets had a plan to jettison Eastern Europe. Had the citizens in Eastern Europe not organized to overthrow the existing regimes, the Soviet leadership—Gorbachev included—would have been quite happy to hold on to Eastern Europe. In the end, the only thing that had changed was the Soviet willingness to pay high costs in order to try to prevent this from happening.

While it is doubtful that the Soviets ever formally and explicitly decided to exit Eastern Europe, this is not to say that they had never weighed the growing costs of using force in Europe prior to 1989. Following the Polish crisis in 1980–81, the Soviet leadership pondered this very question at length. The evidence that has emerged here indicates that the Soviet leadership ruled out direct intervention in Poland as being beyond Soviet capabilities. According to KGB veteran Nikolai Leonov, Yury Andropov opined in 1980 that "the quota for our interventions abroad has been exhausted: . . . The Soviet Union already

"Gorbachev and Shevardnadze had no coherent policy at all for the Warsaw Pact" (8). For another exhaustive review of documentary evidence on this point, see Adomeit, *Imperial Overstretch*, chap. 4.

59. Pravda, "Soviet Policy," 7.

60. Jacques Lévesque, "Soviet Approaches to Eastern Europe at the Beginning of 1989," *Cold War International History Bulletin*, no. 12/13 (fall/winter 2001): 49.

lacked the power for such operations."[61] Available documents on the Polish crisis reveal that the Politburo was deeply reluctant to enforce the Brezhnev
Doctrine and was acutely aware of the punishing costs of doing so.[62] In reviewing the classified documents of the Politburo commission on the Polish crisis,
Georgy Shakhnazarov notes that there was "total unanimity . . . that the use of
our military contingent in Poland should be excluded from our arsenal."[63] The
key point here is that if the Soviets already felt in 1981 that military intervention
in Eastern Europe had become too costly, then the logical expectation is that the
willingness to use force in 1989 would be even lower after a decade more of
decline, after it was clear that this decline was systemic, not simply cyclical and,
most important, when the Soviet economy was in a complete free fall.

Indeed, it is clear that once the depth of economic distress was understood, the punishingly high costs and low benefits of using force were apparent—and not just to Gorbachev and the new thinkers, but to most "old thinkers"
in the Soviet Union as well.[64] The use of force in these circumstances would
have ended the emerging détente with the West, increased the West's allocations for defense, closed off all credits to a Soviet economy in desperate need,
and shut down all hopes of technology transfers or joint ventures. Moreover,
intervention would imply the assumption of direct responsibility for Eastern
Europe's growing foreign debt, whose servicing would have added massive burdens on the Soviet economy—or, of course, a default, which would have further
closed Western markets. As Chernyaev recalls, Gorbachev's resigned response
to worries that Poland was moving away from the Soviet alliance owed much to
his awareness of these economic constraints: "What can we do? Poland has a
$56 billion debt. Can we take Poland on our balance sheet in our current eco-
nomic situation? No. And if we cannot—then we have no influence."[65]

And, to carry the counterfactual further, had Moscow intervened militarily, it would then have had to establish new client regimes whose obvious
dependence on the Soviet Union would have implied even higher governance
costs for the Soviet budget than the old Soviet empire. The use of force would,
in short, have entailed a new Soviet isolation unseen since the 1950s, and it

61. Leonov, *Likholet'e*, 281.
62. See Vojtech Mastny, "The Soviet Non-Invasion of Poland in 1980–81 and the End of the Cold War,"
Cold War International History Project, Working Paper no. 23 (Washington, D.C., September 1998).
63. Shakhnazarov, *Tsena svobody*, 115.
64. See Andrew O. Bennett, "Ideas and the Non-Use of Force in the End of the Cold War" (paper prepared for the Conference "Ideas and the End of the Cold War," Dickey Center, Dartmouth College, June,
2001), 17–18, and sources cited therein.
65. Cited in Zubok, "New Evidence," 10–11.

would have required Moscow to extract 1950s-level sacrifices from its own population. But in the 1950s, the Soviet economy was growing at 8 percent yearly, and Soviet leaders consequently had some confidence in their system's ability to deliver growth. Fifteen years of decline had sapped that confidence, and with it the willingness to die, kill, and impose material hardship in the name of socialism. Given these trends, it is not surprising that no old thinker advocated the use of force in 1989, and none has since suggested that such a decision would have served Soviet interests.[66]

To summarize, the key security benefits of the empire had long ago faded; the economic burdens of the East European empire were rapidly rising; Soviet policymakers across the political spectrum wanted to scale back these growing costs of empire; the costs of using force in Eastern Europe had been deemed unacceptably high as early as 1981; and all decision makers were aware of the prohibitive costs of using force in 1989. In short, there were powerful incentives against the major use of force. Knowledge of these incentives would lead us to expect policymakers to try hard to avoid armed confrontations. Soviet behavior is consistent with this expectation. As Andrew Bennett points out in Chapter 6, "Thus far no evidence has come to light that any top Soviet leader argued for using force in Europe in 1989, or that the military or security bureaucracies were asked for or volunteered operational plans for using force."[67] In fact, Gorbachev took active measures to avert an inadvertent "Kent State" kind of confrontation between armed soldiers and demonstrating civilians.[68] Of course, there was never a guarantee that policymakers would be successful in their efforts to avoid armed confrontation. There is nothing in our analysis that rules out the possibility of policymakers or commanders losing control in a tense situation. Once again, this is a distinction between causation in nature and in social life.

Counterargument 2: The Economic Crisis Was Purely a Consequence of Gorbachev's Particular Economic Policies

Many scholars agree that the Soviet Union's rapid decline in economic fortunes strongly influenced the end of the Cold War, but nevertheless assert that the country's declining material fortunes were merely the result of idiosyncratic

66. See Chapter 6, pp. 200–202.
67. Ibid., 200.
68. Gorbachev's preventive actions are discussed in Kramer, "Ideology and the Cold War," and Lévesque, *Enigma of 1989*.

economic policy choices initiated by Gorbachev after 1985.[69] As noted previously, Gorbachev initially chose to reinvigorate the Soviet economy by massively increasing investment in the machine tools industry, ramping up defense expenditures, tightening discipline, clamping down on corruption, restricting vodka sales, granting enterprises more freedom, and allowing freer flow of information through the system. Far from being simply the brainchild of an idiosyncratic Gorbachev, the policy package was the carefully prepared product of the country's best and brightest policy advisers, and it was thoroughly vetted with critical experts who had spent their professional lives on the problem of reforming the Soviet economy. Of course, it was a catastrophic failure, generating massive fiscal imbalances, no upsurge in growth, and the beginnings of a breakdown in the command system.[70]

Gorbachev's particular economic reforms clearly helped propel the Soviet economy into a severe tailspin by the late 1980s. But the fact that the new economic policies abetted Soviet decline should not be confused with the notion that Gorbachev single-handedly brought the Soviet economy to its knees. As noted in the first section of this chapter, the Soviet economy was in dire straits before Gorbachev assumed power. The systemic decline of the Soviet economy was, in fact, what spurred economic reforms in the first place. Nevertheless, Gorbachev's reform package did make the economic situation even worse. This fact leads immediately to two popular counterfactuals.

First, suppose Gorbachev had not been selected as leader in 1985? As a matter of historical record, most analysts hold that Gorbachev's selection was not a close-run affair. Biology dictated that a transition to the younger generation of leaders was inevitable, and by the early 1980s Gorbachev was the sole representative of that generation who was a full member of the Politburo. Had he met an untimely death, however, the lack of younger leaders with sufficient stature for the top post might have given seventy-year-old Viktor Grishin a chance at power. In Chapter 8, Robert English suggests that a Grishin regime might have continued, and perhaps intensified the Cold War rivalry for another decade or more.[71]

---

69. See the English and Zubok chapters in this volume; also see, for example, Matthew Evangelista, *Unarmed Forces: The Transnational Movement to End the Cold War* (Ithaca: Cornell University Press, 1999), esp. 256.

70. In addition to Sinel'nikov, *Byudzhetnyy krizis*, see also David Kotz, with Fred Weir, *Revolution from Above*.

71. In addition to the English and Zubok chapters herein, see George Breslauer and Richard Ned Lebow, "Contingency and Counterfactuals: How Leaders Matter," in Richard Hermann and Richard Ned Lebow, eds., *Learning from the Cold War* (unpublished manuscript).

The Grishin counterfactual—like the others that have been proposed about the Cold War's end—suggests that other broad outcomes than Soviet retrenchment were possible. But the question is, how probable were they? In this case, how likely was it that a counterfactual General Secretary Grishin would have been able to maintain or intensify the Cold War rivalry for another ten or twenty years? Our analysis suggests that this counterfactual is highly improbable, for it glides over very tough constraints that Grishin would have faced. Most important, the Cold War status quo would have been exceedingly hard to maintain, absent a major turnaround in the economy. Lagging substantially behind the U.S.-led alliance in economic growth, the Soviets would have to devote an increasing share of output to foreign policy just to stay even. Given technological trends, Moscow would also have been hard-pressed to maintain parity as a superpower without some new and expensive program to counter new technology-intensive U.S. weapons and doctrines. Eighty percent of Soviet expenditures on science already went to military purposes. Increasing that proportion yet further might well have worsened the macroeconomic situation just as Gorbachev's policies did. And the new thinkers had a point: given that the trends were toward an even greater Soviet quantitative and qualitative disadvantage, the longer the Soviets waited, the harder and riskier an exit from the Cold War would get. Doing nothing, as the old adage goes, is doing something, and in this case it would simply have produced even more Soviet decline, which would have further skewed odds against easing Moscow's Cold War burdens on good terms. It is not obvious that procrastination—which is what English suggests Grishin would have done—was any safer than the policy package that Gorbachev pursued.

In addition, given underlying trends, some reform effort to boost Soviet economic performance was highly likely. After all, Andropov had begun such a program, his age and conservatism notwithstanding. The pressure on Grishin to turn the economy around would have been intense. The question then becomes, how much would a Grishin program have differed substantively from Gorbachev's initial acceleration policy? Given the popularity of Gorbachev's initial program with many conservatively minded officials, and given its resemblance to Andropov's aborted program, it is likely that a Grishin policy would have been broadly similar, and produced broadly similar results.

This brings us to a second popular counterfactual concerning Gorbachev's reform package. Suppose there had been a different reaction to the failure of the initial reforms? The acceleration policy appears in many ways to have been the system's "default option" response to decline. Thus, any new leader would probably have had to confront its failure. Without resolving very complex and contentious questions of Soviet economic policy, it is difficult to determine what the optimal response would have been. The key point is that any response would have had to confront the basic fact that the Soviet Union's economic crisis was to a significant degree endogenous to the international environment. Nearly a quarter of all economic activity, the best R&D resources, and the best technical and science expertise were all being cannibalized by the massive defense sector. The Central European dependencies were a large and growing burden. Any program for restoring growth and competitiveness to the Soviet economy would have had to confront these realities.

Thus Gorbachev's impulse to retrench internationally and undercut the military's priority claim on resources was not an idiosyncratic impulse on his part, but a response to a deep-seated economic reality. If anything, the most critical blunder Gorbachev made was failing to cut defense fast enough. Instructive on this score is an analysis of the main alternatives to Gorbachev's response to the initial policy's failure. The two economic policy responses that were actually debated—the strategy of "optimizing the planning mechanism" favored by more conservative officials such as Nikolai Ryzhkov, Vitaly Vorotnikov, and Yegor Ligachev; and the strategy of rapid marketization pushed by liberals like Yegor Gaidar, Stanislav Shatalin, and Grigory Yavlinsky—were both weighted even *more* heavily toward cutting back the imperial burden.[72] Both Ryzhkov and Gaidar—coming from two very different perspectives—had the same fundamental criticism of Gorbachev: that he failed to rein in government expenditures (including defense expenditures) fast enough to establish the macroeconomic stability that true reform demanded.[73]

In sum, Gorbachev's initial package of economic reform policies was the Soviet polity's default option. In a counterfactual case involving a different leader, something broadly similar would probably have been attempted—and it probably would have produced similar results. In a counterfactual case involving the adoption of either of the two responses to the initial policy's failure

72. On the "Ligachev/Ryzhkov alternative," see Jerry F. Hough, *Democratization and Revolution in the USSR, 1985–1991* (Washington, D.C.: The Brookings Institution, 1997). On the liberal-market option, see Gaidar, *Days of Defeat and Victory*.

73. The point holds even though the two sides had completely different definitions of "stabilization," as Robert Zoellick points out in Chapter 4, pp. 128.

that appear to have been the most likely alternatives to the course Gorbachev chose, the Soviets would have been even *more* sensitive to the costs of the Cold War status quo than they actually were. Moreover, there is little reason to believe that either plan would have restored growth to the Soviet economy by 1989–90. Thus counterfactuals that feature clear general alternatives to retrenchment or an economically viable Soviet Union in 1990 appear improbable.

Counterargument 3: If Economic Constraints Were So Salient, Then Why Didn't Everyone Agree on Retrenchment?

As the chapters by Bennett, Zubok, and English attest, many scholars who criticize explanations of Soviet foreign policy behavior based on economic constraints highlight the absence of a complete consensus within the Soviet Union on the desirability of retrenchment. The critics are right about the absence of unanimity within the Soviet Union concerning foreign policy. As we stressed above, important elements of the Soviet elite were deeply troubled by Gorbachev's foreign policy course. And a few figures, such as Oleg Baklanov, simply denied that the Soviet Union's foreign policy imposed a massive and escalating economic burden.[74] In short, it is not hard to find domestic disagreement about the advisability of Gorbachev's approach to retrenchment.

Yet it would be surprising to find consensus about any major policy reorientation of any sort in any country. All social science theory tells us that finding such a consensus will be rare indeed, if not impossible. Bureaucratic interests and institutional structures matter; different individuals process information and learn at different rates; leaders at the top of the power structure often see things differently than those at the bottom; and so on. An argument such as ours that highlights economic constraints does not imply that all politics stop the minute certain policies become unsustainably costly. Even in cases where economic constraints are strong, there will still be arguments, persuasion, debates, and controversies.

Despite the lack of theoretical reasons to expect a consensus over the reorientation of Soviet foreign policy, this is exactly the standard of evidence that many accounts use to measure explanations, such as ours, that highlight economic constraints. Most prominently, Matthew Evangelista's influential

---

74. See Skvortsov interview with Oleg D. Baklanov, undated, Moscow (on file at the Institute of General History, Moscow, and the Mershon Center at Ohio State University, 1999).

account of the Cold War's end repeatedly points to the lack of consensus about Soviet retrenchment as a strong indicator of the inherent weakness of any explanation grounded in growing economic pressures.[75] Similarly, all the other scholarly contributors to this volume make much of the absence of consensus within both superpowers. Yet if there is no reason to expect consensus, it is hard to see why a lack of consensus can be counted as evidence either for or against any particular theoretical framework. In short, no matter how strong the economic constraints facing the Soviet Union were, it is unreasonable to expect all Soviet officials to respond to them in an identical manner at the same time.

In addition, the "lack of consensus" counterargument often reflects a preoccupation with a different explanatory problem; namely, accounting for the specific details of individual decisions. When the analytical lens is concentrated on such finely grained decisions, differences of opinion are almost always evident. This is frequently the stuff of policymaking, and it is not surprising that participants focus on it when revisiting their roles in larger events. But explaining, for example, why the Soviets agreed to the inclusion of the "Oka" missile in the INF talks in 1987 is not the same as explaining why the Cold War ended peacefully on largely Western terms, which is the outcome we are seeking to explain here. We have found that the sum total of the dozens of critical decisions that add up to the end of the Cold War are consistent with our argument. Singling out only one finely grained decision from this large series and discovering policy differences does not impugn our basic finding. We do not claim—no responsible analyst can—to account for each microanalytical decision or bargaining position adopted during the Cold War endgame.

The lack of consensus counterargument not only applies an inappropriate standard of evidence, it also ignores the free-rider issue. By free riding we do not mean that conservatives and hard-liners wholeheartedly agreed with Gorbachev's retrenchment policies but stood aside and let him do the tough work of implementing them. Rather, we mean that most of the old thinkers were not in positions where they were forced to confront the trade-offs implicit in any effort to deal with the Soviet Union's growing problems. Much of the evidence of policy differences concerns old thinkers' complaints about Gorbachev's policies, especially concessions in arms control negotiations. But such laments

75. See Evangelista, *Unarmed Forces*, 15, 252, 258, 262.

do not necessarily indicate what these officials would have been able to do had they been in command. They were able to gripe about Gorbachev's course without ever having to face the painful choices between guns and butter and between the present and the future. One example out of many is Yegor Ligachev, who, William Odom shows, "wanted reform but not at the expense of the Soviet Union's international military status."[76] The problem with Ligachev's lament is that in office and in retirement he accepted that the Soviet Union "faced the task of curtailing military spending. . . . the economy could not breathe normally with a military budget that comprised 18 percent of the national income."[77] In short, Ligachev wanted to slash defense outlays without reducing military capabilities. Doubtless Gorbachev would have loved to have been able to do this. What leader wouldn't? Those in opposition are free to advance incompatible policy preferences without having to worry about how to resolve them.

Counterargument 4: The Cold War Endgame
Negotiations Are a Major Puzzle

Many scholars argue that the ease and speed of the negotiations that formally settled the Cold War present a major puzzle for any explanation rooted in economic constraints. They contend that even given the Soviets' parlous economic condition in 1989–90, they could have bargained harder and extracted better terms but for the particular character of Gorbachev (as Zubok contends in Chapter 7), the specific nature of recent Soviet cognitive learning (as Bennett argues in Chapter 6), or the influence of particular ideational dynamics, as Thomas Risse has argued in various analyses.[78]

As with the discussion of the overall reorientation of Soviet foreign policy, any analysis of the role these factors played in influencing particular negotiations during the Cold War endgame requires an accurate estimate of the extent to which economic difficulties constrained Moscow's choices. Given this, what are the logical extensions of our analysis in the first part of this chapter? The first is simply that once Moscow opted for retrenchment, each passing year made a reversal of course less likely. This would be true even if the

---

76. Odom, *Collapse of the Soviet Military*, 92.
77. Ibid.
78. Thomas Risse, "'Let's Argue!' Communicative Action in World Politics," *International Organization* 54, no. 1 (winter 2000): 1–40; and idem, "The Cold War's Endgame and German Unification," *International Security* 21, no. 4 (spring 1997): 158–85.

various trends that we showed were facing Moscow in the 1980s had not accelerated. But, of course, these problems did accelerate: Moscow's already poor economic fortunes changed dramatically for the worse, beginning in 1988. And here, the second logical extension of our analysis is that if a certain magnitude of economic pressures biased the system toward retrenchment, then we would expect an even larger amount of economic distress to generate movement toward a proportionately greater reduction in Soviet foreign policy claims on the international system. In short, if systemic economic decline made retrenchment the most likely outcome, then the utter free fall of the Soviet economy in 1989–91 (see Table 1) would lead to an even greater assault on the Soviets' Cold War foreign policy.

Still our analysis should not be interpreted to mean that there were no differences between new and old thinkers during the Cold War endgame—or that representatives of these orientations would have responded identically to each strategic incentive. As we have noted, we do not claim to account for every microanalytical decision. By outlining a more complete portrayal of the economic constraints facing Moscow in this period, what our analysis provides is the basis for a more productive dialogue concerning how these pressures interacted with ideas and leadership in finely grained decision problems.

To illustrate this point, consider the aspect of the Cold War endgame that has arguably received the most attention from international relations scholars: the reunification of Germany. The Soviet decision to submit to Western terms in negotiations over German reunification was clearly an outcome that the Soviets did not desire but acquiesced in once events conspired to leave them with no better alternative. The key question that needs to be resolved is *why* the Soviets eventually faced no better policy alternatives. The expectation derived from our analysis is that Moscow opted to capitulate to Western terms on German reunification in large part because doing otherwise would have been unacceptably costly. For one thing, taking a hard negotiating line on this issue would have created an environment in which it would have been impossible to sharply cut back Soviet defense expenditures at a time when the Soviet economy was spiraling out of control. In addition, taking this route would have threatened the Soviets' efforts to increase access to the international economy.

For scholars who contend that the endgame negotiations present a major puzzle for our explanation, it is axiomatic that the Soviets had a number of viable potential alternatives concerning German reunification. And as the policymakers' discussion in Chapter 2 indicates, many participants agree. The queries posed by Brent Scowcroft and Robert Zoellick at the conference are echoed by Thomas Risse, who notes:

Although Moscow could no longer influence events or bargaining outcomes in its desired direction, it still could make life quite miserable for the West and for Germany in particular. First, Moscow could have forced the German people to choose between unification and NATO membership, thereby triggering a major domestic dispute in the country during an election year. Second, the Soviet Union could have provoked an international crisis and confrontation with Bonn and Washington by fully insisting on its legal rights over Germany as an allied power. The price to be paid by both sides would have been to start another Cold War just as the first one was about to end peacefully. Third, in the absence of a cooperative agreement with the West, the Soviet Union could have decided to leave its 300,000 troops in East Germany.[79]

Given the extent to which the Soviet economy spiraled out of control after 1989, there is little reason to think that Risse's second option was actually on the table. To the extent that the Cold War was too costly in the 1980s, this economic burden was massively higher in the early 1990s—by which time there was a complete loss of control over the state budget (a deficit of 12–14 percent of GDP in 1989 and over 20 percent in 1990), severe recession (a 5 percent contraction in 1990, 10–15 percent in 1991), hyperinflation (2–5 percent a week in 1991); an overpowering foreign exchange crisis; and a chaotic, empire-wide grab for resources and power by various sub-elites.[80] Given these circumstances, few, if any, policymakers in Moscow thought the Soviet Union had the capacity to start a new cold war at this time.

Concerning Risse's third option, the opportunity cost of taking a firm stance and leaving Soviet troops in Eastern Europe would have been punishingly high. We need more evidence on this period, but there are indications that once the Soviet economy went into a severe tailspin, Gorbachev, Shevardnadze, and a few other top new-thinking officials realized quickly that they simply were not in a position to make strong demands of the West. Given that the GDR's economy was collapsing even faster than the Soviet Union's, it was clear that whoever took responsibility for maintaining order there would be assuming a financial burden far beyond Moscow's means.[81] Publicly, Gorbachev

---

79. Risse, "Let's Argue!" 24.
80. Data from sources in Table 1.
81. For an insider's contemporary assessment of the GDR's economy at this time, see Hans Hermann Hertle, "Staatsbankrott: Der ökonomische Untergang des SED-Staates," *Deutschland Archiv* 25, no. 10 (October 1992): 1019–30. For scholarly treatments that document the economic crisis and the lack of viable

and his aides stuck to the old definition of Soviet interests—no NATO expansion into the territory of the former GDR—but privately they appear to have concluded that dragging out the negotiations would gain less than it would cost in terms of bad faith, fewer loans and grants from the West to ease the foreign exchange crisis, and slower integration into Western political, security, and financial institutions—all of which would serve to impede their efforts to put the Soviet economy back on track. As Chernyaev puts it, had the Soviets continued to stall the negotiations, "Germany would have been united anyway—without us and against us. And we would not have received the compensation that the Germans gave us—both material and political."[82]

Thus, of the counterfactual Soviet policy options Risse mentions, it is the first—a cleverer diplomatic strategy for dividing the U.S.-German alliance—that is relatively plausible. Gorbachev might well have forced Helmut Kohl's hand by agreeing to unification on easy terms in exchange for the new Germany's exit from NATO's security structures, packaged with an appropriate upgrading of the Conference on Security and Cooperation in Europe—the broad security organization Moscow had long favored. Oleg Grinevsky did, in fact, forward the idea in February that Moscow should immediately support unification but insist on a neutral, demilitarized Germany.[83] In this scenario, the Germans would have been forced to confront a trade-off between unity and loyalty to the United States and NATO.

What would have happened if the Soviets had adopted such a tougher bargaining stance? The Western powers did discuss this scenario and resolved to stick to their position if it led to a showdown with Moscow.[84] According to Western officials, Washington and Bonn had contingency plans in case the

---

options, see in particular, Maier, *Dissolution*, and Jeffrey Kopstein, *The Politics of Economic Decline in East Germany, 1945–1989* (Chapel Hill: University of North Carolina Press, 1997).

82. Aleksandr Galkin and Anatoly S. Chernyayev, "Pravdu, i tol'ko pravdu," *Svobodnaya mysl'*, no. 2–3 (1994): 28. For reconstructing Soviet thinking in this period, the authors are grateful to Anatoly Chernyaev, Sergei Tarasenko, Andrei Grachev, and Oleg Grinevsky for granting interviews on this subject conducted at the conference "German Reunification and the End of the Cold War," Wildbad Kreuth, Germany, October 21–24, 1999. Excellent published sources include Philip Zelikow and Condoleezza Rice, *Germany Unified and Europe Transformed: A Study in Statecraft* (Cambridge: Harvard University Press, 1995); Angela E. Stent, *Russia and Germany Reborn: Unification, the Soviet Collapse, and the New Europe* (Princeton: Princeton University Press, 1999); and Adomeit, *Imperial Overstretch*.

83. Oleg Grinevskiy, "Kak nachilos' ob"yednineniye Germanii" (MS, courtesy of Ambassador Grinevskiy). Other alternative diplomatic strategies very roughly along these lines—but vetted later in the endgame—are detailed in Julij A. Kwizinskij, *Vor dem Sturm: Errinerungen eines Diplomaten*, trans. Hilde Ettinger and Helmut Ettinger (Berlin: Siedler, 1993), and Valentin Falin, *Politische Erinnerungen*, trans. Heddy Pross-Werth (Munich: Droemer Knaur, 1993).

84. Zelikow and Rice, *Germany Unified*, chap. 5.

Soviets balked and asserted their residual four-power rights from World War II. The Western three would simply have unilaterally withdrawn their rights, leaving Moscow alone against the Germans. The resulting formula would have been neither "2+4" nor "4+2" but rather "5 (the two Germanys, France, Britain, and the United States) versus 1 (Moscow)." If the West was truly willing to risk a return of Cold War confrontation rather than acquiesce to German neutrality, then there were few policymakers in Moscow who thought the Soviet Union could prevail. If negotiations broke down, the likelihood was that the Soviets' bargaining position would only deteriorate with time as the Soviet and Eastern German economies continued their precipitous decline. Meanwhile, the West German government was busy creating facts on the ground; in effect beginning to provide governance for what was quickly becoming the former GDR, in fact if not yet in law.[85] Moscow simply lacked the resources to counter this influence—unless it was truly willing to crack down forcefully and assume full responsibility for governing the GDR by whatever means necessary, something no one in Moscow wanted to contemplate.

In the end, it thus appears that the new thinkers were probably right to concede on an issue they would lose after a costly diplomatic struggle. But contingency plans do not a policy make. It is conceivable that Kohl would have been faced with intolerable public pressure to accept the Soviet deal, which could have led to a break with Washington. Or it is possible that Kohl and Bush, seeing the trend, would have countered with offers of more restrictions on Germany's role in NATO. While these outcomes were certainly possible, it is not surprising that the Gorbachev team decided not to gamble on them, given the collapse of the GDR, the rapid deterioration of the Soviet economy, and the immense costs to Moscow of actually using its military muscle in Central Europe. Had the Soviets risked an assertion of their power or their residual rights over Germany, in all likelihood they would have had to face an overwhelming diplomatic counter-coalition.

Rational expectations of which side could prevail if negotiations broke down—as well as which side could offer more material rewards in return for concessions—help explain Gorbachev's sudden acquiescence to Western terms

---

85. These measures are detailed in Doris G. Wolfgramm, *The Kohl Government and German Reunification: Crisis and Foreign Policy* (Lewiston, N.Y.: Edwin Mellen Press, 1997). They were part of Bonn's larger policy of using economic incentives in the diplomacy of reunification, which is brilliantly documented in Randall E. Newnham, *Deutsche Mark Diplomacy* (University Park: Pennsylvania State University Press, 2001).

in the spring of 1990. Gorbachev was reluctant to endorse any diplomatic ploy
that banked on the GDR, which by January he had concluded was doomed.[86]
He seems to have concluded that as much as he opposed the inclusion of
Germany within NATO, a concession on this issue would pay off in the future
in terms of better relations with the new Germany. Various factors appear to
have factored into his thinking on this score. For one thing, in 1990 West
Germany ranked first as provider of capital investment to the Soviet Union, as
well as being the number one source of joint ventures in the country.[87] In
short, West Germany was a very lucrative economic partner—and had the
potential to become an even more important one in the future. Moreover, the
growing economic crisis facing the Soviet Union made joint ventures and capital all the more necessary; Gorbachev specifically noted in 1990 that it was
exactly at this moment that Western economic involvement was most urgently
needed.[88] For these reasons, the risks of spoiling the emerging relationship
with Germany seemed high indeed. Of course, beyond these potential costs of
adopting an intransigent position in the negotiations, moving forward on
German reunification also had very substantial, direct economic benefits for
the Soviets, most notably DM 20 billion to offset the costs of repositioning
Soviet troops as well as new grants and loans on favorable terms.[89]

It is here, ironically, that we find the most likely potential alternative to
Gorbachev's policy. In contemporary debates, many old thinkers castigate
Gorbachev, not for allowing German reunification, but rather for not receiving enough financial compensation from the West in return.[90] Thus, the old
thinkers' great alternative on German reunification seems to boil down to a
claim that they would have been sharper bargainers with the West. Adopting a
tougher bargaining strategy in this instance may or may not have meant a
larger inflow of financial capital into the Soviet Union. While adopting such a

86. The January 27, 1990, Politburo meeting at which Gorbachev formally decided to bank on the FRG
is recounted in Chernyaev, *My Six Years with Gorbachev*, chap 7.

87. In March 1990, West Germany provided 13.7 percent of the total number of joint ventures in the
Soviet Union and 12.5 percent of the initial capital investment in the country. See Alan B. Sherr, "Foreign
Direct Investment in the Soviet Union: Status and Trends," Center for Foreign Policy Development,
Briefing Paper no. 5 (Brown University, May 1991), 33.

88. Ibid., 16. Gorbachev described Bonn's willingness to agree to assume financial responsibility for the
GDR and offer Moscow new credits as "oxygen" for perestroika. Quoted in Stent, *Russia and Germany
Reborn*, 126.

89. Newnham, *Deutsche Mark Diplomacy*, is the best source here.

90. Thus, at a conference in Moscow organized by Russia's Institute of General History and the
Mershon Center at Ohio State University, Yazov responded to the question of what he would have done differently regarding German unification by stating, "I would have demanded more money from the Germans!"

ploy might have resulted in a Soviet Union momentarily less strapped for cash, it would not have changed the course of the Cold War's resolution to any meaningful degree.

Counterargument 5: The United States Is Benign

Finally, many scholars and former Bush administration officials contend that the accommodating Soviet stance during the Cold War endgame—and particularly in the negotiations over German unification—were prompted by a U.S. strategy of engaging in concessions and other forms of reassurance that allowed Gorbachev to trust the United States to a remarkable degree.[91] This counterargument raises a simple empirical question: As the Soviets revamped their foreign policy practices and engaged in one concession after another in the late 1980s and early 1990s, did the United States reciprocate? More specifically, did the Soviets submit to Western terms on issue after issue because of the cumulative effect of a cooperative pattern of interaction characterized by mutual concessions and assurances in the late 1980s and early 1990s? Scholars who advance this form of argument are certainly right that Gorbachev desperately wanted his Western partners to match Soviet concessions and that he tried through appeals and gestures to get them to do so.[92] However, the evidence overwhelmingly shows that the Cold War's end simply ratified preexisting foreign policy interests in the West.[93]

As far as Western decision-making elites were concerned, the end of the Cold War was the wholesale collapse of one worldview and the triumph of another. The general pattern that emerges from the evidence is clear: Washington was slow to respond to Gorbachev's concessions, never reciprocated them in kind, and never compromised its basic approach to international security.[94] U.S. decision makers rebuffed Gorbachev's testing moratorium; they insisted on SDI despite a ceaseless campaign by Gorbachev; they held an Afghan settlement hostage to their "right" to arm the mujahedin rebels to the

91. The most recent articulation of this popular argument is Andrew Kydd, "Trust, Reassurance, and Cooperation," *International Organization* 54, no. 2 (spring 2000): 325–57, esp. 350.

92. In his introductory remarks at the Endgame conference, Anatoly Chernyaev noted his surprise that it was the ideologically minded Soviets rather than the pragmatic Westerners who were first to trust their old adversaries.

93. See Shoon Murray, *Anchors Against Change: American Opinion Leaders' Beliefs After the Cold War* (Ann Arbor: University of Michigan Press, 1996).

94. This is the basic theme of Raymond L. Garthoff's magisterial *The Great Transition: American-Soviet Relations and the End of the Cold War* (Washington, D.C.: The Brookings Institution, 1994).

end; they engaged in a prolonged "strategic review" to assess Soviet intentions
even after Gorbachev had made a series of spectacular unilateral concessions;
they would not alter their policy on the Baltics even in 1990, the year in which
U.S.-Soviet relations were the closest they had ever been; and the United
States—together with its West German ally—forced German unification in
NATO against Gorbachev and Shevardnadze's insistent, nearly hysterical
pleading.

The most striking evidence concerning U.S. policy is what is absent from
the policymaking record: any serious argument for doing what Gorbachev
wanted, which was to treat the ending of the Cold War symmetrically, as if the
Warsaw Pact and NATO were equals. The major debate concerns whether
President Bush and Secretary of State Baker, who did change their rhetoric
but never significantly altered any basic Western security institution or practice, went too far in "coddling" Gorbachev. The general alternatives within
U.S. policy circles were strongly weighted toward even less willingness to
bend for Moscow's benefit.[95] The actions of U.S. officials, if not their words,
bespoke confidence that Soviet relative decline had left Gorbachev with few
realistic options other than to make concession after concession to Western
views. The Bush administration's policy toward Moscow, as formulated in
National Security Directive 23 (September 1989), called for "the integration
of the Soviet Union into the existing international system," which required
"fundamental alterations in Soviet military force structure, institutions, and
practices that can only be reversed at great costs, economically and politically,
to the Soviet Union."[96]

If the Gorbachev team balked at U.S. terms, the Americans were apparently ready to revert to a Cold War confrontation in which they knew they
would hold the upper hand.[97] To be sure, President Bush was extremely care-

95. See Robert M. Gates, *In from the Shadows: The Ultimate Insider's Story of Five Presidents and How They Won the Cold War* (New York: Simon & Schuster, 1996); Zelikow and Rice, *Germany Unified*; Robert L. Hutchings, *American Diplomacy and the End of the Cold War: An Insider's Account of U.S. Policy in Europe, 1989–92* (Baltimore: Johns Hopkins University Press, 1997); Jack F. Matlock, Jr., *Autopsy on an Empire: The American Ambassador's Account of the Collapse of the Soviet Union* (New York: Random House, 1996).

96. NSD 23 (9/22/89), "United States Relations with the Soviet Union," from National Security Archive's Briefing Book for its oral history conference "The End of the Cold War in Europe, 1989: New Thinking and New Evidence," Musgrove, St. Simon's Island, Georgia, May 1–3, 1998.

97. Zelikow and Rice, *Germany Unified*, report that Washington was ready to insist that the reunified Germany remain a member of NATO, even at the risk of a crisis in the relationship. In the spring of 1988, the CIA predicted that Moscow would embark on unilateral arms reductions out of economic necessity. Doc. No. 59 in Brown University, "Understanding the End of the Cold War." In September 1989, the CIA

ful to say nothing to humiliate Gorbachev publicly. At Malta, he even agreed to cease talking about uniting Europe based on "Western values," agreeing to use the more neutral "democratic values."[98] But privately the president and his aides believed that the United States had won the Cold War. As Bush told Kohl at the Camp David summit in February, "The Soviets are not in a position to dictate Germany's relationship with NATO. What worries me is talk that Germany must not stay in NATO. To hell with that! We prevailed, they didn't. We can't let the Soviets clutch victory from the jaws of defeat."[99]

This was neither the attitude nor the behavior of people who believed that the Soviet change of heart was in any way contingent upon any foreign policy concessions on their part. Such basic confidence led the Western powers to be extraordinarily tough bargainers with the Soviets. Regarding German unification in particular, former West German and U.S. officials and others argue the West sought successfully to exploit Soviet weakness to achieve German unification "utterly and unequivocally on Western terms."[100]

In sum, the evidence indicates that the United States simply did not adjust its foreign policy practices to any meaningful degree during the Cold War endgame, and that this was in large part because the Soviets were in no material position to push Washington to do so. It is true that personal relationships of trust did evolve among key leaders in the three main governments concerned, the Soviet, West German, and U.S. But these relationships were quite slow in developing. Indeed, the Endgame conference discussions reflect what other available evidence suggests: that the process of the dissolution of communism in Central Europe was well along before relations of trust appeared to take hold among Kohl, Gorbachev, and Bush. In other words, trust emerged when the economic fortunes of the Soviets collapsed and they agreed to Western terms. It is thus difficult to disentangle the importance of interpersonal synergy from the dictates of dire necessity, in the case of

asserted that Soviet domestic instability would "prevent a return to the arsenal state economy that generated the fundamental military threat to the West . . . since World War II" whether or not Gorbachev retained power. Directorate for Intelligence (CIA), "Gorbachev's Domestic Gambles and Instability in the USSR, An Intelligence Assessment" (September 1989); declassified and on file at the National Security Archive, George Washington University.

98. The memorandum of conversation is excerpted in Mikhail S. Gorbachev, *Gody trudnykh resheniy: Izbrannoye 1985–1992* (Moscow: Tortuga, 1993), 172–97.

99. George Bush and Brent Scowcroft, *A World Transformed* (New York: Alfred A. Knopf, 1998), 252.

100. Zelikow and Rice, *Germany Unified*; Hutchings, *American Diplomacy*; Horst Teltschik, *329 Tage: Innenansichten der Einigung* (Berlin: Siedler, 1991).

Gorbachev, and the delights of getting exactly what one wants, in the case of Bush and Kohl.

Of course, in any particular negotiation, one can find instances of U.S.-Soviet give-and-take, and indeed, some concessions on the part of the United States. As stressed above, we make no claim to be able to explain every aspect of each and every negotiation. In the final analysis, however, there is no way to avoid the conclusion that the United States was extraordinarily firm in the positions it adopted and that cooperation during the Cold War endgame was largely the product of a shift by the Soviets, albeit a reluctant one, toward long-standing U.S. positions. For this reason, it is hard to place much weight on the importance of an overall atmosphere of trust and reassurance generated by mutual concessions as an influence on the Cold War endgame.

Conclusion

Our basic finding is that changing economic constraints made the Cold War's end on Western terms the most likely outcome. We do not mean to claim that the agency of key leaders, the role of certain ideas and cognitive processes, or the actions of particular domestic actors or interest groups did not "matter" in the end of the Cold War. We agree with James Baker and the other Princeton conferees, as well as with our scholarly colleagues, that these factors influenced events—as they likely do in all other major cases in international relations. But they all played out against the backdrop of massive and deep economic shifts. Too often, the links between such large-scale changes and ideas, leaders, and domestic politics are not explored. We argue that it is not enough to claim that large-scale economic changes do not determine outcomes and then proceed to analyze other factors as if they were somehow unrelated. Leaders, ideas, bargaining, signaling, domestic struggles, and the evolution of trust were all profoundly affected by shifting economic constraints. By analyzing the intimate connection between economic and political change, it is possible to achieve a more accurate estimate of the relative weight of each factor in producing the outcome.

Why should we care? Why not simply compose a long list of putative causes and be done with it? The answer is that scholarship demands empirical precision. In order to know how ideas, cognitive processes, leadership, and domestic politics matter we need to know how strongly economic incentives shape behavior in various settings. The only way to develop better models of international relations is to test them rigorously against real cases. And the only way to do that is to establish with as much precision as possible how various factors worked together to produce the outcome. In the final analysis, no theory or analytical framework can substitute for careful empirical research; and no argument about the meaning of the end of the Cold War for policy and theory that is unsupported by such research will stand the test of time.

Conclusion

10 Failure or Learning Opportunity? The End of the Cold War and Its Implications for International Relations Theory

Joseph Lepgold

AS THIS VOLUME pointedly illustrates, coming to terms with the end of the Cold War continues to intrigue international relations (IR) theorists and foreign policymakers. It also presents high-stakes challenges to both groups. *If* we can understand why and how this conflict died away, generalizable implications for policy and for analyzing international politics should follow. The purpose of this chapter is to use the conference transcript and scholarly arguments in *Cold War Endgame* to explore what these theoretical conclusions might be.

The Princeton conferees and the academic contributors to this volume agree on several key issues. Although the end of the Cold War was a gradual, multistage process, few foresaw in mid-1989 that it would be wrapped up so quickly or peacefully. All of the former officials and at least some of the scholars also agree that it ended, in former U.S. secretary of state Baker's words, as a "result of a multiplicity of factors."[1] Catalytic and long-term factors were in play within and among Moscow, Washington, and the key European capitals. What the scholars and to a lesser degree the policymakers disagree about is which cause mattered most. Three explanatory arguments are offered: it was the Soviet-American balance of material power resources that drove the outcome; the endgame was largely a product of Gorbachev's vision, leadership, and indecisiveness; the Cold War ended because a new generation of Soviet elites adopted different ideas about the nature of East-West relations in an era of intensified interdependence.

These intellectual disagreements can be interpreted in two ways. One view—by far the most common in the contemporary academic field of IR—is that competing hypotheses are the lifeblood of scholarly progress. By providing contrasting views of social reality, each serves to sharpen and stimulate the others.[2] Moreover, as new evidence about this case becomes available, we can expect that some explanatory arguments will become more plausible at the

---

1. Chapter 1, p. 16.
2. Barry Buzan, "Peace, Power, and Security: Contending Concepts in the Study of International Relations," *Journal of Peace Research*, no. 2 (1984): 110.

expense of others. From another vantage point, viewing these arguments as competitors is not very productive, since each captures a potentially significant piece of the complex story. Much of the academic debate in contemporary IR reflects an "either-or" approach to explaining a multicausal world, but there is no reason to perpetuate that pattern when discussing the end of the Cold War.

My own view is that explaining the end of the Cold War requires an integrative theoretical approach. Each of the contending causal arguments represented in this volume represents a particular piece of a broader set of political processes. Those processes reflect the patterned types of strategic choices actors make in response to domestic and international situational incentives when outcomes are jointly determined. By unpacking such generic political processes and distinguishing them from the values of the explanatory variables that exist at particular times and places, we can see how each scholarly argument in this volume captures *part* of a more complex reality. In this view, theoretical progress depends on ending unproductive intellectual debates among arguments that capture pieces of the larger puzzle, and instead fashioning arguments that examine how the pieces are linked. To illustrate how this objective might be achieved, I summarize some work that has been done on such an argument. Some readers will be skeptical that such an argument will change many minds about a better way to frame world politics. But even these people may be able to agree that a focus on strategic choices across linked domestic and international arenas illuminates pieces of the Cold War endgame that cut across many of our competing arguments.

This chapter is organized in two major sections. I begin by asking what IR theory should (and should not) be expected to tell us about the end of the Cold War. I continue by contending that a broad theory of strategic choice will do a better job than existing analytic approaches in helping us interpret the end of the Cold War and anticipate as well as interpret future threshold changes in world politics.

What Puzzles Does the Cold War Endgame Pose, and What Can IR Theory Tell Us About Them?

The surprising way in which the Cold War ended embarrassed many observers of international politics, practitioners and academics alike. Should it have been better foreseen, especially by scholars? According to John Lewis

Gaddis, IR theories should have allowed analysts to forecast *at least one* of the following outcomes *as likely:* (1) the Cold War's asymmetric result (that is to say, only one superpower lost superpower status); (2) the manner in which it ended (namely, "an abrupt but peaceful collapse of Moscow's authority both within and beyond the borders of the former Soviet Union"); (3) the long-term trends that produced these developments (among others, the weakening of command economies and the inability to compete with the West); (4) the approximate timing of these developments; and (5) "the rough outlines of a world without the Cold War—especially one in which German unification has taken place, NATO has survived, [and so forth]." That these results arose "so unexpectedly" should, as Gaddis sees it, be a source of intellectual embarrassment to theoretically oriented scholars of world politics.[3] The implications Gaddis draws are that IR theory is useless in making sense of the world, and that students should switch from political science to history to anticipate or interpret important events and processes.[4]

How reasonable is it to insist that theories meet such predictive standards? In answering this question, it is important to note that outcomes typically reflect both underlying and triggering causes. The former are cumulative, often long-term developments that establish the potential for war, peace, or other outcomes without specifically producing them. Triggering causes are the specific situational factors that catalyze certain results, given the existing underlying conditions. To use a common metaphor, triggers identify which straw *finally* broke the camel's back without identifying how the ground was laid for that to happen.[5] The Princeton conferees agreed that the end of the Cold War reflected a broad mix of underlying and triggering factors. As former Soviet foreign minister Aleksandr Bessmertnykh put it, "It was a combination of natural forces, of people's involvement on the ground, and the unpreparedness of the leaders. This was a fantastic combination of things that made one of the most important events of the twentieth century happen."[6] The combination was "fantastic" in the sense that long-term developments (such as the weakening of the Soviet economy) and particular, perhaps improbable triggers (such as a Soviet leader's refusal to enforce authoritarian

3. John Lewis Gaddis, "International Relations Theory and the End of the Cold War," *International Security* 17, no. 3 (winter 1992/93): 18, 5 (emphasis in original).
4. Ibid., 53.
5. Kenneth N. Waltz, *Man, the State, and War* (New York: Columbia University Press, 1959), 232, 235.
6. See Chapter 2, p. 61.

rule coercively) had to coincide. It is reasonable to expect theories to make patterned—and thus in many cases long-term—behavior interpretable. But one cannot expect a theory to anticipate the timing or manner by which specific events unfold, unless very precise initial conditions have also been specified. To insist otherwise is to demand point predictions, rather than contingent predictions *given* specified triggering conditions.[7]

These conclusions are based on reasoning that is widely accepted among philosophers of science. To predict an event or explain it post hoc requires at least one empirical generalization and at least one statement describing certain known or possible conditions (at either a past moment, the present, or at some hypothetical future moment, depending on whether one is predicting or explaining). Explanations and predictions are therefore contingent: they apply only when certain conditions are satisfied, even if more general patterned behavior can be adduced.[8] IR theorists should be able to provide substantively appropriate generalizations about important aspects of world politics or at least to have active research programs that might produce them. In that sense Gaddis can reasonably expect them to have been able to anticipate the most important underlying conditions that might have paved the way for an event such as the end of the Cold War (his item 3). (At least one seems to have done so. Drawing on the interdemocratic peace literature, Bruce Russett predicted that outcome considerably before it occurred, contingent on further Soviet liberalization.)[9] But Gaddis cannot reasonably have expected them to anticipate the specific *way* in which the Cold War ended (his item 2), or the timing of its demise (item 4), events that reflected nonsystematic triggering causes as well as more systematic underlying factors.

Whether theorists should have been able to predict post–Cold War unipolarity or other aspects of the new international landscape (items 1 and 5) is less clear.[10] Russia's rapid decline in wealth and international status after 1989 might have been foreseen, if analysts had appreciated how Cold War circumstances helped to make particular types of resources effective tools of

---

7. James Lee Ray and Bruce Russett, "The Future as Arbiter of Theoretical Controversies: Predictions, Explanations, and the End of the Cold War," *British Journal of Political Science* 26, pt. 4 (October 1996): 455.

8. Carl G. Hempel, "The Function of General Laws in History," in Hempel, *Aspects of Scientific Explanation* (New York: The Free Press, 1965), 232, 234; Abraham Kaplan, *The Conduct of Inquiry* (New York: Chandler, 1964), 352.

9. See Bruce Russett, "Causes of Peace," in Caroline M. Stephenson, ed., *Alternative Methods for International Security* (Washington, D.C.: University Press of America, 1982), 191; quoted in Ray and Russett, "The Future as Arbiter," 463–64.

10. For a postdictive outline of the form that a settlement of the Cold War would take, albeit one based only on information publicly known before the events that began in 1989, see Bruce Bueno de Mesquita,

Soviet influence. But other aspects of the post–Cold War strategic environment would have been harder to predict. German unification and NATO's survival and subsequent enlargement have been shaped by the causal beliefs, values, and risk-taking propensities of particular leaders as well as outcomes of the strategic interaction among them. Without good data before the fact on how these leaders might react to a fast-moving, high-stakes situation without historical precedent, it would have been difficult to anticipate what those outcomes would be. Even in hindsight, for example, Bush's skill (or luck) in finding the face-saving concessions that prodded Gorbachev toward a German settlement seems improbable a decade later.[11]

If point predictions about the timing and process of the Cold War endgame are too much to ask of IR theory, can it explain after the fact what occurred? This is the purpose of this volume: to link what we now know about the situation that unfolded between the late 1980s and 1991 with scholarly arguments that identify and help interpret critical puzzles.

There is broad agreement on the key puzzles. Derek Chollet and James M. Goldgeier's chapter on U.S. decision making during Bush's first year and Andrew Bennett's analysis of Soviet actions do a good job of identifying them. On the Soviet side, why did Gorbachev fail to use force to maintain Moscow's outer empire? Why did he quickly accept so lopsided a settlement of the German issue, especially when his key domestic constituencies were urging a harder line? On the U.S. side, why did Bush and his advisers fail to pick up where Reagan and Shultz left off in pursuing a quick end to the Cold War, and what explains the timing of their eventual turnaround?

IR theorists should in principle be able to answer these kinds of questions, since post hoc explanation is easier than point prediction. Post hoc, we may have more information pertaining to the key underlying and triggering causes than was available before the fact. Along with the flow of memoirs, historians' accounts, and declassified archival materials about the decision-making process, the Princeton conferees shed new light on many of the pivotal decision points and choices that arose between the late 1980s and 1991.

There are, however, few generally accepted answers to these questions; scholars' explanations of what transpired are all over the analytic map. These

---

"The End of the Cold War: Predicting an Emergent Property," *Journal of Conflict Resolution* 42, no. 2 (April 1998): 131–55.

11. Jonathan Rauch, "Father Superior: Our Greatest Modern President," *The New Republic*, May 22, 2000, p. 24.

differences are evident in this volume. Stephen G. Brooks and William C. Wohlforth explain Soviet foreign policy choices in 1989 and 1990 in terms of material constraints: by their account, Moscow gave up control of Eastern Europe—particularly East Germany—because it was too weak to keep it by force. Robert English disagrees with this interpretation. He argues that Gorbachev was moving toward a noncoercive view of socialism even before he took power in 1985, and that as early as 1986—three years before the Wall fell—he directed military officials to prepare for a withdrawal of Soviet forces from Eastern Europe. Zubok emphasizes personality-driven factors more than intellectual ones in this transformation, although his conclusions largely coincide with English's. When U.S. behavior is examined, the scholarly interpretations of the Cold War endgame include an emphasis on tight structural constraints at the expense of agency (Brooks and Wohlforth), a focus on actors' perceptions, albeit in their situational context (Chollet and Goldgeier, English), and an emphasis on individual leadership (Zubok).

These differing interpretations are dealt with in two ways, both in this volume and in the broader debates about the nature of international politics. In some cases, the arguments are viewed as competitors. Most striking here is the disagreement about the underlying reasons for Soviet policy changes. According to Brooks and Wohlforth, "Old thinkers . . . agreed that the Soviet economy could not bear the Cold War status quo and that the technological gap was large and widening."[12] By contrast, English argues that the Soviet economy in the early 1980s was strong enough to "sustain the country on a largely status quo course until well into the next century."[13] Similarly, during the climactic changes in 1989 and 1990, Brooks and Wohlforth believe that Gorbachev was consistently negative and reactive on the issue of German unification. Zubok, however, contends that Gorbachev decided unconditionally early on not to use force as a form of bargaining leverage, thereby ruling out any attempt to gain an advantage from Soviet troops stationed in East Germany. From this point of view, Soviet policy had altered in a fundamentally *positive* way, even if the speed of events meant that Gorbachev (no less than Bush, Thatcher, or Mitterrand) was struggling to digest and react to them as they took place.

This kind of intellectual competition can lead to intellectual progress. In IR, realism, liberalism, constructivism, and various decision-making arguments have developed partly in response to stimuli provided by rival schools

12. Chapter 9, p. 286.
13. Chapter 8, p. 245.

of thought. At its best, such competition may spur scholars to improve existing theories or resolve specific puzzles that arise within them. Ideally, it should become possible at some point to determine which arguments have performed best in explaining empirical phenomena. Several criteria have been offered to assess such progress: a theory's capacity to anticipate new puzzles, its ability to account for the successful explanations of weaker theories, and its ability to resolve at least some of the new puzzles.[14]

Yet treating these arguments as competitors also raises problems. Even though political processes take place across multiple arenas and comprise a variety of situational incentives, IR theory is not organized in a way that reflects these connections. The theoretical ideas that have come out of the IR field are insights about different pieces of an interrelated set of political processes. If the end of the Cold War reflected multiple causes, as many of the Princeton conferees believe, each argument captures only a piece. Each is thus likely to "under-explain" the underlying reasons for the various outcomes. For example, even if Gorbachev decided early on to end the Cold War, it is hard to explain from a realist perspective why he made so many concessions. He simply gave away Soviet short-range SS-23 missiles in Europe in 1987, he accepted a one-sided German settlement, and he quickly abandoned a longtime Soviet ally to align with the United States during the Gulf War. Aside from the weakness of the Soviet economy, these choices might have reflected Gorbachev's beliefs about a normatively desirable European order or personality traits that made him take principled ideas more seriously than was tactically expedient.[15] Likewise, the new thinkers could not affect Soviet policy until their ideas were adopted. For that to happen, Gorbachev had to build a policy coalition that included old thinkers as well as those with new ideas. In trying to keep the old thinkers on board politically, he delayed implementing radical economic reform. While Bush would not say so publicly, this decision led him to conclude that unambiguous reform was impossible within the Soviet government. Bush therefore refused to go out on a limb with an ambitious financial aid package for Gorbachev,[16] a decision that cost the Soviet leader key internal support.

14. Imre Lakatos, "Falsification and the Methodology of Scientific Research Programs," in John Worrall and Gregory Currie, eds., *The Methodology of Scientific Research Programmes: Philosophical Papers*, vol. 1 (Cambridge: Cambridge University Press, 1978), 32.

15. Ray and Russett, "The Future as Arbiter," 456; Zubok, Chapter 7 herein, passim; English, Chapter 8 herein, passim.

16. Michael R. Beshloss and Strobe Talbott, *At the Highest Levels: The Inside Story of the End of the Cold War* (Boston: Little, Brown, 1993), 388–92.

These pieces can be treated as intellectual competitors if they happen to combine additively. In that case, one can examine how (as well as how much) each piece affected the outcome. The analytic competition then amounts to a "market share" criterion: which piece explains the most? But if the pieces combine interactively, the *way* in which any causal mechanism shapes outcomes is affected by the way it interacts with others.[17] Realism, for instance, assumes a set of goals that makes a relative decline in military capability unacceptable. If such a decline is occurring and is irremediable in the short run, realism by itself would predict either preventive war or a resentful surrender to a militarily stronger competitor. But if shared norms may also influence leaders' policy objectives, and norm-driven goals can influence how the state's military posture is viewed, one could make sense of the new thinkers' desire to be part of a progressive, norm-governed Europe, even if their state was to be shorn of much of its Cold War status.

In practice, the competitiveness within academic IR is often unproductive. The field has been riven with bitter debates: quantifiers versus methodological traditionalists, realists versus institutionalists, rationalists versus constructivists. Up to a point, such competition can help scholars who work within these intellectual and methodological traditions clarify their approaches and make the best possible cases for the importance of their research results. But beyond a certain point, such competition becomes less useful, as those on each side tend to talk past each other. Opposition to different positions tends to become ritualized, and room to think creatively within partial, often tight, explanatory boxes tends to shrink.[18]

At times, the differing sorts of interpretations found in this book are seen as complementary: since they explain different aspects of a complex case, they can be used as flexibly as needed. This approach is one way to deal with the traditional levels-of-analysis problem. It has been argued that variables operating at different levels address different puzzles, or offer comparable explanations at different levels of detail.[19] Either way, the incomplete nature of these distinct explanations is explicitly acknowledged. This approach thus

17. For a discussion of additive and interactive effects within multicausal explanatory models, see Donald T. Campbell and Julian C. Stanley, *Experimental and Quasi-Experimental Designs for Research* (Boston: Houghton Mifflin, 1963), 16–17.

18. Buzan, "Peace, Power and Security," 110.

19. Robert Jervis, *Perception and Misperception in International Politics* (Princeton: Princeton University Press, 1976), 16–17.

encourages analysts to examine and combine underlying and triggering causes of key outcomes. For example, both Zubok and Chollet and Goldgeier believe that individual-level factors triggered key changes in Soviet and American views of the other side, in each case building on long-term developments that had made Cold War objectives unattractive. As Chollet and Goldgeier put it, although the triggers produced specific turning points in the relationship, "for a more complete explanation, one must consider the interaction between structural conditions and leaders' beliefs and personalities."[20]

If one is willing to assume that these pieces come together additively, choosing an explanatory approach becomes a matter of individual research interests and skills. Alternatively, it could be that the various pieces come together interactively. It seems intuitively that this is the likelier possibility, even if one knows little about the details surrounding the end of the Cold War. Interestingly, even though Chollet and Goldgeier claim that their argument complements structural interpretations, they acknowledge that it was the *interaction* between international situational constraints and individual-level factors that drove key choices.

Unless one is confident that the various explanatory pieces discussed in this book operate independently, it is hard to assess the ultimate value of any of them without understanding how they are connected.[21] In the next section, I suggest how those connections might be made and how such a theoretical lens might improve our understanding of the end of the Cold War.

Toward an Integrated Explanation for the End of the Cold War

An integrated theoretical approach assumes that world politics is linkage politics. The processes that shape actors' choices and the outcomes of strategic interaction (given preferences and perceptions) are systematically linked, even if most existing theories deal with these pieces separately. The task, then, is to link the distinct insights that come out of existing theories so that they explain the interrelated set of political processes that actually exists.

How might this be done? Because world politics involves recurring interaction across domestic and international arenas, a first step would be to

---

20. Chollet and Goldgeier, Chapter 5, p. 169. Zubok presents a similar perspective in Chapter 7.

21. For an argument that theoretical integration will help analysts anticipate nonlinear or threshold changes, see Charles F. Doran, "Why Forecasts Fail: The Limits and Potential of Forecasting in International Relations and Economics," *International Studies Review* 1 (summer 1999): 35 n. 22.

identify and explain those processes. In that way, analysts would not have to choose between interpretations that highlight the individual, domestic, *or* the international sources of foreign policy, but could see how incentives at each level are linked to the others. More ambitiously, one could try to identify common types of political processes that occur within and across all the levels. Doing so would allow scholars to use the same theories to track developments in every arena of world politics simultaneously. In principle, this type of analytic integration would not only help in understanding specific cases such as the end of the Cold War; it could also help officials diagnose the types of situations they confront, making it easier to decide when particular policy tools will be useful.

Examining the Implications of Cross-Arena Linkages

If effective statecraft is the art of reconciling domestic and international incentives, it is clear from the conference transcripts that both of these concerns preoccupied the Soviet and American officials who struggled to work their countries out of the Cold War. Before Secretary Baker or Foreign Minister Shevardnadze could deal effectively with each other, each had to "prove [his] cause, [his] approach inside with . . . friends and colleagues." They discovered that this was at least as difficult as much of the international bargaining.[22] Since Gorbachev had hard-line factions he needed to placate, U.S. officials tried to frame proposals—especially those dealing with the ultrasensitive German issue—that Gorbachev would be able to sell at home.[23] The international incentives confronting decision makers weighed heavily as well. Gorbachev was inclined to resist Iraqi aggression in Kuwait as a way to show that Moscow was ready for partnership with the West, even though that choice hurt him with key internal constituencies.[24] Bush also faced significant external pressures. NATO's traditional priority in U.S. foreign policy and Bush's own individual emphasis on it meant that he would not move boldly to defuse the rivalry with Moscow until an approach had been worked out with key U.S. allies.[25]

Examining the implications of cross-level connections should be a priority in IR theory. But IR scholars have typically avoided efforts to interpret the kinds of linkages illustrated in these examples. Several of the chapters in this

22. See comments by Sergei Tarasenko, Shevardnadze's foreign policy adviser, Chapter 1, pp. 30–31.
23. See comments by State Department Counselor Robert Zoellick in Chapter 2.
24. See Bessmertnykh's comments in Chapter 3.
25. See Zoellick's comments in Chapter 1.

book note the importance of both international and domestic incentives. Bennett argues that any persuasive account of the end of the Cold War must include balance-of-power factors and domestic political constraints (as well as the growth of interpersonal trust and shared goals or norms). Chollet and Goldgeier make a passing reference to domestic as well as international constraints on the U.S. side. By contrast, Brooks and Wohlforth, English, and Zubok make single-level arguments, effectively contending that all of the causal action on the Soviet side operated at *either* the international, domestic, or individual level.

These latter three treatments typify much contemporary scholarly work in IR and, in doing so, reflect how levels-of-analysis distinctions entered the IR field. Beginning in the 1950s, scholars began to distinguish international, state-level, and individual-level sources of foreign policy behavior. This development was part of an effort to sharpen the logic of inquiry in IR, a goal that required more precise and systematic explanations. In *Man, the State, and War* and *Theory of International Politics* Kenneth Waltz made a case for distinguishing the international system, especially its anarchic structure, as a distinct level. For decades, Waltz's treatment remained an influential way to think about these issues, particularly system-level factors. During this time, two notions of "levels" have been used throughout the field, often in the same pieces of work. Levels of analysis are at times interpreted ontologically as actual political locations or arenas—the international environment, the domestic (or at times bureaucratic) arena, and so on. "Levels" have also been seen as distinct kinds or sources of explanation, as in "international-system-level arguments." The widespread failure to unpack these two different senses of the concept may have inhibited scholars from understanding interactions across the levels.[26] Partly by default, then, many analysts have tended to use these distinctions in an eclectic manner, avoiding systematic efforts to link phenomena across international and domestic politics.

There have, however, been some helpful theoretical interpretations of these linkages. Two such analyses take "levels" to denote actual places—political arenas—in which action occurs. Since causal explanation in this usage is *not* arena-specific, one can see how behavior *across* them is linked. Robert Putnam argues that durable international policy requires reinforcing domestic

26. Barry Buzan, "The Levels of Analysis Problem in International Relations Reconsidered," in Ken Booth and Steve Smith, eds., *International Relations Theory Today* (University Park: Pennsylvania State University Press, 1995), 199–210.

incentives. Bargaining occurs at both levels simultaneously, and officials can try to use constraints in one arena as leverage in the other. But unless domestic and international incentives are mutually reinforcing, international bargains will tend to be unstable.[27]

Alan Lamborn reaches similar conclusions but lays out the connection between incentives and policy choices more precisely. He posits three interdependent arenas: an international arena, comprising states and relevant nonstate actors; an arena of factional politics that exists within state-level and transstate policy coalitions; and a constituency arena that connects factional leaders to a base of political supporters. Political leaders face two kinds of risks in making choices: policy risks (the likelihood that their substantive goals will not be achieved even if their policy choices are effectively implemented), and political risks (the likelihood that policy choices will damage their political positions). In foreign policy, policy risks derive from the international arena, while political risks originate in the factional and constituency arenas. The higher the expected value that an actor places on a policy outcome, the more willing that actor will be to invest resources and political position in an effort to achieve that goal. The less control they have over policy choice and implementation, the less willing members of a policy coalition will be to take political risks in an effort to achieve coalition policy goals. The less control they have over policy choice and implementation, the more indifferent coalition members will be to policy failure, *if* policy failure is not seen as politically dangerous.

How people react to political and policy risks also depends on when the costs and benefits attached to those risks are expected to arrive. The higher the expected value actors attach to achieving a specific policy outcome, the less their choices will be affected by discounting. The less control they have over policy choice and implementation, the more actors will prefer future costs over current costs and the more they will discount future benefits relative to current benefits. The higher the immediate risks of preferred policy options, the more willing actors will be to defer policy benefits in return for a reduction in current political risks.[28]

27. Robert Putnam, "Diplomacy and Domestic Politics: The Logic of Two-Level Games," *International Organization* 42, no. 3 (summer 1988): 427–60.

28. Alan C. Lamborn, "Theory and the Politics in World Politics," *International Studies Quarterly* 41, no. 2 (June 1997): 195–97; idem, "Risk and Foreign Policy Choice," *International Studies Quarterly* 29, no. 4 (December 1985): 385–410.

This argument, in sum, suggests that leaders' willingness to take political and policy risks depends on (1) the expected value attached to achieving specific policy goals; (2) whether or not the political and policy risks are mutually reinforcing; (3) how much control they have vis-à-vis other members of their policy coalition over policy choice and implementation; and (4) whether they feel compelled to act quickly, or are willing to wait in the hope that safer policy options will appear.

But the proof of the pudding is in the eating: what can this approach add to those already represented in this volume? I believe that a focus on cross-arena linkages sheds important light on the impetus for ending the Cold War.[29]

By the early 1980s, there were clear international incentives for a change of course in Moscow. As Brooks and Wohlforth point out, it was the relative decline of the Soviet economy that provided the impetus for a shift. Less certain was what the innovations would be. They did not necessarily have to involve domestic liberalization and a fundamental relaxation of tensions with the West. Analysts of major-power conflict have long argued that the most dangerous time in a sustained competition between two large states or blocs is when one side concludes that it can no longer keep up. A preventive Soviet attack on the United States was unlikely in the nuclear age. But Soviet leaders might conceivably have tried to mobilize the country for a renewed arms race with the United States, *if* they had been responding largely to international-security incentives.

Gorbachev's strategy—to seek an end to the Cold War, albeit in an international environment in which the Soviet Union would remain a major player—reflected the nature of his policy coalition as well as his international pressures. His ability to bring new coalition partners into the policymaking arena pushed or allowed him to move toward reform. The importance of these new factions reflected changes in Soviet society since the initial period of de-Stalinization in the mid-1950s. A more educated, urbanized, and prosperous Soviet middle class increasingly demanded that arbitrary rule be replaced by the rule of law and that the government and Party stop micromanaging the economy. Urban mass publics also displayed growing impatience with high

29. The focus in the balance of this subsection is on the changes in Soviet policy, since this was the catalyst for key shifts on both sides after 1986. This discussion draws on Alan C. Lamborn and Joseph Lepgold, *World Politics into the Twenty-first Century: Unique Contexts, Enduring Patterns* (Englewood Cliffs, N.J.: Prentice-Hall, 2001), chap. 6.

military spending and wanted more focus on domestic needs.[30] At the same time, hard-line factions were weakened by the widespread view that an international strategy based on heavy military spending and intervention in the 1970s and early 1980s had failed.[31] Hard-liners—whether committed communists or Russian chauvinists—were not convinced that any long-run change was needed. But there was broad agreement that in the short run the Soviet government needed "a durable and predictable [international] framework for resource choices."[32] That pointed toward a pause in the intense rivalry that Washington seemed to be winning.

Gorbachev's overriding imperative was that the strategy bear fruit quickly. The hard-liners would not indefinitely accept the asymmetric military concessions that were needed to reassure the West, nor were they pleased with the reinforcing liberalizing changes at home; reformers and nationalists across the USSR were increasingly taking matters into their own hands. By the late 1980s Gorbachev was increasingly feeling the impact of factional and public pressure on foreign policy, even as democratization was shrinking his tools for influencing that opinion. His impatience for progress in arms control talks during this period reflected these pressures,[33] which eventually turned out to be more than his system could withstand.

Reframing the End of the Cold War Through a Strategic Choice Lens

Showing how events in one arena are linked to those in others moves us significantly toward an integrated theoretical approach to world politics. Identifying a set of generic processes that occur within and across the arenas would take us even further. Several scholars have recommended this kind of analytic integration. If the levels of analysis are treated as arenas, Barry Buzan argues, each one "contains, in principle, all of the sources or types of explanation." Each causal process thus "can be found as sources of explanation in individuals, states, and the international system."[34] According to Oran Young, a

---

30. Philip Roeder, "Dialectics of Doctrine: Politics of Resource Allocation and the Development of Soviet Military Thought," in William Zimmerman, ed., *Beyond the Soviet Threat: Rethinking American Security Policy in a New Era* (Ann Arbor: University of Michigan Press, 1992), 71–104; S. Frederick Starr, "Soviet Union: A Civil Society," *Foreign Policy* 70 (spring 1988): 29–35; William Zimmerman and Deborah Yarsike, "Mass Publics and New Thinking in Soviet Russian Foreign Policy," in Zimmerman, *Beyond the Soviet Threat*, 3–20.

31. Andrew Bennett, "Patterns of Soviet Military Interventionism, 1975–1990: Alternative Explanations and Their Implications," in Zimmerman, *Beyond the Soviet Threat*, 105–27.

32. Allen Lynch, "Changing Elite Views on the Soviet System," in Zimmerman, *Beyond the Soviet Threat*, 32.

33. Starr, "Soviet Union," 40.

34. Buzan, "Levels of Analysis Problem," 205.

focus on strategic interaction is a powerful way to capture important causal processes:

> It seems likely that viable theories of international relations . . . will often be special cases of more general theories for situations involving strategic interactions among collective entities. . . . [E]ven though the specific techniques for handling strategic interaction, the behavior of individual actors, and so forth may vary to some extent, there is good reason to believe that the basic form and structure of the resultant theories will be quite similar across a number of substantive fields.[35]

Young's position assumes that political choices are necessarily strategic choices—choices about ways to pursue interdependent outcomes. Because political outcomes depend on the goals, perceptions, and relative power of at least two actors, all politics involves strategic choices. The processes of interdependent choice are thus a key part (though not the only part) of politics. Strategic interaction occurs when two or more actors, recognizing that the options available for achieving their goals depend on the preferences and actions of others, evaluate their options according to what they expect the others to do. In other words, the situational incentives actors face affect the consequences of their choices; realizing that, they presumably order their preferences, evaluate the strategic environment, search for options, evaluate the expected consequences of each option, and make choices with those consequences in mind. Such an argument does *not* make assumptions about how actors will carry out these tasks—only that they will behave purposively. It seems, in sum, to capture those aspects of politics consisting of interdependent choices and their consequences, regardless of the political arenas involved.

What is needed, then, are propositions that specify the sources of situational incentives and connect those incentives to the risk-taking calculus by which policy options are assessed. Alan Lamborn has identified three linked sources of generic situational incentives. First, the more compatible actors' preferences, the less strategically important their relative power positions; and conversely, the weaker an actor's relative power position, the less strategically important his preferences.

These relationships provide a starting point for defining actors' strategic situations. But people typically evaluate substantive outcomes and power positions within the context of their beliefs about legitimate relationships. This leads

---

35. Oran Young, "The Perils of Odysseus: On Constructing Theories of International Relations," *World Politics* 24 [Supplement] (spring 1972): 195.

to a second group of incentives. If people value creating and sustaining legitimate relationships *and* if they think the outcomes a political process produces
are legitimate, they are more likely to accept that outcome—even if they would
have preferred something else. If they believe that either the outcome or the
process is illegitimate, they are far likelier to oppose it. The lower the perceived
legitimacy of the political process, the greater the political significance of the
fairness of the substantive outcomes. The lower the perceived legitimacy of an
outcome, the greater the political significance of the process that produced it.

In short, if actors value legitimacy and believe their relationships are
legitimate, they will tend to act less competitively, accepting procedures and
outcomes that adversely affect them. Yet people pay attention, not just to how
power, preferences, and issues of fairness are connected today, but also to how
they expect these factors to evolve over time. Lamborn's third source of situational incentives concerns the effect of anticipated futures on actors' willingness to cooperate. The less stable the strategic context, the more actors' estimates of the strategic implications of different policy options will vary with
the length of their time horizons. The less compatible people expect their
preferences to become over time, the more competitive and power-oriented
their strategic approach is likely to be. The longer the time horizons of actors
who believe there is a high probability of creating stable, jointly acceptable
relationships, the likelier it is that they will follow a cooperative strategy.
Conversely, the longer the time horizons of actors who believe there is a low
probability of creating stable, jointly acceptable relationships, the likelier it is
that they will follow a strategy designed to minimize the risks attached to possible defections.[36]

These three sets of assertions capture the strategic situation confronting
actors within a particular political arena—either international, factional, or
constituency. The assertions about risk-taking preferences in the previous subsection capture actors' reactions to the distinctive combinations of policy and
political payoffs attached to different arena-specific options. This approach
thus allows analysts to focus on either foreign policy or domestic politics,
while taking into account the links between them.

Using the same assumptions about the politics of strategic choice to analyze behavior across arenas yields propositions about enduring patterns in

---

36. Lamborn, "Theory and the Politics in World Politics," 191–95.

world politics. At least implicitly, the major schools of thought seem to share the causal logic of these propositions. What they tend to disagree about are the "typical" values of the variables—the nature, frequency, and importance of different types of issues, actors, arenas, and strategic situations.[37] For this reason, IR theorists have tended to make restrictive assumptions about which variables matter or the range in which they vary. The result has been many implicitly contingent theoretical generalizations, often derived inductively from prominent historical cases. What these propositions often lack is explicit statements that would distinguish what is generic about the model from what is unique about the case. For instance, a spiral model—one reflecting the lessons of the 1914 crisis—claims that threats reinforce security dilemmas and therefore are self-defeating. A Munich-syndrome model claims that threats establish credibility and induce adversaries to retreat. But neither indicates when and why other cases fit these patterns.[38] A truly generic theoretical argument, such as the one outlined here, highlights the effects of stability *and* change in the values of the variables that make up the same generic political processes.

Let us examine how these three interconnected sets of assumptions can be used, along with the propositions about linked arenas, to interpret the end of the Cold War. Consider first Gorbachev's choices. By the early 1980s, he was disappointed with the way the Soviet model had worked under Brezhnev. From this point of view, it was not clear that the state-socialist economy as it was then constituted could be made to grow or innovate as well as capitalist economies.[39] Having reached these conclusions, Gorbachev began after 1986 to pursue very nontraditional domestic and international goals for a Soviet leader—goals more compatible with the West's. Here, recall Lamborn's first set of propositions: the importance of power decreases as compatibility of actors' preferences increases. It follows that Gorbachev's new preferences made Moscow's relative power position less important than before. These changes made it less *necessary* to compete militarily with the West, at least at the level seen in over the previous few decades. Of course, it also follows from

37. Ibid., 188.

38. Robert Jervis, "Models and Cases in the Study of International Conflict," in Robert L. Rothstein, ed., *The Evolution of Theory in International Relations* (Columbia: University of South Carolina Press, 1991), 64, 67.

39. Fred Halliday, "The End of the Cold War and International Relations: Some Analytic and Theoretical Conclusions," in Ken Booth and Steve Smith, eds., *International Relations Theory Today* (University Park: Pennsylvania State University Press, 1995), 49.

Lamborn's first set of propositions that the weaker Moscow's relative power position became, the more important Western, especially American, preferences became to Soviet leaders. Even before he took power in 1985, Gorbachev tried to influence Westerners' preferences and images about his goals; Margaret Thatcher's widely publicized comment that "we can do business with him" laid a foundation for a credible relationship with Ronald Reagan. He also worked to reverse the Stalinist legacy in broader forums. As Zubok notes in his chapter, Gorbachev used a 1988 speech to the U.N. General Assembly to emphasize "the process of demilitarization and humanization of our thinking."[40] Together, these efforts constituted a strategy designed to shape how he was viewed by those who were winning the Cold War.

Realists might reasonably ask what this interpretation adds to theirs. The response is twofold. First, realists assume that foreign policy decision makers respond largely to competitive international incentives. These risks certainly exist in some cases. But as a universal statement about international politics, realism pays too little attention to domestic factional and constituency incentives. Of course, the existence of political groupings coherent enough to deserve the designation of "faction" is contested among specialists on the Soviet Union who view that system through the lens of a totalitarian model. There is, however, disagreement on this point. In his chapter, English contends that Gorbachev systematically consulted various Soviet "new thinkers" who represented a larger domestic constituency that was agitating for change.[41] At the same time, hard-line groups still had influence, which was evident in Gorbachev's economic choices, his 1991 crackdown in Lithuania, high-level appointments of hard-line officials around this time, and his need for quick results in dealing with the West. Realism captures some of the international incentives Gorbachev faced, yet ignores other types of payoffs, especially those originating in the domestic political arenas.

Second, the preference orderings that realists posit for political leaders are too restrictive. Because they assume conflictual preferences, realists see statecraft as inherently competitive. They thus expect leaders to react competitively to a decline in relative resources or status. But if leaders' views about legitimate

---

40. Quoted in Zubok, Chapter 7, p. 224.
41. See also Matthew Evangelista, "The Paradox of State Strength: Transnational Relations, Domestic Structures, and Security Policy in Russia and the Soviet Union," *International Organization* 49, no. 1 (winter 1995): 1–38.

relationships influence the way they view power or status, as Lamborn's second set of propositions suggests, then such expectations may miss the mark.

English and Zubok discuss Gorbachev's cultivation of new thinking inside the Soviet Union and his own normative beliefs, including a distaste for the use of force. Gorbachev and Shevardnadze also encouraged nontraditional international and transnational influences on their policies. Before 1990, by which time changes in the Soviet constitutional structure had made it harder for any leader to impose a policy agenda on the country, a transnational group of scientists and others involved in arms control policy influenced Soviet security policy conceptually and on several specific issues, including a halt in nuclear testing and limiting strategic defenses. This evidence suggests that Gorbachev was trying to build a more legitimate Soviet political culture based on new *kinds* of international goals and relationships. He was thus willing to accept some outcomes, such as the loss of Eastern Europe and unreciprocated military cuts, that adversely affected Moscow's status and power position.

Gorbachev's individual impact as a leader can also be clarified using this approach. He clearly put high priority on instituting a more humane form of socialist governance, including a rejection of the Brezhnev Doctrine. In this sense, Zubok's contention that Gorbachev took ideas "too seriously" can be interpreted as more than just a personality quirk. It highlights a willingness to run certain short-term political risks to achieve valued policy goals. This involved gambling that the power of hard-line Soviet factions, and the strength of their mutually reinforcing links to similar factions in Eastern Europe, could be broken.

Finally, a strategic-choice lens helps clarify the chief U.S. policy puzzle examined in this book: why did Bush wait so long to engage Gorbachev in pursuing an end to the Cold War? Chollet and Goldgeier argue that trust had to develop among U.S. officials. Because National Security Adviser Scowcroft had felt betrayed by Soviet behavior when he served in the Ford administration during the 1970s, trust was at a premium for him (as it was for Bush himself, who had served in several foreign policy posts during the 1970s and seemed to approach these issues with a more *realpolitisch* worldview than Reagan). According to Chollet and Goldgeier, trust involves a recognition of common objectives, as well as predictability and credibility.[42] All these conditions are

42. Chollet and Goldgeier, Chapter 5, p. 000.

captured by Lamborn's three sets of propositions: compatibility of preferences reduces the role of relative power; increased legitimacy of political process decreases the salience of the fairness of the outcome; and actors with longtime horizons and expectations of stable, jointly acceptable relationships will tend to follow a cooperative strategy.

To a skeptical audience, Gorbachev's charm and his ebullience about new thinking in foreign policy might reflect these three requirements, but they also might not.[43] The difficulty in building trust is that people typically see what they expect to see; it is hard to demonstrate shared goals and credibility when the other actor's image is one of mistrust. What began to satisfy Baker and eventually other U.S. officials was a sense that Gorbachev and Shevardnadze had irreversibly broken with the Soviet past for internal reasons. Reducing external tensions, in this view, was a way for them to deal with their domestic problems.[44] In other words, once Bush and his advisers appreciated that *all* of Gorbachev's situational incentives were essentially pushing him in the same direction—toward more legitimate behavior and norms— they began to believe him and acted accordingly.

To be sure, strategic choice is only a partial lens on world politics. To explain fully the fundamental regularities that drive political processes, the individual and community-based sources of cognitive variables that shape perceptions, preferences, and norms must be integrated with the variables that drive strategic choice and interaction. Yet choice under conditions of interdependent outcomes is certainly a basic piece of politics. In principle, therefore, an argument that explains the incentives for choice and the outcomes of collective choice is a good way to combine coherently many implicit assumptions about the processes of politics.

In terms of the broad issues raised in this book, such an argument addresses two problems identified in the conference transcripts and by Gaddis: it synthesizes the multiple causes that produced the end of the Cold War, and it allows us to understand more fundamentally why its end so surprised us.

Unless one is willing to accept one of the single-factor explanations for the key Soviet (or U.S.) decisions, one must conclude, as Baker did, that multiple causes were in play. If one assumes that these causes combine additively,

43. This is what Ambassador Matlock meant in urging U.S. decision makers to counter the effects of Gorbachev's "smile." See the discussion in Chapter 5.
44. See Chollet and Goldgeier's discussion in Chapter 5.

the resulting explanation may be logically overdetermined: several independent factors are given as joint causes, even though some subset might actually
produce most of the outcome.[45] By beginning from the opposite premise—
that the causes are interconnected, in the sense that the impact of relative
power or any other variable on choice *depends on the other linked variables*—the
problem of overdetermined explanations is avoided even when multiple
explanatory mechanisms are invoked.

This becomes evident when one sees that the Cold War grew out of
reinforcing domestic and international incentives, and that it wound down
only when those incentives all began to move in the other direction. As World
War II ended, U.S. and Soviet officials both wanted to create a set of global
arrangements that reflected their domestic and political institutions. The
problem was that these visions were fundamentally incompatible. Stalin's preferences for international and domestic control reinforced each other. To
achieve that control, early in the postwar period he tried "to strengthen further the security of his own regime, first by increasing safeguards against
Western influences inside the Soviet Union; second, by tightening control
over Russia's East European satellites; and finally by working to ensure central
direction of the international communist movement."[46] U.S. leaders sought a
world that they could penetrate economically and ideologically (first set of
propositions). The strategic significance of these conflicting aims was magnified by vastly different standards for creating legitimate political relationships
and by the assumption, built into the ideology of Marxism-Leninism and U.S.
liberalism, that time was on the side of their system (second and third set of
propositions). Domestic and international incentives thus pointed to competition. As George Kennan noted, Soviet leaders bolstered their autocratic rule by
using external enemies to create a state of siege.[47] U.S. officials believed that
their country's security required "an external environment compatible with
their domestic vision of a good society."[48] Only when Gorbachev decided that

45. In principle, it is possible to avoid an overdetermined explanation by dropping out underperforming
explanatory variables one by one, as is done in stepwise regression. However, doing so within the framework
of a qualitative research design would be difficult and might lead to arbitrary decisions about what to include
in the final model. For a discussion of overdetermined arguments, see Jack Snyder, "Science and
Sovietology," *World Politics* 40, no. 2 (January 1988): 176–77, 179–80.

46. John Lewis Gaddis, *Russia, the Soviet Union, and the United States*, 2d ed. (New York: McGraw-Hill,
1978), 189–90.

47. George F. Kennan ["X"], "The Sources of Soviet Conduct," *Foreign Affairs* 25, no. 4 (July 1947): 570.

48. Melvyn P. Leffler, *A Preponderance of Power: National Security, the Truman Administration, and the Cold
War* (Stanford: Stanford University Press, 1992), 13.

his closely controlled system was counterproductive did these patterns begin to reverse. Seen this way, strongly path-dependent outcomes *require* mutually reinforcing incentives in the opposite direction in order to reverse course.

With this in mind, the end of the Cold War might have been less of a surprise if analysts had used a strategic choice lens to think about world politics. "Surprises" occur when something disturbs a situation that had been assumed to be stable. To be fair, distinctive historical periods such as the Cold War are defined by the prolonged stability of a particular set of variables.[49] Analysts who took this stability for granted find it hard even after the fact to account for the end of the Cold War.[50] Political processes can look very different on either side of threshold changes in key variables. We may not be able to predict precisely where those thresholds will be. But if observers are able to recognize that the values of the variables in the relationships that drive strategic choices might be changing, the cumulative impact over time of changes in underlying conditions might be better recognized. If that were the case, it would be easier to anticipate or at least to imagine the effects of possible triggering events.

Gaddis himself conceded the substance of these points, even if he did not use this language. He recognized that the "tectonic plates" of historical change might move so gradually that the inevitable earthquake comes as shock. Nevertheless, he maintained that "events like these are not accidents; they can be understood, accounted for, and at times even predicted. But they often *appear* to us to be random or capricious occurrences, because explanations for them have to be sought in processes that lie outside our normal range of perception."[51] The point here is simply that an explicitly articulated generic theory of strategic choice could help to bring such processes *within* our understanding.

Intellectual Choices and Their Consequences for Historical Interpretation

The end of the Cold War is a complex case, and consensus on a causal interpretation is at a premium. This problem bothers some analysts more than others.

49. Lamborn, "Theory and the Politics in World Politics," 197.
50. Richard K. Herrmann, "Policy-Relevant Theory and the Challenge of Diagnosis: The End of the Cold War as a Case Study," *Political Psychology* 15, no. 1 (March 1994): 112.
51. John Lewis Gaddis, "Tectonics, History, and the End of the Cold War," in John Lewis Gaddis, *The United States and the End of the Cold War: Implications, Reconsiderations, Provocations* (Oxford: Oxford University Press, 1992), 155.

Some people are intrinsically fascinated by the world's detailed complexity, while others are more curious about its underlying order. This fault line typically separates historians from social scientists—in particular from political scientists, with whom they otherwise share a good deal substantively. Yet political scientists specializing in international relations are themselves divided, often bitterly, about the way the world is ordered. Causal arguments in IR typically focus on power *or* norms; arguments pitched at individual, domestic, and international levels are often seen as competitive, and their adherents frequently conduct "debates" that amount to dialogues of the deaf. When these causal factors are not seen as competitors, they are often assumed, just by enumeration, to add up to an explanation for complex historical events or cases. In this chapter, I have argued that these tendencies are not just bad for the intellectual development of the field; they also inhibit analysts interested in specific cases from seeing how various kinds of causes *interact* to produce observed behavior. Although most of the substantive interpretations of the end of the Cold War in this book offer important insights, most of them suffer from this problem. Each tells part of the story but ignores the other parts, setting up what amounts to a misleading intellectual competition with adherents of the other views.

I believe that the best remedy for these problems is a strategic-choice theoretical perspective that tracks the linked incentives actors face in domestic and international politics. That intellectual commitment is likely to remain controversial in political science for some time to come. But, as the particular argument used here should indicate, such an explanation seems to account for much of what we find interesting or puzzling about the end of the Cold War. That—and the degree to which the argument itself is logically compelling— might make it attractive to scholars fed up with the increasingly unproductive debates among the existing theoretical schools.

Causal explanation in international relations tends to be difficult, since one typically finds too many variables in search of too few good data points. It is thus comforting to focus on one or at most a few key variables, rest assured that they provide most of the necessary intellectual traction, and essentially ignore the rest. In part for reasons of mental economy, once analysts are committed to a particular explanatory argument, they will often have reasonable grounds for rejecting the importance of new evidence that would seem to impugn their existing interpretation.[52] For this very reason, one needs a theory that tracks the key variables in world politics and shows how they are connected. Such an argument will still simplify a complex reality, for without such simplification it is impossible to see any underlying order. But it would explain that order without ignoring *either* actors' relative power *or* the political significance of legitimacy *or* the impact of variations in people's time horizons and what they see when they look into the future. Paying attention to these sorts of variables across linked domestic and international arenas would produce fewer surprises about developing trends and more agreement about the fundamental political dynamics at work in important IR cases.

52. William C. Wohlforth, "A Certain Idea of Science: How International Relations Theory Avoids Reviewing the Cold War," in Odd Arne Westad, ed., *Reviewing the Cold War: Approaches, Interpretations, Theory* (London: Frank Cass, 2000), 128.

Participants and Contributors

Conference Participants

James A. Baker III was Secretary of State from January 1989 to August 1992. He previously served as Secretary of the Treasury and Chief of Staff in the White House of President Ronald Reagan, and he led the presidential campaigns of Presidents Ford, Reagan, and Bush. He is the author, with Thomas M. DeFrank, of *The Politics of Diplomacy: Revolution, War, and Peace, 1989–1992* (New York: G. P. Putnam's Sons, 1995), and is the Honorary Chair of the Baker Institute for Public Policy at Rice University.

Jack F. Matlock Jr. was Director of Soviet Affairs on the National Security Council staff in 1983–87 and U.S. Ambassador to the Soviet Union in 1987–91. He was previously U.S. Ambassador to Czechoslovakia. He is the author of *Autopsy on an Empire: The American Ambassador's Account of the Collapse of the Soviet Union* (New York: Random House, 1996). He is currently George F. Kennan Professor at the Institute of Advanced Study in Princeton.

Lieutenant General Brent Scowcroft (USAF, Retired) was the Assistant to the President for National Security Affairs to Presidents Ford and Bush. He also served as Military Assistant to Presidents Ford and Nixon. He is founder and president of The Forum for International Policy. He and former president George H. W. Bush are the authors of *A World Transformed* (New York: Knopf, 1998).

Philip Zelikow was a member of the Directorate for European and Soviet Affairs of the National Security Council during the period considered by the conference with responsibilities for matters bearing on European security and German unification. He was an associate professor of public policy at the Kennedy School of Government, Harvard University, and is currently the Director of the Miller Center for Public Policy at the University of Virginia. He is coauthor with Condoleezza Rice of *Germany Unified and Europe Transformed: A Study in Statecraft* (Cambridge: Harvard University Press, 1995).

Robert B. Zoellick served as Counselor of the Department of State under Secretary of State Baker during the first Bush administration. He had earlier served in the Department of the Treasury in a variety of positions in 1985 and 1986. He is currently the United States Trade Representative.

Aleksandr A. Bessmertnykh was Deputy Foreign Minister of the Soviet Union in 1986–90, Soviet Ambassador to the United States in 1990, and Foreign Minister of the Soviet Union in 1991. Previously he served in the Soviet Embassy in Washington and was in charge of American Affairs at the Soviet Foreign Ministry. He is currently President of the Foreign Policy Association, Moscow.

Anatoly S. Chernyaev was personal adviser on foreign affairs to President Mikhail Gorbachev in 1986–91. Previously he was a senior official of the International Department of the Central Committee of the Communist Party of the Soviet Union. He is currently associated with the International Foundation for Socio-Economic and Political Studies (the Gorbachev Institute), Moscow. He is the author of *My Six Years with Gorbachev*, ed. and trans. Robert D. English and Elizabeth Tucker (University Park: Pennsylvania State University Press, 2000).

Pavel Palazchenko was special assistant and interpreter to President Mikhail Gorbachev in 1985–91. Previously he was an official of the Soviet Foreign Ministry. He is currently associated with the International Foundation for Socio-Economic and Political Studies (the Gorbachev Institute), Moscow. He is the author of *My Years with Gorbachev and Shevardnadze: The Memoir of a Soviet Interpreter* (University Park: Pennsylvania State University Press, 1997).

Sergei Tarasenko was a career diplomat in the Foreign Ministry of the USSR. He served as principal policy assistant to Foreign Minister Eduard Shevardnadze in 1985–91. He is currently with the Institute for Realism in Politics in Moscow.

Don Oberdorfer was diplomatic correspondent for the *Washington Post*. He covered the events that led to the end of the Cold War and interviewed or reinterviewed many of the participants for his book *The Turn: From the Cold*

War to a New Era: The United States and the Soviet Union, 1983–1990 (New York: Poseidon Press, 1991). He is presently a resident scholar at the Paul H. Nitze School for Advanced International Studies of The Johns Hopkins University.

Fred I. Greenstein is Professor of Politics, Princeton University, and director of the John Foster Dulles Program for the Study of Leadership in International Affairs. His most recent book is *The Presidential Difference: Leadership Style from FDR to Clinton* (New York: Martin Kessler Books, 2000).

Contributors

Andrew O. Bennett is an associate professor of government at Georgetown University. He is author of *Condemned to Repetition?: The Rise, Fall, and Reprise of Soviet-Russian Military Interventionism, 1973–1996* (Cambridge: MIT Press, 1999), and coauthor with Alexander George of *Case Studies and Theory Development* (Cambridge: MIT Press, forthcoming).

Stephen G. Brooks is an assistant professor of government at Dartmouth College. Among his recent publications are "The Globalization of Production and the Changing Benefits of Conquest," *Journal of Conflict Resolution* 43, no. 5 (October 1999), and with William C. Wohlforth, "Power, Globalization and the End of the Cold War: Reevaluating a Landmark Case for Ideas," *International Security* 25, no. 3 (winter 2000/2001).

Derek H. Chollet assisted former secretary of state James A. Baker, III with the research and writing of his 1995 book, *The Politics of Diplomacy*. From 1999 to 2001, he served in the Department of State as Special Advisor to Deputy Secretary of State Strobe Talbott and Chief Speechwriter to Richard Holbrooke, the U.S. Ambassador to the United Nations. He is currently a Foreign Policy Advisory to U.S. Senator John Edwards (D-N.C.).

Robert D. English is an assistant professor of international affairs at the University of Southern California. He is the author of *Russia and the Idea of the West: Gorbachev, Intellectuals and the End of the Cold War* (New York: Columbia University Press, 2000).

James M. Goldgeier is Director of the Institute for European, Russian, and Eurasian Studies at George Washington University, where he is an associate professor of political science and international affairs. He is also an Adjunct Senior Fellow in European Studies at the Council on Foreign Relations. His most recent book is *Not Whether But When: The U.S. Decision to Enlarge NATO* (Washington, D.C.: The Brookings Institution, 1999).

The late *Joseph Lepgold* was an associate professor of government at Georgetown University. His most recent publications include *World Politics into the Twenty-First Century* (with Alan C. Lamborn) (Englewood Cliffs, N.J.: Prentice-Hall, 2001) and *Beyond the Ivory Tower: International Relations Theory and the Issue of Policy-Relevance* (New York: Columbia University Press, 2001).

William C. Wohlforth is an associate professor of government at Dartmouth College. He is the editor of *Witnesses to the End of the Cold War* (Baltimore: Johns Hopkins University Press, 1997).

Vladislav M. Zubok is an associate professor of history at Temple University and senior research fellow at the National Security Archive. He is coauthor (with Constantine Pleshakov) of *Inside the Kremlin's Cold War* (Cambridge: Harvard University Press, 1996).

Index